"This volume, analyzing the Kerala situation with a special focus on the manufacturing sector from a historical and sociological perspective, is much-needed, timely, and relevant. This book, impressively edited by P. L. Beena and Thiagu Ranganathan, explains quite well how the accumulated 'human capital,' an educated and healthy population, which includes youngsters who obtain high-paying jobs abroad and send home remittances invests in the services and manufacturing sectors. That said, it could have addressed the demographic situation with an ageing population and the declining numbers in the workforce (equivalent to that in highly developed countries such as those in Scandinavia), but in a relatively poor country."

—Joseph Tharamangalam, Professor Emeritus, *Department of Sociology and Anthropology, Mount St. Vincent University, Halifax, Canada*

"Beyond doubt, the COVID-19 global pandemic affected all countries. However, studies focusing on its impact on subnational economies are few, especially in India, which makes this book of selected essays a useful contribution. Focusing on the Kerala economy set against its rather fast pace of transition resulting from its significant international labour migration and the consequent flow of remittances, the studies provide several lessons on understanding and facing such exogenous shocks as the COVID-19."

—K. P. Kannan, Chairman, *Laurie Baker Centre and COSTFORD,* Former Director and Honorary Fellow, *Centre for Development Studies, Thiruvananthapuram*

"For more than half a century now Kerala's development experience has attracted scholarly attention. It continues to be a fertile and fascinating field of study. Labour and trade mobility from and to Kerala has a long and rich tradition the economic implications of which still remains an inadequately explored area. The collection of 13 papers in this book ably edited by Beena and Thiagu Ranganathan is indeed a useful collection that will contribute to the scholarship in this area that needs more work in greater depth."

—M. A. Oommen, Honorary Fellow, *Centre for Development Studies, Trivandrum,* Distinguished Fellow, *Gulati Institute of Finance and Taxation, Trivandrum* & Emeritus Professor, *Institute of Management in Government, Trivandrum*

"Labour and trade mobility influence regional development and human well-being, vis-à-vis migration, innovation, competitiveness, and skills development. This volume makes a compelling case for addressing Kerala's economic growth through industrialization and public sector involvement. The contributions highlight Kerala's structural transformation from agriculture to services outpacing the rest of India and the need for new paradigms, as multiple labour mobilities increase costs, risks, and vulnerabilities. As Kerala's unique labour market dynamics – the outflux of educated natives and the influx of less-educated migrants – poses new economic and social dilemmas, many relevant findings in this book reassert the need to focus on higher occupational mobility to manage professionals across sectors and adapt to changing demands."

—**Shoba Arun, Reader,** *Work and Organisation Studies, Essex Business School,* **Director,** *Internationalisation and Partnerships (Education),* **Associate Director,** *PGR (OSHRM), Essex Business School*

Kerala Transforming

This book examines Kerala's recent development trajectory and highlights the impact of COVID-19 on its economy. It analyzes Kerala's growth and structural transformation while engaging critically with issues related to employment and migration. The book delves into policies aimed at reintegrating return migrants into Kerala's development process. It examines the implications of Free Trade Agreements and policies initiated by the Government of India under the WTO regime on agriculture. The chapters in the book also investigate the impact of the growth trajectories on distributional aspects of inequality and social mobility.

Timely and topical, the book will be an indispensable resource for students and researchers of economics, development studies, trade, labour and migration, political economy, Kerala economy, and South Asian studies.

P. L. Beena is Professor at the Centre for Developmental Studies, Thiruvananthapuram. She has held positions as Consultant at NCAER, Research Information System for the Developing Countries, New Delhi and South Asia visiting scholar at Queen Elizabeth House, Oxford before joining CDS. Since her PhD at CESP, JNU, her main areas of research are in the field of corporate mergers, inward and outward FDI through CBM&As and anti-trust policies; innovation and competition in the high-tech sectors under the new IPR regime; MSMEs and women entrepreneurship; WTO agreements and its implications on Indian Industries; Contemporary Issues on Indian Economy.

Thiagu Ranganathan is Professor at the Centre for Development Studies, Thiruvananthapuram. Since his PhD at IIT Bombay, he has worked on issues in agricultural economics and development economics including agricultural price risk management, implications of water scarcity on rural livelihood diversification, institutional barriers to employment of higher educated women, and implications of monetary incentives on forest restoration. His work spans across themes of risk, vulnerability, resilience, livelihood diversification, and social mobility.

Kerala Transforming

Labour and Trade Mobility in Times of Pandemic

Edited by P. L. Beena and Thiagu Ranganathan

Routledge
Taylor & Francis Group
LONDON AND NEW YORK

First published 2026
by Routledge
4 Park Square, Milton Park, Abingdon, Oxon OX14 4RN

and by Routledge
605 Third Avenue, New York, NY 10158

Routledge is an imprint of the Taylor & Francis Group, an informa business

British Library Cataloguing-in-Publication Data
A catalogue record for this book is available from the British Library

ISBN: 978-1-032-53901-0 (hbk)
ISBN: 978-1-032-98903-7 (pbk)
ISBN: 978-1-003-60128-9 (ebk)

DOI: 10.4324/9781003601289

Typeset in Sabon
by Deanta Global Publishing Services, Chennai, India

Contents

Foreword

As early as the 1970s, the Centre for Development Studies (CDS) in Thiruvananthapuram had invited academic attention to indications that Kerala has gone through a different development experience from other developing regions. With the CDS's findings that the state achieved important developmental outcomes at low levels of per capita income, Kerala's experience became a matter for wider and deeper analysis. These discussions led to a study on the *Limits to Kerala Model of Development* [George, 1993]. Nevertheless, Kerala's growth performance since 1991, and even if liberalisation is taken as a marker, is also impressive in numerical terms. In this context, international migration and foreign remittances were factors as kick-starters of growth, which became subjects of specific enquiry. The concern over the slow economic growth rate and its lack of productive sector development is slowly disappearing. Nonetheless the better growth performance is not backed by an equally good distribution of income. For a region well known for its earlier distribution mechanism, this is a notable setback. Coupled with it is a comparatively increased unemployment rate. These are some of the major issues that this set of essays tries to understand.

As far as the apparent structural transformation that has been taking place in Kerala over the last few decades is concerned, what is seen is a shift from agriculture to the services sector. Both output and employment, even in the growing factory sector, are dominated by the service sector. The COVID-19 pandemic had its impact in the sense of dwindling remittances and the difficulties that the return migrants had to face in readjusting themselves to the state's labour market. Six chapters, from 4 to 10, address the migration-related labour questions from different points of view. Specific to these questions are the state's increasing educated unemployment and gender disparity in labour participation. The situation is made more difficult in the context of Kerala's labour market, which is already marked by "exporting" skilled and semi-skilled labourers abroad while "importing" unskilled labourers from the rest of the country [see Ch. 5]. The COVID-19 pandemic seems to have adversely affected different subsections of migrants [Ch. 7]. The lockdown seems to have resulted in decreased incomes of all the households surveyed and among them Scheduled Caste and Muslim families being more [Ch. 10]. These are, indeed, indications of a soft underbelly still existing for the emigrants, supposed to have indulged in "conspicuous consumption" [Ch. 9].

These issues take the discussion to a section dealing with structural transformation and distributional issues. Even Kerala, which has made great strides in poverty eradication, has now widened inequality in the post-reform period. In Chapter 11, when Kerala is analyzed along with Tamil Nadu, it is found that Kerala has been more successful in moving the workforce out of agriculture. In terms of quality of employment, Tamil Nadu has had better mobility of SCs and OBCs. Similarly, an inquiry into Madambam settlement in Kannur, Kerala, shows that declining remittances to migrant families remain a major issue, in spite of upward intergenerational educational and occupational mobility [Ch. 12]. Likewise, multidimensional aspects of inequalities still persist in tea plantations in Kerala and Tamil Nadu [Ch. 13]. Though Kerala shows a structural transformation different from that of India, in the inquiries presented in this volume, it should be admitted to be a mixed bag too.

The issues discussed in Chapters 4 to 13 are placed within an overarching analysis of Kerala's manufacturing and agricultural production in Chapters 2 and 3. The first of these analysis, of the manufacturing sector, shows that its recent transformation is mainly due to labour replacing capital investments leading to increased capital intensity [Ch. 2]. Along with this, there is "faltering growth rates" in the factory sector too. Similarly, the study on the "Import surge of agricultural products under the FTAs" [Ch. 3] shows how imported substitutable and value-added products from India's FTA replaced domestic products. In other words, all that glitters is not gold, or that the apparent signs of growth need not be taken to be completely free of problems.

These specific studies, which are brought together in the form of a book, certainly showcase Kerala's present development story with its different aspects. In the context of the several issues brought out, there are also different policy measures suggested. They include planned industrialization that includes the public sector, preventing investments in non-essential production, ensuring demand through procurement policies, and enacting expansionary demand management policies to address the unemployment situation, etc. They are all well taken. The only thing is that they would require further prioritization, in terms of timing, nature, and detailed objectives. That will need further discussion too. As it could happen with any book of this sort, each reader may have his or her suggestions to make towards what is to be done. Nevertheless, attention may be drawn to an important policy suggestion made in the book [Ch. 2] "that a purely market-led pattern of growth cannot satisfy Kerala's aspirations of all-round industrial development".

Since a significant number of specific studies undertaken in this volume position themselves in the post-COVID-19 pandemic situation, further enquiries related to it may be thought of. Post-COVID-19 pandemic situation, along with the post-2018 Flood situation, proved that, in spite of serious setbacks, the people of Kerala are capable of speedy, timely, and empathetic responses in times of major disasters. This was seen even earlier – historically – in the time of the Great Flood of 1924. What is most significant about these kinds of responses to observers from different social sciences is that the people of Kerala are capable of unity across several political and community-based groups and of excellent selfless service, comparable to "Public Action" an important factor in the so-called Kerala Model of Development analysis. These responses were organized and executed largely at the local level under the decentralized leadership of local governments. What was disappointing about these kinds of responses was their apparent short duration. The initial spirit and enthusiasm are not maintained for long. Civic action, however popular and widespread, may not be able to move by its own spirit and in the absence of governmental cooperation. It has already been suggested that the planning for all-round industrial development should not be purely market-led but also include the public sector. Similarly, decentralized and spirited civic action may also be woven into the thinking on Kerala transforming.

Earlier studies on Kerala had already pointed out that interdisciplinary studies are required for a better understanding of the issues involved [Singh, 2015, Tharakan, 2007]. It may not be a pure coincidence that a volume enquiring into labour and trade mobility in times of pandemic has brought about once again the need for interdisciplinary conceptualization on Kerala transforming.

P. K. Michael Tharakan,
Chairperson,
Centre for Socio-economic and Environmental Studies [CSES], Kochi
[Opinions are personal]

Bibliography

K. K. George, Limits to Kerala Model of Development, CDS, Trivandrum, 1993.

Prerna Singh, How Solidarity Works for Welfare, Subnationalism and Social Development in India, cup Delhi, 2017 [2015]

P. K. Michael Tharakan, "Kerala Model Revisited: New Problems, Fresh challenges", in A. Vaidyanathan, K. L. Krishna, [eds], Institutions and Markets in India's Development, Essays for KN Raj, OUP, New Delhi, 2007, 345-59.

Figures

Tables

Contributors

Abhinav Surya L. T. is a research scholar at the Centre for Development Studies, Thiruvananthapuram. A postgraduate in Mechanical Engineering from IIT Madras, he has experience in statistics and machine learning.

Afsal K. is a research scholar in the Department of Migration and Urban Studies at International Institute for Population Sciences, Mumbai. His research interests include international labour migration, Gulf migration, and diaspora philanthropy.

Akansh Khandelwal is an assistant professor of economics at Jindal Global Business School, O.P Jindal Global University , Sonipat, Haryana, and a research scholar in economics at the Indian Institute of Management, Indore. His research interests include development economics and public policy, revolving around issues of poverty and inequality.

Anjali Rajan is an assistant professor of economics at the School of Management, Mahindra University. She earned her PhD in Economics from the Indian Institute of Management, Calcutta. Her research interests include labour economics, economics of inequality and discrimination, and applied macroeconomics.

Govindaprasad P. K. is an assistant professor at the School of Liberal Arts and Applied Sciences, Department of Economics, Hindustan Institute of Technology and Science, Chennai. His research interests include rural development, sustainable development, land use analysis, and migration.

Irudaya Rajan S. is a former professor of CDS and the chairman of the International Institute of Migration and Development (IIMAD), India, and chair of the KNOMAD (the Global Knowledge Partnership on Migration and Development) thematic working group on internal migration and urbanization, World Bank. He has expertise in the demographic, social, economic, political, and psychological consequences of migration.

Jajati Keshari Parida is a professor at the School of Economics, University of Hyderabad. His research interests include labour migration, employment, and development issues.

Jayesh M. P. is an assistant professor in the Department of Economics at Christ University, Bengaluru. He has worked at the Department of Humanities and Social Sciences, Indian Institute of Technology, Delhi, from where he had also secured his PhD in economics with distinction. His areas of interest include econometrics, development economics, and behavioural economics.

Justin Sunny is an economist and consultant at the Indian Political Action Committee (IPAC). He has also worked for the Government of Kerala, IIT Delhi, Central University Punjab, Bhatinda, and Centre for Development Studies, Thiruvananthapuram.

Mritiunjoy Mohanty is an economic adviser to the New Trade Union Initiative (NTUI), Delhi, and a retired professor of economics (Indian Institute of Management, Calcutta). He works in the areas of open-economy macroeconomics, growth and structural change, political economy of growth and development with an emphasis on China and India. Recently, he has also been working in the area of growth trajectory implications of responding to climate change and global warming.

Murali Kallummal is the head of administration at the Centre for Research in International Trade, Indian Institute of Foreign Trade (CRIT) and a professor (Tariffs, Standards, and FTA) at the Centre for WTO Studies, Indian Institute of Foreign Trade (IIFT), New Delhi. He is an expert in international trade and WTO negotiations, market access challenges and issues, FTAs, development economics, and financial economics. He has maintained the database on SBS and TBT measures from 1995 to 2023 with HSN trade linkages.

Murugan G. is a retired officer from the Department of Economics and Statistics, Trivandrum. He has secured a PhD from CDS and was awarded a Senior Research Fellowship by the ICSSR. His areas of interest are environment and water resources economics, the Capabilities approach to well being measurement, and the National Accounts, and many of Socio-Economics issues.

Pooja Batra is an assistant professor of economics at Jindal Global Business School, O. P. Jindal Global University, Sonipat Haryana. She has a PhD in economics from the Indian Institute of Management, Indore. Her research interests include migration, health, education, applied econometrics, development economics, and gender economics.

Pushpangadan K. is a former professor at Centre for Development Studies, Thiruvananthapuram, and honorary professor at the Gulati Institute of Finance and Taxation, Kerala. He is also an executive committee member of the Indian Econometric Society and a visiting professor at the Rajiv Gandhi Institute for Development Studies Thiruvananthapuram.

Ram B. Bhagat is a former professor and head of the department of Migration and Urban Studies, International Institute for Population Sciences,

Mumbai. He has expertise in migration and urbanization, environment and sustainable development, demography, ethnicity, and politics.

Ravi Raman K. is a member of the State Planning Board, Government of Kerala, India. He was formerly a senior fellow at the Nehru Memorial Museum and Library, New Delhi, and visiting faculty at the Centre for Development Studies, Trivandrum.

Sachin Varghese Titty is a research scholar at the Centre for Development Studies, Thiruvananthapuram.

Sajitha A. is an assistant professor of economics in the Department of Economics at Christ University, Bengaluru. She has a PhD in Economics and her research experience includes studying the livelihood strategies of small growers in the natural rubber sector.

Soni T. L. is an associate professor of economics at Sri C. Achutha Menon Govt. College, Thrissur, and an academician specializing in economics under the Directorate of Collegiate Education, Government of Kerala. Her research interests include informal economy, rural development, labour economics, fiscal economics, environmental studies, and sustainable development.

Sulaiman K. M. is a senior research officer at the International Institute for Population Sciences, Mumbai. He has expertise in migration, gender studies, research methodology, public administration, and population studies.

Sumeetha Mokkil Maruthur is an assistant professor Department of Economics, School of Social Sciences and Languages, Vellore Institute of Technology, Vellore. A PhD scholar in Economics from Jawaharlal Nehru University, New Delhi, her research interests include migration, labour process, surveillance, international migration, and the future of work.

Surajit Das is an assistant professor at the Centre for Economic Studies and Planning, Jawaharlal Nehru University, New Delhi. His areas of interest include macroeconomics, econometrics, public economics, macroeconomic policy.

Syam Prasad is an assistant professor in the Department of Economics at the Central University of Kerala, Kasaragod, Kerala. His research interests include health economics, development studies, econometrics, migration studies, and studies on social securities-related issues.

Viswanathan P. K. is a professor of economics and head of the School of Business at Amrita School of Business, Amrita Vishwa Vidyapeetham, Amritapuri, Kerala. His research areas include sustainable energy policy, biodiversity and ecosystems plantation agriculture and commodity trade, economics and management of natural resources, and agrarian transformation.

Acknowledgments

This edited book includes papers presented at a seminar titled "Kerala and the World Economy" organized by the Centre for Development Studies (CDS), Thiruvananthapuram, in February 2021, on labour migration from Kerala and trade between Kerala and other nations, focusing on issues related to return migration to the state in the aftermath of COVID-19.

The seminar, conducted online, was part of research activities by the International Migration Unit at CDS. Seventeen papers were presented in six sessions over two days. Members from the CDS, the Kerala Planning Board, and EPW Research Foundation chaired these sessions. The engaging debates among the participants formed the crux of our decision to publish some of these papers in this edited volume.

We would like to thank R. Nagaraj, Ravi Raman, Mridul Eapen, T. Abhilash, and Dennis Rajakumar who chaired the various sessions. The motivation for this volume came from the productive discussions during every session, the active involvement of the discussants and chairpersons of each session, and rich inputs from seminar presenters and participants. We largely benefited from the remarks on international return migration in Kerala made by Harikrishnan Namboothiri, the CEO of NORKA Roots. We would also like to acknowledge formar chairman, K.M. Chandrasekhar and Sunil Mani, the then director of CDS, whose encouragement helped us organize the seminar amid the pandemic.

The seminar, conducted at zero financial cost, would not have been as smooth had it not been for the many CDS staff members who dedicated their valuable time and effort towards publicizing and organizing it. We would like to particularly acknowledge Ajikumar, Emmanuel, Praveen, Sarath, Satheesh, and Ajayan for their support in organizing the seminar.

We would like to thank Sachin Titty, a PhD scholar, who helped us compile material for the introductory chapter of this volume. We thank Sachin and Abhinav Surya for contributing a chapter to this book right after the seminar. Our special thanks to all the other contributors for their patience through this long-term book project. Only their immense levels of patience through over three years of exchanges could have made this book possible. Thanks are also due to Gayathri and Lalitha for their research assistance and to Meera Menon for her language review of the chapters and valuable inputs through the editing process of this book.

This book would not have been complete without the constant support of many scholars, especially M. A. Ommen, Michael Tharakan, K. P. Kannan, K. N. Harilal, Keshab Das, Mritiunjoy Mohanty, Irudaya Rajan, Jayan Jose, Viswanathan, Mohana Kumar, Syam Prasad, Surajit Das, Murali Kallummal, Pushpangadhan, Shoba Arun, Gilbert Sebastian, and James K. S. Our gratitude also goes to our current chairman, Sudipto Mundle for his encouragement and current director, C. Veeramani, whose initiative to sanction a special grant helped us complete this work and meet our deadline.

Finally, we would like to acknowledge Routledge's external referees for their thought-provoking comments and thank the editors for making this book project possible. We would like to particularly thank Anvitaa Bajaj for her immense patience and support throughout the project.

P. L. Beena and Thiagu Ranganathan,
CDS, Thiruvananthapuram.

1 Introduction

P. L. Beena and Thiagu Ranganathan

The Indian state of Kerala has undergone a distinct trajectory of economic growth and development and this has received widespread attention from academics and policy makers over last 50 years. However, significant contestations exist around the reasons for the state's unique economic track record compared to other states (Roy and Raman 2024). Besides, the persistence of widespread social inequalities despite good social indicators is a perplexing paradox related to the state's developmental outcomes (Kurien, 1995; Raj, 2025 forthcoming). In understanding intelinkages between economic growth, development, and social disparities, Kerala continues to be an idiosyncratic case study and this book focusses on varied issues related to these dynamics in the state.

This chapter lays down the aims and objectives of the book and presents the context underlying Kerala's transition. It also presents a brief outline of the specific themes in this book. In this context, it is important to underline that debates around Kerala's experience of development has a very long history (Kannan 2022). It is imperative to re-visit these debates before discussing the various themes in this book. The next section presents a brief overview of the diverse arguments around Kerala's development course and the dynamics around the shifts in the recent years.

Stories about the Kerala story

Kerala's development has intrigued many scholars, as it appeared to offer an alternative to the conventional understanding that improvements in developmental outcomes have to wait until some level of economic growth is achieved (Harilal and Joseph 2003). Yet, the state seemed to have achieved high developmental indicators related to human capital before its economic growth accelerated in the late 1980s.

Academic curiosity around Kerala's social and economic development started with the publication of a report for a project commissioned by the United Nations (UN) and implemented by the Centre for Development Studies in 1975 (CDS 1975). The report's findings were used to highlight the features of what is now known as the "Kerala model" of development in later years.[1] Given that the state had achieved some critical developmental

DOI: 10.4324/9781003601289-1

yardsticks at low levels of per capita income, it was seen as a potentially "cheap (low-cost)" development model for the backward economies across the world. A study by Franke and Chasin (1992) suggested that Kerala's per capita income was 6/7th of India's, yet its literacy rate was twice that of the country. It also pointed out that if Kerala were to be a country, it would have been the ninth poorest country in the world when it achieved these varied developmental milestones. The UN report prepared by CDS also highlighted some of the challenges in sustaining this unique developmental trajectory, and most of these challenges have persisted in varied forms over the years.

Even today, Kerala's developmental curve is interesting on both social and economic fronts. On the social front, Kerala has the unique distinction of obtaining significant achievements in basic indicators such as adult literacy, life expectancy, infant mortality, and birth rates at low levels of per capita income. Various explanations abound on how Kerala managed to scale these achievements, ranging from historical factors related to early social and religious revolutionary movements, responsive and sometimes adversarial public action, and high public spending (Dreze and Sen 1991; Franke and Chasin 1992; Isaac and Tharakan 1995; Tharakan 2008; Sebastian 2008; Thomas 2021a). The general idea of a decentralized democracy and high public spending propelling social development remains a promising premise for various developing regions in the country .

Compared to the social front, the economic front in Kerala continues to draw attention due to high levels of human migration from the state. Tharakan (1984) notes a tendency towards migration to meet livelihood from as early as 1930s. His study pointed out various reasons for migration during the 1930s–1950s, from Travancore to Malabar, including differences in the price of land, land being cheaper on the Malabar side, economic depression, changes in agricultural practices, and lack of cultivable land post-ancestral succession. During the post-independence period, migration to West Asian countries since the 1970s has been driven by a multitude of push and pull factors .

Subsequently, this tiny state in India has experienced high levels of international migration ever since the 1970s. It is estimated to have about 2.15 million international migrants in 2023 (Rajan and Zachariah 2020). The total remittances have also increased tremendously over the years. In the recent years, the state is estimated to have received remittances in the range of USD 25–26 billion, constituting about 23% of Kerala's net state domestic product (NSDP) (Kannan and Hari 2020; Rajan 2023). The consequences of such high levels of labour migration and remittances on Kerala's economy have been vigorously debated by various scholars (see the latest Kerala Migration Survey [KMS] report of 2023 for trends in the extent of international migration from Kerala; Prakash 1998; Harilal and Joseph 2003; Kannan 2023). While some of these studies have characterized migration to have helped revive Kerala's growth prospects, others seem to characterize it as a "Dutch disease" type phenomenon, where the migration boom in the 1970s might have caused a depression in other goods-producing sectors.

Apart from the labour market, Kerala has also been historically integrated with the rest of the world in terms of commodity markets dating back to the third millennium BC. The state's reputation as a centre for spices attracted traders from various regions, establishing early trade links with foreign countries. The question of sustainability of trade forms an integral part of the age-old debate in Kerala, especially in the era of trade liberalization. The new agreement on agriculture and free trade agreements (FTAs) has adversely affected the plantation sector, especially the natural rubber, coconut, and cashew sectors (Joseph and Viswanathan 2016; Harilal and Dhanya 2015; Harilal and Many 2024).

Despite high migration and trade, umpteen authors have highlighted the shortcomings of economic growth experienced by Kerala – very low investment, rising imports, poor performance of state-level public sector units (PSUs) (Jeromi 2003), higher incidence of consumer services in the service sector, persistence of food production deficits high levels of educated unemployment (Subrahmanian 2006), stagnation of productive sectors (Kannan,1990; Sebastian 2008) among others. Adding to these conundrum, the weakening of remittance inflow (Rajan and Zacharia 2019) and failure to tap into the strong base set up by social indicator performance (Kannan 2005) has added to the challenges to the state. With regard to industrial growth, the state has generally remained a laggard and Thomas (2005) offers path dependence owing to initial investment in select chemical and sectors and hydroelectricity as an explanation for the industrial stagnation.

In this context, the state needs to urgently focus on growth of productive sectors in order to maintain momentum and corroborate developmental achievements. However, the COVID-19 pandemic had a huge impact not only on the domestic economy but also on international migration and remittances. Kerala's handling of pandemic has been considered admirable, but only in phases. As some authors point out much of the excitement of COVID-19 handling in the first phase died down following a not-so-impressive handling in the later waves of the pandemic (Chathukulam and Tharamangalam 2021). Many non-residential Keralites returned to the state following the pandemic. As of July 2020, about 500,000 emigrants returned to Kerala,[2] and there has been a huge impetus to reintegrate these return migrants into Kerala's economy.

International migration appears to have contributed to a varied nature of structural transformation in the state as compared with other parts of the country. Over the years, economic growth in the state has largely been demand driven and propelled by international remittances. The construction and service sectors have contributed more to Kerala's economic growth, while contribution from the manufacturing sector has remained lacklustre (Thomas 2021b). Consequently, the state's structural transformation is atypical and more divergent than India's "stunted" structural transformation.

The challenge of reviving the manufacturing sector is more perplexing in Kerala than in all of India.

Along with the preceding developments on the social and economic fronts, there is now a widespread consensus on some of the peculiar challenges systemic to the Kerala model of development. Some scholars have termed these shortfalls as "spectacular failures" of the model (Kannan 2023). Among the varied shortcomings, three issues have persisted as aspects intrinsic to Kerala's developmental experience. First, despite the appearance of inclusivity, Kerala's development has continuously bypassed wellbeing of Dalits and people from the fishing community (Mencher 1980; George 1990; Tharakan 2008; Sebastian 2008, 2018; Devika 2010; Raj 2022, 2025, forthcoming). Second, the state has time and again fallen into a fiscal crisis, which has caused concerns over the sustainability of state-expenditure-driven welfare (Sebastian 2019). Some scholars have gone so far as to claim that this crisis has the potential to subsume capital investment and bring a perennial growth crisis (George 1990, 1999; Tharamangalam 1998; Prakash 2023). Third, the plantation sector is going through an acute crisis and this raises the question of sustainability of agriculture trade under a new trade regime (Harilal and Many 2024). Fourth, the employment creation potential in the state is drastically low and leads to the perpetual problem of unemployment. The plight of unemployed youth, particularly among the higher-educated men and women, has been highlighted as one of the ominous "spectacular failures" of the Kerala model of development (CDS 1975; Tharamangalam 1998; Kodoth and Eapen 2002; Sebastian 2008; Kannan 2023; Roy and Raman 2024). Given this background, any analysis of Kerala's transition has to account for these challenges that have paradoxically persisted with good social indicators of the state.

The Seminar on Kerala and the World Economy held in February 2021 at the Centre for Development Studies (CDS), Thiruvananthapuram, highlights the above challenges faced by kerala economy at the time of Covid-19 pandemic. The papers articulate the pandemic's impact on employment, emigrants, remittances, and productive sectors of the economy. This edited volume has 12 chapters that are divided into three parts: Structural Transformation and Sectoral Priorities (2 chapters); Structural Transformation and Impact of COVID-19 on Remittances and Labour Question (7 chapters); and Structural Transformation and Distributional Issues (3 chapters).

Part 1 presents Kerala's structural transformation experience over the years and introduces the three chapters that focus on the state's recent sectoral priorities. Part 2 explores the challenges of unemployment in general and specifically those imposed by the COVID-19 pandemic given the high levels of international migration in the state. Part 3 details the developmental concerns in the state and discusses the distributional issues emerging from Kerala's transition.

Structure and scope of the book

Structural transformation and sectoral priorities

Structural transformation in India is a stunted one, where labour shifted from the farm sector to the non-farm sector rather than to more secure jobs with pension and health benefits in the urban economy (Mkhize 2013). Consequently, the gap between labour productivity of the non-agricultural and agricultural sectors since the 1980s has widened due to the steady growth in the non-agriculture sector and comparitively low growth in the agriculture sector. In addition rural–urban migration is very low because of the lower share of manufacturing in the economy and low growth in employment and output. The share of agriculture in gross domestic product (GDP) has been declining while that of the services sector has been increasing at a faster rate. However, the share of the labour force in agriculture is much higher than its share in GDP. These characteristics make the structural transformation of India quite different from the international experience (Sen 2023). The experience of structural transformation though varies across different states in the country. With regard to kerala, two questions become pertinent: How has Kerala experienced structural transformation over the years? Can Kerala be placed differently from India in terms of its structural transformation?

In general, the state of Kerala is appreciated for making a "turnaround" with the emergence of a virtuous cycle of development which seemingly reinforced human development with high economic growth in the post-reform era (Ahluwalia 2000; Kannan 2005). The high aggregate growth rate comparable to all India and a higher per capita income (25% higher than the Indian average) was considered as evidence of the turnaround over the last three decades. But, the onset of COVID-19 seems to have forced a slowdown in 2021–22; though, Kerala recovered quickly to grow steadily through 2022–23. The state's gross state product (GSDP) per capita grew by 6.06% in comparison to the 5.9% growth registered across all India (GoK 2024).

Importantly, Kerala's manufacturing sector has displayed higher growth rate compared to all India. This was not the case earlier, as manufacturing growth rates were generally well below the national averages in the 1980s and 1990s (Subrahmanian and Pillai 1986; Azeez and Subrahmanian 2000) and even in the 2000s. Actually, the distinct divergent behaviour shown by Kerala's manufacturing sector (Subrahmanian and Pillai 1986) had persisted till 2010. It is only in the last decade that Kerala's organized manufacturing has shown signs of revival (GoK 2021). Studies by Veeramani and Arora (2020), Balagopal and Nair (2020), Beena (2018) and Beena, George, and Kumar (2020) have come up with similar observations. Despite being limited by the scale of operation entailing the smaller demographic size of the state, the manufacturing sector was able to display a growth rate above the national average in the past decade, i.e. 2010–20 (Veeramani and Arora 2020, 328). This is attributed to the growth in SMEs and modern sectors in Kerala. Recent study (Beena 2023) has documented an emergence of dynamic women-owned manufacturing enterprises in the state. The study has further observed an association between educational qualification and the upward mobility among those entrepreneurs.

Incidentally, the top industries in Kerala contributing to the value added are chemicals, refined petroleum products, rubber and plastic products, electronic products, and pharmaceuticals & medicinal botanical products (GoK 2021). Kerala's share in national exports by commodity group, highlights the dominance of traditional industries and the emerging role of high-tech products in the revival (Beena 2018; Veeramani and Arora 2020). According to Annual Survey of Industries (ASI) unit level data as of 2016, 73% of the manufactured exported products from Kerala were food products and beverages, textiles (11%), pharmaceuticals and botanical products (5.75%), and apparel (3.5%), which together accounted for about 20% of total manufactured products (Beena 2020). The 1980s and 1990s witnessed establishment of many startups in the modern manufacturing sectors, which have transformed themselves into SMEs (Balagopal and Nair 2020).

These developments warrants attention to analysis of the manufacturing sector in the state. In this context of rekindled interest, a further inquiry has to unleash this domain to identify the nuances and comparative advantages that have been brewing in productive sectors. Considering the importance of structural transformation and its limitations in the economy, this book has devoted two chapters on this topic.

Chapter 2, "Revisiting Kerala's manufacturing sector: New trends in production, labour, and trade" by Abhinav Surya and Sachin Varghese Titty, revisits the state's manufacturing sector and its unprecedented growth in the 2010s, particularly in the factory sector. This study identifies that Kerala's growth in this sector during the phase was primarily led by profitability and marked by growth in the modern sector, with labour-replacing capital investments leading to increased capital intensity. However, despite the buoyant growth rates, the faltering growth rates in Kerala's factory sector towards the end of the last decade suggest that this pattern of unplanned growth aimed at exploiting short-term gains in profitability is unsustainable and raises doubts regarding equity concerns. Hence, this chapter argues that a purely market-led pattern of growth cannot satisfy Kerala's aspirations of all-round industrial development. It suggests revisiting the strategy of a planned growth process with significant interventions by public enterprises to ensure balanced growth.

Chapter 3, "Surge in agricultural products imports under the FTAs: Livelihood concerns by targeting substitutable products" by Murali Kallummal, analyzes the issues and implications of WTO agreements on agriculture, goods, and services as trade agreements between countries on these can alter the domestic economy's delicate balance of commodity prices. The chapter discusses the isolation of price variations after the trade agreement that would alter producers' decisions as intermediaries, users, or consumers. It attempts to trace some linkages from global to local-level price movements and market opportunities for all India and Kerala. It analyzes Kerala's substitutable products (e.g. crude coconut oil and refined coconut oils versus imported palm oils) and their transmission mechanism through price setting and determination for domestic consumption. It also explains the price suppression of the primary products (coconut, pepper, and rubber) as imported substitutable and value-added products from India's FTA replaced the domestic products. It draws attention to the fact that while considering the tariff liberalization of agricultural products, livelihood crops and substitutability both in food and non-food crops also need to be addressed.

Structural transformation and labour question

Tracking the structural shifts in the economy's income in line with employment reveals a relatively better position for Kerala compared to all India. While the primary sector accommodates 26% of the Kerala's working population, it still engages close to 47% of India's working population.

The similarities between Kerala and all India in their trend path extend to even sectoral labour share performance. Reflecting on the performance of GDP share, the tertiary sector in India and Kerala employs more people than the other two sectors. However, a large share of the labour force in India is still dependent on agriculture, whereas the share is much lower in Kerala. Despite this, two issues stand out prominently in the context of Kerala - educated unemployment and gender disparity in labour market participation. Kerala's youth have a much higher unemployment among graduates and postgraduates compared to their national counterparts. The difference seems to be more startling in recent years, with the gap widening between them. Also, the perks of being one of the highest educated societies have not found their way into diminishing gender gaps in labour participation in Kerala. The difference between India and the state remains glaring. Apart from unemployment woes, there are also some discouraging changes in the patterns of migration from the state. Evidently, Kerala's migrants are diversifying into different locations, especially since the 1990s. However, the growth of Kerala's emigration has been much slower since early 2000 compared to other Indian states. The share of Kerala's emigrants in the total Indian emigrants has also sharply declined since 2000 (Kannan and Hari 2020). The second part of this book has devoted seven chapters on the impact of COVID-19 on remittances and labour questions in Kerala.

Chapter 4, "Labour supply behaviour of the return emigrants in Kerala" by Jajati Keshari Parida, Justin Sunny, and K. Ravi Raman, explores the patterns and determinants of the workforce participation of the return migrants in Kerala using secondary data compiled from the Kerala Migration Survey. The study observes that the return migration to Kerala is predominantly occupied by low-skilled migrants from the Gulf Cooperation Council (GCC) region, and a steady increase in the workforce participation rates of the return migrants over the years. The improved standard of living due to the past large-scale inflow of remittances had negative implications on the labour force participation behaviour of the left-behind members. The increased volume of return migrants creates a complex and critical condition in the labour market in Kerala, which is also occupied by domestic migrants from other Indian states. The chapter suggests that should the return migration trends continue to rise, the state must identify and promote self-employment among the return migrants and devise strategies to create job opportunities, especially for female return migrants.

Chapter 5, "Kerala's labour market: The impact of inward and outward migration flows" by Jayesh highlights some of the unique features of Kerala's labour market that exports skilled and semi-skilled labourers to other countries and the rest of India, while importing unskilled workers from other parts of India. While the state's economy fails to provide desired jobs for its youth, the large proportion of remittances received from emigrants is used for the construction of houses and commercial buildings, creating a large demand for unskilled labourers, which in turn is met by the influx of labourers from the eastern and northern regions of India.

The chapter discusses the various factors behind this rare phenomenon, which shapes the duality in the state's labour market. The faster pace of demographic transition, the predominance of the service and construction sectors in the state's GDP, the advancement in the employment structure, and the inflow of remittances are some of the reasons behind the current state of the labour market. This chapter further attempts to analyze the socio-economic background of migrant workers in Kerala based on a field study conducted in Kozhikode.

Chapter 6, "Employer–employee dynamics: The study in return migrants during COVID-19" by Irudaya Rajan, Pooja Batra, and Akansh Khandelwal, discusses the employer-induced reasons for the return migration of immigrants. It delves into the empirical investigation of the employer–employee relation using the novel dataset on the Return Emigrant COVID-19 Survey covering emigrants from Kerala to the Gulf countries who returned home due to the pandemic. The chapter analyzes the impact of COVID-19 on the return emigrants, using the Return Emigrant COVID-19 Survey conducted by the Centre for Development Studies, Thiruvananthapuram.

Chapter 7, "COVID-19 and Gulf return migration: An opportunity to re-orient government strategies" by Sulaiman, Afsal K., and Ram B. Bhagat, analyzes the pattern of migration and the return migration of Kerala during the pandemic. The COVID-19 outbreak directly affected three groups of migrants – migrants who returned to Kerala for break/on leave before the pandemic and couldn't return or lost their jobs; migrants who returned during the pandemic; and migrants at the destination who lost their source of income but did not return. The pandemic and the consequences of the lockdown had self-evident impacts on remittances to Kerala from Gulf countries and the unemployment crisis among NRKs. The chapter analyzes the migration and the return migration patterns of Kerala using Kerala Migration Data, particularly highlighting the recession of 2008. It also covers the socio-economic impact of return migration, including return migration due to the COVID-19 pandemic. The chapter suggests that the state adapt appropriate strategies to enhance the talents of return migrants and feed them to the sectors suffering from a deficit of human resources.

Chapter 8, "COVID-19 pandemic, international remittances and economic growth in Kerala: A macro analysis" by K. Pushpangadan and G. Murugan, develops a macroeconomic framework to estimate the impact of COVID-19 pandemic on economic growth of the sub-national economy of Kerala. The evaluation is based on a simple Solow Growth model for an open economy determined by the stock of physical capital and international remittances. The chapter estimates the comprehensive growth impact on the regional economy and finds a reduction of 39.45% of GDP during the COVID-19 period. During the same period, the reduction in international remittances was about 39.1% due to the slowdown in the economic activity of the Gulf countries, where the migrant population was concentrated, and the return migrants faced job losses.

The overall impact depended on the relative contribution of both components on per capita real output for the COVID-19 period. The growth equation of the region showed that the contribution of physical capital was about 47% and that of international remittances was about 27%, with only the remaining 26% of the growth needing to be accounted for to explain the growth of the regional economy. The investment reduction from the trend value of the capital-output series in 2019–20 was estimated at 22.2%. The weighted average of the investment reduction and reduction in international remittances showed a reduction of per capita income to be 22.4% during COVID-19 period.

Chapter 9, "Remittances and golden Kerala: The economics of productive consumption or conspicuous consumption?" by Sumeetha M. M., analyzes the relationship between remittances in Kerala and the pattern of gold consumption. The chapter tries to answer the following questions: Have remittances changed the consumption pattern of gold in Kerala even at the time of the pandemic? Can gold be considered a productive consumption mechanism in this context? The remittances that flow steadily into the economy of Kerala have earned it the status of a consumption-driven society.

As consumption patterns give an opportunity to analyze the economy through a diverse lens, the economics of productive consumption is taken as the theoretical base to comprehend the significance of gold in migrant households in Kerala. The removal of restrictions on the import of gold has led to large-scale investment in the sector. In Kerala, the majority of investors venturing into the gold industry are mostly non-resident Indians (NRIs). The chapter briefly describes how the Malabar Gold group, Alukkas, and Kalyan group which all had modest beginnings in the early 1990s have now grown into enormous business conglomerates.

Chapter 10, "Economic impact of lockdown on common people in Kerala: A survey report" by Surajit Das and Soni T. L., seeks to understand the impact of the first phase of the COVID-19 lockdown on the common people in Kerala through a primary telephonic survey of 480 sample families conducted in July 2020. The study observed that income came down for 85% of the sample households and by half, on average, for all the sample families. Income fall was universal; however, it was relatively more for the Scheduled Caste and Muslim families. Of the sample families, 59% became indebted, but others could manage with their past savings; 85% got free rations; 17% got some direct benefit transfers into their Jan-Dhan accounts; and only 4% got free cylinders of cooking gas during the first three months of the lockdown in Kerala. Of the respondents, 80% expected reduced income during next six months during the survey, and 70% were convinced they needed some "employment of last resort" programmes in urban areas as well. Based on the comments received from the 480 respondents and the available empirical evidence, the chapter advocates an expansionary demand management fiscal policy by substantially enhancing government expenditure, particularly in the areas of universal employment guarantee, to widen and strengthen the public distribution system, and in the social sector, especially in health, for faster recovery and for overcoming the COVID-humanitarian crisis.

Structural transformation and distributional issues

Analysts have commented on how the state of Kerala has made significant strides in democratizing health and education with the history of collaborative efforts of the state and public action (Oommen 2014). Incidentally, the announcement of the Multidimensional Poverty Index reveals the gains the state has made with respect to poverty eradication (GoI 2021). However, many scholars have recorded the unfavorable impact of globalization on income distribution across class, castes, and gender in the state (Sebastian 2008; 2018). The service-led growth underway in the state also has channelizes earnings in a way that considerably accentuates inequality (Oommen 2014). In this regard, the post-reform widening of inequality is evident in the increasing disparity ratio from 1993–94 to 2009–10. The re-affirmation of widening social inequalities is also reflected in the very low monthly per capita expenditure (MPCE) among the SC/ST communities. In light of these observations, this section deals with three papers related to distributional aspects, especially in the context of COVID-19.

Chapter 11, "Structural change, social groups, and mobility in India: A state-level analysis of Kerala and Tamil Nadu" by Anjali Rajan and Mritiunjoy Mohanty, analyzes the relationship between caste composition and per capita income with a particular focus on Kerala and Tamil Nadu. Based on these stylized facts, the chapter puts forth arguments in the domains of structural transformation, social group differences, and employment mobility in the case of Kerala and Tamil Nadu. In both states, the service sector dominates output and employment. However, industry accounts for a substantially greater share of output in Tamil Nadu than in Kerala.

That being said, Kerala has been much more successful in moving the workforce out of agriculture. Given that in both these states, the scheduled caste (SC) population group was far more likely than any other social group to be employed in agriculture, moving the workforce out of agriculture has benefited them the most, whereas the SC population in Kerala has benefited more from structural change than in Tamil Nadu. Paradoxically, despite Kerala's better performance in terms of structural change, Tamil Nadu affords better mobility to SC and other backward classes (OBC) in terms of quality of employment, largely because inter-social group competition for the best jobs is more muted.

Chapter 12, "Organized peasant migration and intergenerational mobility: A case of Madambam settlement in Kannur district, Kerala" by Govindaprasad P. K. and Syam Prasad, tries to highlight organized peasant migration in Malabar, in an attempt to bridge the gap in discussions on Travancore–Malabar peasant migration, most of which thus far have largely focused on the causes and consequences of unorganized peasant migration.

The chapter explores the causes and consequences of organized peasant migration on the development of the Madambam region in Kannur district, the nature of intergenerational mobility in education and occupation across three generations of members of peasant migrant households, and the impact of the COVID-19 pandemic on these households. Using purposive sampling to select 50 peasant migrant households in the region, the study obtained primary data from these households in a field survey. The analysis of intergenerational mobility using the mobility transition matrix revealed that organized peasant migration and a development strategy of investment in education and infrastructure had led to upward intergenerational educational and occupational mobility, causing the development of the Madambam region and partially transforming it from an agrarian to a non-agrarian settlement. However, with most emigrants not returning to Madambam after the COVID-19 pandemic, remittance income in the migrant families declined slightly.

Chapter 13, "What perpetuates multidimensional inequalities in plantations? A study of tea plantations in Kerala in a comparative setting" by Viswanathan, P. K., and A. Sajitha explores the multidimensional aspects of lingering inequalities in a comparative setting in the tea plantations in Kerala and Tamil Nadu, which continue to bear the brunt of the colonial legacy involving "regimented labour force" and "command and control-based governance regime". The chapter uses mainly primary data to explore the objects in detail, with the survey covering 143 sample respondents from five tea plantation estates in two districts, one each from Kerala (Idukki) and Tamil Nadu (Nilgiri). To examine if fair trade certification has made any impact in addressing the inequalities in tea plantations, both Fairtrade and non-Fairtrade estates were covered in the survey. The chapter also uses a historical analysis of the development and status of tea plantation workers with case studies of working and living conditions from Kerala and Tamil Nadu.

From a policy angle, the chapter concludes that the sustainability of the tea plantation industry in Kerala and other states depends on how the sector can reinvent itself in terms of addressing the challenges posed by the multidimensional inequalities historically faced by plantation workers. The continued dynamism of the tea plantation sector also depends on a thorough overhauling of the production relations and the invention of new models of plantation management with proper collaborations or partnerships between the plantation companies, the emerging segment of small producers, the state and workers, and their associations. Such a process of restructuring both the plantation industry and the key stakeholders becomes imperative in curtailing the historic inequalities perpetuated by the colonial style of plantation management, being followed by the plantation entities even now.

As Kerala's economy follows its own trajectory and structural transformation quite different from that of India, we hope those with an academic perspective and a curious mind to know more about Kerala's economy and how it has fared and faced the challenges posed by the pandemic will find this compilation insightful.

Notes

1 The report itself does not use the word "model" in describing the developmental experience of the state and was much more critical of the state's development than ascribed in some of the future studies referring to it.

2 https://www.livemint.com/news/india/2-384-people-among-4-99-529-returned-to-kerala-so-far-test-covid-19-positive-cm-11594165346005.html

References

Ahluwalia, M. S. 2000. Economic Performance of States in Post-Reforms Period. *Economic and Political Weekly* 35(19): 1637–48.

Azeez, E. A., and Subrahmanian, K. 2000. *Industrial Growth in Kerala: Trends and Explanations*. Working Paper 310. Thiruvananthapuram: Centre for Development Studies.

Balagopal, C., and Nair, R. 2020. "Make in Kerala: The Untold Story of Manufacturing SMEs in Kerala." In *Kerala and the World Economy*, edited by Sunil Mani, 277–301. Thiruvananthapuram: Centre for Development Studies.

Beena, P. L. 2018. "Pattern of International Trade through Kerala State under WTO Regime: Myth and Reality, KASARA". In *A Peer Reviewed Journal of Humanities*, 8(1), January-June, ISSN 2320-2580.

Beena, P. L., George, P., and Kumar, Pradeesh. 2020. "Structure, Direction and Export Contribution of Kerala State: With Special Reference to Cochin Special Economic Zone." In *Kerala and the World Economy*, edited by Sunil Mani, 355–91. Thiruvananthapuram: Centre for Development Studies.

Beena P. L. 2023. "Women-Owned Enterprises in Kerala and its Scalability", Project Report Submitted to ICSSR.

Chathukulam, Jos, and Tharamangalam, Joseph. 2021. "The Kerala Model in the Time of COVID-19: Rethinking State, Society and Democracy." *World*

Development 137(105207): 1–13. https://www.ncbi.nlm.nih.gov/pmc/articles/PMC7510531/.
Centre for Development Studies (CDS). 1975. *Poverty, Unemployment and Development Policy: A Case Study of Selected Issues with Reference to Kerala*. New York: Department of Economic and Social Affairs.
Devika, J. 2010. "Egalitarian Developmentalism, Communist Mobilization, and the Question of Caste in Kerala State, India." *The Journal of Asian Studies* 69(3): 799–820.
Dreze, Jean, and Sen, Amartya. 1991. *Hunger and Public Action*. London: Oxford University Press.
Franke, R. W., and Chasin, B. H. 1992. "Kerala State, India: Radical Reform as Development." *International Journal of Health Services* 22(1): 139156. doi:10.2190/HMXD-PNQF-2X2L-C8TR.
George, K. K. 1990. "Kerala's Fiscal Crisis – A Diagnosis." *Economic and Political Weekly* 25 (37): 2097–2105.
George, K. K. 1999. *Limits to Kerala Model of Development: An Analysis of Fiscal Crisis and Its Implications*. Thiruvananthapuram: Centre for Development Studies.
Government of Kerala (GoK). 2021. Economic Review, Various Issues.
Government of Kerala (GoK). 2024. *Economic Review 2023, Vol. 1*. Thiruvananthapuram: Kerala State Planning Board. https://spb.kerala.gov.in/sites/default/files/2024-02/ER_English_Vol_1_2023.pdf.
Government of India (GoI). 2021. Niti Ayog.
GoI. Various years. NSSO Round and PLFS Data.
Harilal, K. N., and Dhanya, V. 2015. "The WTO Agreements on Tropical Commodities: A Study in the Context of South Asia." *Review of Agrarian Studies* 5(1): 39–60.
Harilal, K., and Joseph, K. 2003. "Stagnation and Revival of Kerala economy: An Open Economy Perspective." *Economic and Political Weekly* 2286–94.
Harilal, K. N., and Many, Rajesh. 2024. "India's Free Trade Agreements and the Political Economy of Deep Integration." *Economic and Political Weekly* 59(40). https://www.epw.in/journal/2024/40/special-articles/indias-free-trade-agreements-and-political-economy.html.
Joseph, K. J., and Viswanathan, ed. 2016. *Globalisation Development and Plantation Labour in India*. New Delhi: Routledge India.
Isaac Thomas and Michael Tharakan (1995). "Kerala: Towards a New Agenda" *Economic and Political Weekly August* 1993–2004.
Jeromi, P. 2003. "What Ails Kerala's Economy: A Sectoral Exploration." *Economic and Political Weekly* 1584–600.
Kannan, K. P. 1990. "Kerala Economy at the Crossroads? *Economic and Political Weekly* 21(35–36): 1951–56.
Kannan, K. P. 2005. "Kerala's Turnaround in Growth: Role of Social Development, Remittances and Reform." *Economic and Political Weekly* 40(6): 548–54.
Kannan, K. P. 2022. *Kerala 'Model' of Development Revisited: A Sixty-Year Assessment of Successes and Failures*. Thiruvananthapuram: Centre for Development Studies.
Kannan, K. P. 2023. "Revisiting the Kerala 'Model' of Development: A Sixty-year Assessment of Successes and Failures." *The Indian Economic Journal* 71(1): 120–51. https://doi.org/10.1177/00194662221145290.
Kannan, K. P., and Hari, K. 2020. "Revisiting Kerala's Gulf Connection: Half a Century of Emigration, Remittances and Their Macroeconomic Impact, 1972–2020." *The Indian Journal of Labour Economics* 63(4): 941–67.
Kodoth, P. and Eapen, M. 2002. *Family Structure, Women's Education and Work: Re-Examining the High Status of Women in Kerala*. Working Paper, No 341. Thiruvananthapuram: Centre for Development Studies.

Mani, Sunil, ed. 2020. *Kerala and the World Economy*. Thiruvananthapuram: Centre for Development Studies.
Mencher J. 1980. "The Lessons and Non-Lessons of Kerala: Agricultural Labourers and Poverty. *Economic and Political Weekly* 15(41–43): 1781–802.
Mkhize Hans P. B. 2013. "The Stunted Structural Transformation of the Indian Economy: Agriculture, Manufacturing and the Rural Non-Farm Sector." *Review of Rural Affairs* 48(26/27): 5–13.
Oommen, M. 2014. "Growth, Inequality and Well-Being: Revisiting Fifty Years of Kerala's Development Trajectory." *Journal of South Asian Development* 9(2), 173–205.
Prakash, B. A. 1998. "Gulf Migration and Its Economic Impact: The Kerala Experience." *Economic and Political Weekly* 33(50): 3209–13.
Prakash, B. A. 2023. "Kerala's Unprecedented Fiscal Crisis and the State Budget of 2023–24." *Economic and Political Weekly* 58(48): 27–9.
Raj, J. 2022. *Plantation Crisis: Ruptures of Dalit Life in the Indian Tea Belt*. London: UCL Press.
Raj, J. 2025. *The Egalitarian Paradox: Dalits and the State in South India*. Forthcoming.
Rajan, S. I. 2023. Kerala Migration Survey 2023. *Kerala Economy* 5(3): 1–12. https://www.gift.res.in/wp-content/uploads/2024/09/Kerala-Migration-Survey-Report-2023-Irudaya-Raj.
Rajan S.I., and Zachariah, K. C. 2019. *Emigration and Remittances: New Evidences from the Kerala Migration Survey, 2018*. Working Paper 483. Thiruvananthapuram: Centre for Development Studies.
Rajan S.I., and Zachariah, K. C. 2020. "New Evidences from the Kerala Migration Survey 2018. *Economic and Political Weekly* 55(4): 41–9.
Roy, T., and Raman, K. R. 2024. *Kerala, 1956 to the Present: India's Miracle State*. Cambridge: Cambridge University Press.
Sebastian, Gilbert. 2008. "Class, Nationality and the Development Process in Keralam Since 1970." Phd Thesis submitted to Centre for Political Studies, JNU.
Sebastian, Gilbert. 2018. "Re-assessing the Development Experience of Keralam: The Case of Land Issues in Big Plantations." In *Kerala History Congress 2015: Selected Papers (from the First Annual Session of the held in Thiruvananthapuram during 29–31 January 2016)*, edited by Gopakumaran Nair.
Sebastian, Gilbert. 2019. 'The Question of Federal Autonomy and Its Changing Contours: The Case of Keralam', in the Session, 'Federalism and Democracy in India' in the All-India Seminar, 'Democratising Democracy: Seventy Years of Experiences and Experiments in India' held during 12–14 December 2019, organised by Institute of Parliamentary Affairs, Government of Kerala and Department of Political Science, University of Calicut, Malappuram, Kerala.
Sen, K. 2023. *Varieties of Structural Transformation: Patterns, Determinants, and Consequences*. Cambridge: Cambridge University Press.
Subrahmanian, K. K. 2006. "Economic Growth in the Regime of Reforms: Kerala's Experience." *Economic and Political Weekly* 41(10): 885–90.
Subrahmanian, K. K., and Pillai, P. M. 1986. "Kerala's Industrial Backwardness: Exploration of Alternative Hypotheses." *Economic and Political Weekly* 21(14): 577–92.
Tharakan, P. K. M. 1984. *Intra-Regional Differences in Agrarian Systems and Internal Migration: A Case Study of the Migration of Farmers from Travancore to Malabar 1930–1950*. Working Paper, No 194. Thiruvananthapuram: Centre for Development Studies.
Tharakan, P. K. M. 2008. *When the Kerala Model of Development Is Historicised: A Chronological Perspective*. Vol. 19 CSES Working Paper Series. Kochi: Centre for Socio-Economic & Environmental Studies.

Tharamangalam, Joseph. 1998. "The Perils of Social Development Without Economic Growth: The Development Debacle of Kerala, India." *Bulletin of Concerned Asian Scholars* 30: 1.
Thomas, Jayan Jose. 2005. "Kerala's Industrial Backwardness: A Case of Path Dependence in Industrialization." *World Development* 33(5): 763–83.
Thomas, Jayan Jose. 2021a. "Kerala's Facilitation Centers: A Success Story." *Indian Journal of Social Work* 82(1): 67–80.
Thomas, Jayan Jose. 2021b. "The Achievements and Challenges of the Kerala 'Model'." *The India Forum*. https://www.theindiaforum.in/article/achievements-challenges-kerala-model.
Veeramani, C., and Arora, M. 2020. "International and Intra-national Trade Flows of Kerala with Special Reference to Manufacturing Sector." In *Kerala and the World Economy*, edited by Sunil Mani, 323–55. Thiruvananthapuram: Centre for Development Studies.

Part I

Structural Transformation and Sectoral Priorities

2 Revisiting Kerala's manufacturing

New trends in production, labour, and trade[1]

Abhinav Surya L. T. and Sachin Varghese Titty

Introduction

Kerala has become the unequivocal example of a counterargument to the neoliberal understanding of growth and development. It has offered an alternative to academic discourse, a trajectory for development entirely different from the Western experience. The continued focus on health and education, dating back to its regal origin, has warranted the state's desire for higher human development levels that outperform national averages.

Amid the laurels, academic debates have highlighted the issues of lopsidedness and sustainability with the development experience of Kerala. Generally characterized by the theoretical framework of unbalanced growth, Kerala's tradable sectors have lagged compared to the services and construction sectors. Migration and remittance have been the buzzwords in Kerala's development debate for most of its independent existence. Existing literature has extensively discussed the different channels of impact these variables have on the economy. The positive channels summarized the effect of these external fund inflows on saving, investment, and consumption patterns, in turn affecting the per-capita earnings of the state (Sunny et al. 2020). The growth in the absolute amount of remittance – despite the fall in the emigrant population over the last 50 years – has contributed to the resilience the state has developed in the face of adversities (Kannan and Hari 2020).

The arguments through the framework of Dutch Disease attributed the inferior performance of tradable sectors to the overt push received by the nontradable sectors. Thus, the same factors – migration and remittance – that acted as chariots of growth and development created a situation of "windfall gains" and deterred the long-run growth prospects of primary and secondary sectors (Harilal and Joseph 2003; Parameswaran 2020).

Recent discussions around migration and remittances signal a declining trend, exposing the critical juncture at which the state stands. The crucial factors that moderated the effect of Kerala's persisting financial crisis appear to be dwindling further. It is evident from the KMS 2018 that the last decade (from 2013) had witnessed a decline of three lakh emigrants (Rajan & Zachariah 2019) and a plunge in the remittance percentage as a

DOI: 10.4324/9781003601289-3

percentage of state gross domestic products (GDP) (Kannan and Hari 2020). This raises questions about the reliability of being heavily dependent on remittance – a standalone mercurial factor – and where the state would look towards to sustain an upward growth trajectory. In this context, the need for reprioritization of other sectors becomes vital.

The services and construction sectors sidelined the prospective growth of Kerala's manufacturing sector. Historically performing under national averages, the state's manufacturing sector occupied an unassuming position in the overall growth story despite a promising start in the 1960s. The influx of sizeable foreign remittance altered the nature of two major factors critical for production activities – land and labour. Higher wages in the nontradable sector characterized wages in the state's labour market as land became an asset class rather than being a factor input. The rising cost of inputs implied that while profit expectations dropped in relation to other states, making it a less attractive destination to produce tradable goods, the demand for nontradable goods had to be met through internal domestic mechanisms (Kannan 1990).

Enquiry into the reasons for the state's inability to maintain the momentum of growth in the manufacturing sector vetted various analytical frameworks to offer an explanation. The high wage-cost hypotheses initially refuted by Subrahmanian and Pillai (1986) reemerged as a plausible explanation in later works such as Subrahmanian (2003). Most analyzes pointed towards labour issues as the major driver of industrial backwardness (Albin 1990; Thampy 1990). Later studies argued that Kerala's industrial-sector backwardness needs to be understood using the "path dependence" framework (Thomas 2005), which refutes the age-old labour-dispute narrative (Thomas 2003).

This chapter explores the historical performance of Kerala's manufacturing sector in the background of these existing studies. It also discusses the changes in the sector on the basis of updated information on the previously discussed parameters. The performance of Kerala's manufacturing sector, which stood above the national average in the last decade, warrants a revisit of the growth patterns in this sector.

The chapter attempts to answer whether the new lease of life in the manufacturing sector reflects a fundamental shift, warranting its reprioritization amid the declining trends in remittance and migration – the previous chariots of development for the state (Rajan & Zachariah 2019).

It also identifies increasing profitability in Kerala's factory sector as leading to the unprecedented growth in Kerala's manufacturing sector, reflected in the significantly large levels of investments, particularly labour-replacing capital investments. But, as the lumpy capital investments induced a downward push on profitability, growth began to taper off. Despite a modest shift in employment away from traditional industries towards modern industries, the significant level of growth, however, was in tandem with a fall in the overall employment level in the factory sector and a rise in the labour exploitation rate in the key sectors that drove the growth. This chapter questions the equity and sustainability of such a process of growth.

Background

Kerala's manufacturing sector growth between 2011–12 and 2018–19

In the post-1991 reform era, Kerala's economy has consistently been less dynamic than the all-India average. Table 2.1 shows the share of Kerala's gross state domestic product (GSDP) (or) gross state value added (GSVA) in India's gross domestic product (GDP) (or) gross value added (GVA). Since the GSDP back-series data is unavailable for the most recent National Accounts Statistics (2011–12 base year series), this chapter provides the share at the beginning and end of three different base year series (1999–2000, 2004–5, and 2011–12). Kerala's output share in India declined across all three series, indicating that Kerala's economic growth consistently lagged the all-India average.

Table 2.1 also provides Kerala's share in India's manufacturing output. The trend matches Kerala's overall GSDP/GSVA until 2010–11. In the 2011–12 series, however, the state bucked the declining trend. Although there was no significant jump in the share, the trend between 2011–12 and 2018–19 could be termed as "nondecreasing".

Table 2.2 shows that since the beginning of the reform period, the share of manufacturing output in Kerala's economy was on a declining trend in the 1999–2000 and 2004–5 series. However, between 2011–12 and 2018–19, the share increased. (Here, we did not compare the magnitudes across the three base year series and observed only the trend.) Tables 2.1 and 2.2 show that while the growth in Kerala's economy lagged India's in the last decade, its manufacturing sector found a new dynamism in its growth pattern, which led to the growth of the state's economy between 2011–12 and 2018–19.

Table 2.1 Share of Kerala's output in India's output

Overall GDP (%)		*Manufacturing GDP/GVA (%)*	
1999–00 Series		1999–00 Series	
1991–92	4.01	1991–92	2.61
2003–04	3.86	2003–04	2.16
2004–05 Series		2004–05 Series	
2004–05	4.01	2004–05	2.26
2010–11	3.86	2010–11	1.9
2011–12 Series		2011–12 Series	
2011–12	4.15	2011–12	2.43
2018–19	3.77	2018–19	2.47

Source: Authors' estimation using National Accounts Data.

Table 2.2 Kerala's manufacturing GSDP/GSVA (%) as a share of Kerala's total GSDP/GSVA

1999–00 Series	
1991–92	9.35
2003–04	8.37
2004–05 Series	
2004–05	8.57
2010–11	7.94
2011–12 Series	
2011–12	10.17
2018–19	11.98

Source: Authors' estimation using National Accounts Data.

Kerala's factory sector between 2011–12 and 2018–19

Table 2.3 presents the growth rates of various components of the economy since 2011–12 and compares Kerala's growth with the all-India average (all growth rates are based on semi-log regression). Between 2011–12 and 2018–19, while Kerala's GSVA grew at an annual rate of 5.26% compared to India's GVA growth rate of 6.92%, Kerala's manufacturing sector grew at an annual rate of 9.35%, which not only outpaced Kerala's GSVA growth rate but also India's manufacturing sector growth rate of 7.97%.

Table 2.3 further disaggregates the growth rates into three sub-periods: between (i) 2011–12 and 2014–15, (ii) 2014–15 and 2015–16, and (iii) 2015–16 and 2018–19. We see that between both 2011–12 and 2014–15 and 2015–16 and 2018–19, Kerala's manufacturing sector growth rate was slower than that of India's. Only for one year, between 2014–15 and 2015–16, Kerala's manufacturing sector grew 28.43% compared to the all-India average of 13.06% (We will see later that the large growth in the GVA of petroleum products industry because of the sharp fall in international crude oil prices contributed to this significantly.) Therefore, Kerala's manufacturing sector was not necessarily more dynamic than India's throughout the last decade.

But Table 2.3 also shows the growth rates in the factory sector (registered manufacturing sector) GVA from the Annual Survey of Industries (ASI) data. Between the entirety of 2011–12 and 2018–19 and in each sub-period, the growth in Kerala's factory sector outpaced India's. While there is still an outlier-level growth between 2014–15 and 2015–16, Kerala's factory sector grew at 6.29% between 2011–12 and 2014–15, which was much higher than India's average of 4.74%. Consequently, between 2011–12 and 2018–19,

Table 2.3 Growth rates: Kerala vs. India (2011–12 constant prices)

	FY12–FY15 (%)		*FY16–FY19 (%)*		*FY15–FY16 (%)*		*FY12–FY19 (%)*	
	Kerala	*India*	*Kerala*	*India*	*Kerala*	*India*	*Kerala*	*India*
GDP/GSDP	4.65	6.19	5.73	6.62	5.34	8.03	5.26	6.92
Industry	3.74	4.58	5.83	6.25	6.60	9.58	5.75	6.53
Manufacturing	2.50	5.98	5.91	7.01	28.43	13.06	9.35	7.97
Registered manufacturing (ASI)	6.29	4.74	4.64	3.86	31.09	11.32	9.57	5.94

Source: Authors' estimation using National Accounts Data.

the overall annual growth rate for Kerala's factory sector was 9.57%, against India's average of 5.94%.

Hence, we conclude that the revival in Kerala's manufacturing sector in the last decade was strongly led by its factory sector (registered manufacturing sector). In the subsequent sections, we delve deeper into the fundamental factors leading to the faster growth in Kerala's factory sector. Since the chapter focuses on the factory sector, we used ASI data.

Data and methodology

Data

Using all-India and state-level data from ASI, as published by the Central Statistical Office (CSO) and compiled by EPW Research Foundation (EPWRF), we analyzed the trends in several variables at the overall organized-manufacuring-sector level and at the two-digit industrial-classification level based on the newly industrialized country (NIC)-2008 classification of industries. This data helped us understand the changes in the production-related aspects of registered manufacturing units in India and assess the drivers of growth.

All the variables, presented in real terms, are in 2011–12 prices. To arrive at the values of variables at constant prices, we deflated output variables (GVA, profits, etc.) using the wholesale price index for manufactured products (WPIMP), workers' wages and benefits using the consumer price index for industrial workers (CPIIW), and the rest of the variables related to capital and investment using the wholesale price index of machinery and machine tools (WPIMM) (The WPIMP and WPIMM are provided by the Office of Economic Adviser, Department of Promotion of Industry and Internal Trade. CPIIW is provided by the Labour Bureau.)

Methodology

We have used Basu and Das (2017) as the theoretical foundation for this study, where they analyzed the state-industry-level panel data on India's factory sector to show that the most important factor impacting investment and capital accumulation, in the short- and long-term, is the "rate of profit".

Based on a Heterodox approach to understanding the dynamics of a capitalist economy, the long-term factor determining growth is "profitability" or "rate of profit" (Marx et al. 1993). In a capitalist economy led by surplus-driven capitalist accumulation, "profitability" is the ultimate factor determining continued capital accumulation (i.e., more investments and expanded production) and continued growth. A decline in profitability slows the pace of capital accumulation, which then considerably hampers growth. However, this does not imply the absence of growth during declining profitability. Instead, declining profitability slows down capital accumulation, making it difficult to sustain growth, which essentially leads the capitalist economy into crisis.

Several studies using the Heterodox approach try to analyze the economy based on the trends in the profitability of the productive sector and its determining role in investments and capital accumulation (Basu and Vasudevan 2013; Basu and Das 2018). Even studies not based on a strict Heterodox approach acknowledge the important role profitability plays in investments and growth (Balakrishnan and Babu 2003). Hence, it is imperative to analyze profitability in the manufacturing sector to understand the growth process.

However, different studies measure "profitability" differently. Conventionally, in literature, most studies measure profitability as the share of profit in total output or sales (profit margin). While other conventional measures such as "return on assets" or "return on equity" also exist, they do not precisely reflect the trends in the process of capital accumulations, because they include "nonproductive assets" such as financial assets. Hence, a Heterodox approach measures profitability as the ratio of profit (surplus) and invested fixed capital, because capitalist decision-making to invest further and enhance capital accumulation depends on the returns on capital invested.

Even the Heterodox tradition measures the invested fixed capital differently (Basu 2013). In this study, we measured profitability as a ratio of profits and the "expended capital-value" or the sum of wages/salaries paid to workers/managers, total cost of inputs, and depreciation. A Marxian understanding suggests that capital accumulation is a continuous process that does not occur in phases. Therefore, the "expended" value of capital, or the value of capital consumed in the production process in each cycle (or the value of capital that goes into determining the production cost of the commodity), and the profitability on that capital determine capital accumulation. Hence, measuring profitability using "expended capital-value" should give a well-rounded picture of the accumulation and growth process, where "expended capital-value" is the sum total of wages and salaries to employees, raw materials consumed, and depreciation.

Hence, our study tries to relate Kerala's factory-sector profitability dynamics to changes and developments in the production method.

Factors driving Kerala's factory sector growth

Profitability

Figure 2.1 provides the factor-sector profitability figures for Kerala and India. After predominantly following India's factory-sector-profitability trends and cycles until the end of the last century, Kerala's factory sector diverged. For a significant period from 2001–2, Kerala's factory-sector profitability remained stagnant even as India's soared. The trends reversed only after the 2007–8 global financial crisis, when from 2009–10 onwards Kerala started

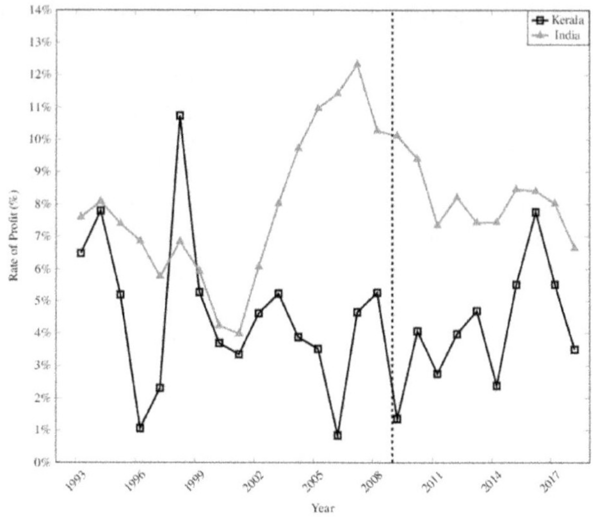

Figure 2.1 Profitability: Kerala vs. India

Source: Authors' estimation using ASI Data (from 1993–94 to 2018–19) from EPWRF.

seeing an increasing trend as opposed to India's declining trend. (The dotted line in Figure 2.1 marks the shift in trend in the last decade.) This continued until 2016–17, after which Kerala's profitability too started declining.

Our study identifies this opposite trend in profitability between the factory sectors of Kerala and India as the key reason behind the differences in growth patterns. The upcoming sections suggest that the subsequent variables characterizing the production process logically follow from this trend.

Gross fixed capital formation

Gross fixed capital formation (GFCF) is an important measure signifying investment activity in the real production sector. Its share in GVA indicates the pace and trends in the capital accumulation process.

Figure 2.2 provides the trend in the GFCF–GVA ratio for the factory sectors in Kerala and India. As profitability in India's factory sector began to decline toward the end of the last decade, the ratio of GFCF to GVA steadily decreased between 2011–12 and 2018–19. Since additional investments are now less profitable, a lower share of the value added is being invested for capital accumulation.

But the trend contrasts with that in Kerala's factory sector. As the profitability started to increase, the GFCF–GVA ratio reflected a sharp increase until 2016–17, then sharply fell with the decline in profitability.

Table 2.2 summarizes the growth rates for the major variables characterizing the production process in the factory sector for Kerala and India between

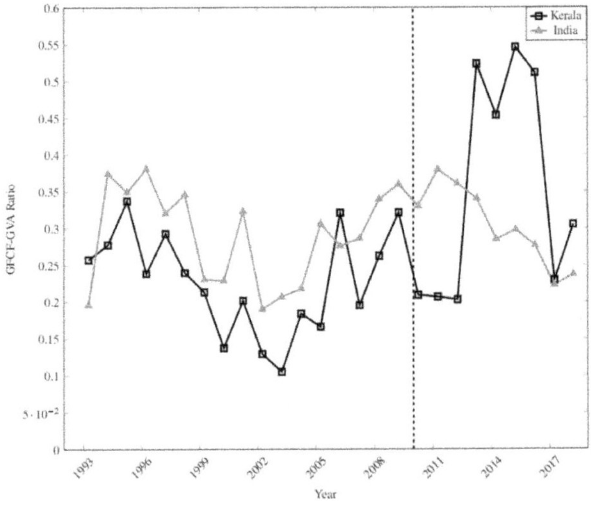

Figure 2.2 Gross fixed capital formation as a share of output: Kerala vs. India
Source: Authors' estimation using ASI Data (from 1993–94 to 2018–19) from EPWRF.

2011–12 and 2018–19. For the GFCF–GVA ratio, against an annual growth rate of 4.19% for Kerala, the magnitude for India contracted at a rate of (–)7.2%. Hence, the pattern of capital accumulation in the last decade has mostly followed the pattern of profitability in the factory sector. Subsequent sections show that the growth in other variables of production also followed this trend and that this trend in investments has been the determining factor in the growth differences between the factory sectors of Kerala and India.

Capital–labour ratio and capital productivity

A positive growth rate in the GFCF–GVA ratio implies the growth of fixed investments outpacing the growth of value added, signifying a fast pace of capital accumulation. Following this, the capital–labour ratio (value of fixed capital per employee) in Kerala's factory sector increased significantly. As evident from Figure 2.3, the ratio rose at a fast pace between 2011–12 and 2016–17, marginally dropping thereafter.

Since the beginning of the reform period, the capital-labour ratio between Kerala's and India's factory sectors began to diverge significantly, as traditionally, labour-intensive industries have dominated Kerala's manufacturing sector. This divergence was accentuated in the first decade of this century when profitability in India's factory sector increased against the stagnancy in Kerala. But since 2011–12, growth in the capital–labour ratio in Kerala's factory sector has significantly outpaced the corresponding growth at the all-India level. Table 2.4 shows that the capital–labour ratio in Kerala's factory

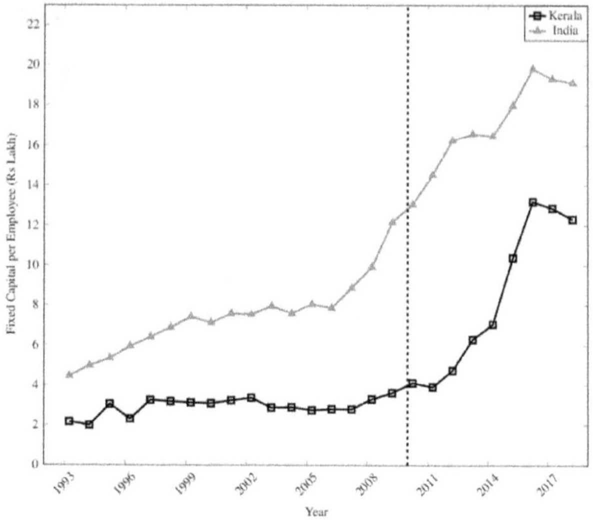

Figure 2.3 Capital–labour ratio: Kerala vs. India

Source: Authors' estimation using ASI Data (from 1993–94 to 2018–19) from EPWRF.

Table 2.4 Factory sector growth rates between FY12 and FY19: Kerala vs. India

	Kerala (%)	*India (%)*
Profitability	6.95	-0.40
Gross value added (GVA)	9.57	5.94
GFCF–GVA ratio	4.19	-7.20
Labour productivity	12.55	2.71
Capital-labour ratio	20.39	4.16
Capital productivity	-6.51	-1.39
Wage rate	6.40	2.04
Total persons employed	-2.64	3.15

Source: Authors' estimation using ASI Data (from 1993–94 to 2018–19) from EPWRF.

sector grew at a large annual rate of 20.39% between 2011–12 and 2018–19 against India's 4.16%.

However, this is not a normal capital accumulation, where the newly invested capital replicates the existing production process, merely increasing in volume. An equally important parameter to observe is the capital productivity (GVA per unit value of fixed capital). Figure 2.4 shows the trends in capital productivity in the factory sector between Kerala and India. Because of the labour-intensive nature of Kerala's factory sector, its capital productivity was higher than the all-India average; however, it dropped significantly since 2011–12 and approached the all-India level. Table 2.4 shows that it plunged at an annual rate of (–)6.51%. Hence, the newly invested capital

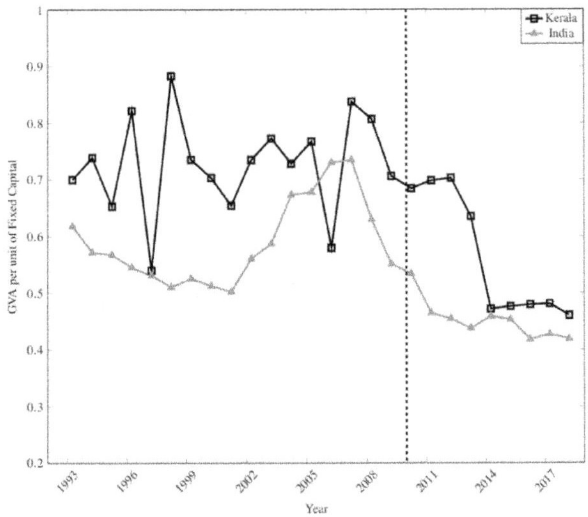

Figure 2.4 Capital productivity: Kerala vs. India

Source: Authors' estimation using ASI Data (from 1993–94 to 2018–19) from EPWRF.

was labour replacing in nature, instead of being a technological upgradation. Such a significantly large investment in labour-replacing capital investments was seen in the first decade of the liberalization era at the all-India level, which was replicated in Kerala.

Declining capital productivity implies that the technological content in the additional capital invested is insufficient to effect a proportional increase in the value-added output. In such a scenario, when a profitability-led capital investment cannot proportionally increase the GVA, profitability cannot either (unless there is a significant squeeze on wages). This led to the decline in profitability after 2016–17, and a subsequent fall in the GFCF–GVA ratio.

Labour productivity, wages, and employment

As Kerala's factory sector invested significantly in labour-replacing technological capital, labour productivity (GVA per employee) also increased significantly, as seen from Figure 2.5. Because of the low capital intensity of the production process in Kerala's factory sector before 2011–12, labour productivity was stagnant since 1998–99, while the productivity at the all-India level increased. However, because of a significant rise in investment in fixed capital, labour productivity quickly approached the all-India level. But it declined after 2016–17 with the fall in both profitability and the GFCF–GVA ratio, possibly indicating low-capacity utilization.

Although labour productivity in Kerala's factory sector increased significantly at an annual rate of 12.55% between 2011–12 and 2018–19 against

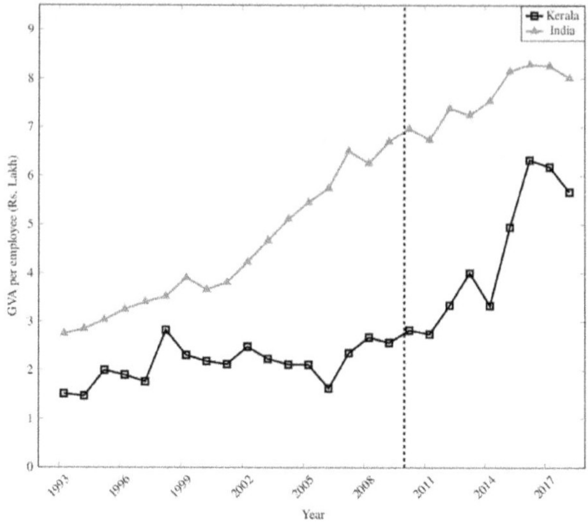

Figure 2.5 Labour productivity: Kerala vs. India

Source: Authors' estimation using ASI Data (from 1993–94 to 2018–19) from EPWRF.

a prolonged rate of 2.71% for India, real wage rates did not increase proportionally (see Table 2.4). It was higher than the all-India level, but it only grew at 6.4%, which was much slower than the rise in labour productivity. A faster growth in labour productivity (at constant prices) compared to real wages indicates an increase in the relative rate of exploitation (i.e., ratio of profits to wages) in real terms. Therefore, the gap between wage-rate growth and labour productivity could have contributed to the increasing trend in profitability in Kerala's factory sector.

Contractualization of work could be a possible reason for such a gap between labour-productivity growth and the real wage-rate growth. The percentage of contract workers in the total number of workers in Kerala's factory sector increased from 12.4% in 2012–13 to 17.1% in 2018–19. Such a rise in the share of contract workers could have resulted in slower growth in wages.

Significant investments in lumpy fixed capital and decreasing capital productivity induce the downward trend in profitability (as the volume of inputs and depreciation increases the denominator). Such a downward push, accompanied by shocks from domestic policies (e.g., demonetization and goods and services tax implementation), led to a decline in profitability towards the end of the last decade, initiating a slowdown in capital accumulation and output growth.

A significant outcome of the sizeable labour-replacing capital investments in Kerala's factories was on employment. From Table 2.4, we see that the total employment in Kerala's factory sector declined in absolute terms at an annual rate of (–)2.64%. Growth in GVA equals the sum of growth in

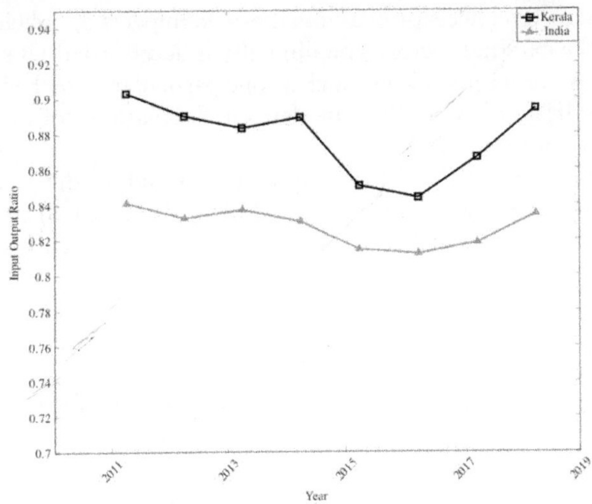

Figure 2.6 Input value as a share of output value: Kerala vs. India

Source: Authors' estimation using ASI Data (from 1993–94 to 2018–19) from EPWRF.

labour-productivity and growth in employment. In the initial years of the last decade, the large capital investments resulted in rapid labour-productivity growth that far outpaced the fall in employment, resulting in fast GVA growth. However, in the later part, with a decline in profitability and capital accumulation, labour-productivity growth slowed down, cementing a slow-down in GVA growth.

Cost of inputs

We briefly discuss the possibility that the profitability rise in Kerala's factory sector was the result of fall in the cost of intermediate inputs. As evident from Figure 2.6, which reflects the input value–output value ratio in the factory sector in Kerala and India, the ratio only declines partially after 2014–15, while increasing again towards 2017–18. But the increasing trend in profitability began much earlier. Input costs in 2015–16 and 2016–17 dropped because of the fall in international crude oil prices. While this may have impacted certain industries that rely heavily on these inputs (e.g., petroleum products and plastic products industries), it could not have influenced the entire factory sector.

Industry-level trends in Kerala's factory sector

Precision in the analysis of an economy's manufacturing sector over a period of time based on the trends in profitability, capital accumulation, and other production-related variables is achievable. However, such accuracy is not possible for an industry-level analysis because of several short-term factors, including micro-level decision-making, lopsided impacts of policies, and fluctuations in the external sector. The difficulty is accentuated when analyzing industries at a sub-national level (such as one particular state) because shocks elsewhere in the country could cause demand fluctuations for products from any industry in a particular region.

While this section delves deeper into understanding the trends in production-related variables at the two-digit (NIC Code-2008) industry level in Kerala, our analyzes and conclusions will be very limited because of the aforementioned difficulties.

For our analysis, we have considered only those of Kerala's factory-sector industries that feature among the first ten in terms of share in GVA. Of these industries, our analysis focuses on those with a higher GVA growth rate than the overall average of Kerala's factory sector between 2011–12 and 2018–19. Table 2.5 presents the top industries and the growth rates in their production-related variables. The analysis also includes the "Food Products" industry, despite a slower growth rate, since it is the largest two-digit level industry in terms of both share in GVA and employment, and therefore, the dynamics in this industry are bound to have a sector-wide impact.

Coke and petroleum, chemical, and transport equipment

Based on the annual growth rate in GVA between 2011–12 and 2018–19, the top three industries are "coke and petroleum products", "chemical products", and "transport equipment". While the first two industries have always played a significant role in Kerala's industrial sector, enjoying more than 10% share in GVA, the transport equipment segment has grown to significant levels in recent years.

A look at the production-related variables reveals profitability-led growth in these three industries. While the coke and petroleum products industry witnessed this phenomenon in the first half of the decade, the chemical products industry did it in the second half. Therefore, these two industries witnessed significant growth in labour productivity and very high growth rates in GVA in these corresponding periods. The transport equipment industry witnessed a growth in profitability throughout the sub-periods. While profitability was sustained due to labour-replacing capital investments and labour-productivity rise in the first half, technologically advanced investments kept afloat in the second half, which increased the capital productivity.

The real wage rate in these three industries has either declined or remained stagnant, but labour productivity has shown significant high growth. Therefore, among other factors, the profitability growth in these industries has been induced through a squeeze in wages, thereby increasing the rate of exploitation (ratio of profit to wages) in both relative and absolute terms. On average, the share of contractual workers in the total workforce is well above 60% in the coke and petroleum products and transport equipment industries,

Table 2.5 Industry-wise growth rates of various attributes of Kerala's factory sector

Industry	*Capital productivity (%)*				*Labour productivity (%)*			
	FY12–FY15	*FY16–FY19*	*FY15–FY16*	*FY12–FY19*	*FY12–FY15*	*FY16–FY19*	*FY15–FY16*	*FY12–FY19*
Coke and petroleum products	3.85	-13.35	106.39	-3.49	11.53	2.50	110.09	8.20
Chemical products	-10.12	21.76	10.65	14.47	-22.89	36.51	16.75	14.49
Transport equipment	2.05	-5.39	28.67	2.17	23.15	4.05	6.10	8.82
Pharmaceuticals products	-6.09	-7.90	29.58	-0.50	10.31	-1.30	29.36	5.65
Non-metallic minerals	-2.07	15.75	-55.06	-3.54	10.94	7.89	-7.28	9.16
Food products	-0.17	-4.24	-16.61	-4.28	14.12	4.34	46.32	15.48

Industry	*Wage rate (%)*				*Total persons employed (%)*			
	FY12–FY15	*FY16–FY19*	*FY15–FY16*	*FY12–FY19*	*FY12–FY15*	*FY16–FY19*	*FY15–FY16*	*FY12–FY19*
Coke and petroleum products	-19.21	19.82	-5.78	-4.85	31.80	-9.55	36.51	15.29
Chemical products	-8.09	0.22	20.15	-0.47	10.09	2.68	-22.02	0.50
Transport equipment	4.28	-7.49	5.11	-1.40	-0.09	6.80	1.87	3.47
Pharmaceuticals products	19.22	-1.61	-20.49	3.94	18.80	4.50	-11.58	7.97
Non-metallic minerals	6.25	5.71	0.47	4.91	-1.41	0.61	12.23	0.84
Food products	11.11	7.22	15.21	10.81	-5.84	-2.73	-22.66	-9.05

Source: Authors' estimation using ASI Data (from 1993–94 to 2018–19) from EPWRF.

whereas it increased from 15.7% in 2012–13 to 21.8% in 2018–19 in the chemical products industry.

Pharmaceuticals and non-metallic minerals

The pharmaceuticals and non-metallic minerals were two other industries that led the growth in Kerala's factory sector. However, these industries did not observe profitability growth.

Kerala's pharmaceuticals industry started with a very low level of capital intensity (capital–labour ratio) compared to the all-India level. Hence, any additional investment in capital could be expected to create a large growth in the capital–labour ratio and labour productivity. This growth in labour productivity resulted in the industry's GVA high growth rate of 19.22% between 2011–12 and 2014–15. But considering growth not led by profitability cannot be expected to sustain the labour-productivity growth, the labour productivity in this industry stagnated (declining marginally) and the GVA growth rate slowed down between 2015–16 and 2018–19.

The scenario was similar in the non-metallic minerals industry. But here, the labour-productivity growth and the GVA growth rate remain afloat in the second half as well because of a sudden and very large investment between 2014–15 and 2015–16.

Food products

In the food products industry, the GVA growth rates were slower than the state average throughout, and the profitability grew only in the second half of the last decade. But this industry, too, had a much lower capital intensity than the all-India average. Therefore, investments in this industry led to a very large increase in labour productivity.

Although the growth in real wage rates in this industry closely followed the growth in labour productivity, employment suffered the most significant impact. The large labour-replacing capital investments meant a decline in absolute terms in the total employment in this industry. The industry, which employs approximately 46% of all the employees in Kerala's factory sector, witnessed a decline in employment at an annual rate of (–)9% between 2011–12 and 2018–19. Therefore, the volume of profits in this sector was kept afloat through workforce reduction and labour intensification.

Possibility of trade-led growth

The preceding discussions have shown that the growth in Kerala's factory sector was led by a profitability rise. To understand if such a rise in profitability was triggered by a boom in international trade, matching the growth pattern of the all-India level in the first decade of the twenty-first century, we analyzed the pattern of exports from Kerala's factories. ASI unit-level data shows the share of output directly exported by the firms.

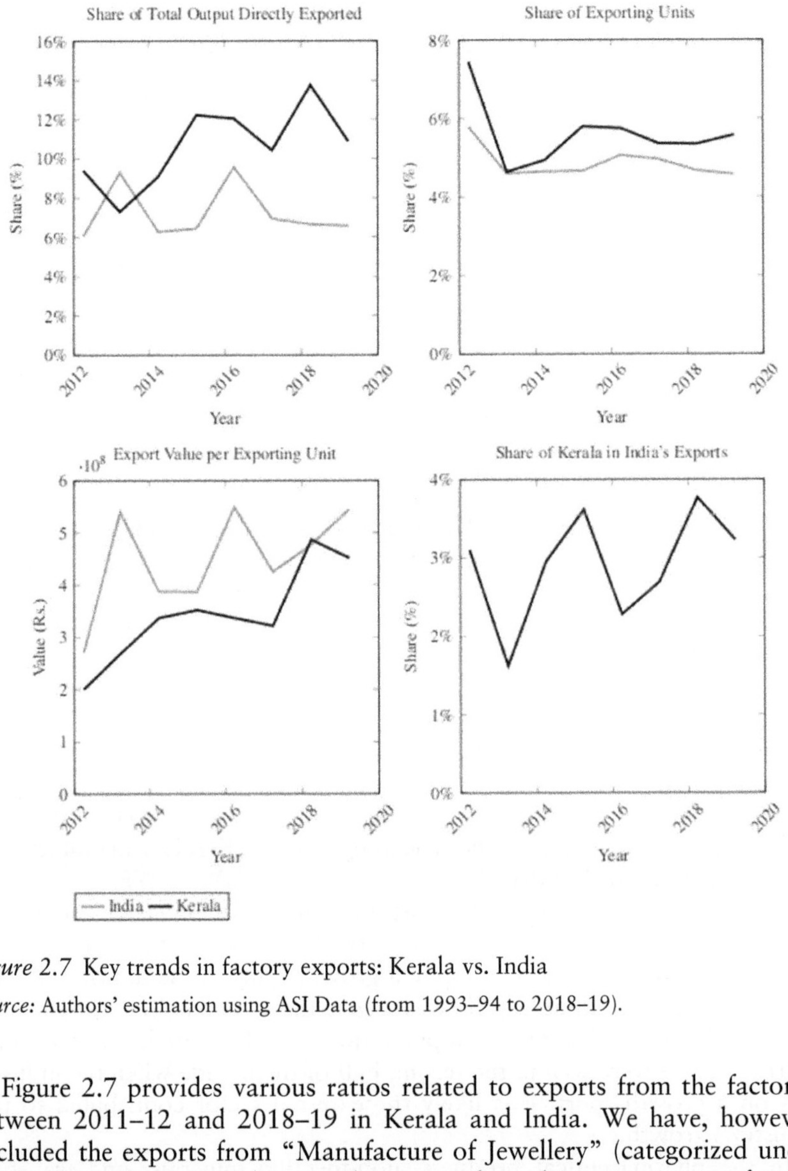

Figure 2.7 Key trends in factory exports: Kerala vs. India

Source: Authors' estimation using ASI Data (from 1993–94 to 2018–19).

Figure 2.7 provides various ratios related to exports from the factories between 2011–12 and 2018–19 in Kerala and India. We have, however, excluded the exports from "Manufacture of Jewellery" (categorized under "Other Manufacturing") because the exports from this sector were performed by a handful of firms (mostly less than 5) and the highly fluctuating trends in exports along with the large values of output distorted the analysis of overall trends.

Figure 2.7 shows that in Kerala's entire formal sector, the directly exported share of output saw a marginal upward trend beginning 2011–12. Such a trend shows that "exported" output grew faster than "non-exported" output in Kerala's factories, a case which has been absent at the all-India level. Similar trends were also seen in the share of exporting units in Kerala, a trend not

Table 2.6 Top exporting industries in Kerala (2015–16)

Industry	*Share in total exports (%)*	*Export–output ratio (%)*
Food products	64.44	28.03
Chemical products	9.52	26.48
Coke and petroleum products	7.54	2.80
Textiles	5.84	27.99
Wearing apparel	3.28	66.46
Rubber and plastic products	3.09	4.15
Computer and electronic products	2.21	14.63
Electrical equipment	0.97	14.39
Wood products	0.97	11.17
Basic metals	0.67	3.80

Source: Authors' estimation using ASI Data (from 1993–94 to 2018–19).

observed at the all-India level. The export value per exporting unit, in nominal terms, has also been increasing, both at the Kerala and all-India levels.

But the share of Kerala in India's export basket from the formal manufacturing sector has not changed dramatically, seeing a very marginal upward trend. As trade at the all-India level has been sluggish over the past decade, there is only partial evidence that could point to the external sector's role in contributing to the growth in Kerala's factories.

Disaggregating this into industry-wise trends, firstly, we see the share of various industries in Kerala's formal manufacturing sector's export basket in Table 2.6. Among the top 10 industries, only coke and petroleum products and chemical products have been leading (top 5) Kerala's manufacturing sector growth in the last decade.

Figure 2.8 shows the share of exports in total output for various industries. In the coke and petroleum products industry, hardly any output was exported in the first half of the decade despite a growth spurt in the industry; a brief phase of exported output (2–4%) was seen in the second half. In the chemical products industry, the export-output ratio trend fluctuated; however, high shares (>20%) were seen in the second half of the decade when the industry was on a growth spurt. It is likely the external sector contributed to this industry's growth.

In the pharmaceutical products, non-metallic minerals, and transport equipment industries, which were top contributors to growth, the share of exports to output remained on a fluctuating trend and could not be claimed to have contributed to growth.

Food products, the biggest exporting industry in Kerala's factory sector, had an average growth rate lower than Kerala's in the last decade. This industry saw a partially increasing trend in the export–output ratio in the first half, but it declined thereafter. The external sector could likely have played a role.

Therefore, we cannot conclusively claim that the faster pace of growth in Kerala's entire factory sector was the result of significantly increased demand

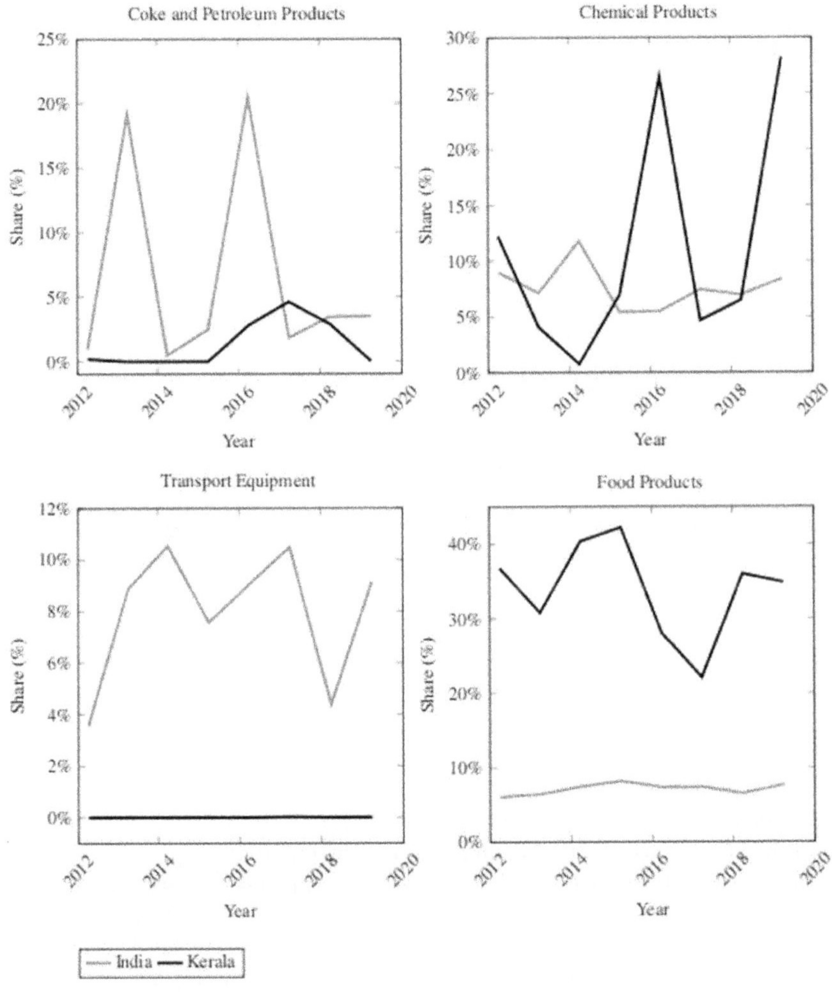

Figure 2.8 Industry-wise export–output ratio: Kerala vs. India

Source: Authors' estimation using ASI Data (from 1993–94 to 2018–19).

from the external sector. However, the external sector could have played a role in the growth in certain industries during certain periods. This situation is unlike the all-India case in the 2000s, when the boom in world trade significantly contributed to the manufacturing sector growth.

Discussion on the growth pattern in Kerala's factory sector in the last decade

Starting from 2003, India's manufacturing sector rode the wave of significant expansion in international trade. Growth rates in the manufacturing sector neared the double-digit mark, with the registered manufacturing sector growing at over 10% annually. Boosted by increasing profitability, both capital intensity and labour productivity increased significantly.

During this period, Kerala's manufacturing sector was a typical example of a victim of unplanned growth with severe regional disparities. Its factory sector remained relatively labour intensive. Of the several explanations that could be provided for this trend, one could be Myrdal's phenomenon of cumulative causation taking shape. Taking advantage of the rise in profitability and expanded world trade, Indian industries focused their investments on the traditional industrial centres, and Kerala was at the lower end of the industrialization level. Another possible explanation could be the boom in the construction sector in Kerala, with resources and credit being redirected to this sector, away from manufacturing. Altogether, Kerala's manufacturing sector, especially the factory sector, severely lagged the all-India levels.

But towards the end of the last decade, after the global financial crisis, as profitability in India's factory sector declined, capital found profitable investment in Kerala's low capital-intensive factory sector. Labour-replacing capital investments led to fast growth in labour productivity and value-added output. The capital intensity and labour productivity of Kerala's factory sector began to narrow the gap with the all-India level.

Yet, such a growth process in Kerala's factory sector was concerning, considering the unplanned growth, with the short-term aim to exploit the opportunity for profitable investment, it was bound to end in a crisis. As lumpy investments in fixed capital increased, it induced a downward push on profitability, which ultimately started to decline after 2016–17. The factory sector growth began to slow down towards the end of the last decade because of the slowdown in capital accumulation, stagnant capital productivity, drop in capacity utilization, and declining labour productivity.

But more importantly, as previous sections suggest, it was also a period of "jobless growth". As a result of the increase in capital intensity, despite a segment of the jobs lost in the low-productivity and labour-intensive sectors being absorbed in the capital-intensive sectors, employment in the factory sector declined as a whole. Moreover, as discussed earlier, these highly productive and capital-intensive sectors where a portion of the job losses were absorbed saw a decline in real wage rates along with a significant rise in labour productivity, indicating an increase in the rate of exploitation in absolute and relative terms.

Therefore, such a pattern of "jobless growth", although accompanied by increased productivity and capital intensity, raises concerns about the effectiveness in initiating a structural transformation in the economy that would enhance Kerala's capacity towards a steady long-term process of development accompanied by improved welfare. It also puts the focus back on the need for a planned process of industrial growth and a strong industrial policy in the developing world.

Conclusion

The "revival" in Kerala's factory sector growth in the last decade can be termed as an attempt by the state to "play catch-up" with the factory sector at the all-India level. It was a typical profitability-led growth that led to faster capital accumulation and growth in labour productivity.

But the "catching-up" process also brought with it the pitfalls of the neoliberal growth pattern witnessed at the all-India level. As is the case with all unplanned growth processes, it was bound to be crisis-ridden, with the fall in profitability towards the end of the decade triggering a slowdown. Moreover, it was a "jobless growth", with increased contractualization and the major industries driving growth witnessing an increase in the rate of exploitation. Hence, the vulnerabilities and unsustainability associated with the neoliberal growth path were imported into Kerala's factory sector as well.

Several studies point to the need for effective state intervention to counter such unfavourable tendencies associated with a purely market-led process of growth (Chandrasekhar 2015). Planning the path of industrialization; imposing controls on capacity creation to direct the pattern of growth and ensure effective structural transformation in both output and employment; establishing backward and forward linkages through public sector intervention and controls on finance; preventing investments into the production of non-essentials; ensuring demand through procurement policies, public investment in infrastructure, counter-cyclical public expenditure, a long-term innovation policy to build domestic research capabilities and move up the value chain, etc., are generally regarded as essential measures the state must take in developing countries for sustainable industrialization (Andreoni & Chang 2019).

In the neoliberal era, however, the capacity of the provincial (state) governments is greatly restricted in terms of both resources and policies. Most are merely left to compete with each other to attract private investments. As a result, these governments attempt to reduce taxes, amend labour and environmental regulations, and ease land acquisitions to ensure the profitability of private investments, thereby only feeding on to the vulnerabilities of the neoliberal growth process. An effective and planned process of industrialization at the national level is necessary, not just for sustainable growth but also to reduce regional disparities.

Scope for further research

In this study, we attempted to understand the growth in Kerala's manufacturing sector – specifically the factory sector – to identify the sources and patterns of "revival" in growth in the past decade. We performed this exercise purely by analyzing the production-related aspects of the factory sector.

But we must also understand the demand side of the growth process. The demand-related factors that spurred the growth in Kerala's factory sector could have originated due to a multitude of factors, including government policies and economic factors in other regions of the country. These need to be researched for a well-rounded understanding of this growth process.

Moreover, several production-related aspects discussed here, such as "labour-replacing capital investment", "increase in rate of exploitation", etc., are deeply associated with the economic and political environment of the region and the state of class struggle in various industries. This aspect needs to be understood in the context of the political economy of the growth process.

Note

1 The preliminary versions of this chapter were presented at the Kerala and the World Economy Conference 2024, Centre for Development Studies, Thiruvananthapuram.

References

Albin, Alice. 1990. "Manufacturing Sector in Kerala: Comparative Study of Its Growth and Structure." *Economic and Political Weekly* 2059–70.

Andreoni, Antonio, and Chang, Ha-Joon. 2019. "The Political Economy of Industrial Policy: Structural Interdependencies, Policy Alignment and Conflict Management." *Structural Change and Economic Dynamics* 48: 136–50.

Balakrishnan, Pulapre, and Babu, M. Suresh. 2003. "Growth and Distribution in Indian Industry in the Nineties." *Economic and Political Weekly*, 3997–4005.

Basu, Deepankar. 2013. "Replacement Versus Historical Cost Profit Rates: What Is the Difference? When Does It Matter?" *Metroeconomica* 64(2): 293–318.

Basu, Deepankar, and Das, Debarshi. 2017. "Profitability and Investment: Evidence from India's Organized Manufacturing Sector." *Metroeconomica* 68(1): 47–90.

Basu, Deepankar, and Das, Debarshi. 2018. "Profitability in India's Organized Manufacturing Sector: The Role of Technology, Distribution and Demand." *Cambridge Journal of Economics* 42(1): 137–53.

Basu, Deepankar, and Vasudevan, Ramaa. 2013. "Technology, Distribution and the Rate of Profit in the US Economy: Understanding the Current Crisis." *Cambridge Journal of Economics* 37(1): 57–89.

Chandrasekhar, C. P. 2015. "Promise Belied: India's Post-Independence Industrialization Experience." *Economics: Indian Industrialization* 1.

Harilal, K. N., and Joseph, K. J. 2003. "Stagnation and Revival of Kerala Economy: An Open Economy Perspective." *Economic and Political Weekly* 2286–94.

Kannan, K. P. 1990. "Kerala Economy at the Crossroads?" *Economic and Political Weekly* 1951–56.

Kannan, K. P., and Hari, K. S. 2020. "Revisiting Kerala's Gulf Connection: Half a Century of Emigration, Remittances and Their Macroeconomic Impact, 1972–2020." *The Indian Journal of Labour Economics* 63: 941–67.

Marx, K., Fernbach, D., and Mandel, E. 1993. *Capital: Volume 3: A Critique of Political Economy. Capital Series*. London: Penguin Publishing Group.

Parameswaran, M. 2020. "Migration, Remittances and Dutch Disease: Evidence from Kerala Economy." In *Kerala and the World Economy* edited by Sunil Mani. Thiruvananthapuram: Centre for Development Studies.

Rajan, S. I., and Zachariah, K. C. 2019. "Emigration and Remittances: New Evidences from the Kerala Migration Survey 2018." Working Papers id:12989, eSocialSciences.

Subrahmanian, K. K. 2003. *Regional Industrial Growth under Economic Liberalization: A Case Study of Selected Issues with Reference to Kerala State*. New Delhi: Manak Publications.

Subrahmanian, Kalarickal Kumaran, and Pillai, P Mohanan. 1986. "Kerala's Industrial Backwardness: Exploration of Alternative Hypotheses." *Economic and Political Weekly* 577–92.

Sunny, Justin, Parida, Jajati K, and Azurudeen, Mohammed. 2020. "Remittances, Investment and New Emigration Trends in Kerala." *Review of Development and Change* 25(1): 5–29.

Thampy, M. M. 1990. "Wage-Cost and Kerala's Industrial Stagnation: Study of Organised Small-Scale Sector. *Economic and Political Weekly* 2077–82.

Thomas, Jayan Jose. 2003. "Labour and Industrialisation in Kerala." *Indian Journal of Labour Economics* 46(4): 575–92.

Thomas, Jayan Jose. 2005. "Kerala's Industrial Backwardness: A Case of Path Dependence in Industrialization?" *World Development* 33(5): 763–78.

3 Surge in agricultural products imports under the FTAs

Livelihood concerns by targeting substitutable products

Murali Kallummal

Introduction

Multilateral trade agreements are not merely deals between countries that impact domestic trade flows. When countries form trade agreements for goods and services, it can alter the delicate balance of commodity prices within their domestic economies. The price variations that can be isolated after signing a trade agreement will alter producers' decisions as intermediaries, users, or consumers. There can be gradual changes over the years, as well as sudden changes around trade agreements that affect a product's price. Such a change will be particularly demanding for the sector or partner, resulting in a more significant price cut. Such products can be categorised under two heads based on the impact on price and the quantum of the difference: the "complementary" products and the "substitute" products. The commodity markets are said to be "more competitive" with a lower price.[1] For consumers, as a direct outcome of the trade agreements, which imply a decrease in market power due to reduced price-cost margins. India has had some significant free trade agreements (FTAs) from 2010 to 2011, and price behaviour would be essential to understanding the economy's dynamics.

India is expanding its mandate on the coverage and scope of trade agreements through fast-paced bilateral deals, while continuing to maintain its pace in the multilateral process. The hastened pace across many of the bilaterals requires additional focus economic activities and their associated challenges. One immediate challenge is that, multilateral negotiations, there is a need for more time to develop a domestic narrative about the financial activities and associated challenges of the bilateral trade deal. The gains would depend on specific key governance parameters, such as the level of representation (feedback mechanism and interconnectedness), the stage of development, and legislative strength (Dhar and Kallummal, 2007).

The chapter is divided into three sections. The first provides the theoretical underpinning of establishing substitutable and complementary products based on trade flows. The second assesses the treatment of the agricultural sector under India's Free Trade Agreement (FTA). To understand market access issues, the chapter also analyses India's tariff profiles and its FTAs separately. The third section deals with the Kerala economy, highlighting the importance

DOI: 10.4324/9781003601289-4

of the agricultural sector in providing livelihoods across the economy, and identifying coconut as a key livelihood crop. About Kerala, the analysis is based on agricultural value-added products such as crude coconut oil (CCOs) and refined coconut oils (RCOs). It also highlights Kerala's livelihood concerns because of imported crude palm oils (CPOs) and refined palm oils (RPOs) at reduced tariffs under the ASEAN–India Free Trade Area (AIFTA). India has provided market access to substitute products for CPOS and RPOS. Both these products showed a spike in India's imports from the ASEAN partners.

The chapter attempts to contextualise the varying implications that the price of products (raw or finished) can have on agricultural products in general, as well as at the most disaggregated levels, such as coconuts and coconut oil. It points to the overall ecosystems beyond the natural and otherwise (health advisories based on "scientific research"),[2] which influenced consumption habits. The livelihood of coconut farmers came under stress due to not just the ASEAN FTA but also the overall policies and the prevailing ecosystem. The impact is owing to the overall changes in the prices of raw coconut, nuts, and other value-added products.

The chapter also attempts to trace some linkages from the global to local-level price movements and market opportunities for national states (India) and the federal units (Kerala). It explores sustainability-based trading relationships and sustainability issues, aiming to understand how Kerala can fit into the national framework of trade agreements.

Methodology

This chapter delves deeper into understanding the content of agricultural tariff line participation in the FTA. Across most of India's FTAs until 2012, a considerable share of agricultural and allied products was not considered for preferential duty treatments through duty elimination or reduction commitments. All existing literature on India established that some of the agricultural and allied sectors had been negatively impacted despite such products being categorised in the negative list of the FTAs. Therefore, the chapter shifts away from the usual calculations (such as the balance of trade or terms of trade) to the actual impact of changing prices and the challenges they pose for a largely agrarian economy. The first possibility lies in understanding the price variations that can be isolated after a trade agreement is signed, which may alter producers' decisions as intermediaries, users, or consumers.

1. Substitutable products: Two goods are substitutes if they can be used by the user (industries and consumers) for the same purpose. Users perceive both goods as similar or comparable, so having more of one good causes the consumer to desire less of the other good.[3]
2. Complementary products: A complementary good is one whose appeal increases with the popularity of its complement. It displays a negative

cross-elasticity of demand, meaning that it increases demand for itself when the price of another sound decreases.

3. Value-added products: Value-added refers to the extra value created beyond the original value of the commodity. In the agricultural and allied products sector, transformation from primary to value-added products can be achieved by establishing agro-processing units, resulting in investments and employment within the domestic or local territory.

This chapter examines the agricultural trade complementarity of ASEAN countries in the global agrarian market from 1997 to 2015.

The results indicate that (i) the ASEAN countries' agricultural export patterns are weakly complementary in matching the regional import demands; (ii) they are relatively complementary in exporting agricultural products to the world market; (iii) the countries' agricultural competitiveness patterns are more affected by and benefitted from the global integration than the regional integration; and (iv) the countries, moreover, tend to become more substitutable over time (Hoang 2018).

Hoang's paper of 2018 proposed a cooperative strategy when competing with the international market, suggesting a process of internalisation. Since its formation, ASEAN has initiated a process of integration guided by a single market and joint production base (ASEAN n.d.). Before entering into any trade agreement, the welfare of 10 ASEAN nationalities was brought together under a common regional welfare through internalisation and balancing acts. In theory, the understanding of international trade is a manifestation of the change in national welfare (NW); each partner negotiating a trade deal would like to see a positive movement or minimise the losses. However, NW is the aggregation of the producer's and the consumer's welfare; in this context, the social accounting matrix (SAM) becomes prime for understanding a trade agreement.

This chapter covers 7 of the 13 trade agreements in Table 3.1 in the section India's FTAs. It examines how much of the 15% (approximately 1,700 products) is comprised of agricultural and allied products. The terms of trade (TOT) refer to a country's quantity of imports compared to that of its exports. Therefore, it is measured as a ratio of export price to import price, indicating what domestic goods a country can export or sell in exchange for imported goods. Viner (1950) proposed and introduced two concepts, trade creation and trade diversions, for the analysis of FTAs. While analysing trade agreements, studies continue to give utmost importance to these concepts today. Across all trade theories, consumers have remained at the centre, and it was never the producers – the reason being, as a template, it was the free trade theories adopted by the developed world that were imposed.

This chapter employs simple statistical tools, such as moving averages, to understand the role of opportunity cost. Concepts like intra-industry trade are not suitable for analysis as the primary task, and opportunity cost is also not considered, as the agricultural sector is protected for its other functions, such

as food and nutritional security roles. Therefore, the focus is on (i) whether the FTAs led to the loss of livelihood in Kerala or the India–Malaysia barter deal, which predates the WTO; (ii) establishing how trade does not enable livelihood concerns and whether they are disconnected from one another; and (iii) analyzing how vital internal dynamics are when it comes to trade deals.

Theoretical underpinning of price competitiveness

Mercantile and neoliberal theories have focused primarily on product competitiveness from the point of view of price. Using the available theoretical framework, the trade negotiators viewed the possible variations in cost associated with the product's tariff. The reduction in tariff was primarily considered to directly alter the price, thereby further enhancing the competitiveness of the product. Such an approach always led the negotiators to quickly list identifiable cost-impacting variables, such as the tariffs or duties imposed when goods move from one territory to another. Under the FTA, the pricing policies, driven by the race-to-the-bottom concept, did not account for all-off or sometimes some aspects of the list of unpaid bills, and most often, such costs were social and are, in some cases, economic costs too.

From the intergenerational implications point of view, land and labour costs are two factors of production that face a considerable amount of unpaid bills and are, therefore, always underpriced. Unfortunately, this is reflected in the final price of agricultural products, as the two variables significantly influence the main factors in determining prices. Another example is the cost of natural resources, such as water, air, soil, minerals, flora, fauna, and climate, which are utilised in product development. The human effort used in the production also includes technical and marketing expertise.

The payment for someone else's labour and all income received from one's delivery is wages. Labour can also be classified as an employee's physical and mental contribution to the production process's goods. The landowner's payment is rent, loyalties, commission, and goodwill with capital and labour.

Intellectual property rights and contracts in today's age and time are part of the capital and an integral part of the production factor. Capital, considering it is in a lesser proportion, including machinery, tools, and buildings, is of two types – fixed and working. While fixed investments are typically one-time investments in goods, such as machines and tools, working investments consist of liquid cash or money on hand, as well as raw materials.

Global accounting systems have primarily been designed to capture investments made at the working stages. The intrinsic values of fixed investments are not fully captured, except for intellectual property rights and contractual obligations. The initiatives of developed countries triggered a discussion on the externalisation of costs, and the divide between the North and the South became increasingly apparent. The imbalance between the goods sector and the services sector has been highlighted by Kallummal

(2020). Further, global negotiations have favoured the services sector's non-transparent modes of transaction (Kallummal and Francis 2020). Such unpaid bills are referred to as an "externalisation of price" and have continued to be an integral part of price fixation and have distorted domestic and international trade (Kallummal 2015). Although all investments had the issues of externalization of the project costs, it got a shot in the arm with the increased flow of foreign direct investments (FDIs) to the newly industrialized countries (NICs) within which a large quantum of capital was routed under the overseas development assistances (ODAs). This was supplied a decade ago.[4]

In the later decades, the surge in the FDIs further accentuated traceability problems and made matters worse with each and every untraceable flow of investments. In 2002, the OECD analysed the FDIs for development and suggested that most of the negative impacts do not factor in the positive linkages with the local communities and the harmful environmental effects of the FDIs (especially in the extractive and heavy industries). Accounting addresses the totality of FDIs, but it is found to be less favourable than domestic investments. (Kallummal 2001) Additionally, the social disruptions of the accelerated commercialisation in less developed countries and their effects are faced in terms of increased competition in the national markets (OECD 2002). One reason could be that the developed markets have higher shares of the services sector compared to other economies, and the second is that these economies have surplus capital for the FDI flows. Therefore, it is essential to analyse and understand which income groups (countries) benefited from the growing imbalance and restructured economic activity under the new paradigm, driven mainly by price competitiveness (Figure 3.1). The world is divided into four groups based on per capita income, and the WITS provides trade data (see Annex Table 3.1).

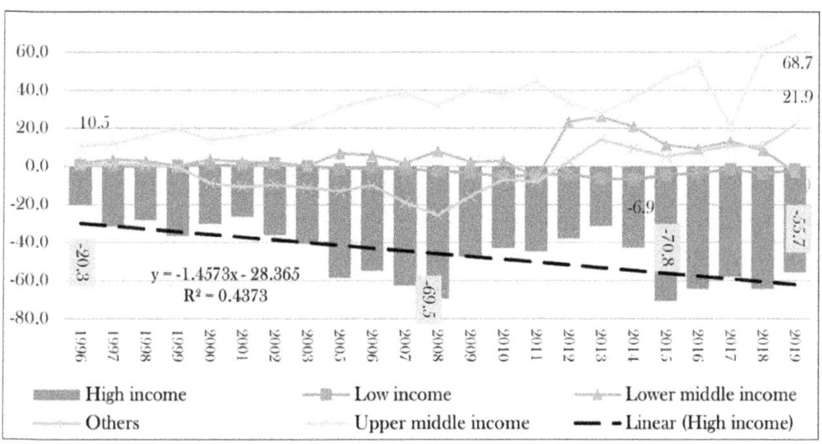

Figure 3.1 Global agricultural trade balance (income category-wise) (USD bn)

Source: WITS COMTRADE.

Figure 3.1 suggests a departure from when the WTO Agreement was signed in 1995, the agricultural trade balance across the main four income groups. High-income countries suggested growing market access up to 2008, reflected in increased trade deficits, from USD 20 billion in 1996 to USD 70 billion in 2008. After this, it fell and only bounced back in 2015. It suggested that the high-income group, with its predictable market (as indicated by the linear trend line), provided a perfect market for the upper-middle countries. In terms of gains in the agricultural sector, upper-middle-income countries, including China, Brazil, Russia, Peru, Malaysia, Mexico, and Thailand, among others, achieved a trade balance of USD 10.5 billion in 1996, which increased to a high of USD 69 billion in 2019. This is the only group that has consistently recorded a trade balance in the agricultural sector; therefore, it can be said that the dominant countries have benefited from it. Income category analysis revealed an increase in agricultural product exports after 2010, peaking in 2013 at USD 26 billion, after which their exports fell below imports. This is reflected in the decline in the trade balance from its 2013 peak (USD 26 billion) to a deficit of USD 3 billion in 2019. India is one of the countries that belong to this income category. Domestic production suggested an upward movement in both food and nonfood crops' prices, as suggested by the increased production and yield indices. A falling trade balance could result from increased importing of agricultural and allied products or reduced exports as products find it challenging to find an international market (see Annex Table 3.2).

The middle-income group is the only group with a consistent trade balance in the agricultural sector. Therefore, the dominant countries benefited from it. The analysis of the lower-middle income category showed an increase in agrarian product exports after 2010, peaking in 2013 at USD 26 billion. After that, its exports fell below imports, resulting in a negative trade balance with a value of $ 0.3 billion.

At the macro level, India's indices on all crops, food crops, and non-food crops indicated that during the period of 1993–94 to 2006–07 (with 1993–94 =100), it was food crops that had the upper hand over the nonfood crops in terms of production indexes, while in the second period of 2007–08 to 2019–20 (with 2007–08 =100), the nonfood crops had the upper hand over the food crops in production indexes (Annex Figures 3.1–3.3). The analysis of the two phases suggested that the yield graphs did not convey any apparent domination across both periods or shocks. Annex Figures 3.1–3.3 show that India's agricultural sector (food and nonfood) has been showing an increase in production and yield indices. Strategically, India should have sought external markets to export its surpluses. This meant that India did not face any reduction in the production or yield of agricultural commodities.

India has FTAs with four high-income economies, two of which are small markets and the other two are industrially developed, with a very high incidence of SPS and TBT barriers.[5] (Kallummal 2020). On the other hand, nine of India's FTA partners belong to its income group, accounting for nearly 50% of the 19 partners.

India's FTA and treatment of agricultural sector

Trade agreements driven by globalisation are usually defined as increasing the volume of cross-border economic interactions and resource flows, producing a qualitative shift in the relations between national economies and welfare-enhancing for both trading nations. Therefore, such agreements must be carefully analysed when a considerable proportion of the economy is in the informal sector; the data availability is primarily derived rather than absolute. Price movements and their direction determine the foundation of cross-sectoral linkages and the quality of interaction.

Agriculture: WTO and FTA[6]

The WTO's Agreement on Agriculture came into force on 1 January 1995. The agreement established a programme for the gradual reform of trade in agriculture. Members made specific commitments across three pillars – domestic support, export subsidies, and market access – resulting in a reduction in overall support and protection for agricultural products. The agreement also outlines procedures for addressing non-trade concerns, including food security and environmental protection. It also provided unique and differential treatment for developing countries, including improving the opportunities and terms of access for agricultural products of export interest to the developing members. The programme under the Agreement on Agriculture (AoA) aimed to establish a "fair and equitable, market-oriented agricultural trading system" by requiring countries to adopt new disciplines governing border measures and to use export subsidies and other related forms of support.

The Doha Round negotiations were conducted under three main pillars, which built upon commitments made in the Uruguay Round and outlined in the members' General Agreement on Tariffs and Trade (GATT) schedules: market access, domestic support, and export subsidies. The Doha Ministerial mandate in market access was to reduce and, where appropriate, eliminate the tariffs and non-tariff barriers (Figure 3.2).

Tariff commitment negotiations under the Doha Round remained static, so all tariff commitments undertaken under the Uruguay Round were considered final. The negotiations of the FTA differ from the approach taken by the WTO. Under the FTA, the modalities are to "eliminate" tariffs on almost all products, barring a few product lines (the coverage of which is negotiated) that form part of a Sensitive or Negative List. The elimination of tariff means that the reduction in duties starts on the actual most favoured nation (MFN) applied rate of duties and not on the WTO binding commitments (the gap between the WTO bound rate and the applied MFN tariff rates is also referred to as "water" or the "policy space"). Under the FTAs, the profound

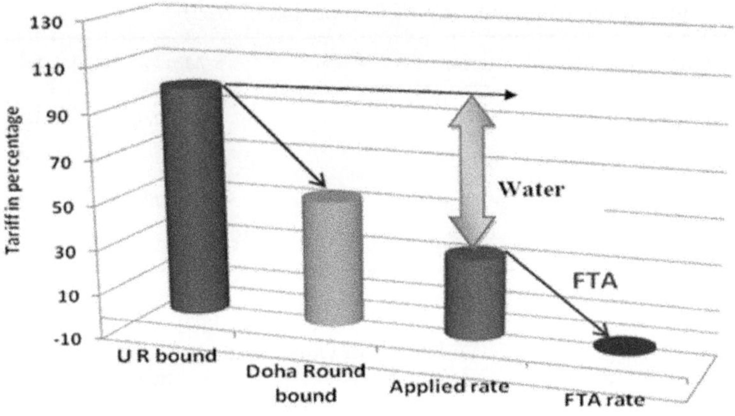

Figure 3.2 WTO and FTA commitments: a comparison

Source: Rajan S. R., Kallummal, M., and Sharma, S.K., 2016.

nature of tariff elimination is bound to reduce WTO members' policy space. An alternative to the conditions under FTAS could be achieved by providing the proper product-process standards, such as the sanitary and phytosanitary (SPS) and technical trade barriers (TBT) measures.

Discussions on removing nontariff measures did not progress well under the Doha Round. The WTO members were engaged in the WTO Committees of SPS and TBT measures. The approach that members followed was to seek recourse through harmonization, equivalence, mutual recognition arrangements, conformity assessment procedures, etc. – measures provided under the SPS and TBT agreements.

In terms of reducing the nontariff barriers under the FTA, the approach is similar to that of the WTO – to seek bilateral or regional harmonisation (or harmonisation bilaterally or regionally), the equivalent of mutual recognition arrangements (MRAs). In some instances, the FTAs provide a faster means to resolve issues relating to non-tariff barriers through harmonisation or MRAS - often these require careful and considerable attention to details, particularly with respect to trade and production dynamics. The WTO Doha Round negotiation discussed how to reduce or eliminate domestic support and export subsidies. Unfortunately, the FTAs did not include any provisions relating to disciplining domestic support or export subsidies. Thus, while the FTA aims to eliminate tariffs on agricultural goods and certain aspects address nontariff measures through harmonisation, exchange of information, etc., it did not address trade distortions due to subsidies.

India's FTAs

Market access for agricultural and nonagricultural products for all FTAs is an average of 85% of India's total tariff lines (Table 3.1). Compared to nonagricultural products, a substantial portion of India's agricultural tariff lines

Table 3.1 India's trade in goods and FTAs (updated in 2020)

S. No.	*Acronym*	*Member countries*		*Market Access in Tariff Lines (India's Offer)*	*FTAs/ PTAs*[(1)]
		No.	*Names*		
1	APTA	7	Bangladesh, China, India, Laos, Rep. of Korea, Sri Lanka, and Mongolia	MOP (3142 Tariff lines)	PSA
2	AIFTA	11	Brunei, Cambodia, India, Indonesia, Laos, Malaysia, Myanmar, Philippines, Singapore, Thailand, and Vietnam	Ap. 89%	FTA and EIA
4	GSTP	43	List of countries# (2)	MOP	PSA
5	MERCOSUR India	5	Argentina, Brazil, Paraguay, Uruguay, and India	MOP (450 Tariff Lines)	PSA
6	Chile	2	India and Chile	MOP (178 Tariff Lines)	
7	DFTP-2008	34+ (49)	List of countries* (2)	Ap. 96%	Unilateral
8	SAFTA	8	Afghanistan, Bangladesh, Bhutan, India, Maldives, Nepal, Pakistan, and Sri Lanka	Ap. 96% ($)	FTA
9	ISLFTA	2	India and Sri Lanka,	Ap. 91%	FTA
10	ISCECA	2	India and Singapore%	N/A	FTA and EIA
11	IMCECA	2	India and Malaysia	Ap. 84%	FTA and EIA
12	JICEPA	2	India and Japan	Ap. 86%	FTA and EIA
13	IKCEPA	2	India and Rep. of South Korea	Ap. 84%	FTA

Source: Author, based on the Ministry of Commerce (various trade agreements).

Note 1: Partial Scope Agreement (PSA)/Preferential Trade Agreement (PTA), Free Trade Agreement (FTA), and Economic Integration Agreement (EIA), Ap. = approximately.

Note 2: # = Algeria, Argentina, Bangladesh, Benin, Bolivia, Brazil, Cameroon, Chile, Columbia, Cuba, Democratic People's Republic of Korea, Ecuador, Egypt, Ghana, Guinea, Guyana, Iran, Indonesia, Iraq, Libya, Malaysia, Mexico, Morocco, Mozambique, Myanmar, Nicaragua, Nigeria, Peru, Pakistan, Philippines, Rep. of Korea, Romania, Singapore, Sri Lanka, Sudan, Thailand, Trinidad and Tobago, Tunisia, Tanzania, Venezuela, Vietnam, Zimbabwe, * = Angola, Benin, Burkina Faso, Burundi, Central African Republic, Chad, Comoros, DR of Congo, Djibouti, Equatorial Guinea, Eritrea, Ethiopia, Guinea, Guinea-Bissau, Gambia, Lesotho, Liberia, Madagascar, Malawi, Mali, Mauritania, Mozambique, Niger, Rwanda, Sao Tome and Principe, Senegal, Sierra Leone, Somalia, Sudan, Togo, Uganda, Tanzania, Zambia, Afghanistan, Bangladesh, Bhutan, Cambodia, East Timor, Kiribati, Lao PDR, Maldives, Myanmar, Nepal, Samoa, Solomon Islands, Tuvalu, Vanuatu, Yemen, and Haiti, ($) = only for LDCs in SAFTA, + = only the LDCs which seek for Market access are provided, % = Singapore had two separate India's tariff concession schedules as Singapore is a zero duty country.

belong to the negative list – in other words, they are allowed market access only under the MFN route. Approximately 15% of tariff lines are traded outside the FTA rules, commonly referred to as negative tariff lists under WTO rules. The WTO rules are continuously negotiated every two years and are subject to change in response to evolving conditions. How much of the 15% belongs to agricultural and allied products?

It is a lesser-known fact that under the Asia-Pacific Trade Agreement (APTA), India has liberalized 3142 tariff lines, accounting for 26.2% of the tariff lines. The margin of preference (MOP) ranges from 10% to 100% tariff concessions. It should be recalled that China is an integral part of APTA. India's Duty-Free Tariff Preference (DFTP) Scheme of 2008 provided unilateral trade preferences for the least developed countries (LDCS) as mandated by the Hong Kong Ministerial Declaration of 2005. Thirty-four LDCs have sought permission from the Government of India to seek the benefit of the DFTP Scheme. An analysis of the trade balance of the DFTP scheme indicates that the agricultural and allied products trade balance increased from USD -0.3 billion in 2009 to USD 2.0 billion in 2013, after which it decreased to a marginal amount of USD 0.8 billion (Figure 3.3).

The AIFTA agricultural and allied sectors turned negative starting in 1997. It started with USD 1 billion and reached USD 3 billion in 2012. After that, it fell and remained negative, with a value of USD 0.9 billion in 2019. India is self-sufficient in meeting its domestic demands. Still, it has witnessed considerable pressure at the sectoral level, especially in the oilseeds, fats, and oils, as well as in other agricultural product groups. The add-on is the fall in tariffs up to 89% of national tariff lines imposed by India on the AIFTA partners, which is either eliminated or reduced – in categories like the sensitive tracks (ST) and unique products (SP). It meant that for 89% of tariff lines, the new FTA tariffs would be applicable.

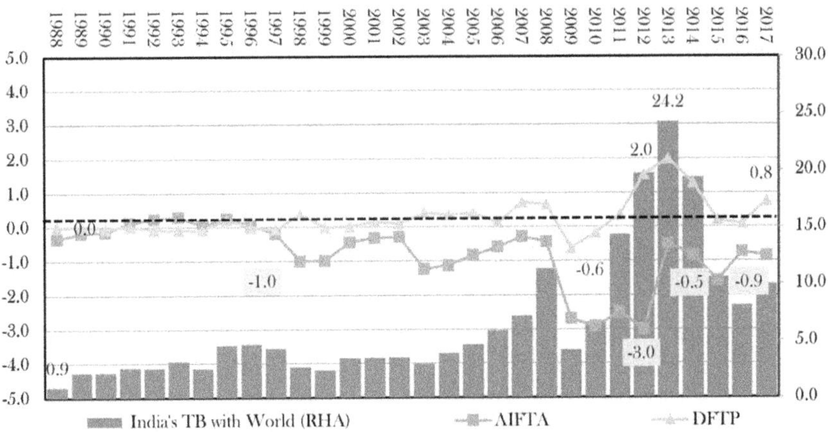

Figure 3.3 India's trade balance in ag. and allied sector (USD Bn.)

Source: WITS Comtrade.

Production and consumption imbalances were further aggravated by the macro level in India's total exports and imports. The trends observed in the exports and imports ratio to GDP, as the GDP is the indicator of any economy's market size, have been taken as one of the parameters to mark a country's demand. The ratio of merchandise exports to India's gross domestic product would indicate the exports relative to India's GDP (Figure 3.4).

The merchandise exports do not account for the contribution of the services exports; on the other hand, the GDP accounts for it, and therefore, this ratio would be much lower in India's context. India's total exports of goods to GDP (in % cent) increased from 9.6% in 2000 to 19.5% in 2013, after which it decreased at a secular rate to a low of 12% in 2019. Including services exports with goods did not alter the overall trends observed in Figure 3.4.

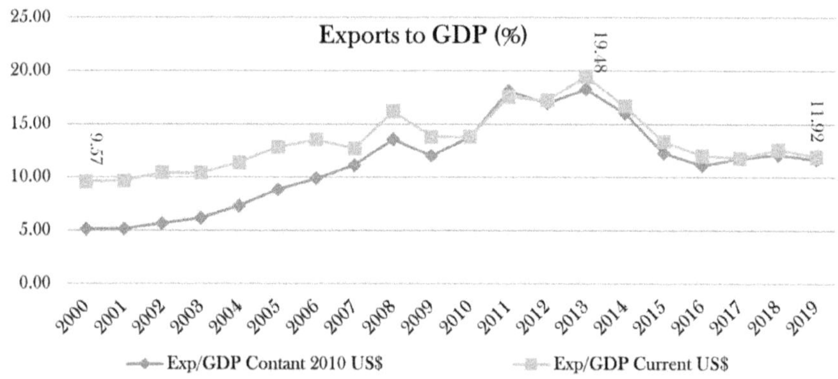

Figure 3.4 India's exports to GDP, current and constant 2010

Source: World Bank.

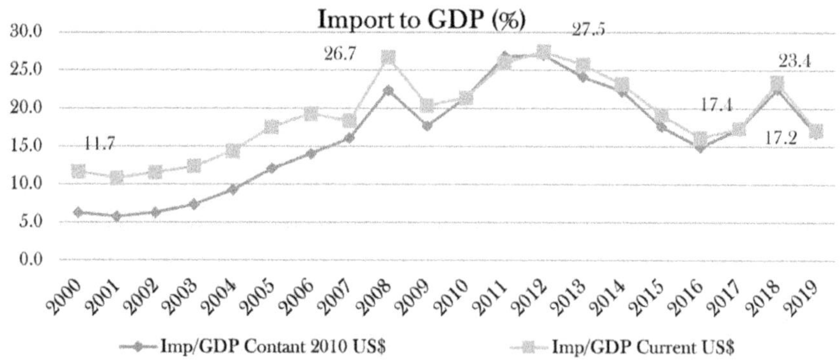

Figure 3.5 India's imports to GDP, current and constant 2010

Source: World Bank.

However, the inclusion of service did increase the values by three percentage points (13%) in 2000. It increased by five percentage points (25.4%) in 2013 and fell to 7 percentage points (20%) in 2019, see Annex Figure 3.4. The potential for India's gains from exports has been a consistent decrease since 2013. This would have created increased pressure in terms of the prices of commodities; this phenomenon is more pronounced in Micro, Small and Medium Enterprises (MSMEs). Small and scattered, it does not have global linkages and deep pockets (working capital) to address cost-enhancing new regime under the tariff measures, which have been notified since the WTO formation but were initiated post-2012, the reason being the stalemate of the Doha Round.[7]

India's total goods imports recovered in 2017 (17.4%) and 2018 (23.4%), recovering from a falling trend after the 2012 peak of 27.5% of GDP, which again dropped sharply to 17.2% in 2019 (Figure 3.5). A similar observation can be seen in India's total imports with services' inclusion; see Annex Figure 3.5. It suggested that the Indian economy was shrinking in terms of its trading possibilities.

Imports from India's 19 FTAs in agricultural products

India's terms of trade seem adversely affected in the agricultural and allied sectors based on the analysis of exports and imports under the harmonised system nomenclature (HSN).

Export-to-import ratios from the 19 FTA partners (Figure 3.6) declined from 2.2 in 2000 to 1.6 in 2019, exhibiting a W-shape pattern from 2000 to 2013 with three distinct peaks. Figure 3.6 shows that for the period from 2014 to 2018, the ratio remained at an average of 1.3, increasing by only 0.3 points in 2019 to a ratio of 1.6. Imports continued to flow into India from the 19 FTA partners, with India's exports remaining either static or decreasing marginally from 2015 to 2018. The 19 FTA had AIFTA, South Asian Free Trade Area (SAFTA), India–Japan Comprehensive Economic Partnership Agreement IJCEPA, and India–Korea Comprehensive Economic Partnership Agreement (IKCEPA) as significant suppliers, and there is almost complete domination of imports, 90% from AIFTA and 10% from SAFTA during the post-FTA period. This highlights the significance of imports from AIFTAS and their potential impact on India's agricultural commodity prices.

The surge in imports from AIFTA and the 19 FTAs is reflected in the rigidities across the nine MTNS sub-product groups. Of the nine products, only three have negative growth rates, with sugar and confectioneries having the highest (12%), followed by fish and fish products (3.3%) and animal products (1.3%) (Figure 3.7). The rest of the six MTN product groups are beverage and tobacco (15.3%); the other agricultural products (14.6%); fruit, vegetable, and plants (13.9%); cereals and preparations (10.8%); and coffee and tea (8.2%).

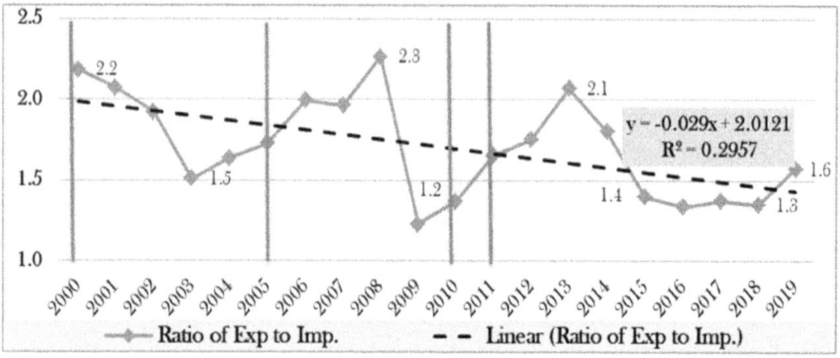

Figure 3.6 India's total export-to-imports ratios: 19 FTA partners
Source: WITS Comtrade.

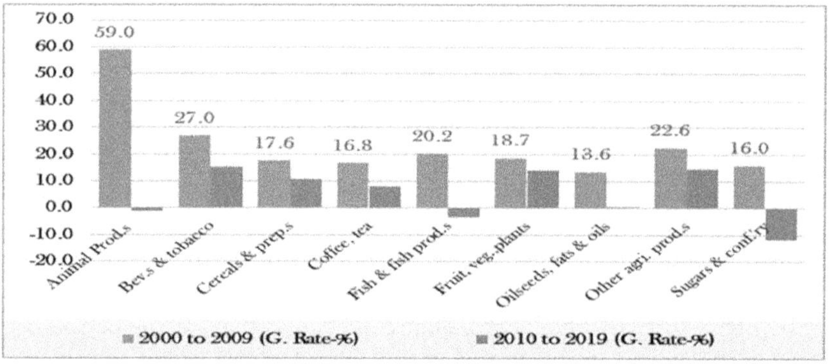

Figure 3.7 Growth rate of 19 FTA partners share to total India's imports (%)
Source: WITS Comtrade.

Average imports from the 19 FTA partners account for more than one-fifth (20%) of the total imports in six MTN product groups. The highest share among the six was in product groups such as oilseeds, fats, and oils (63.3%), followed by animal products (56.2%) and five other MTN product groups within the agricultural and allied sectors, which collectively accounted for shares above one-fifth of India's total imports (Figure 3.8). There is increased pressure on domestic substitute agrarian products, with more than one-fifth of the total imported products falling in seven of the nine product groups.

Therefore, there is sufficient evidence to suggest that imported palm oils have been exerting downward pressure on coconut oil prices at the national level. It can be suggested that, when considering tariff reduction under a trade agreement or allowing imports of a primary product, the impact on substitutable agricultural products' argument must be factored in and assessed.

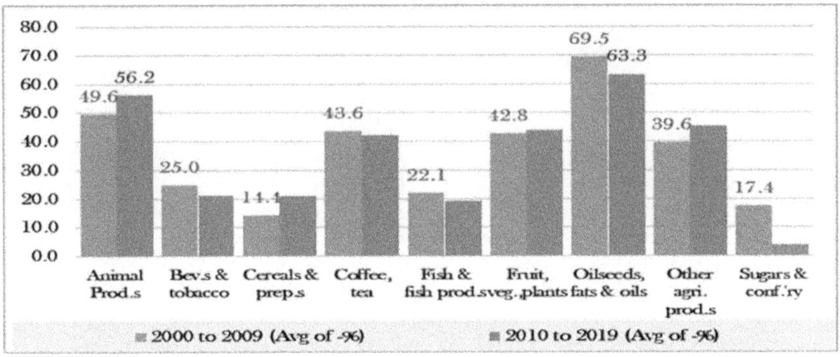

Figure 3.8 Average of 19 FTA partners share to total India's imports (%)

Source: WITS Comtrade.

Furthermore, there is a need to address the livelihood concerns of farmers who produce the commodity, which must be done in conjunction with one another. Additionally, considering the average income, there is a need to explore solutions in the value-added segments of products. Furthermore, it is evident from Figure 3.9 that India's FTA had a detrimental impact, indirectly suppressing the price of coconut oil, a direct value-added crop product.

There is a widespread perception across a wide range of academic chapters, popular media, and newsprints that the AIFTA is the primary reason for depressing the competitiveness of some unique Kerala products such as pepper, coffee, and rubber (ASEAN Ratna et al. 2010; Francis 2011; Veeramani and Saini 2011; Francis and Kallummal 2013; Ratna and Kallummal 2013) All these studies indicated that the exact nature of Kerala's agricultural products competitiveness could not be identified but could be associated with the lack of agrarian competitiveness owing to the very high cost of farming linked to high labour cost in Kerala.

The India–Sri Lanka Free Trade Agreement (ISFTA) can be blamed for the price slump in pepper. Figure 3.9 illustrates that the FTA with Sri Lanka resulted in a sharp decline in pepper prices. The price of pepper fell from a high of INR 540 per quintal to INR 295 per quintal in 2001. Rubber prices fell thrice from just below INR 300 per quintal to INR 100 per quintal in 2006 and continued to increase to INR 150 per quintal in 2015, slightly. However, under the AIFTA, many of the primary crops are on the negative list, which means they are traded at the MFN tariffs with no preferential concessions.

The increased use of imported crude and refined palm oils for stickiness in the prices of coconut oils in the AIFTA trade deal cannot be blamed totally. There is also a need to evaluate the stickiness observed in the coconut oil prices relative to the livelihood crop syndrome versus commercial crops (Government of Kerala 2016). Other challenges include the need for further technological upgradation of small-holding crops (Dhillon and Moncur, 2023).

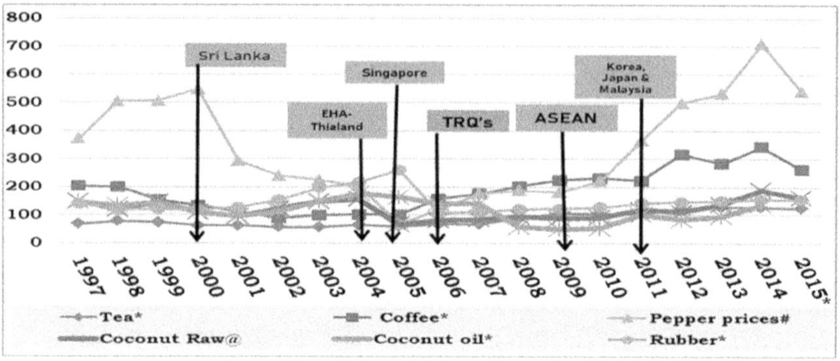

Figure 3.9 Trends in commodity prices (raw materials and value-added products)

Note: * = per kilogram/litre # quintal @= Wholesale Price Index.
Sources: Various commodity boards and the INDIASTAT online database.

Livelihood crops cannot be neglected solely because of their productivity. We need to expand our understanding to link these crops to substitute products and various other reasons mentioned in the above paragraph.

Kerala economy

The economy of Kerala is the ninth largest in India, with an annual gross state product (GSP) of INR 9.78 lakh crore (USD 138.88 billion) in 2020–21. The per-capita GSP of Kerala during the same period, 2020–21, is INR 205,484 (USD 2917.97) and is the sixth largest in India. Kerala has undergone significant economic transformation, as evidenced by its gross state domestic product (GSDP) compositional shares, which indicate a substantial shift since independence. The share of the primary sector in Kerala's Gross State Domestic Product (GSDP) in 1960–61 was 51.1%. Its share decreased to 44.5% in 1980–81; thereafter, it declined every decade to a low of 8.4% in 2019–20. Since the 1960s, Kerala's economy has experienced a decline of nearly 22% in the primary sector. Kerala recorded a positive growth of 8% and 9.4% in the secondary and tertiary sectors, respectively. It suggests a significant fall in the number of people dependent on agricultural and related primary sector activities, hinting at the growing pressure on livelihood. Combined with the annual report of the periodic labour force survey (2017–18), pages A-138 suggested that Kerala has one of the highest unemployment rates at 11.4% compared to the all-India unemployment rate of 6.1% (Government of India, 2019).

Kerala can effectively utilise its large pool of educated, unemployed youth for the modernisation needs of the agricultural sector and crop diversification. The survey conducted by the Kerala government's planning board on the changing trends in the composition of the state's principal crops suggested an increase over the years for other crops, from 10% (1990–91) to 23% in 2005–06 (Government of Kerala, 2022). The attitude of unemployed, educated youth towards employment has been driven by the availability of high daily wages in the informal sector and the abundance of food in various forms. Until December 2019, Kerala's economy had received a very high share of India's total remittances. We can observe that Kerala will face a unique dilemma of being caught in a "remittance trap", with almost 30%–40% of the state's income derived from it. Unlike other states, Kerala has been blessed by nature with a diverse range of horticultural crops and seasonal vegetables, which have helped cushion the population against food scarcity.

Livelihood and agrarian concerns: a case of Kerala

The area under the horticultural crops decreased by 67 thousand hectares, from 1658 thousand hectares in 2011 to 1591 thousand hectares in 2018. On the other hand, the production increased by 56,574.0 thousand tonnes, from 2,57,277 thousand metric tonnes in 2011 to 3,13,851 thousand metric tonnes in 2018 On the other hand, production increased by 56,574.0 thousand tonnes, from 257,277 thousand metric tonnes in 2011 to 313,851 metric tonnes in 2018. A detailed analysis needs to be carried out to understand the exact reasons for this trend; however, it does suggest that the probable intensification of horticultural production could be achieved through mechanisation and the adoption of modern cropping methods. Table 3.2 illustrates the changes in Kerala's shares in terms of area and production across various horticultural crops, including fruits, vegetables, plantation crops, aromatics, medicinal plants, flowers (both loose and cut), spices, and honey (Government of India, 2011, 2018).

Kerala's share in the total area fell by up to 2 percentage points in the plantation crops (tea, rubber, coffee, cardamom, and pepper) (Table 3.2). Plantation crop production increased by eight percentage points from 25.5% in 2011 to 33.1% in 2018, with 26.4% of the area and 32% of the production, followed by honey production with a share of 3% in India's total production. In terms of area, it was followed by spices with 5% and 2% shares of production. Spices, which accounted for almost 8% of India's total area, decreased by four percentage points; the observed increase was nominal, at 0.2 percentage points.

Table 3.3 provides details on the share of each of the 19 crops in Kerala, India, in terms of area and production for 2014. In Kerala, the top two crops in terms of area cropped are coconut (807 hectares) and rubber (548 hectares). The top four crops, including the two mentioned, accounted for a total of 1656 hectares. Of these, coconut alone constituted nearly 50%. In terms of relative shares, the top five crops are rubber, with 70% of the area and 84% of India's total production. It is followed by pepper, cloves, cardamom, and coconut, each of which accounts for more than 35% of India's total area and 27% of the production share. The only exception to this is the share of cloves in total production, which accounts for 7%. Clearly, there are six other crops with more than 10% of India's total area of cropping, and they are tapioca (30%), tamarind (23%), areca nut (22%), coffee (21%), cocoa (19%), and papaya (13%).

Table 3.2 Kerala's share in total India's horticultural crops: 2011–18

S. N.	*Kerala's Horticultural Crops*	*Area (000 hectares)*			*Production (000 M. ton)*		
		2011–12	*2016–17*	*2018–19*	*2011–12*	*2016–17*	*2018–19*
1	Fruits	4.4	3.9	4.8	3.2	2.8	1.9
2	Vegetables	1.7	1.4	1	2.3	1.2	1.6
3	Plantation	26.8	26.4	24.9	25.5	31.8	33.1
4	Aromatics and medicinal	–	0	0	–	0	0
5	Flowers – Loose	–	4.6	17	–	0	0
6	Flowers – Cut	—	–	–	–	0.1	5.6
7	Spices	7.9	4.8	3.9	1.9	1.8	2.1
8	Honey	–	–	–	–	2.9	1.8
Kerala's share in India		**7.1**	**6.3**	**6.2**	**4**	**3.5**	**3.4**

Source: Compiled from various reports of National Horticulture Board, Ministry of Agricultural, GoI.

Table 3.3 Share of Kerala's 19 crops in the total production – 2014

S. N.	*Crop*	*All India*		*Kerala*		*% share of Kerala in*	
		Area	*Production*	*Area*	*Production*	*Area*	*Production*
1	Coconut*	2140.5	22088	808.6	5921	37.8	26.8
2	Rubber	778.4	774	548.2	648.2	70.4	83.8
3	Paddy	43950	106540	199.6	564.3	0.5	0.5
4	Arecanut	451.9	622.3	100	100	22.1	16.1
5	Coffee	409.7	304.5	85.4	66.6	20.8	21.9
6	Pepper	123.8	50.9	84.1	29.4	67.9	57.8
7	Mango	2516	18431.3	77.2	457.1	3.1	2.5
8	Tapioca	228.3	8139.4	67.6	2479.1	29.6	30.5
9	Banana	802.6	29724.6	62.3	531.3	7.8	1.8
10	Cashew	1010.9	753.2	49.1	33.4	4.9	4.4
11	Cardamom	92.8	21.3	39.7	12.9	42.8	60.7
12	Tea	564	1208.8	35	63.5	6.2	5.3
13	Papaya	133.4	5639.3	16.6	103.4	12.5	1.8
14	Cocoa	71.4	21.1	13.3	12.3	18.6	58.3
15	Tamarind	58.6	188.1	13.2	44.7	22.5	23.8
16	Pineapple	109.9	1736.7	8	75.6	7.3	4.4
17	Ginger	132.6	655.1	4.5	21.5	3.4	3.3
18	Turmeric	232.7	1189.9	2.4	6.3	1	0.5
19	Clove	2.1	1.1	1	0.1	49	6.5

Source: Agricultural Statistics at a Glance 2014 and Indian Horticulture Database 2014, M/o Agriculture, Govt of India, https://desagri.gov.in/wp-content/uploads/2014/04/Agricultural-Statistics-At-Glance2014.pdf
Note: * Production of coconut in Million Nuts; Area – Hectares; Production – Tonnes

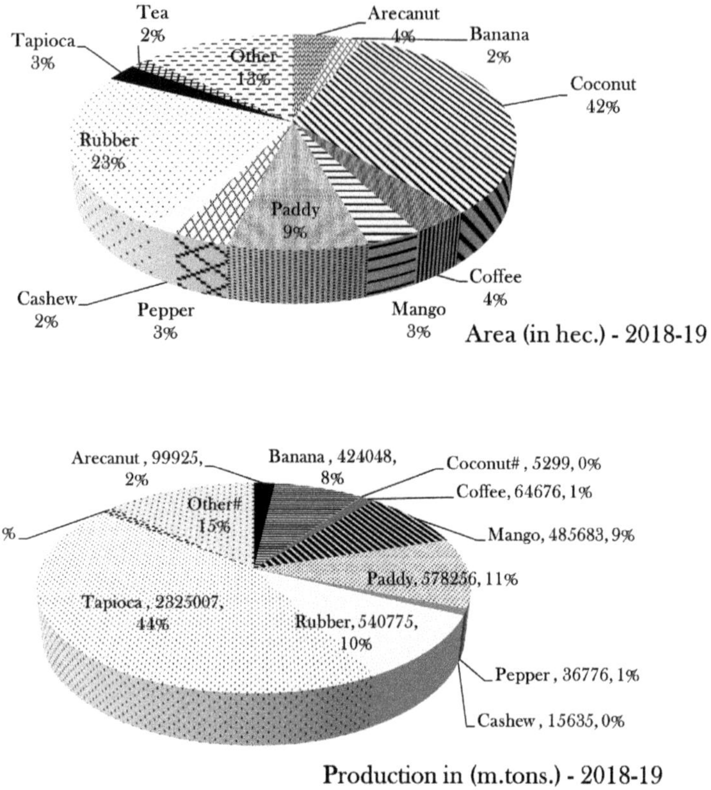

Figure 3.10 Agricultural crops in Kerala Comparison of area and production 2018–19

Note: # coconut production in a million nuts

Source: Agricultural Statistics at a Glance 2014 and Indian Horticulture Database 2014, M/o Agriculture, GoI.

The land utilization in the area and total production across 11 major crops are analyzed in Figure 3.10, which will help us further understand Kerala's dominant agricultural crops. In terms of area, 65% is accounted for by two crops – coconut (42%) and rubber (23%). In terms of production, the dominant crops are tapioca (44%), followed by paddy (11%), rubber (10%), mango (9%), banana (8%), and coconut#, which is widespread across the state as indicated by the coverage in the area.

Most analyses point towards the importance of coconuts as a crop in Kerala.

Cost of labour and livelihood issues

Compared to many other states in India, Kerala is blessed with the highest annual rainfall of 3055 mm, and therefore, the land is blessed with all kinds of possibilities. Agricultural land is used for the cultivation of multiple crops, including jackfruit, mango, pepper, coconut, areca nut, betel leaves, ginger, turmeric, tamarind, and tapioca. Kerala was the second-highest state, with a high urban population share of 47.7% in its total population of 33.4 million, as of 2011. (Government of India 2011) Therefore, the cost of labour is higher in agricultural activities because many landowners are urban or semi-urban dwellers. Moreover, the land and housing in Kerala are so well-connected that the daily cost of labour is relatively higher. Due to Kerala's high mobility, once wages are set in urban centres, they become the norm across rural areas. A study by Kumar (2002) found very high mobility of the labour force in the Kerala economy. The study also found that the infrastructural and institutional development in the village has facilitated gathering information about job availability, work environment, and access to a place of work, thus increasing their ability to move. Many mobile workers are daily commuters (Kumar, 2002).

The chapter analyses the selected crop in Kerala based on the input costs. The components that led to the determination of cost, namely, hired human labour, animal labour, machine labour, the cost towards seed/seedlings, farmyard manure and chemical fertilizers, plant protection, land tax and irrigation cess, repair and maintenance charges of implements, machinery and building, interest on working capital, other expenses, interest on fixed capital and finally the imputed value of household labour.[8] To address livelihood concerns, there must be an increase in the imputed value of household labour over the years of FTA-led liberalisation.

Most of Kerala's crops are labour-intensive and thus show an average share of above 40% across the six crops. Tapioca is the most labour-intensive crop, accounting for 60% of the sum of hired labour and imputed household labour. At the same time, ginger has the least labour intensity, with a 40% share for the period from 2004 to 2013. Coconut and pepper have an average labour usage of almost 56%, including both hired human labour and imputed household labour. The share of labour continued to grow at a rate of above 2% for all but turmeric, which has a negative growth rate of 0.03% (Figure 3.11).

The growth rates in labour from 2004 to 2013 are shown in Figure 3.12, which suggests that the average shares of imputed household labour in the total labour have increased across coconut, tapioca, banana, pepper, and ginger, with both measures, including the average values and their growth rate, indicating positive values. The highest recorded shares are in crops such as turmeric (29%), banana (28%), pepper (25%), and tapioca (24%). In areca nut and turmeric, the average share is positive, while the growth rates are negative. At the same time, coconut registered the lowest share of labour at 15% of the crop's total cost of production, suggesting a crisis across the coconut crop.

The imputed household labour cost increased in the coconut from 13% in 2004–05 to 18% in 2013–14, with an exponential growth rate of nearly 3%. With a 6% growth rate, only ginger imposed household labour cost, and with 5%, tapioca was higher than coconut. Therefore, with high imputed

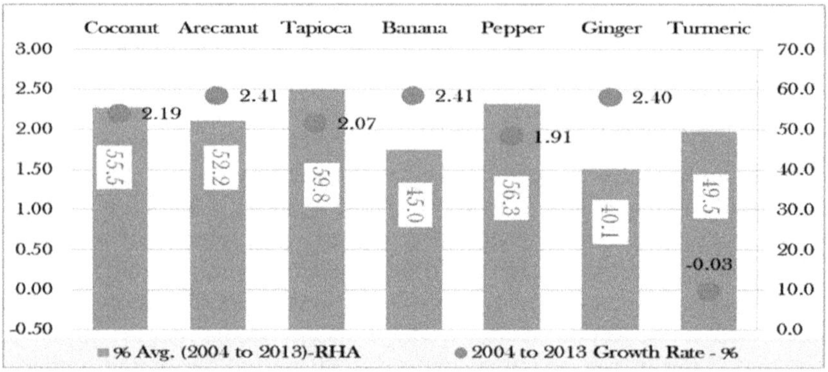

Figure 3.11 Labour shares in the main seven Kerala's crops (2000–13)

Source: 2016, An Analytical Study on Agriculture in Kerala, Monitoring and Evaluation Division, Directorate of Agriculture, Thiruvananthapuram, Government of Kerala.

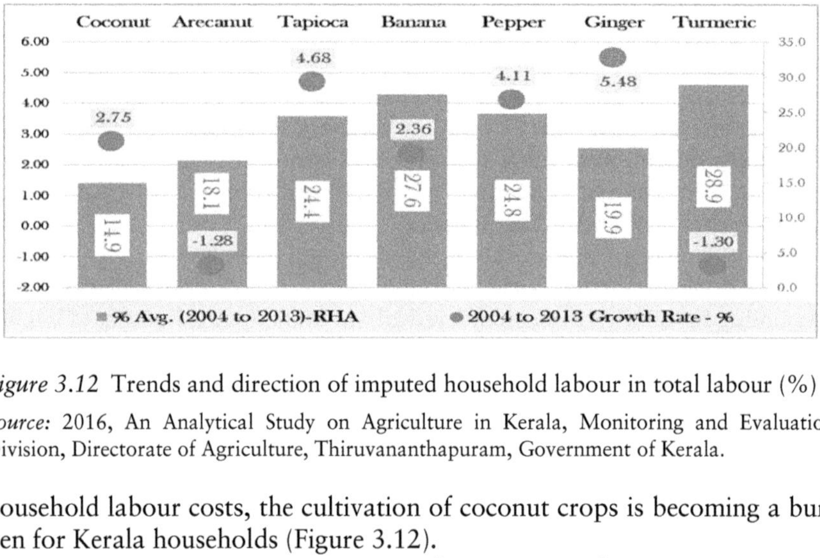

Figure 3.12 Trends and direction of imputed household labour in total labour (%)

Source: 2016, An Analytical Study on Agriculture in Kerala, Monitoring and Evaluation Division, Directorate of Agriculture, Thiruvananthapuram, Government of Kerala.

household labour costs, the cultivation of coconut crops is becoming a burden for Kerala households (Figure 3.12).

However, a two-year comparison of 2004–05 and 2013–14 suggested some clear trends. Except for bananas, all the other six crops of Kerala registered an increase in the imputed household participation share in the total labour (Table 3.4). The farmer's reluctance to use hired labour suggests the increasing strain in continuing with production, which could be reflected in the price pressures.

Exportable surplus

Trade is a combination of exports plus imports, when negotiating agricultural products, an element of sensitivity related to food security or inflation

Table 3.4 Imputed household labour as a share of total labour input – 2004–13

Select Kerala crop	*2004–05*	*2005–06*	*2006–07*	*2007–08*	*2008–09*	*2009–10*	*2010–11*	*2011–12*	*2012–13*	*2013–14*
Coconut	13	13.5	12.1	15	16.8	15.4	15.2	15.2	14.4	18.1
Arecanut	20.8	17.6	19.9	15.6	22.5	16.2	13.3	18.8	16.9	19.2
Tapioca	20.4	20.6	21.3	23.5	22.4	24.5	24.4	25.4	31.8	29.9
Banana	31.3	22	26.1	21	27.5	25.4	30.2	30.1	33.2	28.7
Pepper	16.2	19.2	28.5	24.9	28.6	23.9	27.6	23.9	25.5	29.5
Ginger	7.8	24.2	19.2	19	22.1	19.4	24.7	20.7	21.6	20.3
Turmeric	11.7	34.5	35.8	38.1	37	32.4	41.3	16	21.7	20.5

Source: 2016, An Analytical Study on Agriculture in Kerala, Monitoring and Evaluation Division, Directorate of Agriculture, Thiruvananthapuram, Government of Kerala.

can put additional pressure on a decision to liberalise a tariff line/commodity. There is a need to have a figure on the exportable surplus for all commodities produced within the territory of a nation with a large domestic market. The exportable surplus in any agricultural commodity can be calculated based on a simplified formula:

> Exportable Surplus = Total Production – (Domestic Consumption + Strategic Reserves)

In the formula, the most challenging is the decision on the *strategic reserves* needed, and several variables influence it. One of the most critical concerns is food security, which aims to ensure the sufficiency of supply in case of shortages or emergencies. The second variable is the need to maintain price stability, which involves managing market price volatility. A related factor is also the seasonality, leading to production fluctuations. One of the most important parts would be to account for off-season periods or crop failures. The last variable is the obligations under various international trade agreements undertaken in the past, as well as the compliance with them, which may require certain reserve levels.

An indicative figure on the exportable surplus is missing across the developing countries. Figure 3.13, therefore, provides details on the simple trade surpluses, which are calculated as the difference between exports and imports. In India's case, it is coconut oil, and in ASEAN's case, it is palm oil – these are used as proxies.

India registered a fall from 35,000 metric tonnes to 13,000 metric tonnes in coconut oils but a secular increase in palm oils by the ASEAN countries. The fall should not be associated directly with ISFTA, but there was no increase under the AIFTA. Therefore, India needs to focus attention on data gathering as they are an important part of any meaningful signing of a trade agreement.

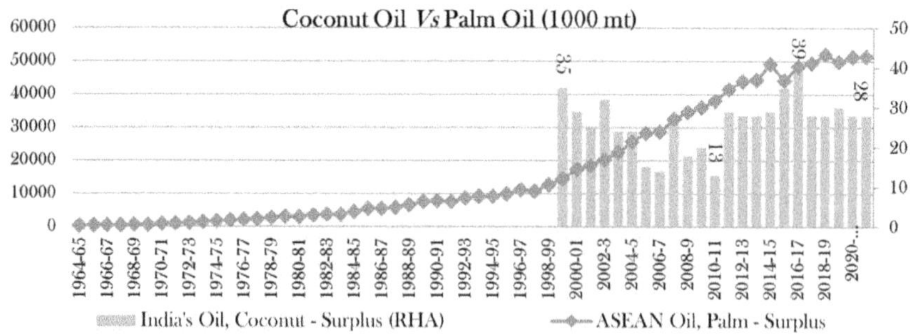

Figure 3.13 Surplus of CPOs vs. CCOs: ASEAN* and India

Note: * = ASEAN palm oil accounted by Indonesia, Malaysia and the Philippines.
Source: Author calculation based on https://apps.fas.usda.gov/.

Kerala's agricultural substitutable and value-added products

An ideal trade agreement should address the livelihood concerns of the economy, as modern trade deals harmonise two economic entities (pre-FTA) into a seamless single entity (post-FTA) within an agreed level of interaction as specified in the free trade agreement. Today, such agreements have become increasingly complex, as evidenced by the number of chapters in any new trade agreement, with almost 22 chapters, most of which are non-trade concerns. Maintaining the support of domestic constituencies[9] is crucial for sustaining stable socio-economic conditions and political stability. Therefore, a harmonised list of agricultural commodities and value-added products needs to be prepared at a sub-federal level.

Such a simple listing of the total crops based on livelihood concerns of Kerala is provided in Table 3.5. There is a need to address some of the gaps in data transparency and accounting practices. The nature of accounting practices differs across the agriculture, manufacturing, and services sectors; therefore, the level of data accuracy in these sectors also varies.

The agricultural sector has exceptionally high levels of informality,[10] and it remains largely unstandardised (Murthy 2001). At the national level, the data suggest that the share of informal/unorganised sector GVA to total GVA, as shown, is more than 50% across all years, and the share of the unorganised sector is highest in agriculture, as holdings are small and fragmented (Murthy 2020). However, tracing the value-added process becomes vital in India's agricultural sector, as it is the sector with the most tremendous potential for employment. Therefore, it becomes crucial from the perspective of livelihood, and this practice has been observed as online trade gains significance in recent years; these efforts have faced some challenges (see https://keralacalling.kerala.gov.in/?p=2511).

Table 3.5 Kerala: Raw commodities, substitutable products and value added

Kerala's products	*Raw commodities*	*Substitutable products*	*Value added*	*Kerala sub-total*
Cassava	1		2	3
Coconut and Palm	3	32	20	55
Fisheries	176		102	278
Pepper	9		5	14
Rubber	3	128	98	229
Tea		16	9	25
Coffee		8	8	16
Milk and Dairy	16		12	28
Total Kerala's Products	208	184	256	648
% share	32.1	28.4	39.5	100
India's National Tariff Lines (11,960)				

Source: Author based on India's Tariff Classification.

Table 3.5 presents Kerala's livelihood concerns, comprising a total of nine products categorised into six crops, one animal husbandry sector (milk and dairy), and aquatic products (fisheries). In the case of Kerala, the author could list out a total of 208 (8-digit HS-ITC) products with a share of approximately 32 per cent as products to be protected by using trade policies under the FTAs, tariff and nontariff measures. However, the same is to be used for an additional approximately 68 per cent of products which can be segregated into two product categories like 184 substitutable products with approximately 28 per cent and 256 value-added products accounting for approximately 40 per cent of Kerala's agricultural products, which has an indirect impact in terms of the price determination. Therefore, a totalitarian impact on protecting livelihood can only be addressed if the 648 products are effectively addressed in terms of balancing the import surge and promoting exports. (See Annex Tables 3–5.).

Conclusion and policy recommendations

The negative trade balance has been draining the much-needed forex, which is crucial for India – as it is attempting to move to a status of a developed nations. Trade deficits increased from USD 9.8 billion in 2000 to USD 294.2 billion in 2018, after which it fell by nearly USD 150 billion to USD 151 billion in 2019 – the sharp falls have been a direct outcome of a fall in exports and imports. This trade balance scenario leads to the direct outflow of USD 3 billion worth of production to the ASEAN economies.

It is in this context that the chapter analyses Kerala's substitutable products, such as crude coconut oil and refined coconut oil, *versus* imported palm oil and their transmission mechanism through price setting. Which would then determine the choice of domestic consumption in India. Price suppression in the primary product (coconut, pepper and rubber) since the formation of FTAS has led to a surge in imports of direct substitutes (coconut and rubber) or similar products (pepper), causing serious injury at the sub-federal level.

Therefore, when considering the tariff liberalisation of agricultural products, another element that needs to be addressed is how to address some of the livelihood crops and their substitutability, both in food and non-food crops. Considering that India has a large informal economy, its trade policies should integrate this understanding into its overall tariff liberalisation initiative. From this perspective, it is crucial to make a meaningful assessment of India's imports of primary crops and intermediate products like crude vegetable oils. By binding and eliminating tariffs, it is evident that macroeconomic tools are being used to address microeconomic issues, such as substitutability versus complementarity and value-added products.

Policy recommendations

- The FTAs are increasingly integrating two or three economies into one single entity, where the impacted nation-state has minimal sovereign control. Therefore, the FTAs should have a compulsory review provision after two years.

- In the context of rubber, the Rajya Sabha recommended that a "Livelihood Clause" be incorporated in all trade agreements to protect the interests of small and marginal growers (Rajya Sabha Secretariat 2017).
- All commitments under the FTAs should be evaluated based on at least three criteria: their intergenerational impact concerning the dependent population, the cross-sectional ecosystem (investment possibility, quality, technological upgradation, etc.) and finally, the economy-wide overall effects of its implications on terms of trade (TOT) at the sectoral level or more disaggregated levels, wherever applicable.
- Considering the author's experience of non-availability of recent data while analysing the chapter (trade versus economic), the author would like to suggest the creation of separate data tracking, along the lines of the Goods and Services Tax, that records the HS codes for all transactions. A similar mechanism will be introduced to track a harmonised set of data points for production, consumption, exportable surplus, and import surges for each of the identified negative list products and their substitutable and value-added products.
- Finally, any negotiation involving tariff rates and other NTMs/Bs and their implementation should be reflective of an assessment of at least a few of the important aspects like the livelihood concerns of the tariff line which are being negotiated by incorporating variables like the production, consumption and the livelihood linkages based on the size of farms, dependence, and issues of substitutability vs. complementarity. The total number of primary commodity tariff lines across the agricultural sector should be mapped accordingly. As and when tariffs are liberalised, an appropriate policy decision should be made to address any concerns that may arise from the trade agreement.

Notes

1 Lower price can be achieved by both FTA partners agreeing to reduce or eliminate tariffs across significant number of tariff lines. It can also be driven by easing the domestic regulations, processes, and procedures, harmonising between partners, impacting costs, and indirectly being reflected in prices.

2 Høstmark et al. (1980) referred in the coconut board report compared the effects of diets containing 10 per cent coconut fat and 10 per cent sunflower oil on lipoprotein distribution in male Wistar rats. Coconut oil feeding produced significantly lower levels (p = <0.05) of pre-beta lipoproteins (VLDL) and significantly higher (p = <0.01) alpha-lipoproteins (HDL) relative to sunflower oil feeding. The referred in the CDB Reports titled "Health and nutritional benefits from coconut oil and its advantages over competing oils", Coconut Development Board, https://www.coconutboard.in/docs/English-Article-MaryEnig.pdf.

3 Substitutable products are olive oil, safflower oil, coconut oil, sunflower oil, almond oil, cottonseed oil, corn oil, soybean oil, peanut oil, and canola oil.

4 Korea received ODA from foreign countries, amounting to a total of $ 12 billion for structural adjustment programs. The ODA significantly contributed to Korea's economic and social development. In the 1960s, "growth" and "foreign

investment" replaced "humanitarian relief" and "reconstruction" as the primary focus in war-torn countries, as Korea underwent a dramatic transformation of its economic structure.

5 These are non-tariff measures/barriers that require processes and procedures to be factored in before a market is integrated into FTA.

6 Some portions of this subsection are credited to a conference paper presented in 2016 by Rajan R. S. Kallummal M., Sharma S. K. (2016).

7 The Doha Round discussions came to a halt during a meeting in Potsdam due to a serious deadlock between the United States, the European Union, India, and Brazil. Issues regarding agricultural trade between the United States, India, and China led to the failure of discussions that began in Geneva in 2008, which continued until late 2011. It was an outcome of two groups level of ambition the developed wanted complete liberalization of Non Agricultural sector and the developing countries wanted more market access in Agricultural products.

8 Refer to https://www.ecostat.kerala.gov.in/storage/publications/422.pdf.

9 These are a group of stakeholders like the farmers and producers, consumers (availability and affordability of foods and other products), government agencies, traders' associations, and the nongovernmental organisations (NGOs) and civil society groups.

10 Imports of synthetic rubbers from China and ASEAN Partners.

References

ASEAN Secretariate. (n.d.). https://investasean.asean.org/asean-economic-community/view/670/newsid/758/single-market-and-production-base.html.

CDB. (undated). CDB Reports Titled "Health and Nutritional Benefits from Coconut Oil and Its Advantages Over Competing Oils." *Coconut Development Board.* https://www.coconutboard.in/docs/English-Article-MaryEnig.pdf.

Dhar, Biwajit, and Kallummal, Murali. 2007. "Trade Policy Off the Hook: The Making of Indian Trade Policy Since the Uruguay Round." In *Process Matters: Sustainable Development and Domestic Trade Transparency*, edited by Mark Halle and Robert Wolfe, 183–240. Manitoba: IISD. ISBN 978-1-895536-95-9.

Dhillon, Rajveer, and Moncur, Qianna. 2023. "Small-Scale Farming: A Review of Challenges and Potential Opportunities Offered by Technological Advancements." *Sustainability* 15(21): 15478. https://www.mdpi.com/2071-1050/15/21/15478.

Francis, Smitha. 2011. "A Sectoral Impact Analysis of the ASEAN-India Free Trade Agreement." *Economic and Political Weekly* 46(2).

Francis, Smitha, and Kallummal, Murali. 2013. "India's Comprehensive Trade Agreements: Implications for Development Trajectory." *Economic and Political Weekly* August 48(31).

Government of India. 2011. *National Horticultural Board.* http://nhb.gov.in/Statistics.aspx.

Government of India. 2018. *National Horticultural Board.* http://nhb.gov.in/Statistics.aspx.

Government of India. 2019. *Periodic Labour Force Survey.* Ministry of Statistics and Programme Implementation. National Statistical Office. https://mospi.gov.in/sites/default/files/publication_reports/Annual%20Report%2C%20PLFS%202017-18_31052019.pdf.

Government of Kerala. 2016. *An Analytical Study on Agriculture in Kerala.* Thiruvananthapuram: Monitoring and Evaluation Department of Kerala. https://www.ecostat.kerala.gov.in/storage/publications/56.pdf.

Government of Kerala. 2022. *Economic Review Volume 1.* Thiruvananthapuram: Kerala State Planning Board. https://spb.kerala.gov.in/sites/default/files/2023-02/ENGLISH%20FINAL%20PRESS%2004.02.2023.pdf.

Hoang, Viet. 2018. "Assessing the Agricultural Trade Complementarity of the Association of Southeast Asian Nations Countries." *Agricultural Economics* 64(10). https://agricecon.agriculturejournals.cz/artkey/age-201810-0005_assessing-the-agricultural-trade-complementarity-of-the-association-of-southeast-asian-nations-countries.php.
Høstmark, A. T., Spydevold O., Eilertsen E. 1980. Plasma lipid concentration and liver output of lipoproteins in rats fed coconut fat or sunflower oil. *Artery,* 7(5):367–83.
Kallummal, Murali. 2001. *An Alternative to Investment Promotion in Developing Countries: A Case Study of the Indian Primary Market.* New Delhi: Research and Information System for the Non-Aligned and Other Developing Countries.
Kallummal, Murali. 2015. "India's Re-industrialisation at Cross Roads: Developmental Issue vs. Green Challenges." *Xplore—The Xavier Research Journal* 6(1).
Kallummal, Murali. 2020. "Market Access and Issues of Data Gaps and Transparency and Information Asymmetry: A Case of RCEP Negotiations." *International Finance eJournal* 12(45).
Kallummal, Murali, and Francis, Smitha. 2020. FDI Screening: Need of the Hour in the Time of Non-Transparent Capital Flows. https://www.ecostat.kerala.gov.in/storage/publications/660.pdf.
Kumar, Mahesh. 2002. *Labour Mobility in Rural Areas: A Village-Level Study.* Thiruvanthapuram: CDS.
Murthy, S. V. R. 2001. "Measuring Informal Economy in India: Indian Experience." Session II: Traditional Estimation Practices: Determining the Level and Growth of the Informal Economy.
Organisation for Economic Co-operation and Development (OECD). 2002. *Foreign Direct Investment for Development: Maximising Benefits, Minimising Costs.* Paris: OECD.
Rajan Sudesh Ratna, and Kallummal, Murali. 2013. "ASEAN–India Free Trade Agreement (FTA) and its Impact on India: A Case Study of Fisheries and Selected Agricultural Products." *Foreign Trade Review* 48(4).
Rajan Sudesh Ratna, Kallummal, Murali, and Sharma S. K. 2016. Conference paper presented at the Centre for WTO Studies.
Rajan Sudesh Ratna, Kallummal, Murali, and Moitra, Snigdha. 2010. *Implications for Development Trajectory: A Case Study of Fisheries and Commercial Crops and its Impact on the Rural Economy.* Thiruvananthapuram.
Rajya Sabha Secretariat. 2017. *Trade with Association of South-East Asian Nations (ASEAN).* 137th Report. Department-Related Parliamentary Standing Committee: Rajya Sabha Secretariat.
Veeramani, C., and Saini, G. K. 2011. "Impact of ASEAN-India Preferential Trade Agreement on Plantation Commodities: A Simulation Analysis." *Economic and Political Weekly,* 5 March 46(10).
Viner, J. 1950. *The Customs Union Issue.* New York: Carnegie Endowment for International Peace.

Further Reading

Government of Kerala. 2014. Agricultural Statistics at a Glance 2014 and IndianHorticulture Database 2014. Thiruvananthapuram: Ministry of Agriculture, Govt of India.
Government of Kerala. 2023. Report On the Cost of Cultivation of Important Crops in Kerala 2020–21. Thiruvananthapuram: Department of Economics & Statistics. https://www .ecostat .kerala .gov .in /storage /publications /660 .pdf.

Annex Table 3.1 WITS grouping of countries

High income			
Antigua and Barbuda	Estonia	Kuwait	Saudi Arabia
Aruba	Faeroe Islands	Latvia	Seychelles
Australia	Finland	Lithuania	Singapore
Austria	France	Luxembourg	Slovak Republic
Bahamas, The	French Polynesia	Macao	Slovenia
Bahrain	Germany	Malta	Spain
Barbados	Greece	Netherlands	St. Kitts and Nevis
Belgium	Greenland	New Caledonia	Sweden
Bermuda	Hong Kong, China	New Zealand	Switzerland
Brunei	Hungary	Norway	Trinidad and Tobago
Canada	Iceland	Oman	Turks and Caicos Isl.
Chile	Ireland	Palau	United Arab Emirates
Croatia	Israel	Panama	United Kingdom
Cyprus	Italy	Poland	United States
Czech Republic	Japan	Portugal	Uruguay
Denmark	Korea, Rep.	Qatar	
Low income			
Afghanistan	The Gambia	Mali	Syrian A. Rep. c
Benin	Guinea	Mozambique	Tanzania
Burkina Faso	Guinea-Bissau	Nepal	Togo
Burundi	Haiti	Niger	Uganda
Central African Republic	Madagascar	Rwanda	Yemen
Eritrea	Malawi	Sierra Leone	
Ethiopia(excl. Eritrea)			
Lower middle income			
Angola	Egypt, Arab Rep.	Lesotho	Sao Tome & Principe
Bangladesh	El Salvador	Mauritania	Senegal
Bhutan	Eswatini	Micronesia, Fed. Sts.	Solomon Islands
Bolivia	Fm Sudan	Moldova	Tunisia
Cambodia	Ghana	Mongolia	Ukraine
Cameroon	Honduras	Morocco	Uzbekistan
Cape Verde	India	Myanmar	Vanuatu
Comoros	Indonesia	Nicaragua	Vietnam
Congo, Rep.	Kenya	Nigeria	Zambia
Cote d'Ivoire	Kiribati	Pakistan	Zimbabwe
Djibouti	Kyrgyz Republic	Papua New Guinea	
East Timor	Lao PDR	Philippines	
Others			
Andorra	Mayotte	Occ.Pal.Terr	
Belgium-Luxembourg	Montenegro	Other Asia, nes	

(*Continued*)

Annex Table 3.1 (Continued)

Cook Islands	Montserrat	Serbia, F.R. (Ser./ Mont.o)	
European Union	Netherlands Antilles	Sudan	
Upper middle income			
Albania	Cuba	Kazakhstan	South Africa
Algeria	Dominica	Lebanon	Sri Lanka
Argentina	Dominican Republic	Libya	St. Lucia
Armenia	Ecuador	Malaysia	St. Vin. & the Grenadines
Azerbaijan	Fiji	Maldives	Suriname
Belarus	Gabon	Mauritius	Thailand
Belize	Georgia	Mexico	Tonga
Bosnia and Herzegovina	Grenada	Namibia	Turkey
Botswana	Guatemala	North Macedonia	Turkmenistan
Brazil	Guyana	Paraguay	Tuvalu
Bulgaria	Iran, Islamic Rep.	Peru	Venezuela
China	Iraq	Romania	
Colombia	Jamaica	Russian Federation	
Costa Rica	Jordan	Samoa	

Source: WITS Comtrade
Note: Shaded cells are India's 19 FTAs partners.

Annex Table 3.2 India's trade balance with the world and 19 FTA partners (USD bn.)

India FTA partners	*2000*	*2005*	*2006*	*2007*	*2008*	*2010*	*2011*	*2012*	*2014*	*2015*	*2017*	*2018*	*2019*	*Growth* %	*COV-* %
World	−9.8	−38.9	−54.2	−68.9	−126	−127.4	−153.6	−186.6	−132.8	−123.1	−148.6	−294.2	−150.7	19.5	−75.2
Singapore	−0.5	2.4	1	−0.4	0.7	1.9	7.6	5.9	2.8	0.6	4.4	−6.7	−4.4	**16.1**	**275.9**
Bhutan	0	0	−0.1	−0.2	−0.1	0	0	0	0.1	0.2	0.2	0.4	0.5	**21**	**226.6**
Vietnam	0.2	0.7	1	1.6	2.2	2.1	2.9	2.7	4.4	2.9	4.4	−1.6	−1.6	**14.6**	**107.3**
Nepal	−0.2	0.4	0.6	0.8	1.1	1.5	2.2	2.5	4	3	5.7	7.4	6.8	**22.4**	**104.7**
Cambodia	0	0	0	0	0.1	0.1	0.1	0.1	0.2	0.1	0.1	0.1	0.2	**15.9**	**74.2**
Afghanistan	0	0.1	0.1	0.2	0.2	0.2	0.4	0.4	0.2	0.2	0.2	0.2	0.4	**19**	**66.3**
Bangladesh	0.8	2	1.8	2.5	3.8	3.1	3.5	5.3	6.8	5.4	7.3	8.3	7.3	**11.7**	**60.7**
Pakistan	0.2	0.5	1.4	1.5	1.6	2.7	1.6	1.4	1.9	1.7	1.4	1.8	1.2	**13.7**	**59.4**
Sri Lanka	0.6	1.3	1.6	2.2	2.5	2.9	4.1	3.4	6.2	4.8	4	3.2	3.3	**11**	**58.8**
Maldives	0	0.1	0.1	0.1	0.1	0.1	0.1	0.1	0.2	0.2	0.2	0.2	0.2	**11.9**	**57.5**
Philippines	0.1	0.3	0.5	0.5	0.6	0.5	0.7	0.8	1.2	0.9	0.9	1.1	1.2	**10.5**	**53.8**
Malaysia	−1.3	−1.5	−3.5	−3.8	−4.2	−2.9	−6.3	−8.7	−8.5	−6.8	−4.7	−8	−6.2	**12.3**	**−62.9**
Korea, Rep.	−0.3	−2.8	−2.4	−2.7	−4.2	−6	−7.6	−9	−8.2	−9.1	−11.5	−14.6	−11.1	**18.9**	**−72.5**
Indonesia	−0.9	−2.6	−2.5	−4	−5.5	−8.7	−11.8	−12.4	−14.1	−14.5	−17.5	−19.3	−13.6	**19.6**	**−74.3**
Japan	−0.3	−1	−1.7	−2.3	−3.7	−3	−5	−5.5	−4	−4.9	−5.8	−10.3	−7.8	**20.3**	**−79.3**
Brunei	0	0	−0.2	−0.2	−0.3	−0.2	0.2	−0.9	−0.9	−0.6	−0.5	−0.5	−0.5	**38.9**	**−102.8**
Thailand	0.2	−0.1	−0.1	−0.4	−0.5	−1.8	−2.1	−1.7	−2.2	−2.5	−2.9	−5.4	−2.7	**20.4**	**−116.4**
Myanmar	−0.1	−0.4	−0.6	−0.6	−0.7	−0.8	−0.8	−0.8	−0.4	0.1	0.6	0.9	0.5	**4.5**	**−213.2**
Lao PDR	0	0	0	0	0	0	−0.1	−0.1	0	−0.1	−0.2	0	0	**26.6**	**−229.7**
19 FTA partners of India	**−1.4**	**−0.5**	**−2.8**	**−5.3**	**−6.1**	**−8.4**	**−10.2**	**−16.4**	**−2**	**−10.4**	**−18.2**	**−15.1**	**−13.6**	23.5	**−112.2**

Source: WITS Comtrade.

Note: COV- The coefficient of variation (CV) is statistical measure that indicates the relative variability of a dataset compared to its mean. The significance lies in the fact that COV expresses variability as a percentage, which enables comparisons across different datasets, even if they have different units or scales.

Annex Table 3.3 Kerala's agricultural products and AIFTA tariff concession categories

Agricultural crops	*NL*	*NT-1*	*NT-2*	*Special products*	*ST*	*HSL**	*No Tariff Line#*	*Six-digit HS.*
Coconut	4							4
Coffee	6			1				7
Fish and fish products	37	73	9		3			122
Natural rubber	4	14			1			19
Pepper	1			1				2
Tea	4			1				5
India	**56**	**87**	**10**	**3**	**4**			**159**
Coconut		4						4
Coffee	1	2			4			7
Fish and fish products		105					17	122
Natural rubber		19						19
Pepper		2						2
Tea	2				3			5
Brunei	**3**	**132**			**8**		**17**	**159**
Coconut	2	2						4
Coffee		6			1			7
Fish and fish products	11	103			8			122
Natural rubber		17			2			19
Pepper		2						2
Tea		2			1	2		5
Cambodia	**13**	**132**			**12**	**2**		**159**
Coconut		3			1			4
Coffee		6			1			7
Fish and fish products	18		67		7	30		122
Natural rubber		15			4			19
Pepper		2						2
Tea	2	1	1		1			5
Indonesia	**20**	**27**	**68**		**14**	**30**		**159**
Coconut					4			4
Coffee					7			7
Fish and fish products		103			19			122
Natural rubber		19						19
Pepper					2			2
Tea					5			5
Lao PDR		**122**			**37**			**159**
Coconut		3	1					4
Coffee		7						7
Fish and fish products		120	2					122
Natural rubber		8	6		5			19
Pepper		2						2
Tea	2	3						5

(*Continued*)

Annex Table 3.3 (Continued)

Agricultural crops	*NL*	*NT-1*	*NT-2*	*Special products*	*ST*	*HSL**	*No Tariff Line#*	*Six-digit HS.*
Malaysia	2	**143**	9		5			**159**
Coconut	4							4
Coffee	6					1		7
Fish and fish products	43	47	26		6			122
Natural rubber	4	15						19
Pepper	1	1						2
Tea		1	4					5
Philippines	**58**	**64**	**30**		**6**	**1**		**159**
Coconut	4							4
Coffee	6				1			7
Fish and fish products	22	80	2		18			122
Natural rubber		19						19
Pepper	2							2
Tea	4				1			5
Thailand	**38**	**99**	**2**		**20**			**159**
Coconut		4						4
Coffee		4	3					7
Fish and fish products#		11	62		14	18	17	122
Natural rubber		19						19
Pepper			2					2
Tea					1	4		5
Vietnam		**38**	**67**		**15**	**22**	**17**	**159**

Source: Based on AIFTA Tariff Schedules

Note: * = highly sensitive list, # = National tariff lines that do not follow HS3 (2007) standard (the first six digits should be based on the standard subheading nomenclature of the country's HS version) are listed.

Annex Table 3.4 Kerala's agricultural products and AIFTA base (MFN – 2007) tariffs

Agricultural crops	*0–5*	*6–15*	*20–30*	*Above 35*	*Specific duties*	*No T.L.s*[#]	*Total six-digit H.S.*
Coconut	–	–	–	4	–	—	4
Coffee	–	–	2	5	–	–	7
Fish and fish products	–	1	121	–	–	–	122
Natural rubber	1	14	3	1	–	–	19
Pepper	–	–	–	2	–	–	2
Tea	–	–	1	4	–	–	5
India	**1**	**15**	**127**	**16**	–	–	**159**
Coconut	4	–	—	–	–	–	5
Coffee	3	–	–	–	4	–	7
Fish and fish products	105	–	–	–	–	17	122
Natural rubber	19	–	–	–	–	–	19
Pepper	2	–	–	–	–	–	2
Tea	1	–	–	–	4	–	5
Brunei	**135**	–	–	–	**8**	**17**	**159**
Coconut	–	4	–	–	–	–	4
Coffee	–	2	–	5	–	–	7
Fish and fish products	4	87	–	31	–	–	122
Natural rubber	–	19	–	–	–	–	19
Pepper	–	2	–	–	–	–	2
Tea	–	4	–	1	–	–	5
Cambodia	**4**	**118**	–	**37**	–	–	**159**
Coconut	4	–	–	–	–	–	4
Coffee	7	–	–	–	–	–	7
Fish and fish products	105	17	–	–	–	–	122
Natural rubber	19	–	–	–	–	–	19
Pepper	2	–	–	–	–	–	2
Tea	5	–	–	–	–	–	5
Indonesia	**142**	**17**	–	–	–	–	**159**
Coconut	–	–	4	–	–	–	4
Coffee	–	–	2	5	–	–	7
Fish and fish products	102	–	20	–	–	–	122
Natural rubber	19	–	–	–	–	–	19
Pepper	–	–	2	–	–	–	2
Tea	–	–	1	4	–	–	5
Lao PDR	**121**	–	**29**	**9**	–	–	**159**
Coconut	3	–	1	–	–	–	4
Coffee	6	–	1	–	–	–	7
Fish and fish products	98	23	1	–	–	–	122

(*Continued*)

Annex Table 3.4 (Continued)

Agricultural crops	*0–5*	*6–15*	*20–30*	*Above 35*	*Specific duties*	*No T.L.s#*	*Total six-digit H.S.*
Natural rubber	11	–	8	–	–	–	19
Pepper	2	–	–	–	–	–	2
Tea	2	2	1	–	–	–	5
Malaysia	**122**	**25**	**12**	**–**	**–**	**–**	**159**
Coconut	–	4	–	–	–	–	4
Coffee	–	1	2	4	–	–	7
Fish and fish products	34	88	–	–	–	–	122
Natural rubber	19	–	–	–	–	–	19
Pepper	1	1	–	–	–	–	2
Tea	4	1	–	–	–	–	5
Philippines	**58**	**95**	**2**	**4**	**–**	**–**	**159**
Coconut	–	–	4	–	–	–	4
Coffee	–	–	6	1	–	–	7
Fish and fish products	91	2	29	–	–	–	122
Natural rubber	19	–	–	–	–	–	19
Pepper	–	–	2	–	–	–	2
Tea	–	–	5	–	–	–	5
Thailand	**110**	**2**	**46**	**1**	**–**	**–**	**159**
Coconut	–	1	1	2	–	–	4
Coffee	–	–	2	5	–	–	7
Fish and fish products	5	2	84	14	–	17	122
Natural rubber	19	–	–	–	–	–	19
Pepper	–	–	2	–	–	–	2
Tea	–	–	–	5	–	–	5
Vietnam	**24**	**3**	**89**	**26**	**–**	**17**	**159**

Source: Based on AIFTA Tariff Schedules

Note: # = National tariff lines that do not follow HS3 (2007) standard (the first six digits should be based on the standard subheading nomenclature of the country's HS version) are listed.

Annex Table 3.5 Kerala's agricultural products and India's tariff category

Kerala products/category (CLMV and Philippines)	*EL*	*NT-1*	*NT-2*	*SP*	*ST*	*Six-digit tariff lines*	*% Share*
EL	**56**	–	–	–	–	**56**	**35**
Coconut	4	–	–	–	–	4	7.1
Coffee	6	–	–	–	–	6	10.7
Fish and fish products	37	–	–	–	–	37	66.1
Natural rubber	4	–	–	–	–	4	7.1
Pepper	1	–	–	–	–	1	1.8
Tea	4	–	–	–	–	4	7.1
NT-1		**87**				**87**	**54.4**
Fish and fish products	–	73	–	–	–	73	83.9
Natural rubber	–	14	–	–	–	14	16.1
NT-2			**10**			**10**	**6.3**
Coconut	–	–	1	–	–	1	10
Fish and fish products	–	–	9	–	–	9	90
SP				**3**		**3**	**1.9**
Coffee	–	–	–	1	–	1	33.3
Pepper	–	–	–	1	–	1	33.3
Tea	–	–	–	1	–	1	33.3
ST					**4**	**4**	**2.5**
Fish and fish products	–	–	–	–	3	3	75
Natural rubber	–	–	–	–	1	1	25
Six-digit tariff lines	**56**	**87**	**10**	**3**	**4**	**160**	**100**

Source: Based on the Trade Agreement, ASEAN Indian Free Trade Agreement, DOC

Note: # = National tariff lines that do not follow the HS3 (2007) standard (the first six digits should be based on the standard subheading nomenclature of the country's HS version) are listed.

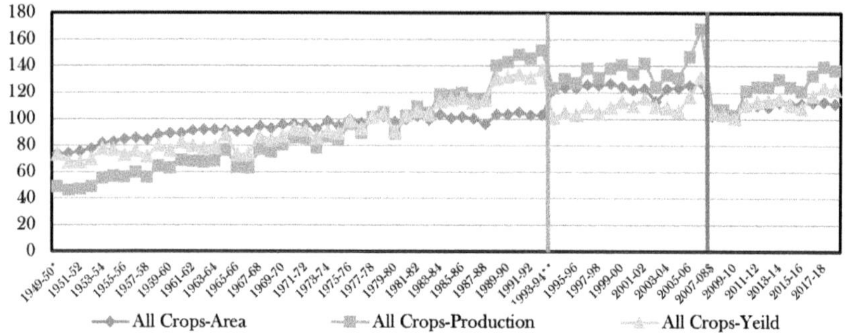

Annex Figure 3.1 Performance of food and non-food crops of agricultural sector (area, production, and yield)

Source: RBI database (Real Economy)

Note: Base-triennium ending * =1981–82 = 100, ** = 1993–94 = 100 and $ = 2007–08 = 100.

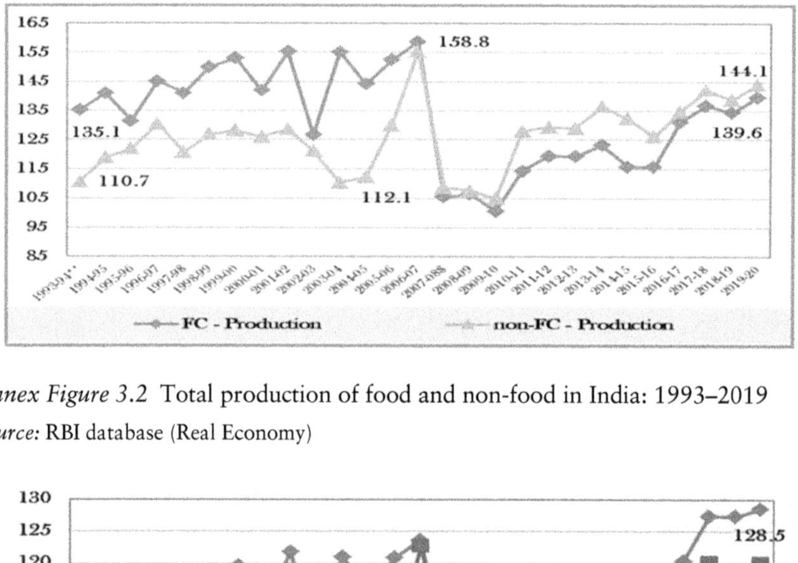

Annex Figure 3.2 Total production of food and non-food in India: 1993–2019

Source: RBI database (Real Economy)

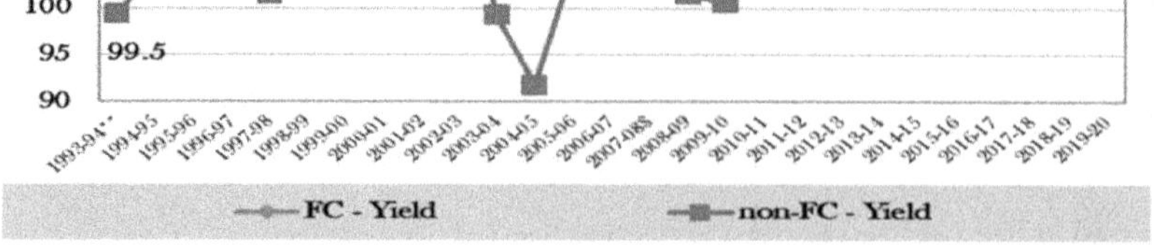

Annex Figure 3.3 Yield-based difference between food and non-food crops: 1993–2019

Source: RBI database (Real Economy)

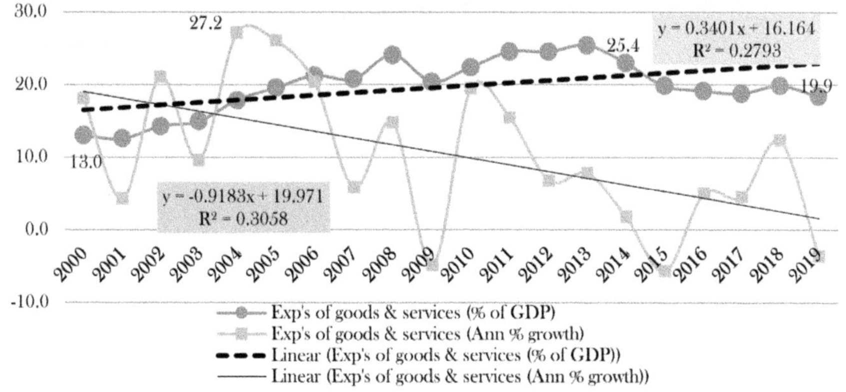

Annex Figure 3.4 India's export competitiveness: 2000–2019

Source: World Bank

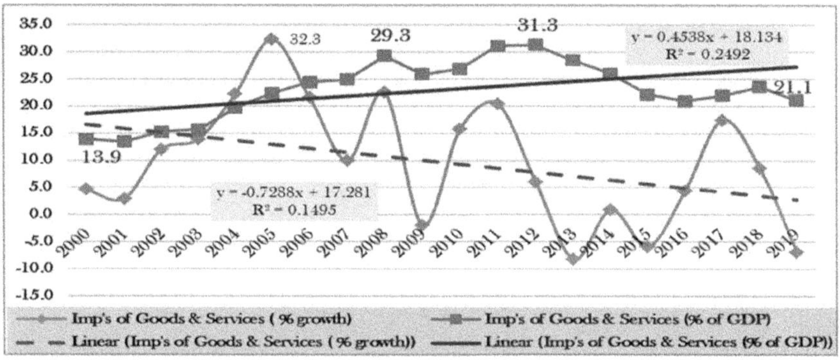

Annex Figure 3.5 India as a market: 2000–2019

Source: World Bank

Part II

Structural Transformation and Impact of COVID-19 on Remittances and Labour Question

4 Labour supply behaviour of the return emigrants in Kerala

Justin Sunny, Jajati Keshari Parida and K. Ravi Raman

Introduction

Kerala is one of the states with social development indicators comparable to those of developed countries. Kerala's attainment of higher living standards and social development without achieving higher economic growth has been debated for several years. Kerala ranks the highest among Indian states in terms of reporting emigration and remittance receipts (Parida 2019; Parida & Raman, 2018). For the past five decades, the uninterrupted remittances might have resulted in higher social development in Kerala. Remittances improved living standards, reduced poverty, and helped Kerala advance as one of India's developed states (Chakraborty 2005, Kannan 2005, Raman 2012). Increased remittance inflow helped reduce the overall incidence of poverty and boosted investments in land, assets, and human capabilities (including education and health). However, the most recent data (KMS 2018) shows that the number of return migrants (from abroad) is rising in Kerala.

The Kerala Migration Survey (KMS) estimated the number of return migrants in Kerala to be around one million in 2000 (Zachariah et al. 2001); however, this number went up drastically during COVID-19, with the estimated number of return migrants during COVID-19 in Kerala touching more than two million (Rajan and Pattath 2022). In 2001, the percentage of return migrants who were self-employed was higher (Zachariah et al. 2001). The other two sectors were construction and transport. The number of return migrants increased in 2018; it was about 1.2 million (Rajan and Zacharia 2019). The primary reason reported for the return of migrants in recent years is job loss. A significant number of migrants return to Kerala because of poor or deteriorating health conditions or family matters, including marriage, care, and assistance for dependent members (Rajan and Zacharia 2019).

The COVID-19 crisis has also added to this trend of return migration. This chapter explores the following questions: What will happen if this trend continues in Kerala? What will be the employment pattern of these return migrants, given that other state domestic migrants already occupy a large number of low-paid jobs in the state? Do improved living standards or existing wage rates significantly determine their workforce participation behaviour?

DOI: 10.4324/9781003601289-6

The primary objectives of this study include examining (i) the trends and broad patterns of emigration from and return migration to Kerala and (ii) the pattern of workforce participation and exploring the socio-economic factors determining it in Kerala.

Data and methodology

We used the KMS conducted by the Centre for Development Studies (CDS), Thiruvananthapuram (2018), to estimate the labour supply behaviour of return migrants in Kerala. The survey used a multistage sampling framework to cover the entire Kerala. The KMS provides information on various socio-demographic and economic indicators, such as emigration, return migration, remittances, household income, and expenditure. Information on remittances includes the amount of remittance received during the last 365 days and the different heads under which households use the remittances. The study's regression results are based only on the KMS 2018 round.

The workforce participation function of return migrants was estimated using the KMS data and compared across various sections. We used the Probit and IV Probit regression models to estimate the workforce participation function of the return migrants. Probit Regression, or the Probit Model, is used to model the dichotomous or binary-dependent variable. In the Probit Model, the inverse standard normal distribution of the probability is modelled as a linear combination of the predictors. We estimated four different Probit models for determining workforce participation.

We used the instrumental variable method to overcome the endogeneity bias between workforce participation and either consumption expenditure or income. Endogeneity occurs because workforce participation can influence consumption expenditure or income; simultaneously, consumption expenditure or income can influence workforce participation. This mutual influence makes it hard to determine the exact cause-and-effect relationship. We used specific household-level characteristics as an instrumental variable to address the endogeneity issue of household expenditure and workforce participation (including household size, landholding, head of the household, and dummy variables for religion in household income and expenditure functions). Test statistics suggest that our IV Probit estimates are appropriate.

Findings

Trends of emigration and return migration from Kerala

Kerala has a long, centuries-old history of emigration. However, current trends reflect changes in destination, occupation, and demographic patterns. These are visible both in terms of magnitude and inflow. The early-age migration from Kerala was mainly towards the Middle East countries. Recently, emigration from Kerala shows a more pluralistic pattern. Yet, the trends have been consistent. The percentage of emigrating families from Kerala started

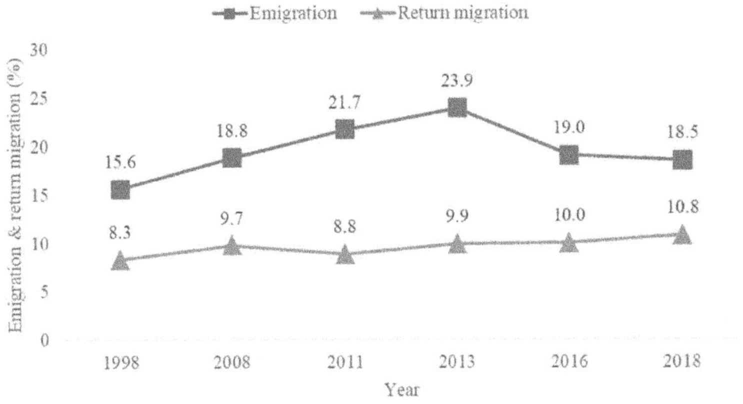

Figure 4.1 Households reported emigration and return migration in Kerala, 1998–2018

Source: Authors' estimation from KMS Survey Data.

declining in 2013. The percentage of households that reported emigration peaked in 2013 and declined in the following years (Figure 4.1). However, the percentage of households that reported return migration has consistently risen. The rate of increase is slow, but it is steady.

Although the emigration pattern is changing from Gulf Cooperation Council (GCC) countries to the Global North and Oceania, GCC countries continue to be the foremost destination. As the dominance of GCC emigration is rooted back in the cultural hegemony shared through the Arabian trade route, about 90% of the migrants prefer to choose the GCC region as their preferred destination. These trends imply that low-skilled emigration still dominates the emigration stream even though the human capital base of the state has improved substantially. This might even be reflected in the changing pattern in the occupational structure of emigrants from Kerala. There exists an interlinkage between the past remittance investment and the new emigration trends (Sunny et al. 2020). Past remittances channelled and stimulated public funding, which resulted in considerable investment in health and education in Kerala. Higher levels of human capital formation have triggered skilled emigration to GCC countries, the Global North, and the Oceania region (Figure 4.2).

The return migration trends show that the districts that reported a higher rate of emigration also reported a higher rate of return emigration (Table 4.1). Malappuram reports the highest percentage of return migration in Kerala. Rates of households reporting return migration are consistent with the emigration trends.

However, the urban–rural differentials show a different picture (Table 4.2). A sharp difference exists between the percentage of urban and rural households reporting return migration. The percentage of households reporting

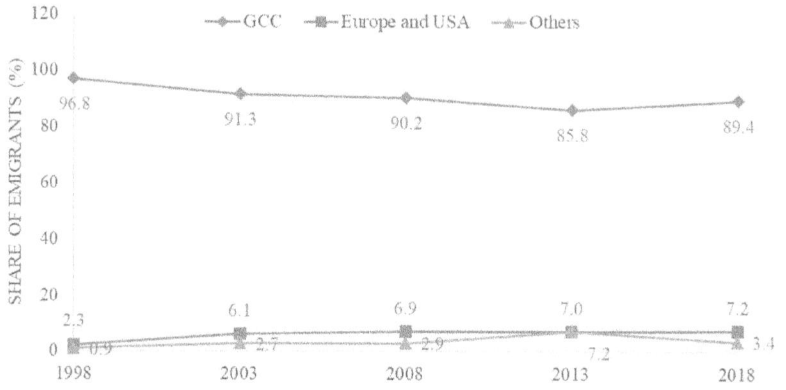

Figure 4.2 Major emigration destinations of Kerala emigrants, 1998–2018

Source: Authors' estimation from KMS Survey Data, various years from 2011 through 2018.

return migration is higher in rural areas across the districts of Kerala except for the districts of Thrissur, Palakkad, and Kasaragod (Table 4.1). The existence of the urban–rural differential could be attributed to the educational qualification and destination countries (Table 4.2). Households from urban areas are more likely to migrate to non-GCC countries and will be skilled migrants. All these factors provide more stability to emigration from urban regions, and these migrations will be more permanent than temporary.

Workforce participation of the return migrants

The factors attributing to return migration are pluralistic and vast. Anything from disruptions in the local economy of the receiving country to necessities in the households can cause return migration, push factors in host countries, and changes in labour policies and macroeconomic fluctuations. One of the best ways to analyze these is by measuring the WPRs of return migrants. The workforce participation of return migrants in Kerala has been very high and has continued to rise over the years.

The WPR of return migrants in Kerala was about 60% in 2011, which consistently increased to about 69% in 2018 (Table 4.3). A consistent increase in return migrants to the domestic labour market can also disrupt the local economy. While several reasons drive the workforce entry of return migrants, we tried to estimate the determinants of workforce participation. Return migrants from North Kerala and South Kerala reported higher WPRs compared to those from other parts of the state. While districts like Thiruvananthapuram and Kollam in the southern part reported higher WPRs, in North Kerala, Kasaragod, Kannur, Kozhikode, and Malappuram districts had higher rates. These districts also report higher rates of unskilled emigration to GCC countries.

Table 4.1 District-wise emigration and return migration scenario in Kerala, 1998–2018

Name of the district	*Household reported emigration (%)*						*Household reported return migration (%)*					
	1998	*2008*	*2011*	*2013*	*2016*	*2018*	*1998*	*2008*	*2011*	*2013*	*2016*	*2018*
Thiruvananthapuram	18.4	24.61	23.6	23.5	22.2	15.2	14.3	17.2	18.6	18.7	24.0	12.1
Kollam	14.1	20.39	23.6	24.7	18.0	23.4	8.6	10.1	13.4	12.8	18.0	17.8
Pathanamthitta	22.7	19.7	16.2	30.6	19.0	17.9	12.5	4.0	4.0	7.1	7.9	9.8
Alappuzha	10.5	13.09	14.9	15.7	15.4	16.9	5.5	8.9	7.0	9.8	9.9	11.6
Kottayam	6.7	11.12	10.7	12.2	13.8	13.5	3.4	4.8	1.8	5.1	1.2	5.3
Idukki	1.9	1.25	2.0	6.3	1.0	6.3	1.7	2.8	2.0	0.8	0.3	1.9
Ernakulam	12.4	8.54	8.7	13.6	8.8	4.1	6.3	7.2	4.8	5.4	4.0	2.1
Thrissur	17.0	25.72	27.6	22.3	17.9	17.4	9.9	11.2	12.8	12.4	6.9	9.4
Palakkad	13.8	19.76	20.2	10.0	8.5	10.5	4.8	7.0	7.7	1.5	2.6	6.2
Malappuram	32.4	40.29	44.0	49.8	32.1	35.8	15.2	18.4	11.2	21.0	8.4	22.3
Kozhikode	18.4	20.55	25.3	26.4	23.9	22.9	9.1	9.1	12.3	10.3	15.7	12.3
Wayanad	2.9	6.18	11.7	11.5	9.9	11.8	2.1	5.6	6.6	5.8	3.4	4.9
Kannur	16.9	18.66	35.8	39.7	33.7	25.3	6.1	6.4	11.0	9.9	17.6	10.2
Kasaragod	12.7	19.55	30.5	29.5	30.5	22.6	5.2	10.7	7.1	10.0	15.1	17.1
Total	**15.6**	**18.78**	**21.7**	**23.9**	**19.0**	**18.5**	**8.31**	**9.73**	**8.8**	**9.8**	**9.9**	**10.7**

Source: Authors' estimation from KMS Survey Data, various years from 2011 through 2018.

Table 4.2 Sector-wise return migrants' scenario in Kerala

Name of the district	*2011*		*2013*		*2016*		*2018*	
	Rural	*Urban*	*Rural*	*Urban*	*Rural*	*Urban*	*Rural*	*Urban*
Thiruvananthapuram	19.6	17.2	18.5	18.8	27.7	18.2	13.2	10.4
Kollam	14.3	9.0	11.5	14.4	19.0	13.1	20.6	16.2
Pathanamthitta	4.2	2.7	8.6	5.7	8.2	5.6	10.5	6.8
Alappuzha	8.4	3.7	8.3	12.5	11.0	7.5	12.2	9.7
Kottayam	1.8	2.0	5.4	3.8	1.4	0.0	4.1	2.1
Idukki	2.0	2.0	1.0	0.8	0.3	0.0	2.2	1.8
Ernakulam	4.0	5.7	5.7	4.8	3.4	4.5	2.8	1.4
Thrissur	13.4	10.4	12.5	12.3	6.2	9.5	8.4	10.5
Palakkad	7.9	6.7	2.0	1.0	2.3	4.7	5.2	7.6
Malappuram	10.7	14.7	21.9	20.0	8.7	5.1	22.0	19.9
Kozhikode	13.9	8.6	9.1	12.5	17.5	11.9	14.2	10.8
Wayanad	5.7	2.4	9.0	2.3	3.1	0.8	4.6	3.2
Kannur	11.1	10.5	7.6	12.0	14.4	25.1	12.1	8.3
Kasaragod	7.1	7.0	11.0	9.2	14.2	18.0	14.4	20.4
Kerala	**8.8**	**8.9**	**10.0**	**9.7**	**9.7**	**11.0**	**10.4**	**10.9**

Source: Authors' estimation from KMS Survey Data, various years from 2011 through 2018.

Table 4.3 Workforce participation rate (WPR) of the return emigrants in Kerala, 2011–18

Name of the district	*Workforce participation rate (%)*								
	2011			*2013*			*2018*		
	Rural	*Urban*	*Total*	*Rural*	*Urban*	*Total*	*Rural*	*Urban*	*Total*
Thiruvananthapuram	67.8	60.8	65.1	65.1	63.6	64.4	68.6	60.8	77.6
Kollam	65.7	64.5	65.5	69.2	68.8	69.0	71.0	75.0	75.2
Pathanamthitta	48.7	45.5	48.3	50.0	36.2	43.9	67.3	33.3	48.6
Alappuzha	50.0	59.5	52.1	56.8	63.6	59.7	72.8	53.9	54.4
Kottayam	30.0	16.7	27.8	66.1	80.0	68.1	64.3	0.0	42.3
Idukki	63.6	75.0	64.6	0.0	33.3	25.0	50.0	0.0	72.2
Ernakulam	71.7	52.1	59.1	71.1	71.4	71.2	85.7	60.0	63.6
Thrissur	54.0	47.5	52.9	65.3	63.8	64.6	69.1	55.6	67.3
Palakkad	58.8	31.2	53.5	46.7	80.0	55.0	65.2	0.0	73.2
Malappuram	70.9	69.6	70.6	76.6	64.6	72.0	58.2	57.1	73.8
Kozhikode	86.4	54.3	75.0	75.3	68.1	72.2	76.6	82.2	75.2
Wayanad	80.6	100.0	82.9	83.7	66.7	80.8	72.7	75.0	95.5
Kannur	60.8	48.8	57.3	60.2	65.2	63.2	79.0	59.8	65.7
Kasaragod	59.5	60.0	59.5	68.3	62.7	65.1	71.1	62.2	72.4
Kerala	**62.8**	**54.2**	**60.8**	**67.7**	**63.7**	**65.9**	**71.0**	**61.8**	**68.6**

Source: Authors' estimation from KMS Survey Data, various years from 2011 through 2018.

The differences are not limited to geographical proximity. The urban–rural difference in the WPR is drastic. Return migrants residing in rural areas are more likely to be engaged in the workforce, as they are not well off compared to those from urban areas. These rates have been consistent over the years. Understanding the employment pattern and the determinants of workforce participation among return migrants will develop further insights.

Employment pattern of the return migrants in Kerala

Distress-driven factors prominent in rural areas push return migrants to join the workforce. Sectoral employment patterns and the types of employment of return emigrants show that the service sector holds the largest share at about 65% (Table 4.4). This sector also holds a significant share in the overall employment pattern of Kerala. Moreover, return migrants depending on employment in the service sector is increasing over these years. While about 16% of return migrants are engaged in the agriculture sector, the percentage of those in the manufacturing sector is consistently declining, with only about 3% working in the sector in 2018. About 17% of the return migrants are engaged in the non-manufacturing sector, including construction and utilities (Table 4.4). Construction sectors have a prominent role in all of Kerala's migration episodes. Emigrants from Kerala predominantly migrated to the GCC regions to work in the construction sectors. The resulting remittance receipts were primarily invested in land and buildings. Remittance receipts played a crucial role in the construction boom in Kerala (Parida et al., 2020). The share of the non-manufacturing sector has seen a decline in accommodating return migrants over the years. However, an interesting coincidence is that this sector, which has grown because of the remittances, is absorbing return migrants. The decline is due to the large influx of domestic migrants from different parts of India occupying a significant share in the domestic labour market.

Table 4.4 Occupation pattern of the return emigrants in Kerala, 2011–18

Sector of employment	*Share of workers (%)*			
	2011	*2013*	*2016*	*2018*
Agriculture	16.8	15.5	14.0	16.0
Manufacturing	5.0	5.1	4.4	3.0
Non-manufacturing	14.7	16.5	18.5	14.6
Service	61.1	59.1	62.1	64.5
Others	2.5	3.9	1.0	1.9
Total	**100**	**100**	**100**	**100**

Source: Authors' estimation from KMS Survey Data, various years from 2011 through 2018.

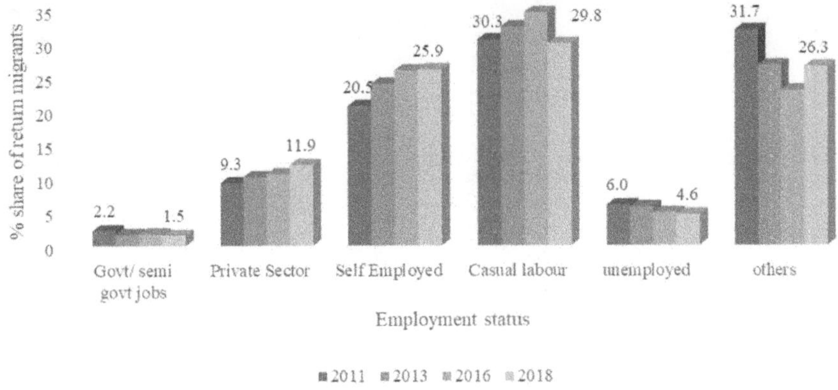

Figure 4.3 Employment pattern of the return migrants in Kerala

Source: Authors' estimation from KMS Survey Data, various years from 2011 through 2018.

On investigating the distribution of the types of employment among the return migrants, the broad types of employment patterns show that the quality of jobs is poor and questionable. About 30% of the return migrants are engaged in casual daily labour (Figure 4.3) and about 25% are self-employed.

Higher self-employment rates among return migrants could be a relief for policymakers. Promoting self-employment among return migrants will be mutually beneficial for the state and returnees. The return migrants will not only get an opportunity to highlight the knowledge and skills they have acquired during migration but also create further employment in the state, which will be a massive relief to the distressed labour market in Kerala.

About 12% of the return migrants are engaged in the private sector, and a marginal number is engaged in government jobs. Also, about 5% of the return migrants are unemployed. The number of return migrants engaged in daily labour is alarming and requires urgent attention. Several factors force them to join the labour force. From the employment pattern, it is evident that distress factors trigger them to engage in casual labour. Policy measures should be taken to provide social security and employment security benefits to them; however, we need to identify the determinants to define the factors responsible for the workforce participation of return migrants.

Factors determining the workforce participation of the return emigrants

From workforce participation and employment patterns, we noted that the return migrants from vulnerable sections are more likely to be engaged in the labour market. To examine the factors determining their workforce participation, we estimated the determinant function. We estimated both Probit and IV Probit regression (Tables 4.5 and 4.6).

Table 4.5 Determinants of workforce participation of the return emigrants in Kerala (Probit regression results)

Variables	*Model I*		*Model II*		*Model III*		*Model IV*	
	Coefficient	*Z Value*	*Coefficient*	*Z Value*	*Coefficient*	*Z Value*	*Coefficient*	*Z Value*
Constant	−1.247645	6.26***	* 1.876089	−3.64***	−2.675854	−4.41***	−2.047792	−3.86***
Age	0.134802	−7.42**	0.135456	6.17***	0.136931	6.21***	0.136468	6.13***
Age square	−0.001702	−5.24***	−0.001707	−7.31***	−0.00174	−7.43***	−0.001734	−7.32***
Log MPCI					−0.08718	−2.21***		
Expenditure dummy (reference category – **MPCI Class 1**)								
MPCI Class 2							0.052337	0.55***
MPCI Class 3							0.140891	1.58***
MPCI Class 4							−0.254528	−2.56***
MPCI Class 5							−0.153469	−1.59***
Log MPCE	−0.088287	−1.7***						
Expenditure dummy (reference category – **MPCE Class 1**)								
MPCE Class 2			0.085398	0.9***				
MPCE Class 3			0.113878	1.22***				
MPCE Class 4			−0.08224	−0.85***				
MPCE Class 5			−0.230336	−2.31***				
Remittance (reference category – **non-receipt**)								
Receipt of remittance	−0.377715	−5.04***	−0.373588	−4.97***	−0.421986	−5.54***	−0.428263	−5.59***
Sex (reference category – male)								
Female	−1.238337	−11.77***	−1.240536	−11.76***	−1.269465	−11.76***	−1.268035	−11.73***
Marital status (reference category – **unmarried**)								
Married	0.322784	2.86***	0.319199	2.81***	0.352218	3.03***	0.353771	3.06***
Level of education (reference category – illiterate)								
Primary	0.177101	0.64**	0.180587	0.65*	0.181617	0.62*	0.178295	0.61*
Secondary	0.277253	1.02*	0.279636	1.03	0.256257	0.89	0.256203	0.89
Higher secondary	0.069503	0.25	0.0684	0.24***	0.08718	0.29***	0.081365	0.28**

(Continued)

Table 4.5 (Continued)

Variables	*Model I*		*Model II*		*Model III*		*Model IV*	
	Coefficient	*Z Value*	*Coefficient*	*Z Value*	*Coefficient*	*Z Value*	*Coefficient*	*Z Value*
Graduation and above	−0.154361	−0.55**	−0.146096	−0.52*	−0.226463	−0.76	−0.214546	−0.73
ITI/diploma	0.016044	0.06*	0.024472	0.08**	0.004443	0.01*	−0.012076	−0.04
Landholding dummy (reference category – 0–0.25 acres)								
0.25–0.75 acres	−0.224958	-2.68***	−0.22566	-2.69***	−0.250463	-2.94***	−0.252156	-2.96***
0.75–1.5 acres	-0.023441	-0.17***	-0.020878	-0.15***	-0.069516	-0.49***	-0.075912	-0.53***
1.5–5 acres	0.111929	0.58***	0.104743	0.54***	0.032222	0.17***	0.020342	0.11***
Above 5 acres	-0.126487	-1.53***	-0.128011	-1.54***	-0.107513	-1.27***	-0.114918	-1.35***
Religion group dummy (Reference category – Christian)								
Hindu	0.198713	2.24***	0.196758	2.21***	0.181709	2.01***	0.178568	1.98**
Muslim	0.108383	1.18***	0.103345	1.12***	0.133606	1.43***	0.132194	1.41***
Pseudo R2	0.256		0.257		0.2626		0.2638	
Wald Chi (2)	439.28		436.98		422.56		433.18	
Max. log likelihood	−1168.349		−1166.852		−1114.5148		-1113.2715	
Observations(*N*)	2523		2523		2443		2445	

Note: *,** and *** imply the statistical significance levels at 10%, 5% and 1% respectively.
Source: Authors' estimation from KMS Survey Data, various years from 2011 through 2018.

Table 4.6 Determinants of workforce participation of the return emigrants in Kerala (IV Probit regression results)

Variables	*IV Probit Model I*		*IV Probit Model II*	
	Coefficient	*Z Value*	*Coefficient*	*Z Value*
Constant	-0.649044	-0.48***		
Age	0.1355301	6.31***	0.134348	6.09***
Age square	-0.0016992	-7.42***	-0.00166	-7.01***
Predicted log MPCI			-0.22829	-1.77***
Predicted log MPCE	-0.1665012	-1.03***		
Remittance (reference category – non-receipt)				
Receipt of remittance	-0.3687857	-4.82***	-0.35206	-4.34***
Sex (reference category – male)				
Female	-1.235125	-11.69***	-1.25269	-11.51***
Marital status (reference category – unmarried)				
Married	0.3091892	2.69**	0.273829	2.31***
Level of Education (reference category – illiterate)				
Primary	0.1801581	0.65*	0.163674	0.55**
Secondary	0.2850842	1.04**	0.280376	0.96***
Higher secondary	0.0776252	0.27**	0.132968	0.44*
Graduation and above	-0.123264	-0.42*	-0.04187	-0.13*
ITI/siploma	0.0423971	0.14**	0.102259	0.33
Landholding dummy (reference category – 0–0.25 acres)				
0.25–0.75 acres	0.2182215	-2.58***	0.221552	2.61**
0.75–1.5 acres	-0.0106144	-0.08*	-0.03612	-0.26***
1.5–5 acres	-0.1305128	0.67**	-0.1104	0.58***
Above 5 acres	-0.1366457	-1.6**	-0.12842	-1.52*
Religion group dummy (reference category – Christian)				
Hindu	0.1895734	2.1***	0.181407	2.01***
Muslim	0.0962448	1.03***	0.063236	0.66***
Athrho	0.0468397	0.51***	0.25142	2.5***
Lnsigma	-0.6586386	-32.36***	-0.36573	-13.08***
Rho	0.0468055		0.2462531	
Sigma	0.5175555		0.6936921	
Wald test	0.26	0.6091***	6.24	0.0425***
Wald Chi (2)	439.26		438.91	
Max. log likelihood	3086.41		3683.45	
Observations (*N*)	2523		2443	

Standard of living appears to be one of the major push factors among return migrants within the push and pull factors. As the returnees migrated and households received remittances, their spending pattern also changed. Kerala migration scenario is deeply connected with the spending pattern skewed towards durable goods and human capital formation. Households are expected to maintain the improved living standards and spending patterns. All these factors could also be attributed to factors driving the workforce participation of the return migrants.

Different models have been estimated under Probit regression. While age is positively associated with the workforce participation of the return migrants, age square turns out to be negatively associated. The return migrants are more likely to participate in the labour market if they return after a short time, but those belonging to a higher age group are less likely to participate in the workforce. Similarly, elderly return migrants who are retired are less likely to be engaged in the labour market. These results are consistent across all Probit and IV Probit models (Tables 4.5 and 4.6)

To begin with, for factors related to living standards, we used the logarithm of monthly per capita income (MPCI) and per capita expenditure (MPCE). We also used quintiles of MPCI and MPCE to examine the effects of return migrants belonging to different quintiles. Across all four models and IV Probit regression, we observed a negative association between MPCI and MPCE. Return migrants with higher MPCI are less likely to participate in the workforce. We used MPCI and MPCE as proxies for the living standards of the return migrants. Return migrants with relatively better living standards are less likely to participate in the workforce. Economically vulnerable return migrants are forced to join the domestic workforce due to the distress in the household.

The relatively higher spending capacity enjoyed by the household while the returnee was staying abroad is also a significant factor. The MPCE of those households is lesser than before, and the households intend to remain in that expenditure strata. Households prefer to remain in their improved living standard, which they were enjoying as the benefits of remittances. Along with the distress factors, the household's tendency to avoid reducing their consumption with the fall in income pushes the return migrants to enter the workforce again.

We further investigated the distress factors using the coefficients of MPCE quintile dummies and MPCI quintile dummies. The results showed the first three quintiles to be positively associated and the upper two quintiles to be negatively related and statistically significant. Results imply that the return migrants belonging to lower economic quintiles have a higher chance of joining the workforce, whereas those in a relatively higher income group have a lower chance of joining the workforce in Kerala. The positive signs of the lower economic quintiles show that economic vulnerability in the household is a major pushing factor. All these results substantiate the employment pattern of the return migrants in Kerala. Return migrants who belong to the lower economic category are forced to engage in daily labour, which does not have any social security benefits.

Moreover, we also investigated the results of the landholding dummies to verify these results further. All the landholding dummies, except the 0.25–0.75 acres dummy, are negatively associated with workforce participation. The higher landholding dummies are negative and statistically significant. Results imply that return migrants who own at least one acre of land are less likely to join the workforce. It also shows that about 16% of the return migrants are engaged in agricultural jobs. Those with landholdings are expected to rather depend on the earnings from landholdings than join the workforce. The return migrants owning marginal landholdings feel forced to join the workforce to sustain their living. Moreover, with the increase in landholdings, return migrants in Kerala are less likely to join the workforce.

Otherwise, we can also conclude that household-level distress has pushed the return migrants' probability of joining the workforce.

Furthermore, along with economic vulnerabilities, social factors are also strong enough to determine and push return migrants' workforce participation in Kerala. Participation of marginalized communities in Kerala's entire migration scenario is minimal. These social factors are highly inclined towards the religious aspects of the return migration. Hindus and Muslims are more likely than Christians to be engaged in workforce participation. Nurses occupy a significant share of emigration among Christians from Kerala, with Europe and the Oceania region as their preferred destinations. Factors like these place Christian return migrants in a relatively better standard of living, which hinders them from joining the workforce.

Female return migrants are less likely than their male counterparts to participate in the workforce. Considering a significant number of return migrants are engaged in casual labour activities (on a daily wage basis), female workers are less likely to engage in these sectors. Also, the patriarchal stigma associated with women working after a certain age lowers the participation of women in the workforce in Kerala. Female participation in the Kerala migration experience is predominantly limited to nurse migration. Gender differentials in the WPR of return migrants show a drastic difference. An increase in the WPR of female return migrants shows that women feel forced to engage in daily or casual labour even though their working conditions are very pathetic and require urgent attention. Female return migrants are less likely to join the workforce because of all these factors. The state needs to pay special attention to accommodating female return migrants.

The study shows married return migrants as being more likely to join the workforce than those unmarried. This could be because dependent members of married return migrants, including children and elderly parents, are likely to be high, and they also have the added responsibility of having to take care of their families. These factors also stop them from migrating further or leaving their family to look for jobs elsewhere. However, return migrants find suboptimal jobs nearby with meagre daily wages. Household-level distress, social factors, gender differentials, and a higher dependency ratio force return migrants to join the workforce. The consistent addition of return migrants to the workforce will burden the domestic labour market and eventually create cheap labour in the state. One of the primary reasons is the supremacy of low-skilled temporary emigration to GCC countries, which needs to be channelled to high-skilled emigration.

Migration and sustainable development in Kerala – discussion

Recent evidence points out that emigration from Kerala is dominated by low-skilled emigration to the GCC countries. However, recently the emigration pattern has changed. Emigration from Kerala has been directed towards more skilled emigration in terms of education and employment. The emigration destination is shifting from the GCC region to the Global North, Europe, and the Oceania region. Even though the emigration patterns are changing, the rate of change is slow and marginal.

Besides, emigration to the GCC is predominantly low-skilled in the Kerala emigration scenario, hence low-skilled return emigration is also large, and the educational qualification of these return migrants is also very low.

The level of education dummies also shows that return migrants with lower levels of education are more likely to participate in the workforce. Also, return migrants with technical skills from ITI and diplomas are likely to enter the workforce. However, return migrants who are graduates or have higher educational qualifications are less likely to join the workforce. Evidence from the association suggests that low-skilled return emigrants are more likely to join the workforce. Empirical evidence matches the employment pattern of the return migrants. A significant number of low-skilled return migrants are engaged in casual labour, whereas ITI-educated skilled return migrants are likely to join the workforce as employees in the private sector.

All these factors suggest that the temporary migration from Kerala is turning out to be a blessing in disguise. While low-skilled emigration to the Gulf region is temporary, the emigration towards the Global North, Europe, and the Oceania regions appears more permanent. The receipt of remittances is high in the case of temporary migration, whereas the remittance receipt is low in the case of permanent migration.

The driving factors for temporary migration are household-level distress and poverty. Temporary emigration is often accompanied by higher rates of remittances to households, and higher rates of remittance receipts often improve living standards and investment in human capital. The problem arises when the emigrants return to the state, and these rates increase over the years. A higher number of return migrants in the state will destabilize the local labour market, which domestic migrants from other states of India currently occupy. If the state decides to promote permanent migration, it will eventually result in falling remittances, which will negatively impact Kerala's economy. Considering the number of return migrants has increased more rapidly since the COVID-19 crisis, it is imperative that the state identify and promote self-employment among the return migrants. If the return migration trends continue to rise, it should also emphasize accommodating female return migrants and prioritizing job-creation strategies.

Conclusion

Household-level distress and various social and individual-level factors determine workforce participation of return migrants. While the emigration pattern is changing, low-skilled emigration to the GCC region is predominant and a significant number of the return migrants also belongs to this category.

Household-level economic vulnerability is forcing return migrants to join the workforce in Kerala. The receipts of remittances in the past have increased household consumption expenditure. Considering consumption expenditure does not drop as much as the fall in income, return migrants feel compelled to join the local labour market. However, with domestic migrants from other states currently occupying the local labour market because of their arrival into the state following the construction sector boom and excessive emigration, return migrants have to compete for space in the casual labour market.

Distress factors and a higher dependency ratio force return migrants to accept jobs with suboptimal wages in nearby vicinities. A significant number of return migrants are engaged in casual labour, with no social security benefits and job security. Hence, it is important that policies that help accommodate return migrants emphasize job creation. The state must also promote self-employment among return migrants and create a framework for that purpose.

References

Chakraborty, B. 2005. "Human Capital, Education Policy and Economic Growth." *Productivity* 46(1): 13–20.

Kannan, K. P. 2005. "Kerala's Turnaround in Growth: Role of Social Development, Remittances and Reform." *Economic & Political Weekly* 45(1): 548–54.

Kerala Migration Survey (KMS). 2018. Thiruvananthapuram: Centre for Developments Studies.

Parida, J. K. 2019. "Rural–Urban Migration, Urbanization, and Wage Differentials in URBAN INDIA. In *Internal Migration, Urbanization and Poverty in Asia: Dynamics and Interrelationships*, 189–218. Singapore: Springer.

Parida, J. K., and Raman, K. R. 2018. "India: Rising Trends of International and Internal Migration." In *Handbook of Migration and Globalization*, edited by A. Triandafyllidou, 226–48. Northampton: Edward Elgar Publishing.

Parida, J. K., John, M. E., and Sunny, J. 2020. "Construction Labour Migrants and Wage Inequality in Kerala." *Journal of Social and Economic Development* 22(2): 414–42.

Rajan, S. I., and Zachariah, K. C. 2019. "Emigration and Remittances: New Evidences from the Kerala Migration Survey 2018 (Working Chapter No. 12989). *eSocialScience*. https:// ideas.repec.org/p/ess/wchapter/id12989.html

Rajan, S. I., and Pattath, B. 2022. "What Next for the COVID-19 Return Emigrants?: Findings from the Kerala Return Emigrant Survey 2021." In *India Migration Report 2021*, edited by S. Irudaya Rajan, 181–95. India: Routledge.

Raman, K. R. 2012. "'Currents and Eddies': Indian-Middle East Migration Processes." *Cambridge Journal of Regions, Economy and Society* 5(2): 189–206.

Sunny, J., Parida, J. K., and Azurudeen, M. 2020. "Remittances, Investment and New Emigration Trends in Kerala." *Review of Development and Change* 25(1): 5–29.

Zachariah, K. C., Mathew, E. T., and Rajan, S. I. 2001. "Social, Economic and Demographic Consequences of Migration on Kerala." *International Migration* 39(2): 43–71.

5 Kerala's labour market

The impact of inward and outward migration flows

M. P. Jayesh

Introduction

Kerala's labour market has reached a unique stage in its evolutionary path, where a significant portion of its workforce migrates to other countries (overseas) and other Indian states and a significant portion of migrant workers immigrate into the state from other Indian states. The major labour resources states such as Odisha, West Bengal, Bihar, Uttar Pradesh, Jharkhand, Assam, and Madhya Pradesh have been sending their labourers to Kerala to engage in various economic activities informally since the beginning of the 1990s (Sambasivan 2013; Sumeetha 2015; Prasad 2016; Raunaq 2016; Thomas and Jayesh 2019; Jayesh 2020; Peter et al 2020; Parida and Raman 2021). Kerala has been known for the emigration mainly of largely the less-educated unskilled workforce to Gulf regions since the early 1970s (Zachariah, and Rajan, 2005; Zachariah and Rajan 2010; Zachariah and Rajan 2012). However, after the mid-2000s, the nature of outward migration has undergone a paradigm shift from an unskilled to a more skilled labour force (Raman 2012; Thomas and Jayesh 2019).

Various state government agencies estimate approximately four (4) million Keralites work outside the country, and 1.4 million work outside the state but within the country. Meanwhile, as many as 3.5 million workers, predominantly male migrants from other Indian states, seek employment in Kerala. It is to be noted here that a large number of students join higher education in other countries such as Canada, Australia, Russia, the United States, and the United Kingdom. According to state government agencies, to get global exposure and quality higher education, approximately 15,000–18,000 students from Kerala move to other countries and around 30,000 students seek admission in other Indian states for various higher education programmes. Many of those students who migrate to these countries anticipate permanent employment and wish to settle in those countries. There is a clear shift in the emigration pattern observed in the late 2000s from circular migration to permanent migration by switching the destination from Gulf regions to Europe, Canada, the United States of America, and Australia, to name a few developed regions in the world.

DOI: 10.4324/9781003601289-7

This chapter attempts to describe and analyze various aspects of the inflow of migrant workers from other Indian states, particularly from the eastern and northern regions of the country. Based on the secondary sources of data, the chapter also attempts to understand the outflow of migrant workers from Kerala to other countries and Indian states and its impacts on the state's economy. After providing a brief description on the data and methods used in this study, the chapter broadly describes the trends in migration across Indian states with a special focus on Kerala, based on Census and NSSO data. It also gives an estimate of the outflow of migrant workers from Kerala to other countries and Indian states and compares this estimate with the state's workforce. The chapter examines various aspects of inward migration, including workers' year of entry into Kerala, their socio-economic conditions, literacy, and educational status. The chapter concludes with policy prescriptions for the dynamic Kerala labour market.

Data and methods

This chapter is partly based on an analysis of secondary data on the Kerala labour market, including migration data from the Census of India; National Sample Surveys on employment, unemployment, and migration; and the periodic labour force surveys (PLFS). It also relies on the field survey conducted between January and March 2021 in different towns and cities across Kerala, including Thiruvananthapuram, Perumbavoor, Alappuzha, and Kollam. To describe the various aspects of inward migrant workers, we used inputs from an earlier survey conducted among migrant construction workers in Kozhikode district between December 2015 and May 2016. In that first survey, 260 sample migrant workers were interviewed with a structured questionnaire. The sample workers were selected from all four taluks in the district. Apart from field study, we used evidence gathered through direct and telephonic interviews with industry leaders, heads of various government departments, and trade union leaders.

Migration across Indian states with special reference to Kerala based on census 2011 and NSSO 2007–08

An analysis of trends in migration across Indian states shows significant variations across Indian states concerning the proportion of migrants to the population (Jayesh 2020). According to the Census of India 2011, the average proportion of migrants to the population was 49.0% for the three western states and 42.2% for the four southern states (see Jayesh 2020, 54). The corresponding measure for the (three) eastern states were 31.9% and the (eight) northern states were 35.2%. If we consider male migrants as a proportion of the male population, the southern and western states are markedly ahead of the rest of India. In 2011, the proportion was relatively high in Delhi (44.2%), Kerala (40.2%), Tamil Nadu (34.8%), and Punjab (33.5%), and relatively low in Bihar (8.2%), Uttar Pradesh (UP) (11.6%),

Jammu and Kashmir (11.9%), Rajasthan (12.9%), Odisha (16.6%), and Chhattisgarh (18.6%) (Jayesh 2020).

The Census data on migrants in a particular state does not include migrants who migrated out of the state (to another state or another country) (Jayesh 2020). So, the Census data shows that the southern and western states, which are economically more advanced than the rest of India, attract a considerable number of migrants, including migrants from other states. On the other hand, states such as Bihar, UP, Rajasthan, Madhya Pradesh, Odisha, Chhattisgarh, and Jharkhand send large numbers of workers to other Indian states. Yet, as already noted, migrant proportion of the population is quite low in these states. This is because the outward migration of workers from a particular state (say Bihar) to other states goes unreported in that state's (Bihar's) migrant data (Jayesh 2020).

Workforce, human capital, and outward migration from Kerala

The employment condition in a state can be analyzed through the labour force participation rate (LPR) and workforce participation rate (WPR). The LPR is a measure of the proportion of the population that actively engages in the labour market. It includes both people currently working and those looking for employment. The LPR indicates the unemployment condition in the state.

As per the Periodic Labour Force Survey (PLFS), in 2017–18 (NSO 2019), LPRs (or those in the labour force as proportions of the population, all ages) of males in rural and urban areas of Kerala were 54.1% and 53.6% respectively (see Table 5.1). These proportions were less than the corresponding LPRs among men in the country (54.9% and 57.0% in the case of rural and urban men respectively). It is to be noted that, male LPRs in Kerala were lower than the male LPRs in states such as Tamil Nadu, Karnataka, Gujarat and Maharashtra (see Table 1, cited in Jayesh 2020).

According to PLFS 2017–18 (NSO 2019), LPRs among females (of all ages) are low in the state at 20.7% and 22.1%, respectively, in rural and urban Kerala (see Table 5.1). It is puzzling that female participation in the labour force is low in Kerala despite the progress that the state has made in reducing gender disparities. Nonetheless, it is important to note that the female LPRs in Kerala are still higher than the corresponding rates in the country. In 2017–18, while the LPR among females in urban Kerala was 22.1%, the corresponding rates were only 12.7% in Gujarat, 16.2% in Maharashtra, 18.1% in Karnataka, and 15.9% in India (see Table 5.1).

Workforce participation rate (WPR)

As per PLFS 2017–18 estimate (NSO 2019), the share of workers in the total population (WPR) of men was lower in rural and urban areas of Kerala when compared to India. The WPRs of rural and urban men in Kerala were 50.9% and 50.0%, respectively, in 2017–18 as against WPRs of 51.7% and 53.0%

Table 5.1 Labour force as a proportion of population (all ages) or labour force participation rates in Kerala and India, in per cent, 2011–12 and 2017–18

States	*Rural male*		*Urban male*		*Rural female*		*Urban female*	
	2011–12	*2017–18*	*2011–12*	*2017–18*	*2011–12*	*2017–18*	*2011–12*	*2017–18*
Kerala	58.3	54.1	56.7	53.6	25.8	20.7	22.2	22.1
Tamil Nadu	60.7	61.3	59.9	60.6	38.6	31.3	21.1	22.5
Karnataka	62.0	60.9	59.4	57.8	28.9	21.9	17.1	18.1
Maharashtra	58.2	57.8	56.0	44.1	38.9	29.8	17.2	16.8
Gujarat	60.2	58.5	60.7	59.2	27.9	17.2	13.5	12.7
India	55.3	54.9	56.3	57.0	25.3	18.2	15.5	15.9

Source: Cited in Jayesh 2020.
Note: Labour Force defined according to usual principal and usual subsidiary status of persons (PS+SS).

in rural and urban India, respectively (see Table 5.2). On the other hand, the WPR of an urban female is relatively high in Kerala (16.0% in Kerala and 14.2% in India). But in the case of rural females, the WPR is less (16.6%) in Kerala than the corresponding measure in India (17.5%) (see Table 5.2).

Between 2011–12 and 2017–18, there was a marked decline in WPRs in the case of rural and urban men in India and Kerala, but the decline is stark in the case of Kerala (see Table 5.2). Rural male WPR in Kerala was 56.5% in 2011–12 and 50.9% only in 2017–18. On the other hand, there was no remarkable change in WPRs in the case of rural and urban females in Kerala. At the same time, there was a marked decline in WPR in the case of rural females in India (see Table 5.2).

It would be interesting to compare WPRs according to NSSO and the Census of India. As shown already, according to the NSSO, WPRs in Kerala were higher than the corresponding national averages in the case of males and females in urban areas in 2011–12. However, according to the Census of India, in 2011, WPRs in Kerala were lower than the corresponding national averages in the case of both males and females (see Table 5.2).

Marginal workers as a proportion of the population are particularly low in Kerala relative to the national averages. In 2011, Kerala was ahead of the country with respect to main workers as a proportion of the male population (44.8% and 43.8% in Kerala and India, respectively). However, marginal workers as the proportion of male population was 7.9% in Kerala compared to 9.4% in the country. As a result, Kerala lagged the rest of the country with respect to (main and marginal) workers as a proportion of the male population (52.7% and 53.2% in Kerala and India, respectively) (see Table 5.2) (Thomas and Jayesh 2019).

Census of India provides estimates of WPRs for various age groups. It is indeed striking that the WPRs among the working-age population (15–59

Table 5.2 Workers as a proportion of population (all ages) or workforce participation rates in Kerala and India, according to NSS, in per cent, 2011–12 and 2017–18

Male	*Kerala*		*India*	
	PS+SS		*PS+SS*	
	2011–12	*2017–18*	*2011–12*	*2017–18*
Rural	56.5	50.9	54.3	51.7
Urban	55.2	50	54.6	53
All Regions	56.2	50.5	54.7	52.1
Female				
Rural	16.1	16.6	24.8	17.5
Urban	16.1	16	14.7	14.2
All Regions	16.1	16.4	21.9	16.5

Source: Estimates based on NSSO (2014) and NSO (2019) (cited in Jayesh 2020).

years) in Kerala are lower than the corresponding rates in the country. Kerala's distance (regarding WPRs) from the national averages is more in the case of females and marginal workers. In 2011, main workers as proportions of the female population in the age group of 15–59 years were 17.8% in Kerala and 22.6% in India – the difference between the two rates being 4.8 percentage points. At the same time, main and marginal workers combined as proportions of the same category of population (females, 15–59 years) were 26% and 37.4%, respectively, for Kerala and India (see Table 5.3). The difference between Kerala and the national average rises to 11.4 percentage points in the latter case, mainly on account of relatively smaller proportion of marginal female workers in the state (Thomas and Jayesh 2019).

Compared to the rest of the country, the proportion of students in the population in the 15–29-year age group is relatively high in Kerala. In 2011, this proportion was 38.9% among males and 34.7% among females in the state, while the corresponding national averages were 29.8% and 25.2%, respectively (see Table 5.4). Given that the proportion of students is relatively high, the proportion of workers is relatively low in the population in the 15–29-year age group in Kerala. This is a factor behind the relatively low-level of WPRs in Kerala among the population in the working-age years (Thomas and Jayesh 2019).

Table 5.3 Main and marginal workers as proportions of populations, in per cent, for various age-categories, Kerala and India, 2011

		Kerala		*India*	
Age-categories	*Years*	*Main*	*Main & marginal*	*Main*	*Main & marginal*
Male					
15–29	2011	39.0	48.4	45.5	59.3
30–59	2011	79.8	91.6	81.9	94.7
15–59	2011	64.4	75.3	65.1	78.4
May–14	2011	0.50	0.9	2.0	4.1
60+	2011	33.7	41.9	49.4	60.4
All Population	2011	44.8	52.7	43.8	53.2
Female					
15–29	2011	9.1	14.0	16.5	29.7
30–59	2011	22.7	32.8	27.6	43.8
5–59	2011	17.8	26.0	22.6	37.4
5–14	2011	0.30	0.70	1.4	3.6
60+	2011	6.10	10.1	14.0	23.4
All population	2011	12.4	18.2	15.2	25.5

Source: Census of India 1991, 2001, 2011 (cited in Jayesh 2020).

Table 5.4 Students as a proportion of the population, in per cent, Kerala and India, 1991–2011

Age-categories		*Kerala*		*India*	
		Male	*Female*	*Male*	*Female*
5–14	1991	86.4	86.6	82.1	57.8
	2001	89.9	90.2	68.3	61.9
	2011	90.1	90.2	77.3	75.9
15–29	1991	26.4	22.5	22.4	10.8
	2001	26.2	24.6	22.6	15.6
	2011	38.9	34.7	29.8	25.2
5+ population	2011	26.9	23.5	28.1	25.5

Source: Estimates based on Economic Tables of the Census of India (cited in Jayesh 2020).

Human capital formation in Kerala

The term "human capital" refers to the economic value of a worker's experience and skill, which includes assets like education, training, intelligence, skills, and health.[1] This section describes the health and education status of the state compared to India. Kerala continues to hold a leading position among Indian states concerning advancements in social indicators and human capital formation (Drèze and Sen, 2013, 214–18). In 1961, infant mortality rates of Kerala and India were 52 and 115 per thousand live births, respectively (Ramachandran 1996). By 2020, these rates declined to 6 and 27[2] per thousand live births for Kerala and India, respectively (GoK 2021, 303). Kerala witnessed a sharp decline in fertility and birth rate from the middle of the twentieth century onwards (Ramachandran 1996). In 2017, birth rate in Kerala was 13.5 births per thousand populations, whereas the corresponding figure for the nation was 19.7 births per thousand populations (GoK 2022 304). During the period 1951–61, while an average woman lived up to 35.7 years in India, an average woman in Kerala could live up to 45.3 years (Ramachandran 1996, 225). By 2021, the life expectancy at birth of an average woman in India and Kerala was 70.7 and 77.9 years, respectively (the corresponding figures for men were 68.2 and 72.5 years, respectively (GoK 2022, 304).

Kerala holds the top position among Indian states in terms of literacy levels of the population. By 2011, literacy rates for males and females in Kerala were 96.0% and 91.6%, respectively (Jayesh 2020). The corresponding Indian averages for males and females were 82.1% and 65.5%, respectively (a difference of 17.6 percentage points). Kerala's record has been remarkable both in achieving near-universal literacy rates and in reducing the gender gap in this area (Jayesh 2020).

Kerala's labour force is a relatively well-educated one. According to the NSS report on employment and unemployment in India in 2007–08, mean years of schooling (MYS) for Kerala's labour force was 8.5 years compared to the corresponding figures of 5.5 years for the country, 6.2 years for Tamil Nadu, 4.3 years for Andhra Pradesh, 5.5 years for Karnataka, and 5.8 years for Gujarat (GoI 2014, 244).

According to data from the Ministry of Human Resources Development, Government of India, the total number of students who pursued higher education in Kerala in 2015–16 was a little less than 1 million (0.94 million), which comprised 0.41 million male students and 0.53 million female students. As a proportion of all students pursuing higher education in the country, students in Kerala were 2.2% in the case of males and 3.3% in the case of females in 2015–16 (In 2011, the proportion of Kerala's population to India's population was 2.8%.) (Thomas and Jayesh 2019, 489). Women's participation in higher education is higher than that of men in Kerala (see Table 5.5). Despite the large expansion in education in Kerala, there are concerns regarding the quality of skills attained by youth in the state, especially to perform in the labour market.

Outward migration from the state

Kerala has been one of the source regions for migrant workers to other Indian states and foreign countries, especially to countries in the Middle East. The massive migration to foreign countries started in the 1970s, particularly towards the Gulf countries followed by the oil boom in the region (Rajan and Zachariah 2018). Recognizing the importance of out-migration on Kerala's economy, the Centre for Development Studies (CDS) Thiruvananthapuram had started conducting surveys to collect information about out-migrants at the household level and the impact of remittances on the economy since 1998. According to Kerala Migration Surveys (KMS), conducted by the CDS,

Table 5.5 Students enrolled in higher education in selected Indian states (in thousands) and as proportion of population in the age group of 18–23, 2015–16

States/India	*Numbers of students (1000s)*		*As proportions of 18–23 population (%)*	
	Male	*Female*	*Male*	*Female*
Kerala	405.6	533.6	26.6	35
Maharashtra	2247.8	1739.5	32	27.6
Gujarat	865.4	621.7	22.9	18.3
Tamil Nadu	1690.4	1544.9	46.3	42.4
West Bengal	1034.1	892.4	19.1	16.2
India	18594.7	15990.1	25.4	23.5

Source: GOI 2016, cited in Thomas and Jayesh 2019, 489.

the estimated number of migrants from the state increased from 1.4 million in 1998 to 2.4 million in 2013. As per the Kerala Migration Survey 2013, the highest number of emigrants was from the district of Malappuram (4.6 lakh) and the lowest number was from Wayanad (22,568). Out of the 14 districts in Kerala, outward migration was high in all districts except in Idukki and Wayanad, both hilly districts. Districts that send large numbers of migrants include Thiruvananthapuram, Kollam, Ernakulam, Thrissur, Kozhikode, Kannur, and Malappuram (CDS 1998–2013) (Jayesh, 020).

The earlier emigrants from Kerala were relatively less-educated and low-skilled workers. For instance, during the 1990s, almost 41% of the workers given emigration clearance were unskilled workers (Zachariah et al. 2002). Over the years, the migrant cohort from Kerala have comprised more educated workers, and new destination countries have emerged, too, for these workers (Zachariah and Rajan 2010). Nowadays, a large share of migration from Kerala is of professionally skilled workers, including nurses, engineers, teachers, accountants, doctors, and so on, and their destination regions include the United States, Australia, Singapore, and Canada apart from the Gulf countries (Mani 2011, 309–315).

Migration from Kerala from the 1970s onwards helped to reduce the massive unemployment problem in the state. At the same time, it became a cause of unemployment in 1990s and 2000s. Zachariah and Rajan (2005) identified four important factors that contributed to the unemployment problem in the state from the 1990s onwards: influx of females into the labour market, ageing, educational expansion, and emigration (Zachariah and Rajan 2005). The remittances received by the household were partly used for higher education purposes, which enhanced the reserve price of labour in Kerala. Given their affinity towards white-collar jobs, the young and educated labourers from Kerala prolong their entry into the workforce. At the same time, the high levels of investment in the state in the construction of houses, commercial complexes, and other real estate construction businesses increased demand for low-skilled manual workers. Migrant workers from other Indian states have filled this gap. Earlier inward migration to Kerala was mainly from the states of Tamil Nadu, Karnataka, and Andhra Pradesh, which has been replaced by the eastern, northern, and northeastern parts of the country.

Inward migration and emerging trend in Kerala labour market

Kerala's economy entered a phase of revival from the late 1980s onwards (Thomas and Jayesh 2019). With economic growth in the state gaining further speed during the 2000s, demand for labour increased, particularly in sectors such as construction. At the same time, Kerala's economy began to face a shortage of manual workers in various sectors (GoK, 2017). The state's economy is now dependent on the inflow of migrant workers, especially from the eastern and northern Indian states, including Bihar, West

Bengal, and Odisha. According to estimates by the Gulati Institute of Finance and Taxation (GIFT), the number of migrant workers in Kerala from other Indian states was 2.5 million in 2011. The number of inward migrants may have increased further to 4 million in 2016 as per *Economic Review 2016* (GoK 2016). Given that Kerala's total workforce numbered 12.7 million in 2017–18, the size of inward migrants in Kerala could be as high as 31.5% of the state's total workforce in that year (Jayesh 2020; Thomas and Satheesha, 2018).

This section focuses on understanding the nature and impact of inward migration from other Indian states to Kerala by taking inputs from a previous detailed study on migrants conducted in one of the districts, Kozhikode, Kerala. The study found that 1,59,485 migrant workers were engaged in around 21 economic activities spread across four taluks of the district[3] (Jayesh 2020). In the primary sector, migrant workers were (and continue to be) engaged in works in paddy fields, dairy farms, fisheries, quarrying, and plantations. In the secondary sector, migrant workers have been working in the footwear industry, garments manufacturing, manufacture of steel plates and rods, furniture making, engineering industries, agro-processing industries such as atta (wheat flour), maida (refined flour), biscuits, bread, and oil manufacturing industries, and bakery food production. In the services sector, migrant workers have been working in barber shops/beauty parlours, hotels and restaurants, shops selling beverages, bakeries, as salespersons in supermarkets, grocery shops, and other shops. The construction and infrastructure sector continues to absorb the largest share of migrant workers (68.4%) (Jayesh 2020). It is to be noted that the study conducted by GIFT (Gulati Institute of Finance and Taxation) shows that more than 60.0% of migrant workers in the state were in the construction sector.

The Kerala Migrant Welfare Scheme 2010 was established by the Government of Kerala for all migrant workers engaged in various economic activities in the state. Ironically, the number of registered construction workers in the labour department of Kerala was below 2000 in 2015–16. However, the COVID-19 pandemic and the consequent lockdown exposed the vulnerability and the size of the migrant workforce in the state. According to the government, the aggregate number of migrant workers in the shelter camps during the lockdown induced by the pandemic was 4.3 lakhs in Kerala. This is an underestimated number of migrant workers in the state for two reasons – (i) many workers were given safe shelter by the employers in Kerala, which was not counted in the official estimate and (ii) many migrants working in Kerala returned to their villages before the lockdown announcement on 25 March 2020, because of a lockdown-like situation in Kerala even before the Government of India lockdown official announcement, because of the early presence of the COVID-19 virus infection in the state.

Meanwhile, in Kerala, the return migration from other countries was estimated around 2.4 million as per the Vande Bharat Mission as of 31 October 2021 (Rajan and Pattath 2022). However, during the interaction with employers in Kerala, limitations in employing the return emigrants in the available employment opportunities in Kerala were observed. The kind of job opportunities available were not suited to the experienced, relatively educated emigrants from Kerala. Most engaged (or would like to be engaged) in self-employment activities such as plying autorickshaws or car taxis, being entrepreneurs in small businesses, or working in workshops, car service outlets, highway side fast-food shops, vegetable shops, supermarkets, etc.

Some features of migrant workers from other Indian states

This section primarily relies on a primary survey conducted in two stages as mentioned in "Data and methods" earlier. Previous studies pointed out that, the initial spell of inflow of migrant workers to Kerala occurred in the plywood industry at the beginning of the 1990s as a consequent prohibition of felling trees in Assam (GIFT 2013). In our study, the number of sample workers comprises 260. We obtained information regarding the year of entry of each migrant worker into Kerala, their travel destination, difficulties in their finding work, and their socio-economic conditions in their villages. The following section explains the details of the geographical mobility and the socio-economic characteristics of migrant workers in Kerala.

Workers' entry into Kerala

In our study conducted in 2015–16, we asked every sample migrant worker their history of migration and the year they reached Kerala to gain an understanding of the beginning of the new migration phenomenon. There were two types of migrants – one set migrated to Kerala after working in many other states in India (we called them "indirect migrants") and the other set reached Kerala without having worked in any other place in India (we called them "direct migrants") (Figure 5.1). Factors from the demand and supply sides affect the huge presence of migrant workers in Kerala labour market.

Figure 5.1, based on the sample of workers in Kozhikode, shows that migration of workers into Kerala accelerated after the year 2005. Of all the sample workers, only 21 had reached Kerala until 2005. However, over the next two years, 2006 and 2007, another 31 workers in the sample started working in Kerala for the first time. The entry of workers into Kerala appeared to have slowed down in 2008 and 2009 following the general recession in the economy on account of the global financial crisis. Migrant workers' entry into Kerala resumed in 2010. From mid-2010 onwards, the number of workers who migrated directly to Kerala also began to increase. In 2015, of the 50 workers who started working in Kerala, the number that migrated directly to Kerala was 14. The rate of migration of workers into Kerala appeared to have accelerated after 2011. The number of workers in the sample who first started working Kerala was 23 in 2010, which increased to 50 by 2015.

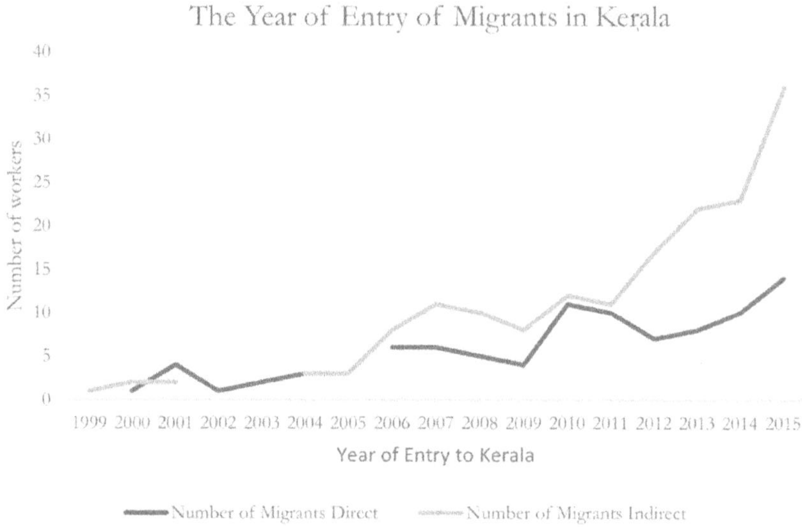

Figure 5.1 Distribution of direct and indirect migrant workers, by the year of entry into Kerala as a worker, in numbers

Source: Field survey in Kozhikode, 2015–16 (cited in Jayesh 2020).

Many real estate builders and small-scale contractors reported that the financial crisis of 2008 had affected businesses in the Middle Eastern countries and cities, particularly Dubai. The rich non-resident Indians (NRIs) including non-resident Keralites (NRKs) partially shifted their business interests and investments to India, particularly to cities such as Bangalore, Chennai, and Kochi. Their investments were mainly in the areas of health, education and tourism, and this gave a boost to the construction sector in Kerala. For instance, business groups like KEF and PARCO made large investments in Kozhikode in the health sector (multi-speciality hospital projects) after 2010.[4] At the same time, relatively small investors were interested in constructing commercial and residential buildings in small towns and villages across the state.

To understand the factors that affect the labour supply, each indirect migrant worker in the sample in Kozhikode was asked about their reasons for shifting the location of work in their previous jobs. The major reported reasons were the following: low wages (the workers received in their previous jobs), long working hours without adequate payment, nonpayment of wages, poor living conditions (lack of good food and water, and lack of proper accommodation), risky nature of work, extreme weather conditions, and higher wages offered at alternate locations. The reasons also include the completion of the projects or shutdown of the industries in which the workers had been engaged. The main regions in which the migrant workers in the sample had worked (other than Kerala) were Mumbai (38 workers) and Pune (10 workers) in Maharashtra, Surat and Ahmadabad in Gujarat

(28 workers), Delhi (29 workers), Kolkata (24 workers), and Bangalore (18 workers)

The first instance of migration into Kerala among all samples of workers in Kozhikode was in 1999. Jeevan Biswas, who hailed from Gopal Nagar village of North 24 Parganas, was the first migrant worker to start working in Kerala. Before coming to Kerala, he had worked in Kolkata and many other towns in West Bengal.

Lal Muhammed, aged 24 years at the time of the survey, hailed from Malda district of West Bengal. Muhammed had first migrated in 2009 to Vashi in Mumbai to work in the construction sector. He received INR 200 per day in Mumbai (in 2009). However, he left Mumbai within a year and returned to Malda, after being afflicted with jaundice. Subsequently, he migrated to Kerala in 2010 with the help of his elder brother.

Goutam Das, belonging to the scheduled caste community, aged 35 years at the time of the survey, migrated from South 24 Parganas to Mumbai in 2008 to work in the construction sector. The contractor who recruited Das exploited him, paying him very low wages (INR 100) for the first seven months of his employment in Mumbai. Eventually, in 2011, Das returned to his native place, unable to sustain a living on low wages and lack of good water and accommodation. In 2014, he migrated to Kerala with the help of a village friend, finding employment in the spot labour market in Kozhikode. In 2014, his wage was INR 550 per day for eight hours of work in Kozhikode. At the time of the survey in March 2016, his daily wages (in Kozhikode) had increased to INR 650.

Nirakar Bisul, aged 32 years at the time of the survey, hailed from Ganjam district of Odisha. Bisul had first migrated to Gujarat in 2008 to work in the garment industry (embroidery works). He had found employment through a contractor. In the initial few months, he had to work without any wages for 12 hours a day as an apprentice. Unable to cope with the strenuous working conditions, he left that job after working for 10 months in Gujarat.

In summary, both demand and supply-side factors affect the current huge number of migrant presences in Kerala's economy. The next section examines the socio-economic nature of the migrant workers in Kerala.

Social and economic background of the migrant workers

To understand the impact of the inflow of migrant workers in the state, one way of analysis is to examine the social and economic conditions of migrant workers from other Indian states. In the sample survey, we asked each migrant worker about their religion and caste identity to understand the social background and obtained information about the possession of land. We also analyzed the literacy and educational attainment of migrant workers engaged in the construction sector.

Out of the 157 workers in the sample who migrated from West Bengal to Kozhikode, 79 (50.3%) belonged to the Muslim community and 49 (31.2%) were Dalits. Muslims and Dalits, together, accounted for 81% of all workers in the sample who migrated from West Bengal to Kozhikode. Muslim workers in the sample came mostly from Bardhaman, Nadia, Murshidabad, and Malda. Dalit workers in the sample originated mostly from two 24 Parganas and Jalpaiguri[5] (see Table 5.6).

The pattern of migration from Assam appears to match that of West Bengal. Out of seven workers in the sample from Assam, six were Muslims, and one belonged to the SC community. Dalits and Muslims constituted a large share of migrant workers in the sample from Bihar and Jharkhand as well. All six migrants from Jharkhand in the sample were Muslims.

Muslims and Dalits, together, accounted for 56% (9 out of 16 sample workers) of all migrant workers from Bihar and 38.5% (5 out of 13 sample workers) of all migrant workers from Uttar Pradesh. Three out of all four migrant workers in the sample from Rajasthan were Dalits. Five out of 10 migrants in the sample from Madhya Pradesh belonged to the scheduled tribe (ST) community. Migrant workers from Madhya Pradesh in the sample also had three Dalits (see Table 5.6).

Thus, communities facing some degree of social disadvantage – Dalits, Muslim, STs – accounted for the bulk of migrant workers from West Bengal, Bihar, Assam, Jharkhand, Rajasthan, Madhya Pradesh, and Uttar Pradesh in the sample in Kozhikode.

However, the pattern is different in the case of migrant workers from Odisha. Of the 42 migrant workers in the sample from Odisha, 27 (64.3%) were general caste Hindus belonging to the general category (see Table 5.6).

Distribution of workers by land ownership and state

Of the 260 workers in the sample, 125 workers (48.1%) were landless and the rest 57 (21.9%) owned plots of land that were less than 1 acre in area. Thus 70% of all workers in the sample were either landless or owners of marginal land holdings (see Table 5.7).

Table 5.6 Distribution of workers in the sample in Kozhikode, by caste/religion and states of origin, in per cent

Districts/States of origin	*SCs/STs*	*Other Hindus*	*Muslims*	*Others*	*Total*
West Bengal	35	12.1	50.3	2.5	60.4
Odisha	16.7	76.2	0	7.1	16.2
Uttar Pradesh	23.1	61.5	15.4	0	5
Madhya Pradesh	80	20	0	0	3.8
Assam	14.3	0	85.7	0	2.7
Jharkhand	0	0	100	0	2.3
Rajasthan	75	25	0	0	1.5
All sample workers	31.9	26.9	38.1	3.1	100
All sample workers in numbers	**83**	**70**	**99**	**8**	**260**

Source: Field survey in Kozhikode, 2015–16 (cited in Jayesh 2020).

Table 5.7 Distribution of workers, in the sample in Kozhikode by land ownership and states in per cent

Districts/State	*Landless*	*Less than 1 acre*	*1 to 3 acres*	*3 acres and above*	*All workers*
West Bengal	57.3	20.4	17.2	4.5	60.4
Odisha	23.8	21.4	31	21.4	16.2
Bihar	75	18.8	0	6.3	6.2
Uttar Pradesh	7.7	23.1	46.2	15.4	5
Madhya Pradesh	30	20	40	10	3.8
Assam	28.6	28.6	14.3	28.6	2.7
Jharkhand	50	33.3	0	16.7	2.3
Rajasthan	0	75	0	25	1.5
All sample workers	48.1	21.9	18.8	10	100
All sample workers in numbers	125	57	49	26	260

Source: Field survey in Kozhikode, 2015–16 (cited in Jayesh 2020).

The proportions of the landless and marginal landholders among all workers were relatively high in the case of the sample from West Bengal, Bihar, and Jharkhand. Among all workers in the sample who migrated from West Bengal, 57.3% were landless (90 out of 157 workers) and the rest 20.4% (32 out of 157 workers) owned small plots of land (that were less than one acre in area). The proportion of landless workers was the highest (12 out of 16 or 75%) in the case of sample workers from Bihar. Five out of all 6 sample workers from Jharkhand were either landless or marginal landowners (see Table 5.7).

Contrary to the preceding pattern, the proportion of landless and marginal landholders was relatively low in the case of workers in the sample who migrated from Odisha, Uttar Pradesh, Madhya Pradesh, and Rajasthan. For instance, of all the 42 workers from Odisha in the sample, only 10 were landless (nearly 24.0%) and 9 (21.4%) were marginal holders. Among the 13 sample workers from Uttar Pradesh, only one worker did not have any plot of land and three (23%) had marginal land holdings. The number of landless workers was 3 out of 10 sample workers (30%) from Madhya Pradesh, and there were no landless workers in the sample from Rajasthan (see Table 5.7).

Literacy and educational achievements of workers across districts/state

Migrant workers in the sample in Kozhikode were characterized by relatively poor educational achievements. Out of 260 migrant workers in the sample, 69 workers (26.5%) did not have any formal schooling. While the remaining 191 workers (73.5%) received some formal education, not all the workers who received formal education considered themselves literate (see Table 5.8). Out of 260 workers, only 143 workers (or 55% of the total) reported that they could read as well as write in any language. The remaining 117 workers (or 45% of the total sample workers) could not read and write and were categorized as "illiterate".

Table 5.8 Distribution of workers in the sample workers in Kozhikode by educational achievements and districts/states of origin, in numbers

District/State of origin	*Illiterate*	*No formal school*	*Primary*	*Secondary and above*	*Total in numbers*
Bardhaman	58	52	8	40	50
West Bengal – all workers	51	31.8	20.4	47.8	157
Ganjam	40	20	6.7	73.3	15
Odisha – all workers	23.8	14.3	7.1	78.6	42
Bihar – all workers	31.3	25	12.5	62.5	16
Uttar Pradesh – all workers	69.2	15.4	23.1	61.5	13
Madhya Pradesh – all workers	70	30	20	50	10
All sample workers in numbers	117	69	44	0	260

Source: Field survey in Kozhikode, 2015–16 (Cited in Jayesh 2020).

Out of 157 workers in the sample from West Bengal, only 107 (68.2%) had some formal schooling and only 77 (49%) were literate. These rates are way below the official literacy rates. As per the Census of India, 2011, West Bengal's male and female literacy rates were 81.7% and 70.5%, respectively (77.1% for all persons).

The educational achievements of workers in the sample from Bihar, Uttar Pradesh, Madhya Pradesh, and Jharkhand were also quite poor. The literacy rates of workers in the sample from Bihar and Uttar Pradesh were 62.5% and 61.5%, respectively. All five workers from Katni district in Madhya Pradesh, which is a drought-affected region, were illiterates.

On the other hand, the educational achievements of workers in the sample who migrated from Odisha were better than the average educational levels of workers in the sample. Thirty-three out of all 42 workers (or 78.5%) in the sample from Odisha had completed secondary education or even higher levels. The corresponding figure for workers in the sample from West Bengal was 47.7%. The literacy rates of workers in the sample from Assam was also high, 85.7% (see Table 5.8).

Summary and policy suggestions for Kerala's labour market

This chapter described and analyzed some of the unique features of Kerala's labour market. One of the remarkable features of the Kerala labour market is that it sends skilled and semi-skilled labourers to other countries and the rest of India and simultaneously hosts huge unskilled workers. The chapter began with a brief description of the Kerala labour market, focusing on labour force participation based on secondary data. It also discussed Kerala's human capital and the changing nature of outward migration from its earlier path. It introduced the nature of inward migration and its impact on the Kerala labour market, showing that the influx of migrant workers from other Indian states has had a positive impact by keeping a check on wage rise in all sectors, including the construction industry. The contractors and other employers find a regular supply of labour due to this internal migration, which has helped them complete the projects in time.

The wages the workers received for agricultural and non-agricultural activities in Kerala were higher than the corresponding wages in the place of origin or other migrant destinations. The wage rate received by a skilled construction worker working with large-scale private builders or labour contract cooperative society was INR 550 per eight hours in 2015. The wage rate received by similar workers working with small-scale contractors and in the spot labour market was INR 650 per eight hours. The migrant workers were paid overtime wages at the regular hourly wage rate.

The wage rate for the migrants improved over time. Our second survey conducted in 2020–21 showed that the wage rate increased to INR 950 for the skilled worker and INR 850 for the unskilled workers.

An important socio-economic feature of inward migrants in Kerala is that the vast majority of sample workers faced twin disadvantages on account of their social background (belonging to Muslim or Dalit communities) and lack of land ownership. The educational standards of migrant workers were also very poor.

Migrant workers contribute to economic activities that help to maintain economic growth across sectors. Because of the huge presence of migrants, the economy could finish both public and private infrastructure projects without lagging and smoothen other industries such as footwear manufacturing.

The average age of the inward migrants is in the 25–30 years range, which can balance the highest ageing population state in the country (12% of the population is above 60 years as per the 2011 Census of India). However, the rapid urbanization in the state put additional pressure on the government to provide basic services such as health care, education, and sanitation. The absence of proper data about migrant workers is a pertinent problem that the state faces to take evidence-based policies that affect migrant workers. In this direction, the state can adopt innovative practices to manage the migrant workforce.

One of the probable directions in this issue is seeking the help of the local self-government in identifying and capturing the migrant workforce and maintaining a proper database at the panchayath level. Another way towards managing the influx of migrant workers is upgrading the technology of production in all sectors, which would be a welcome move to attract educated state youth to engage in economic activities in the state itself. However, Kerala is lagging in using state-of-the-art technology in various economic activities to ease the daily life of the larger society, instead highly depending on relatively low-skilled manual labour in the economic activity and hence locked in a low-level technology trap.

Notes

1 https://www.worldbank.org/en/publication/human-capital/brief/the-human-capital-project-frequently-asked-questions#HCI8
2 https://data.worldbank.org/indicator/SP.DYN.IMRT.IN?locations=IN
3 For a detailed description of the methodology of estimation of the size of the migrant work force please see Jayesh 2020, pp.96–110.
4 KEF is a Singapore-based multinational holding company owned by a native of Kozhikode. See for details https://www.kefholdings.com/. PARCO is another Kozhikode-based business group which has operations in the health sector in UAE. See for details https://www.parcointl.com/hospital.html
5 See Jayesh, (2020) for a district-wise migrant workers' detailed table of information.

References

Drèze, Jean., and Sen, Amartya. 2013. *Uncertain Glory: India and Its Contradictions*. London: Penguin.
Government of India. 2014. Data-book Compiled for use of Planning Commission, Planning Commission of India, Retrieved fromhttp://planningcommission.nic.in/data/datatable/0306/Databook_June2014.pdf.
Government of Kerala (GoK). 2016. *Economic Review 2015*. Thiruvananthapuram: State Planning Board, Government of Kerala.
Government of Kerala (GoK). 2017. *Economic Review 2016*. Thiruvananthapuram: State Planning Board, Government of Kerala.
Government of Kerala (GoK). 2021. *Economic Review 2020*. Thiruvananthapuram: State Planning Board, Government of Kerala.
Government of Kerala (GoK). 2022. *Economic Review 2021*. Thiruvananthapuram: State Planning Board, Government of Kerala. https://spb.kerala.gov.in/sites/default/files/2022-03/ECNO_%20ENG_21_%20Vol_1.pdf
Jayesh, M. P. 2020. "Inter-State Migration for Employment in India: A Study on Construction Workers in Kerala." Unpublished Ph.D. Thesis. New Delhi: Indian Institute of Technology Delhi (IITD).
Mani, Sunil. 2011. "High-Skilled Migration from India: An Analysis of Its Economic Implications." In *India Migration Report 2011: Migration, Identity, and Conflict*, edited by Rajan, S. Irudaya, 309–30. New Delhi: Routledge.
Narayana, D., Venkiteswaran., C. S., and Joseph, M. P. 2013. *Domestic Migrant Labour in Kerala*. Thiruvananthapuram: Gulati Institute of Finance and Taxation (GIFT), Government of Kerala.
National Statistics Office (NSO). 2019. "Public Labour Force Survey (July 2017–June 2018." Annual Report. Government of India Ministry of Statistics and Programme Implementation and National Statistics Office. May 2019.
Parida, J. K., and Ravi Raman, K. 2021. *A Study on In-migration, Informal Employment and Urbanisation in Kerala*. Thiruvananthapuram: State Planning Board (Evaluation Division), Government of Kerala.
Peter, Benoy, Sanghvi, Shachi, and Narendran, Vishnu. 2020. "Inclusion of Interstate Migrant Workers in Kerala and Lessons for India." *The Indian Journal of Labour Economics* 63: 1065–86.

Prasad, Mythri. 2016. "Migration and Production of Space Labour, Capital and The State in Kerala, India." Unpublished PhD thesis, Jawaharlal Nehru University (JNU). Thiruvananthapuram: Centre for Development Studies.

Rajan, S. Irudaya, and Zachariah, K. C. 2018. *International Migration*. Geneva: International Labour Organization. http://cds.edu/wp-content/uploads/2018/05/ILO-CDS-Thematic-Chapter-3.pdf.

Rajan, S. Irudaya, and Pattath, Balasubramanyam. 2022. "Distress Return Migration Amid COVID-19: Kerala's Response." *Asian and Pacific Migration Journal* 31(2): 176–89. https://doi.org/10.1177/01171968221115259.

Ramachandran, V. K. 1996. "On Kerala's Development Achievements." In *Indian Development: Selected Regional Perspectives*, edited by Jean Drèze and Amartya Sen, 205–330. New Delhi: Oxford University Press.

Raman, K. Ravi. 2012. "Currents and Eddies: Indian-Middle East Migration Processes." *Cambridge Journal of Regions, Economy and Society* 5: 189–205. https://doi.org/10.1093/cjres/rss003.

Raunaq, M. S. 2016. "Working Conditions of Migrant Workers in Kerala: A Study of Construction Workers in Thrissur." MPhil thesis, Jawaharlal Nehru University.

Sambasivan, S. 2013. "Beyond Un-free Labour and Income Augmentation Strategy: Rethinking Inter-State Migration Based on the Study of Construction Sector Workers in Ernakulam District of Kerala." MPhil thesis, University of Hyderabad.

Sumeetha, M. 2015. "Labour in Globalised World: In-migration in the Gold Jewellery Making Industry in Kerala, India. Unpublished PhD thesis, Jawaharlal Nehru University (JNU), Thiruvananthapuram: Centre for Development Studies.

Thomas, J. J., and Jayesh, M. P. 2019. "Labour Market in Kerala: Examining the Role of Industrial and Employment Policies." In *Globalization, Labour Market Institutions, Processes and Policies in India*, edited by K. R. Shyam Sunder. Singapore: Palgrave Macmillan.

Thomas, J. J., and Satheesha. B. 2018. "Wages, Internal Migration and Labour Markets: An Analysis of Indian States." An unpublished research document.

Zachariah, K. C., Prakash, B. A., and Rajan, S. Irudaya. 2002. *Gulf Migration Study: Employment, Wages and Working Conditions of Kerala Emigrants in the United Arab Emirates* (Working Chapter 326). Thiruvananthapuram: Centre for Development Studies. http://www.cds.edu/wp-content/uploads/2012/10/326.pdf.

Zachariah, K. C., and Rajan, S. Irudaya. 2004. *Gulf Revisited: Economic Consequences of Emigration from Kerala-Emigration and Unemployment* (Working Chapter 363). Thiruvananthapuram: Centre for Development Studies. http://www.cds.edu/wp-content/uploads/2012/10/363.pdf.

Zachariah, K. C., and Rajan, S. Irudaya. 2005. *Unemployment in Kerala at the Turn of the Century: Insights from CDS Gulf Migration Studies* (Working Chapter 374). Thiruvananthapuram: Centre for Development Studies. http://www.cds.edu/wp-content/uploads/2012/10/374.pdf.

Zachariah, K. C., and Rajan, S. Irudaya. 2010. *Migration Monitoring Study, 2008 Emigration and Remittances in the Context of Surge in Oil Prices* (Working Chapter 424). Thiruvananthapuram: Centre for Development Studies. http://www.cds.edu/wp-content/uploads/2012/09/wp424.pdf.

Zachariah, K. C., and Rajan, S. Irudaya. 2012. *Inflexion in Kerala's Gulf Connection-Report on Kerala Migration Survey, 2011* (Working Chapter 450). Thiruvananthapuram: Centre for Development Studies. http://www.cds.edu/wpcontent/uploads/2012/11/WP450.pdf.

6 Employer–employee dynamics

The study on return migrants during the COVID-19 pandemic

S. Irudaya Rajan, Pooja Batra, and Akansh Khandelwal

Introduction

COVID-19 has led to severe labour market disruptions, specifically affecting immigrant workers from low- and middle-income countries. Immigrant workers have faced not only vulnerabilities in terms of health but also in terms of the costs and risks due to economic shocks in terms of job loss, work from home, return to the home country during the pandemic, or reduced/forfeited remunerations (Akhil and Rajan 2020, Borjas and Cassidy 2020, Behbahani et al. 2020, Gelatt 2020). The global pandemic led to an unprecedented wave of return migration across the globe (Boillat and Zähringer 2020, IOM 2020, Migration Data 2021, World Bank Group and KNOMAD 2020, 2021). This is very much the case for lower-middle-income countries like India. Evidence suggests that an estimated 1.4 million (14.33 lakh) emigrants originating from India, especially from the south Indian state of Kerala, returned to India between May 2020 and April 2021 (Rajan and Pattah 2022).

Various research studies unanimously echo that COVID-19 devastated the economies. All social and economic activities were brought to a standstill for an infinite period by the state to restrict the outspread/outbreak. Many important industries like airlines, manufacturing, and hospitality were brought to a sudden halt indefinitely. This led many firms to total shutdown, rendering millions jobless due to the sudden and unprecedented disruption of businesses. From the viewpoint of development economists, the labour market disruptions caused by the pandemic reversed the decade-long achievements in poverty alleviation. Millions of people were pulled back into a state of poverty and economic distress. People were not only facing health hazards but became more vulnerable than before.

The International Labour Organization (ILO) estimates put the number of international migrant workers worldwide in 2017 at 164 million (ILO 2018). This shows the importance of migration for the livelihoods of millions of people, including migrants and their families, households, and other people who are dependent on them. Global as well as internal migration is crucial for people's livelihoods in many developing countries in Africa and Asia. However, the global context of migration within and between countries

DOI: 10.4324/9781003601289-8

shows significant shifts due to restrictions on movement since the initial outbreak of COVID-19.

This chapter reflects on the implications of the COVID-19 outbreak in the field of employment relations. The impact of the pandemic was severe on international emigrant workers, particularly low-skilled emigrant workers on short-term contracts working in the informal economy and undocumented workers. Loss of jobs, wage theft, issues with visa extension, closure of border crossings, lack of access to any social protection mechanisms, and the cost of repatriation all took a heavy toll on them. Incomes also declined for those emigrants who continued in employment. The ILO estimates that global labour income losses, without income support measures, declined by 10.7% during the first three-quarters of 2020 compared to the same period in 2019 (ILO 2018).

The World Bank (Ratha et al. 2020) currently estimates that international remittances would decline by 7.2% in 2020, followed by a further decline in 2021. High-return migration and low prospects of new emigration are estimated to cause an absolute decline in the total number of emigrants, more severe than the 2008 global crisis (Ratha et al. 2020). For India, international migration is voluminous, and India is the highest earner of international remittances, which, however, is projected to decline by about 9% in 2020 (Ratha et al. 2020). On the other hand, India also has a significant volume of migration from other countries, although most of this is from countries India shares a border with (Srivastava and Pandey, 2017). There is scanty literature on the impact of the pandemic on these migrants. In contrast, we know more about the actual and possible impact of the pandemic on international migrants, particularly worker migrants in the Gulf and other regions.

With the help of a few studies, the present work identifies three major pandemic-led shocks to the immigrant labour market – (i) the return migration to the native country in case of sudden job loss in the destination country, (ii) the unexpected increase in the burden on the families and the state due to return emigrants (REM), and (iii) huge remittance loss to the households and the economy.

The Kerala Return Emigration Survey 2021, a study by Rajan and Batra (2022) on Vande Bharat returnees, suggests that a large number of long-term and highly skilled employees immigrants from Kerala were fired during COVID-19. This led to emigrants returning home, increasing the burden on the families and state. The family's economic burden increased because of loss of income and the additional unexpected burden of REM. The REM often sought the support of their families for ticket purchases, bearing the costs incurred for quarantining, etc. Moreover, the burden of the government increased during the crisis period in planning for the return and institutional quarantine and safety measures for the REM. This led to a loss of remittance to the household and the economy. Kerala is a remittance-dependent economy, with 36% of its GDP being remittance-based (Kannan and Hari 2020, Prakash, 2020). The remittance income has a major developmental role to play for the emigrants' families, as it contributes to investment decisions like house construction, social consumption in terms of education, social participation, and the provision of health facilities. Moreover, as mentioned, there has been a flow of reverse remittances from the families to the emigrants. Thus, the remittance shock has decelerated human development and progress towards sustainable development goals (SDG) in such economies.

A study conducted by the Centre for Development Studies (CDS) and the International Institute of Migration and Development (IIMAD) (Rajan and Pattah 2022) showed that roughly 50% of the sample lost their jobs as a result of COVID-19, while 25% of the respondents returned because of the adverse social protection conditions for migrant workers, as several migrant workers live in accommodations and settings that could worsen their health vulnerabilities during a pandemic (Martin 2016). While migration occurs for a variety of reasons and takes a number of forms, it mostly aims at improving the livelihood and employment prospects of the movers and supports the growth and development of the areas towards which the movement occurs. But this does not happen without significant stress and costs. Patterns of unequal development, demographic changes, wars, and conflicts play a key role in migration.

This chapter focuses on a particular aspect of COVID-19 and migration. The study orients itself on the impact of the COVID-19 pandemic on the relationship between the employer and the employee in the context of international migration. It highlights the international emigrants who returned home during COVID-19, also called return emigrants (REM). It emphasizes the employer's concern for employees during this adversity by supporting the emigrants in the form of financial help to purchase tickets, social distancing, and sanitizing within the premises to work, and a work from home option for some migrants depending on their industry of work.

To reflect on the implications of the COVID-19 outbreak in the field of employment relations, the chapter uses the data from the Return Emigrant COVID-19 Survey conducted by the CDS. As many as 850 emigrants came to India (Kerala) via the Vande Bharat Mission and private chartered flights through Gulf countries. The survey contains a detailed description and vital information on the impact of COVID-19 on migrants and their households based on their consumption patterns, employment, and earnings abroad. The emigrants share their initial experiences about the COVID-19 pandemic and its repercussions on the remittances provided to their left-behind families. Additionally, the survey also contains a brief description of the attitude and knowledge on preventive care measures taken by the government and civil societies to protect the migrants and their households during COVID-19.

The findings help us to visualize the overall impact of COVID-19 on emigrants who returned to Kerala during the pandemic. They provide a comprehensive understanding of the emigrant experiences from two perspectives at the individual and household levels during the spread of COVID-19. The data reflects the careful decisions made by emigrants and their households during the pandemic. At the individual level, COVID-19 has severely affected the labour market and disrupted the lives of many. Because of prolonged lockdowns, many people became jobless and faced a reduction in or a complete loss of their livelihood. There were layoffs, reduction in working hours, and wages. Thus, leaving a negative impact on unemployment, labour force participation, hours of work, and wages of return emigrants in Kerala. The majority of REMs experienced a drastic fall in their wages and were able to get economically engaged in their native land. Thus, it can be seen how the pandemic negatively impacted the economic activities at the individual and household levels. At the individual level, it might have led to forgoing consumption, purchase of certain goods and services, medical and hospitalization costs, loss of labour, and disruption of services and travel. At the household level, it led to a sudden increase in their pandemic-related spending. The pandemic-related spending included costs incurred for health concerns along with money spent by households in financing the tickets and quarantine of the REMs. The increased expenditure needs to be viewed along with the drastic fall in the household incomes due to fall in remittances.

The chapter focuses on the context and details of the literature, presents the data, and reports the descriptive statistics, discusses the findings, and, finally, touches on the policy measures and provides the conclusion.

The context

Migration is a global phenomenon, driven not only by economic needs but also by various push and pull factors that include social, political, cultural, environmental, health related, and educational issues. The United Nations Migration Agency defines migrants as people who are moving or have moved across an international border or within the borders of a state, away from their habitual place of residence, regardless of their legal status, whether the movement was voluntary or involuntary, the causes of the movement, or the length of stay.[1] The World Migration Report of 2020 states that there are an estimated 272 million international migrants (IOM 2020).

The broad pattern of Indian emigrants abroad was dominated by middle and high-income states in the north, west, and south of the country in the past. Over time, the pattern of worker migration tilted towards the eastern states of the country – Uttar Pradesh, Bihar, and West Bengal (Srivastava and Pandey 2017). The pandemic, with its impact on oil revenues, likely had a significant impact on the Gulf Cooperation Council (GCC) countries, which depend on oil exports due to falling oil revenues. Abella and Sasikumar (2020) observed that trends in aggregate worker emigration closely mirror (albeit with a lag) the growth trends in the Gulf economies. They pointed out that the Government of India's Vande Bharat mission brought back nearly 60,000 stranded Indians from various countries abroad, of whom 170,000–180,000 were migrant workers. Since the journeys involved a direct travel cost of USD 350–400, many workers could not avail of them. Nonetheless, the likely scenarios of employment loss on incomplete contracts or wage loss for those migrants continuing to be employed implied a loss of earnings for the migrants and a loss in remittances.

This loss increased when the "sunk costs" of migration in terms of recruitment costs are factored in. Abella and Sasikumar (2020) considered the segment of low-skilled workers migrating to Saudi Arabia to be engaged in the construction sector. Based on the distribution of the length of contract and earnings of this group, they projected the estimated loss in earnings and remittances under assumptions of job loss or lower wages. They pointed out that two counter tendencies could imply that the actual decrease in remittances may not be as high as anticipated: (i) the tendency of employed migrants to remit a higher proportion of wages during crises and (ii) the loss in employment may eventually not be very high due to the irreplaceability of low-skilled migrants in some sectors. Kerala continues to have a large stock of migrants abroad, more than two million, particularly in the Gulf states. Kannan and Hari (2020), in this issue, offer a long-term view of emigration from Kerala and hypothesize the impact of the pandemic on emigration and remittances in Kerala. Migrant workers from Kerala are currently estimated to be about 17%–18% of its workforce. Kannan and Hari (2020) estimate the number of migrants from Kerala and total remittances over nearly half a century. Although emigration peaked around 2012–13, remittances have shown a steady increase, but their contribution to state income declined from over a fifth at the beginning of this decade to about 14% between 2015 and 2020, mainly due to the rapid growth in Kerala's state income. Significantly, the secular increase in remittances was not reversed either by the Gulf wars or by global economic crises, including the 2008 crisis. According to Kannan and Hari (2020) the total remittances increased despite a decline in the total number of migrants because of the changing educational and skill composition of the emigrant workforce, with a much smaller proportion engaged in manual and low-skilled jobs.

The chapter also analyzes the macro-economic implications of emigration for the state's economy over different phases, its impact on the labour market, on household income and consumption, and (increasing) interpersonal inequality, despite the state's low multidimensional poverty index (MPI) and high human development index (HDI). The negative aspect of Kerala's development is the persistence of educated unemployment, especially among women, despite the safety valve of emigration. The third negative aspect is the declining tax collection effort shown by the share in net state domestic product (NSDP) of own tax revenue. The chapter notes that the economic crisis precipitated by the pandemic confronts the state with multiple challenges and possibilities. As far as emigration is concerned, the crisis could be a turning point in terms of a sharp decline in Kerala's large-scale labour migration to the Gulf countries, but alternatively, it could set off the beginning of a change in the composition of emigration if the demand for healthcare personnel increases in the Gulf as well as in other countries.

Abraham (2020) examined the Kerala migration story from another perspective, which could throw light on the long-term prospects open to the return migrants affected by the crisis (assuming that the short-term prospects could be overshadowed by the severity of the economic crisis and unemployment). Using the Kerala Migration Survey data, Abraham examined the occupational mobility of international migrants pre-, during, and post-migration. The major destination for migrants in Kerala was the GCC, and 95% of the migrations to the Gulf countries were on temporary contracts, Kerala still accounted for the highest Indian emigrant stock in the GCC. It is also the state with the highest return emigrant stock in India, and a high proportion of return emigrants are still in the working-age group and active in the labour force. The contractual jobs are mostly low-skilled but offer a much higher earning potential to the migrants, although at the cost of deskilling for many, and downward occupational mobility. Their post-return occupational choices in the home labour market would be dependent on their level of human and physical capital and re-migration intentions, but termination or nonrenewal of the migrant's contract could have an adverse impact on the occupational choices of the return migrants (Abraham 2020).

Using data from the 2011 Kerala Migration Survey, Abraham constructed three mobility matrices over the three phases of geographical mobility of return migrants in the economically active age group. The study found that skilled blue-collar workers were in a higher proportion in all three stages of migration, and they, along with elementary workers, formed the largest proportion of return emigrants in Kerala. However, the proportion of workers was twice in the service sector abroad, as compared to that in the source region. The proportion of higher-skilled workers (professionals, associates, and technicians) were more or less stable over the three phases. At the same time, there was a significant rise (from negligible) in the percentage of workers reporting as managers/self-employed post-return. The data showed a high occupational persistence among pre-emigration and post-return occupational choices, indicating that work experience abroad did not lead to a significant level of occupational mobility for return emigrants in Kerala. Around a fifth of the return migrants showed upward mobility, while 10% moved to a lower occupational category. Only about 10% were engaged in self-employment (mainly as proprietors and managers). The chapter concludes that international migration does not lead to upward occupational mobility for most migrants and that there is limited skill augmentation ensuing from foreign work experience.

Data

The CDS Return Emigrant COVID-19 Survey was used to analyze the impact of COVID-19 on the return emigrants. Initially, a total of 850 return emigrants were interviewed via mobile phones, with the interviews lasting for around 25–40 minutes. Due to overlapping and some error while collecting the data, the sample size was reduced from 850 to 830. The survey was conducted in Malayalam between November 2020 and January 2021, and each interview lasted 25–40 minutes. All the interviews were translated into English before entering the data. The telephone numbers of the respondents were provided by NORKA (Non-Resident Keralites Affairs), a department of the Government of Kerala.

Descriptive statistics

Characteristics of REM

An overwhelming majority of 96% of the return emigrants returned from the Gulf countries. In the sample size of 830 emigrants, around 90% of the respondents were males within the 25–59-year age group. The REMs to Kerala predominantly belonged to the Muslim community, comprising 63% of the total sample surveyed (see Figure 6.1 for more details). The sample was representative as the majority of the emigrants in Kerala were from the Muslim community. All three communities – Hindu, Muslims, and Christians – the majority of the population who re-migrated were married. In total, 97% of the re-migrants were married. However, the re-migrants were overwhelmingly males, with only 9.7% constituting the female population in the survey, and more than 90% of female re-migrants were married. Religion-wise, the majority of the women REMs were Christians (39%), followed by Hindus and Muslims. Whereas among men, the majority of them

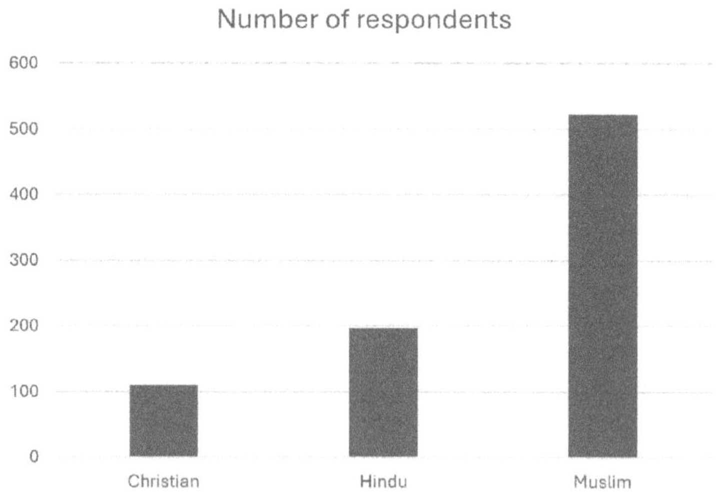

Figure 6.1 Religious group of respondents

Source: Author's calculation using microdata from the Return Emigrant COVID-19 Survey.

Table 6.1 Industry engagement of the Return emigrants

Type of industry	*Freq (%)*
Agriculture, forestry, and fishing	6 (0.72)
Accommodation and food service activities	76 (9.16)
Information and communication	21 (2.53)
Financial and insurance activities	42 (5.06)
Real estate activities	39 (4.70)
Professional, scientific, and technical activities	80 (9.64)
Administrative and support service activities (*including travel agency, tour operator, and other reservation services*)	15 (1.81)
Public administration and defence; compulsory social security	1 (0.12)
Education	12 (1.45)
Human health and social work activities	31 (3.73)
Arts, entertainment, and recreation	8 (0.96)
Mining and quarrying	14 (1.69)
Activities of households as employers; undifferentiated goods- and services-producing activities of households for own use	9 (1.08)
Others#	132 (15.90)
Manufacturing	36 (4.34)
Electricity, gas, steam, and air conditioning supply	36 (4.34)
Water supply; sewerage, waste management, and remediation activities	15 (1.81)
Construction	62 (7.47)
Wholesale and retail trade; repair of motor vehicles and motorcycles	88 (10.60)
Transportation and storage	72 (8.67)
not answered	35 (4.22)
	830 (100)

Source: Author's calculation using microdata from Return Emigrant COVID-19 Survey
#others include shipping yard, textile, supermarket, oil company, and jewellery industry

were from the Muslim community (67%), followed by Hindus (22%) and Christians (10%).

Most of the emigrants were engaged in construction, wholesale and retail trade, repair of vehicles, transportation and storage, and other industries like shipping yard, textile, supermarket, oil company, and jewellery industry (see Table 6.1 for details).

The employer plays a crucial role in the emigrant employees decision-making process of whether to stay or return to their home country. This shows the relationship dynamics between the two entities in a contract and how the employer extends support to the emigrant employees in situations of unprecedented health hazards like COVID-19. To gauge this aspect of the employer–employee relation, the survey asked the respondents the following: "Whose decision was it for you to return home?" As shown in Table 6.2, for around 75% of the population, the decision was driven by self or family considerations. In contrast, only 24% of the cases was the decision for re-migration that of the employers/sponsors. This indicates that though the employees had agency in deciding about the continuation of their stay in

Table 6.2 Decision to return to Kerala

	Frequency	*Percentage*
Employer	196	23.61
Host country	8	0.96
Self/Family	619	74.58
Others (joint decision)	7	0.84
Total	830	100

Source: Author's calculation using microdata from Return Emigrant COVID-19 Survey

Table 6.3 Response of REM on employer's support to go home

Employer support on decision to go home	*Frequency*	*Percentage*
No	34	4.1
Yes	689	83.01
Not Answered	107	12.89
Total	830	100

Source: Author's calculation using microdata from Return Emigrant COVID-19 Survey

the destination country, the agency was not available and exercised by all the employees.

Using descriptive statistics, we tried to understand the scenario regarding the re-migration of the employees. On asking if *the employer was supportive of the decision to go back home* (irrespective of the job loss or the decision to return was the respondents' own), 83% of the respondents replied in an affirmative (see Table 6.3). They believed that their employer was supportive about their decision to return to their home country, whereas, for 13%, the employers' support was not readily observed. Further analysis showed that irrespective of whose decision it was to return home, employers' support was available to the majority of the respondents. When the employer decided that the employees return to their home country, they provided support in 95% of the cases. In contrast, when the emigrants decided to return due to their family's decision or on their own accord, employers' support was provided only in 79% of the cases.

The survey enquired the respondents about the reason behind returning to their home country. While COVID-19 might have appeared to be the obvious reason, it was still important to investigate to ascertain if a factor other than COVID-19 drove the return migration. As per Table 6.4, 80% of the REMs decided to return home due to COVID-19 scenarios in the host countries. As mentioned, though the cause for REM was clear and obvious, it was of interest to know the specific factors in the COVID-19 scenario that

Table 6.4 Did you (REM) return home because of the COVID-19 pandemic?

Pandemic the cause for REM	*Frequency*	*Percentage*
No	165	19.88
Yes	665	80.12
Total	830	100

Source: Author's calculation using microdata from Return Emigrant COVID-19 Survey

Table 6.5 Reasons for return for emigrants

Particulars	*Frequency*	*Percentage*
Reason for return		
Was scared to remain in the host country	59	8.87
Employment issues	545	81.95
Felt more secure to go back to the home country	39	5.86
Lack of money and other resources	4	0.6
Other reasons	18	2.71
Total	665	100

Source: Author's calculation using microdata from Return Emigrant COVID-19 Survey

led to the decision to return home. The motivation for this question came from the following: people re-migrated during the first COVID-19 wave for multiple reasons. The reasons for REM could be health related (e.g., illness during COVID-19), personal (e.g., family emergency during COVID-19), security related (e.g., feeling safer in the native land), economical/labour market issues (e.g., loss of employment opportunity due to COVID-19), or political (e.g., government's mandate to work from home). In our sample, it was found that the majority of those who returned home due to COVID-19, the main stressor was labour market disruption, i.e., the employment issue. Most of the respondents (82%) mentioned that the employment issues drove them back to their home country, while only around 6% of the respondents returned home because they felt more secure in their home country, and a meagre 0.6% returned home due to lack of money and other resources (see Table 6.5). Thus, it establishes that employment issues were the major factors disincentivizing emigrants to continue living in host countries during COVID-19. This indicates that COVID-19 itself was not the issue, but the labour market shocks under the COVID-19 situation were the major reason for the REM.

The REMs faced economic hardships in terms of the sudden costs they had to incur when returning to their home country and spending on quarantine facilities, apart from the job loss. Of the REMs, 74% had to purchase tickets for the return to their home country, whereas around 20% were funded by

Table 6.6 Do you currently have paid employment abroad?

Current employment abroad	*Frequency*	*Percentage*
No	662	80.63
Yes	56	6.82
My job has been temporarily suspended	91	11.08
My job has been permanently suspended	12	1.46
Total	821	100

Source: Author's calculation using microdata from Return Emigrant COVID-19 Survey

their employers. In the case of quarantine, the majority of the respondents had to self-fund their quarantine (72%), while only three of the respondents' employers funded their quarantine.

While analyzing the employment scenario of emigrants abroad, the results in Table 6.6 reveal that majority of the REMs (81%) did not have employment abroad. In contrast, only a meagre 7% managed to maintain their employment in the host country. Of the respondents, 11% had their jobs temporarily. In contrast, around 2% had their jobs suspended permanently. Of those who were still employed abroad (56 respondents), only 25% (14 respondents) engaged in work from home (WFH), while 75% (42 respondents) were not engaged in WFH.

To further clarify the preceding discussion on the impact of COVID-19 on employment loss, the survey asked: "Did you lose your employment because of COVID-19?" The figures in Table 6.7 show that of the 763 respondents who responded, 79% replied in the affirmative. This implies that 603 of the respondents lost their jobs due to COVID-19 reasons.

An important aspect of the study on labour market disruptions is often the response mechanisms of those affected. It is pertinent to understand REMs in our context absorbed and adapted to the labour market shocks due to COVID-19. Table 6.8 shows that of the 830 REMs, only 85 were employed in Kerala at the time of the survey. That implies that a substantial number (745 REMs) were not employed in Kerala at the time of the survey. Of the 85 REMs, 41% (35 respondents) were employed in daily waged work, 31% (26

Table 6.7 Did you lose your employment because of COVID-19?

Did you lose your employment because of COVID-19	*Frequency*	*Percentage*
No	160	20.97
Yes	603	79.03
Total	763	100

Source: Author's calculation using microdata from Return Emigrant COVID-19 Survey

Table 6.8 Employment scenario of REMs

Are you employed in Kerala or not?	*Frequency*	*Percentage*
No	745	89.76
Yes	85	10.24
Total	830	100
Current economic activity the REMs are engaged in	*Frequency*	*Percentage*
Self-employed/business	26	30.59
Daily wage	35	41.18
Agriculture	8	9.41
Others specify	16	18.82
Total	85	100

Source: Author's calculation using microdata from Return Emigrant COVID-19 Survey

Table 6.9 Work schedule of REM 30 days prior return to Kerala

Work schedule 30 days prior return	*Frequency*	*Percentage*
No work	261	66.08
Some work, but less than usual	79	20
The usual work	47	11.9
More than usual work	8	2.03
Total	395	100
Present work schedule	*Frequency*	*Percentage*
No work	315	88.73
Some work, but less than usual	24	6.76
The usual work	14	3.94
More than usual work	2	0.56
Total	355	100

Source: Author's calculation using microdata from Return Emigrant COVID-19 Survey

respondents) were self-employed or in business, and only 9.4% (8 respondents) engaged in agricultural activities (see Table 6.8 for details).

The survey enquired about the work schedule of the REMs over the last 30 days prior to their return. It asks, "In the 30 days prior to your return, what has been your work schedule like?" Table 6.9 reveals that the majority (66%) of respondents had no work in the 30 days before they returned from the destination country, while only 2% had had more than usual work before their return to the homeland. Only 12% of respondents had usual work, while 20% had some amount of work over the 30 days prior to their return. This again reiterates the excessive cost to the respondents in staying in the host country without any job, compelling them to return to their homeland.

Table 6.9 also captures their current work schedule, where 89% of return emigrants had no work and 7% had some work, but less than usual. On being asked, "In the 30 days prior to your return, what have your wages been

Table 6.10 Scenario of wages of REMs prior to their return

Wages prior return	*Frequency*	*Percentage*
No wages	256	63.84
Some wages, but less than usual	79	19.7
The usual amount	66	16.46
Total	401	100
Present wages state	*Frequency*	*Percentage*
No wages	321	86.52
Some wages, but less than usual	29	7.82
The usual amount	20	5.39
More than usual	1	0.27
Total	371	100

Source: Author's calculation using microdata from Return Emigrant COVID-19 Survey

like?" around 64% of the respondents said they had no wages, 21% had less than usual, and 16% had usual wages (see Table 6.10 for details). Compared to this, the questionnaire enquired about the work schedule of the REMs post their return to their home country. The percentage of REMs with no work increased to a mammoth 89%. Less than 1% of REMs had more than usual work, and only 4% (14 REMs) had usual work as before (Table 6.9). Moving in tandem with the work schedule, 87% of REMs had no wages compared to just 5% (20 REMs) who had the usual wages (Table 6.10).

The REM had a collective view that the pandemic enforced several changes in the environment at the workplace of emigrants. Precautions were taken to avoid the spread of the virus, including stopping unsafe activities; reducing the number of workers working at the same time at the workstation; mandating the use of masks, sanitizers, and soaps; and enforcing physical distancing. Also, people who were sick were not allowed to come to work. Around 50% of respondents reported that unsafe activities were stopped, 20% verified that fewer people were working at the same time, and 14% agreed on soaps and sanitizers being provided on a massive scale at the workplace. In a few organizations, social distancing (7%) norms were maintained, and masks (2%) were distributed, and for the remaining, the organizations assured that people who were sick to not come to work.

Conclusion and policy recommendations

In March 2020, the spread of the COVID-19 pandemic led the World Health Organization (WHO) to declare a global public health emergency. The pandemic worsened everyone's lives, making it tougher for businesses to survive, slowing down the economy at a rapid rate, and increasing job insecurities, especially among migrant workers, as a vast number of them lost their jobs. It robbed people of a proper workplace, teamwork spirit, and leadership. People faced poor working environments and stagnant salaries, which lowered their morale. Individuals struggled to attain targets, be it at a personal or professional level. Considering all this, the pandemic was too alarming a situation to maintain harmonious employee relations.

The policy responses taken by the governments, included lockdown measures, which resulted in an economic downturn, particularly affecting certain sectors that employed large numbers of workers, and self-employed in both formal and informal economies. The ongoing COVID-19 episode changed the working scene significantly. WFH, wearing a mask, maintaining physical distancing, sanitizers at every nook and cranny of the workstation became common. It was not just for the worker, individually, each association, the general public, and the world became attuned to this new circumstance (Prasad et al., 2020). People were compelled to live in social isolation and maintain emotional and physical distancing due to the lockdown. Industries and organizations were compelled to WFH during COVID-19. Online platforms were used to facilitate a range of services to the employee relations programmes that are ordinarily part of a human resource procedure intended to guarantee the best utilization of individuals to achieve the mission of a business firm (Rea and Shinn 2015).

There is an interrelationship between both the factors – employee engagement and relations. To survive in a better mode with both the factors, an analysis is required to have a better understanding of the scenario, where it was hard to keep employees engaged for extended periods of time due to rampant WFH. Though some of the zones were becoming free from lockdown, physical distancing was not completely eliminated. It called for support for each other for better survival in organization and the smooth running of business activities. In a way, the narrative boiled down to making efforts towards maintaining better employee relations and employee engagement. After the dramatic shutting down of offices, people gradually started WFH and tried to recover from the financial and psychological losses, emerging stronger by the day. All employers understood the importance of taking care, and being concerned about their employees and customers and turn all the threats into opportunities with positivity and an energetic mindset.

According to Abrol and Madan (2020), employers need to take up some responsibilities if they want to maintain good employee relations and provide a strengthened support system and social security to their employees: overseeing and directing all business-related exercises to guarantee the well-being and assistance of employees; advancing video conferencing for gatherings over face-to-face meetings and creating a sense of belongingness among the employees; giving a sheltered workplace and proper assets for remote working that are arranged, sorted out, and kept up; setting up plans in case of crises and emergencies.

Some general recommendations are highlighted in the literature that could help in such a scenario, mitigating the strain in employer–employee relations and ensuring security to both parties. First is bettering communication to reduce the gap of misunderstandings among individuals. Second is taking the help of technology to ensure face-to-face interactions and stay connected with clients and colleagues. Third is ensuring employee engagement.

In the context of Kerala migration studied in the present work, the study makes two major observations:

1. The employer–employee relations studied through the survey do not indicate any lack of cordiality in the relationship between employers and emigrant employees. It is indicated by the fact that in the majority of the cases, the decision to re-migrate was not determined by the employers but by the employees themselves. Moreover, the employers were generally found to be supportive of their decision. However, it doesn't discount the fact that the reason for re-migration was the loss of jobs during COVID-19 for the majority of the respondents. Hence, the emigrants stood highly vulnerable to the pandemic and bore disproportionate hardships due to the labour market disruption. It can be assumed, at the risk of simplifying the issue, that the employers were not able to protect the employment of the emigrants.
2. We can conclusively say that emigrants were the worst hit. They not only faced the disruption of their lives in the host country but also experienced a drastic fall in their standard of living. Emigrants not only lost their jobs, but they also had to voluntarily/involuntarily leave their host country as well. This was accompanied by the economic burden of travel and quarantine costs, and most detrimentally, the loss of their jobs. They were not economically/gainfully employed in their native land and hence, seemed to have lost all sources of income. This, in turn, created further pressure on the REMs and their families, as they lost the source of income through remittances, along with difficulty in meeting household needs.

Countries across the world have resorted to various mechanisms to provide support to the returning emigrants. World Bank report (2020) stressed on the need for better social safety nets for the REMs to safeguard them from negative labour market shocks. The prerogative was on the destination country as well to include the emigrants in the social safety nets of their country. Countries like Portugal, Ireland, New Zealand, and Australia among the developed world took measures to safeguard their migrants. Fortunately, developing countries such as Myanmar, Brazil, and Thailand also took several initiatives, including providing cash transfers and benefits to the vulnerable sections (internal and international REMs). Some countries also arranged cash grants to compensate for the income loss of the migrants. An important aspect to note is that given the public nature of the problem, the remedies were mostly put forth by the state, i.e., at the macro level. There is no denying that the state has a significant role in providing relief in such situations; however, initiatives at the micro level were also needed to combat the multifaceted problems raised by COVID-19. In this regard, solutions also needed to come from the decision-making bodies at the local level. In our context, the employer's role was crucial in providing urgent effective solutions to the problem of emigrants. The solutions mentioned previously were intended to address the same issue. Singapore, China, and South Korea followed the approach of providing incentives to employers to retain their workers. This is an example of how a state could function as an enabling body to ensure the betterment of both the employers and the employees (Moroz et al. 2020).

In brief, the COVID-19 pandemic period was a period of examination related to relationships in both professional and personal dimensions. Every individual, directly or indirectly, fought for the improvement in the relations surroundings. So, it was the responsibility of all the persons (employees and employers) to give their best to maintain harmony and peace in the organizational relationships for the smooth running of business activities. It was a time to fight back against all odds with determination and commitment. It was a challenging time to keep morale high, have contented relationships, and engage towards accomplishing goals. If, on the one hand, COVID-19 impacted business organization and economy in a negative way, it also forced companies to look at alternative ways to run operations through remote connections. The adoption of digital technology was a positive change for many people as it kept employees productive even as they maintained work-life balance.

Note

1 See Human migration in India, 2019, Drishti IAS, https://www.drish tiias.com/to -the-points/paper1/human-migration-in-india.

References

Abella, M. I., and Sasikumar, S. K. 2020. "Estimating Earnings Losses of Migrant Workers Due to COVID-19." *The Indian Journal of Labour Economics* 63(4): 921–39.

Abraham, A. 2020. "International Migration, Return Migration and Occupational Mobility: Evidence from Kerala, India." *The Indian Journal of Labour Economics* 63(4): 1223–43.

Abrol, S., and Madan, V. 2020. "Coronavirus: Employer and Employee Relationship." https://lakshmisri.com/insights/articles/coronavirus-employer-and-employeerel ationship/.

Akhil, C. S., and Rajan, S. I. 2020. "Exploitative or Ethical?: Understanding the Labour Recruitment Practices in the 21st century from Kerala." In *India Migration Report 2020*, edited by S. Irudaya Rajan, 280–92. New Delhi: Routledge India.

Behbahani, S., Smith, C. A., Carvalho, M., Warren, C. J., Gregory, M., and Silva, N. A. 2020. "Vulnerable Immigrant Populations in the New York Metropolitan

Area and COVID-19: Lessons Learned in the Epicenter of the Crisis." *Academic Medicine* 95(12): 1827–30.
Boese, M. 2015. "The Roles of Employers in the Regional Settlement of Recently Arrived Migrants And Refugees." *Journal of Sociology* 51(2): 401–16.
Boillat, S. and Zähringer, J., 2020. "COVID-19, Reverse Migration, and the Impact on Land Systems." Global Land Programme. https://glp.earth/news-events/blog/covid-19-reverse-migration-and-impact-land-systems.
Borjas, G. J., and Cassidy, H. 2020. *The Adverse Effect of the COVID-19 Labor Market Shock on Immigrant Employment* (No. w27243). Cambridge, MA: National Bureau of Economic Research.
Gelatt, J. 2020. *Immigrant Workers: Vital to the US COVID-19 Response, Disproportionately Vulnerable.* Washington, DC: Migration Policy Institute.
International Labour Organization (ILO). 2018. *Global Estimates on International Migrant Workers.* Geneva: International Labor Organization.
International Organization for Migration (IOM). 2020 *World Migration Report 2020.* https://www.un.org/sites/un2.un.org/ files/wmr_2020.pdf. Accessed June 23, 2020.
Kannan, K. P., and Hari, K. S. 2020. "Revisiting Kerala's Gulf Connection: Half a Century of Emigration, Remittances and Their Macroeconomic Impact, 1972–2020." *The Indian Journal of Labour Economics* 63(4): 941–67.
Martin, S. 2016. "Conflict or Natural Disaster: Does It Matter for Migrants" [Issue Brief, p. 12]. *Migrants in Countries in Crisis Initiative.* https://micicinitiative.iom.int/sites/micicinitiative/files/brief/issue_brief_conflict_vs_natural_disaster_0.pdf.
Migration Data, P. 2021. "Migration Data Relevant for the COVID-19 Pandemic." *Migration Data Portal.* http://migrationdataportal.org/themes/migration-data-relevant-covid-19-pandemic.
Moroz, H., Shrestha, M., and Testaverde, M. 2020. *Potential Responses to the COVID-19 Outbreak in Support of Migrant Workers.* Washington, DC: World Bank.
Prakash, B. A. 2020. "The Impact of COVID-19 on Kerala's Economy: A Preliminary Assessment."
Prasad, D. K., Mangipudi, D. M. R., Vaidya, D. R., & Muralidhar, B. 2020. Organizational climate, opportunities, challenges and psychological wellbeing of the remote working employees during COVID-19 pandemic: A general linear model approach with reference to information technology industry in Hyderabad. International Journal of Advanced Research in Engineering and Technology (IJARET), 11(4).
Prasad, K. D. V., Rao, Mruthyanjaya Mangipudi, Vaidya, Rajesh, and Budumuru, Muralidhar. 2020. "Organizational Climate, Opportunities, Challenges and Psychological Wellbeing of the Remote Working Employees during COVID-19 Pandemic: A General Linear Model Approach with Reference to Information Technology Industry in Hyderabad." *International Journal of Advanced Research in Engineering and Technology* 11(4): 372–89. http://www.iaeme.com/IJARET/issues.asp?JType=IJARET&VType=11&IType=4.
Rajan, S. I., and Batra, P. 2022. "Return Migrants and the First Wave of COVID-19: Results from the Vande Bharat Returnees in Kerala. In *India Migration Report 2021*, edited by S. Irudaya Rajan, 57–76. New Delhi: Routledge India.
Rajan, S. I., and Pattath, B. 2022. "What Next for the COVID-19 Return Emigrants?: Findings from the Kerala Return Emigrant Survey 2021. In *India Migration Report 2021*, edited by S. Irudaya Rajan, 181–95. New Delhi: Routledge India.

Ratha, D. K., De, S., Kim, E. J., Plaza, S., Seshan, G. K., and Yameogo, N. D. 2020. "COVID-19 Crisis Through a Migration Lens." *Migration and Development Brief 32*.

Rea, A., and Shinn, J. 2015. "What Are Employee Relations? Definition & Concept." https://study.com/academy/lesson/what-is-employee-relations-definition-lesson-quiz.html

Srivastava, R., and Pandey, A. K. 2017. "Internal and International Migration in South Asia: Drivers, Interlinkage and Policy Issues. *United Nations Educational, Scientific, and Cultural Organization (UNESCO)*, 1–62.

World Bank Group and KNOMAD. 2020. "COVID-19 Crisis Through a Migration Lens." Migration and Development Brief no. 32." World Bank Group & KNOMAD.

World Bank Group and KNOMAD. 2021. "Kerala Return Emigrant Survey 2021: Insights and Way Forward." https://blogs.worldbank.org/en/peoplemove/kerala-return-emigrant-survey-2021-insights-and-way-forward.

7 COVID-19 and Gulf return migration

An opportunity to reorient government strategies

Sulaiman, K. M., Afsal K., and Ram B. Bhagat

Background

According to the World Migration Report 2020, India has the highest number of international migrants in the world (IOM 2020). Of the total population of 272 million international migrants, almost 6% (~17 million) of them are Indians, of which 3 million are from Kerala alone. This includes students, workers, and their families (spouses, parents, etc.).

The outbreak of the COVID-19 pandemic brought into focus the major international migration corridors India shares with the globe, including the Gulf, Europe, and North America. Many of the Stage 1 COVID-19 infections imported to India came through these corridors as emigrants returned to their families. News reports related to Indian emigrant workers and significant recruiters in Middle Eastern countries revealed a frantic desire to return to their home regions.

At the start of the COVID-19 crisis, India evacuated its citizens multiple times, first from China and then from Italy, totalling about 842, according to a press release (2020). There was considerable return migration from countries in Europe, America, and the Gulf. In Kerala, for instance, conversations with migrant welfare workers revealed that anywhere from 60,000 to 80,000 Gulf emigrants returned during the lockdown phase and were quarantined. The initial few weeks saw 413,000 NRKs living outside India register to return to Kerala due to the pandemic. Half of the Indians registered with the Indian Embassy in the United Arab Emirates to return were NRKs. The majority were blue-collar workers willing to return to India due to the loss of their jobs. NRKs, as the largest migrant community in the Gulf, suffered the worst from job losses and pay cuts.

As the Gulf countries locked down non-essential industries, migrants faced the loss of jobs and income, hence, were desperate to return home. Their return led to a spur in COVID-19 cases in Kerala, in particular. The COVID-19 crisis also highlighted Kerala's active international migration network, with India's first three cases imported from Wuhan, China, being reported in the state in January 2020.

This chapter tries to understand the migration and the return migration pattern of the people from Kerala to the Gulf, based on the Kerala Migration

DOI: 10.4324/9781003601289-9

Survey 2014 and 2018 conducted by the Centre for Development Studies, Thiruvananthapuram. This chapter also covers the socio-economic impact of return migration, highlighting the current wave of return migration due to the COVID-19 pandemic from the Middle East region.

Return migration to Kerala

Trends in migration and return migration

The emigration of the Keralites to the Gulf countries started with a few thousand in 1973, but it continuously increased, making a far-reaching impact on the development scenario of Kerala's economy. Contract workers constitute the major type of migration of workers from Kerala to the Middle East, and they are expected to return home at the end of the contract period. The emigration of workers from Kerala to the Gulf region has made a significant impact on the economy of Kerala for the last four decades. Kerala is the largest supplier of migrant workers to the Gulf Cooperation Council (GCC) countries, accounting for nearly 2.5 million.

Gulf remittances also contribute a major part of the state's annual gross domestic product (GDP). In 2018, Kerala received approximately INR 30,717 crores in Gulf remittances. Researchers and institutional agencies have executed numerous efforts to calculate the number of emigrants from Kerala to the Gulf nations, which certify that the number of emigrants has constantly been increasing, regardless of the decrease in the rate of growth in emigration to the GCC region. Figure 7.1 shows the trend of migration and return migration of Keralites from 1998 to 2018. According to an estimation, there were 1.86 lakh Keralites in the Gulf region during the year 1980,

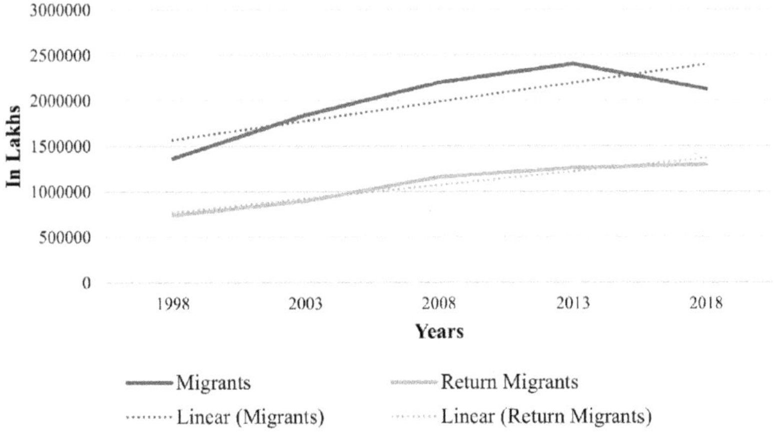

Figure 7.1 Trend of migration and return migration

Source: Various rounds of Kerala Migration Survey, 2007.

which increased to 2.30 lakhs within a year in 1981 (Nair 1989). In 2000, the estimated stock of emigration from Kerala to Gulf countries was 11.04 lakhs, which accounted for about 35.75% of the total emigrants from India to the Gulf countries (Kannan and Hari 2002). Other research pointed out that the number of migrants from Kerala to the Gulf countries was 21.93 lakhs in 2008 (Zachariah and Rajan 2010a), and another study estimated the stock of migrants from Kerala to the Gulf countries to be about 23.31 lakhs in 2011 (Zachariah and Rajan 2012) and about 25 lakhs in 2018.

As per the 1998 study on Kerala migration (Zachariah et al. 2001), the stock of return migrants in that year was more than seven (7) lakhs. From 2003 to 2008, there was an unexpected increase in both emigration and return emigration; coupled with that in remittances, the global economic crisis periods did not deeply affect emigrants from Kerala in Gulf countries. However, there was a negative impact on emigrants in developed countries and female migrants during this period. Most returnees were from the United Arab Emirates (UAE), followed by Saudi Arabia and Qatar. The trend of return migrants during the post-global crisis period 2008–11 showed a decrease from 11.6 lakhs to 11.5 lakhs, while it was 8.9 lakhs in 2003 (Zachariah and Rajan 2010a, 2011, 2012; Zachariah et al., 1999; Prakash, 1998, 2013). After 2011, the returnees increased from 11.5 lakhs to 12.5 lakhs. (Figure 7.1).

Among the majority of the return migrants, in the above-35-year-old age group, males outnumbered females. Still, the proportion of female return emigrants was primarily on the increase compared to women during the economic crisis (Zachariah and Rajan 2012). By considering the marital status of returnees, above 70% were married, in contrast to their first migration time, when they were not married. The educational quality of migrants was better than that of the general population. Still, the number of return migrants with low levels of education, such as primary, secondary, and higher secondary, was higher than that of highly educated migrants. Based on religion, Muslims were 44%, followed by Hindus at 39%, and Christians at 16% (Zachariah and Rajan 2015).

Table 7.1 shows the percentage of migrants who returned during the 2008 recession, the return migrants by destination countries, and the number of COVID-19 cases in those countries reported by December 10, 2020. Nearly 90% of Kerala emigrants go to the Gulf countries. The UAE has the highest share of Kerala migrants at 39%, while 23% of Kerala's international migrants are in Saudi Arabia. Oman and Qatar are the destinations for nearly 20% of Kerala migrants. However, the most significant number of return emigrants came from Saudi Arabia, followed by the UAE and Oman, mainly due to their new labour policies. Saudi Arabia lost about 3% of its share, especially after the Nitaqat crisis (KMS Report 2014).

The six major destination countries mentioned in Table 7.1 accounted for 4% of the total COVID-19 cases in the world, and Saudi Arabia and Qatar were the worst affected. One of the significant waves of return migration

Table 7.1 Percentage of migrants and return migrants by destination countries and number of COVID-19 cases

Country of return	*Percentage of migrants*	*Migrants returned*	*No of COVID-19 cases by December 10*	*Percentage of migrants returned (recession 2008)*
United Arab Emirates	39.1	33.1	184,949	46.4
Saudi Arabia	23	38.0	359,888	22.7
Oman	8.6	12.0	126,240	6.9
Qatar	8.7	4.9	140,961	5.3
Kuwait	6	4.3	146,218	10.5
Bahrain	3.8	4.7	89,143	2.6
Other countries	10.8	3.1		5.6
Total	100	100	4% (World)	100

Source: Kerala Migration Surveys 2008, 2018, Johns Hopkins.

experienced before was during the economic recession of 2008. As many as 173,339 people returned due to the recession, according to the Kerala Migration Survey 2009. The UAE and Saudi Arabia contributed 69% of the total return migration. Kuwait was also one of the major countries from which migrants returned in 2008. The return migration due to COVID-19 will raise the same challenges raised by the 2008 return migration due to the economic recession in Kerala (Zachariah and Rajan 2010b).

Reasons for return

The principal cause for the return of emigrants to Kerala was labour-related issues such as the expiry of the contract, compulsory repatriation, low salary, non-payment of wages, harsh behaviour of the employer, and lousy work atmosphere (Reshmi 2008; Prakash 2013). Another study found that the reasons for the return were contract expiry, low wages at the destination, ill health, new labour policies, problems at home, Nitaqat issues, and compulsory expatriation. (Zachariah and Rajan 2012, 2015; Rasheed 2017). Figure 7.2 shows the reasons for the return of Kerala migrants from the Gulf region in both 2014 and 2018. The year 2014 was used to show the importance of the Nitaqat issue, a significant crisis Kerala migrants faced after the 2008 economic recession.

Work and related financial issues functioned as primary reasons for the return migration from the Gulf region. From 2014 to 2018, the percentage of people returning because of job loss increased six times (Figure 7.2), whereas, in 2014, the proportion of returns from Saudi Arabia was high (KMS 2014) due to compulsory expatriation and Nitaqat issues (4% returned from Saudi Arabia (Figure 7.2), as well as other fixed reasons such as poor working conditions, low wages, and problems at home. Those who returned due to

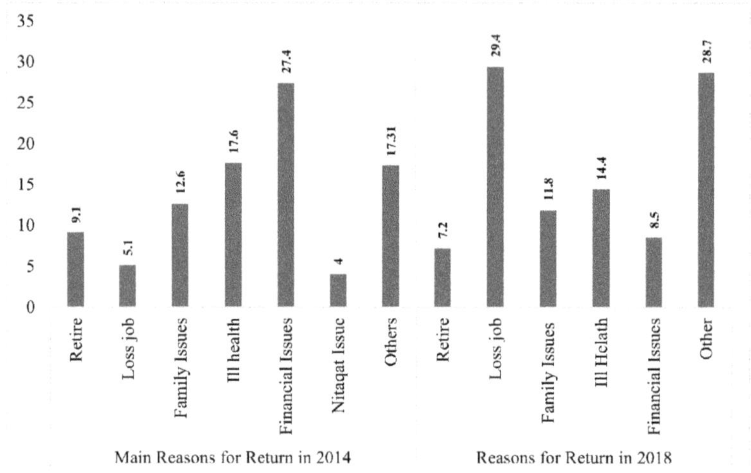

Figure 7.2 Reasons for return migration from the Gulf region (in percentage)
Source: Kerala migration survey 2014 and 2018.

the Nitaqat issues mainly worked in the private sector and engaged in self-employment. The new rule compelled the companies to replace foreign citizens with natives, and the proportions of return with low-level education in the semi-skilled and unskilled sectors were very high (Zachariah and Rajan 2015).

Remittances and migrant households

Dependency on migrants is high in Kerala. When a person migrates, the whole family becomes dependent on that person; in other words, the migration was a household decision to improve the overall well-being of its members. Figure 7.3 shows the household use of remittances received. Of the remittances, 37% were used for household day-to-day expenses, 15% for household assets, and 8% on children's education. Around 13% of remittances are used to repay debts, and only 19% of remittances go into savings (Figure 7.3). Taken together, 60% of total remittances are directly spent on household needs, showing the dependence of households on the money sent by the migrant.

It is essential to know-how many families having migrants/return migrants. Table 7.2 shows that in Kerala, 24 of the 100 households have at least one migrant, and a district-wise analysis shows that Malappuram has migrants in 40 out of 100 households, contributing to 20% of the total migrants from Kerala to the Middle East. Besides that, districts like Kollam, Pathanamthitta, Kottayam, and Kannur have more than 30 out of 100 households with migrants outside. The maximum number of return migrants

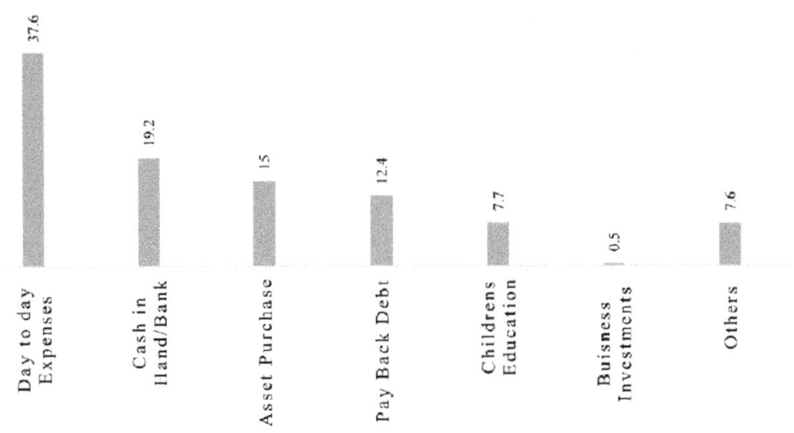

Figure 7.3 Household use of remittance 2018

Source: Kerala migration survey 2018.

was in Malappuram district, followed by Thiruvananthapuram, and the minimum number of return migrants was in Idukki, followed by Wayanad. Malappuram again accounts for 24% of the total return migrants to the state. Of 100 households, 32 had return migrants, while Kerala had, on average, return migrants in 14 of 100 families. In Kollam and Kasaragod, over 20 households of the 100 had returned migrants. Nearly 8% of migrants returned during the 2008 great economic recession, and significant migrant-sending districts had an equal share of returnees in the same period (Table 7.2). Most emigrants returned after just one migration episode; the average migration period was seven years (KMS Report 2020).

The reason for dwindling return migration in some districts of the southern region in 2018 was the decline in the return of, especially, skilled migrants from the western and the Gulf countries, and the decrease of female returnees from abroad (Zachariah and Rajan 2012, 2015; Prakash 2013). After the economic recession of 2008, from 2011 to 2018, the number of return emigrants primarily increased, especially from Saudi Arabia, due to the Nitaqat Law (which is a plan the Saudi Government implemented to increase the number of their citizens in all enterprises and companies) that mainly affected the semi-skilled and unskilled labourers and self-employed persons.

Life after return migration

Return migration, due to various reasons, has serious consequences on the lives of migrants. Life after returning to home society directly depends on the nature and context of their return migration. The impact of forced or involuntary return makes their lives more vulnerable, with the immediate loss of jobs and not having pre-departure planning for their home society. There

Table 7.2 Migrants, return migrants, and remittances received in Kerala, district-wise

District	*Percentage of emigrants*	*Emigrants/100 household*	*Percentage of return migrants*	*Return migrants/100 household*	*Percentage of migrant returned (2008)*
Thiruvananthapuram	6.5	15.2	7.2	10.4	16.7
Kollam	11.3	32.8	12.8	22.6	6.9
Pathanamthitta	5.2	31.9	4.2	15.8	3.9
Alappuzha	6.4	23.6	7.7	17.3	6.1
Kottayam	7.9	31.3	3.2	7.9	3
Idukki	1.6	11.3	0.5	2.1	0
Ernakulam	2.5	5.8	1.8	2.6	3.9
Thrissur	11.4	27.9	7.3	10.9	13.5
Palakkad	4.2	12.2	4.5	7.9	11.3
Malappuram	19.1	42.1	23.9	32.1	14.1
Kozhikode	7.6	19.7	11.7	18.5	11
Wayanad	1.4	14.5	0.9	5.7	0.5
Kannur	11.8	38.8	7.3	14.7	6.5
Kasaragod	3.2	21.3	6.9	28.4	2.8
Kerala	**2121887**	**24**	**1294796**	**14.6**	7.7

Source: Kerala Migration Surveys 2008, 2018.

are many cases where the average NRK returning home after decades does nothing and sinks into depression. The state is also struggling with a compound range of socio-economic problems faced by Gulf returnees without having systematic supporting mechanisms and policy plans. Return migrants are likely to be more vulnerable to exoticism due to their long-time absence as migrants in another country, due to the changing socio-cultural and economic environment of the home society (Shekhar, 1997).

The majority of migrants from Kerala are unskilled, or semi-skilled labourers. Transition in the occupation and employment sector from before emigration to after returning home is one of the factors that could help study the impact of emigration on occupations in Kerala. In contrast to occupational mobility, most return emigrants joined the same sector they worked in before the migration, mainly in the non-agricultural sector and the private sector after their return. The percentage of persons who were self-employed increased greatly among return migrants. The incidences of unemployment among the return emigrants were high, and most returnees faced economic and employment problems after return (Reshmi 2008; Zachariah and Rajan 2011, 2012; Prakash 2013).

With the local labour market system having undergone rapid change over the last few years, trained and untrained jobs are being filled with immigrant workers from other states such as Uttar Pradesh, West Bengal, Bihar, and Tamil Nadu. This affects the economic reintegration of return migrants. The present low wages in Kerala, comparable to those in the Gulf, will also change the total financial management of families after return.

As entrepreneurial opportunities are very low in Kerala compared to other states, it has led to many migrant returnees being forced to remain unproductive for the rest of their lives. Overall, the investment activity of the return emigrants was minimal after the return. Very few had tried to start any kind of economic activity. Other than a few trading shops, taxi services, and agricultural processing establishments, the return emigrants of Kerala did not involve themselves in any investment activity. Those who tried were not very successful (Zachariah and Rajan 2011).

The proportion of savings and the investment of remittances was much lower among migrants, and utilization of remittances was mainly for the construction of houses, daily expenses, and marriage. The earnings and expenditures of return migrants decreased compared to those before return (Zachariah and Rajan 2012; Rasheed 2017). Rehabilitation programmes for return migrants from the government did not help to improve their living standards (Zachariah et al. 2001). Jabir (2014) suggests a framework of multidimensional policies that could address all problems of return immigrants, such as information-based policies, economy incentive policies, and institution-based policies. However, another positive aspect of emigration is that return emigrants have acquired several skills while working abroad, including technical, marketing, managerial/supervisory, and financial management skills (Zachariah and Rajan 2011, 2012).

Table 7.3 Revenue receipts and revenue expenditures

Year	*Annual growth rate (AGR)*		*Annual growth rate of main sources of revenue receipts*			*Share of revenue expenditures*	
	RR (%)	*RE (%)*	*SOTR (%)*	*SNTR (%)*	*SCTG (%)*	*DE (%)*	*NDE (%)*
2017–18	9.79	27.02	10.15	15.46	6.85	53.01	46.99
2018–19	11.84	21.01	9.00	5.21	19.98	51.48	48.52

Source: Various issues of Economic Review and Budget in Brief, Government of Kerala, 2020.
Note: RR = Revenue receipts, RE = Revenue expenditure, SOTR = State's own tax revenue, SNTR = State's own non-tax revenue, SCTG = Share of central taxes and grants, DE and NDE = Development and non-development expenditures; and AGR = Annual Growth Rate.

Kerala during unprecedented challenges

Natural disasters like floods, cyclones, and landslides, and public health challenges like epidemic diseases (e.g., viral fever, chikungunya, dengue, Nipah virus, and H1N1) have posed severe threats to the fiscal stability of the state in the last few years. Despite all these challenges, Kerala maintained reasonably good fiscal stability in 2017 and 2018.

Table 7.3 shows that the annual growth rate of the total revenue receipts increased to 11.8% in 2018–19 from 9.8% in 2017–18. The annual growth rate of the state's share in central taxes and grants has risen sharply from 6.85% to 19.98% between 2017–18 and 2018–19, though the annual growth rates of the state's tax revenue and the state's non-tax revenue have declined. The revenue deficit decreased to 2.2% in 2018–19 from 2.4% in 2017–18 due to the decline in the annual growth rate of the revenue expenditure (RE), but the annual growth rate of the receipts had increased (Manikandan and Sulaiman 2020).

During local calamities, the central government's total transfers play a vital role in adjusting the state's fiscal and revenue deficits. But as in the current global pandemic, return migration (loss in remittances) could also affect fiscal stability. Kerala may have to supplement the anticipated drop in remittances with other kinds of revenue.

Return migration during the pandemic and challenges

As the Middle Eastern countries slowly shut down non-essential industries, migrants, facing job loss and no income, were desperate to return. The COVID-19 pandemic highlighted Kerala's strong and active international migration networks, with India's first three active cases in January 2020 being imported ones from Wuhan. Subsequently, a new outbreak of cases erupted in Kerala at the end of March, with the northern districts of Kasaragod and Kannur registering more active cases.

KMS (2018) data shows that Malappuram and Kollam ranked the highest in terms of emigration as well as return migration (Table 7.2). Kasaragod and Kannur rank relatively lower in migration and return migration compared to other districts, but like the other districts, they share the most robust migration linkages with UAE and Saudi Arabia (worst affected in the GCC). Earlier reports about Kasaragod's high number of cases could have been due to its special connection with Dubai: the district, with 121 cases as of 1 April 2020, sends migrants to the textile sector of Deira Naif, Dubai, from where almost every return migrant had been testing positive, according to a 25th March 2021 based on the report in the online journal, *Lede*.

Even though return migration is a predictable feature of temporary or contract migration, adequate data to gauge its magnitude and impact is sparse. In the case of Kerala, government authorities did not record the number of migrants returning, particularly during the pandemic. Nonetheless, it is clear that COVID-19 has imposed additional burdens on state agencies to screen and trace returnees from the Gulf while taking steps to avoid rumours that could lead to the latter facing social rejection and discrimination of return migrant. Moreover, returning migrants who lost their jobs were expected to add to the unemployed population in Kerala. Previous similar situations that had resulted in sudden job loss and large-scale returns from the Gulf (e.g., the economic recession of 2008 and Saudi Arabia's Nitaqat Policy, 2012) did not necessarily provide a bright idea as to how much less or how good returnees in the COVID-19 context would be re-absorbed into their communities, what the extent of their reintegration would require of the Government of Kerala and local authorities' attention.

As many as 4,13,000 Non-Resident Keralites (NRKs) living outside India registered to return to Kerala due to the pandemic in the first few months of the pandemic. Why do people returning after losing their jobs and income matter? Consider the case of Malappuram, where one in three households is an NRK household. The district boasts of the highest number of migrants and gets 21% of Kerala's total remittances. But the flow of returnees was also the highest – almost a quarter of the total, with about one in four households having a returnee. The phenomenon of migration was not individual but concerned with migrants' families, as families of migrants in Kerala have long been depending on remittances to meet their expenses. Before the crisis, migrants would remit to support their spouses and family, to meet children's educational and medical expenses, and to repay loans. The return migration of an individual also affects the household and the community.

This raises another critical question: Does it only affect the families with migrants who returned during the pandemic? It directly affects three of the following groups of people, including persons who returned during the pandemic:

1. **Migrants who returned to Kerala before the pandemic for break/ on leave:** These people were stuck and were in danger of losing their

livelihoods, and had no source of income. The prevailing situation halted large infrastructure projects in the Gulf and caused oil prices to fall drastically. As the Gulf was facing a severe economic crisis, it did not recruit migrants shortly. This hit Kerala's economy and migrants' livelihoods the hardest.

2. **Migrants who returned during the pandemic:** Migrants returned during the lockdown due to job loss and even opted for voluntary retirement due to the instability they faced in their destination. Most lost their source of income and were rethinking their future endeavours. This group also included the early migrants who went to the Middle East on a short visit in search of jobs by making investments (taken as loans or debts).
3. **Migrants at the destination who lost their source of income but did not return:** These migrants ran out of money and could not find an income-generating activity. In some cases, workers were not provided adequate financial support for food or rent. Still, they believed it was better to stay back and wait until the pandemic ended than return to their homeland, which would cost a considerable amount.

Experts expected more than three lakh people to lose their jobs from the three groups, which accounted for 16% of the current Kerala migrants in the Gulf region. It could directly affect the migrant or remittance-dependent households and the state economy as well, suggesting an interconnection between migrants and remittances. Remittances are the lifeblood of Kerala's economy and have steadily increased over the last two decades. However, the real global economic slowdown triggered by the pandemic was expected to lead to remittance losses. It was estimated that 15% of Kerala's annual remittances were expected to decline as the crisis had further heightened the livelihood concerns of returning migrants and the NRKs who remained in the Gulf. It was pertinent to mention that most Indians abroad infected by COVID-19 were from the Gulf countries. Due to shutdowns or quarantines, their earnings decreased, their families faced a difficult time, and their remittances were affected.

The majority of return migrants were employed either on a part-time or full-time basis. Studies on return migrants (2014) show that nearly one-fifth of the return migrants remain unemployed. Similarly, they get only a small amount of monthly income from self-employment and wage employment. Studies also observe that the socio-economic status of 40% of return emigrants due to emigration to the Gulf countries has not improved. Two-thirds of households face several financial problems. Similarly, migrations of the head of the household creates social tension and problems for return emigrant households. Emigration has adversely affected the education, as well as character formation of the children, and has created mental stress and challenges for wives of emigrants. Return emigrants also feel that they are isolated from society due to their long-term emigration. Return emigration also produces a mild or moderate recession in the economic activities in the localities having a high concentration of immigrant households, as was experienced at the time of the recession (2008) and Nitaqat (KMS 2014).

Policy recommendation

Briefly, Kerala could address the return migration in two ways: first, economically reintegrating the return migrants and second, facilitating a secure and safe future migration.

For economic reintegration, return migrants in Kerala have already availed some incentive-based policies like the Santhwana Financial Scheme, Pravasi Welfare Fund, and Initiative for Entrepreneurship Development. The initiative for entrepreneurship development could further improve as a support fund for the investments of return migrants like the Senegalese government's programme called FAISE (Support Fund for the Investments of Overseas Senegalese). This would technically provide all return migrants in Kerala with financial support, in the form of loans ranging between INR 5 and 50 lakh, to implement an income-generating, development-oriented project in key sectors upon their return. This would help the return migrants use their skills to develop an employment-generating business in their homeland.

Facilitating a secure and safe migration and re-emigration should be prioritized during economic and pandemic emergencies. Proposing a complete institutionalized migration has its limitations, but it would create a safe migration environment. In the Philippines, the government-created Philippine Overseas Employment Administration (POEA) is responsible for processing workers' contracts and pre-deployment checks and licensing, regulating, and monitoring private recruitment agencies. Another government agency, the Overseas Workers Welfare Administration (OWWA), provides support and assistance to migrants and their families. All processes and requirements up until the point of departure are managed by the POEA, while the OWWA assumes responsibility for the workers' welfare while employed abroad.

Kerala could follow this model by taking the suggestions put forward by the International Organization of Migration (IOM), which include collecting better data on the skills of migrant workers before departure and on return, Recognition of Prior Learning (RPL) (skill testing and training) for migrant workers, developing a recruitment chain ensuring longer-term career opportunities (re-emigration), training the returning migrants to be future trainers (Bangladeshi model of ICT application), and an internet-based network of illustration of triumphant return. A formal network of skilled returnees who have set up businesses could offer a forum for idea sharing, support, advice, and the provision of mentors for new returnees, safeguard the well-being of the left-behind family members, and create bilateral agreements with countries of destination. Kerala cannot simply stop people from leaving, and the state will need to explore how migration can be an instrument for development through appropriate policies and programmes. In this matter, Kerala can learn much from international discussions and reflections on migration and development from other countries.

Conclusion

The return of a large number of migrants in any health emergency is likely to create severe economic consequences, especially in employment, unemployment, consumption, savings, investment, and the general well-being of the people. So, both the state and the central governments should give high priority to the issues of return migration and the rehabilitation of return emigrants. Though Kerala could plan more policies and implement programmes, it poses challenges in the reintegration process of returnees. The unhealthy economic scenario of the state due to COVID-19 carries a significant role in creating challenges. The nature of problems and difficulties may be personal or situational. Though individual issues, like lack of adjustment with family or home society, are a problem, the challenges regarding the excessive return migration and lack of alternative systems become a significant challenge to the government and other related departments.

The pandemic and the consequences of lockdown had self-evident impacts on remittances to Kerala from the Gulf countries and an unemployment crisis among NRKs. Kerala may have to supplement the anticipated drop in the remittances with other revenue. However, the more significant consequence will unfold over the coming years. Only then can the state understand how far this pandemic has hit Kerala's remittance economy. While the Government of Kerala had organized medical facilities for the returning NRKs, it would need to do more to overcome migrants' financial difficulties due to the loss of livelihoods. Kerala could mobilize the skill sets of returnees in sectors suffering from a deficit of human resources. Furthermore, enhancing the talents of returning migrants may also facilitate further international migration to new destinations or to the Gulf itself. However, this proposal would require comprehensive research to examine the best feasible ways to integrate the returning NRKs economically. For quite some time in Kerala, return migration and integration strategies have lost their pertinence. It could use the COVID-19 experience to reorient these strategies to address the current demands.

References

Government of Kerala (GoK) Dashboard. 2020. "Kerala Fights COVID-19." https://dashboard.kerala.gov.in/index.php.

Government of Kerala D of H and FW. 2020. "Testing Strategy: Strategy for COVID-19 Testing in Kerala State." https://health.kerala.gov.in/2020/06/.

International Organization for Migration (IOM). 2020 *World Migration Report 2020*. https://www.un.org/sites/un2.un.org/ files/wmr_2020.pdf.

Jabir, M. M. 2014. "Reintegration of Return Migrants in Kerala: Policy Initiatives and Challenges." *International Journal of African and Asian Studies* 4: 112–23.

Kannan, K. P., and Hari, K. S. 2002. *Emigration, Remittances and Their Macro Economic Impact*. Working Paper No. 328. Thiruvananthapuram: Centre for Development Studies.
Kerala Migration Survey (KMS) Report. 2007. Thiruvanathapuram: Centre for Development Studies.
Kerala Migration Survey (KMS) Report. 2014. Thiruvanathapuram: Centre for Development Studies.
Kerala Migration Survey (KMS) Report. 2018. Thiruvanathapuram: Centre for Development Studies.
Kerala Migration Survey (KMS) Report. 2020. Thiruvanathapuram: Centre for Development Studies.
Manikandan, A. D., and Sulaiman, K. M. 2020. "Fiscal Challenges in the Aftermath of Natural Disasters and Public Health Challenges in Kerala." *Indian Journal of Applied Business and Economic* 2(1): 25–35.
Nair, P. R. G. 1989. "Incidence, Impact and Implications of Migration to the Middle East from Kerala." In *To the Gulf and Back: Studies on the Economic Impact of Asian Labour Migration*, edited by Amjad Rashid, 343–64: New Delhi: ILO-ARTEP.
Prakash, B. A. 1998. "Gulf Migration and Its Economic Impact: The Kerala Experience. *Economic and Political Weekly* 33(50): 3209–13.
Prakash, B. A. 2013. *Return Emigration of Indian Emigrant Workers from the West Asia: Report on a Survey of Return Emigrants in Kerala*. Thiruvananthapuram: Rajiv Gandhi Institute of Development Studies & New Delhi: Ministry of Overseas Indian Affairs.
Rasheed, C. K. 2017. "International Return Migration to Kerala: A Socio-Economic Analysis." *International Multi-Disciplinary E-Journal* 6(6).
Reshmi, R. S. 2008. "Labour Migration of Women from Kerala: Socio-Economic Impact on Migrants and Their Families." Unpublished Ph.D. Thesis, IIPS Mumbai.
Shekhar, T.V. 1997. *Migration and Social Change*. New Delhi: Rawat Publication.
Zachariah, K. C., Mathew, E. T., and Rajan, S. I. 1999. "Impact of Migration on Kerala's Economy and Society. *International Migration* 59(1): 23–41.
Zachariah, K. C., Mathew, E. T., and Rajan, S. I. 2001. "Social, Economic and Demographic Consequences of Migration on Kerala." *International Migration* 39(2): 43–71.
Zachariah, K. C., and Rajan, S. I. 2010a. *Migration Monitoring Study, 2008, Emigration and Remittances in the Context of Surge in Oil Prices*. Working Paper 424. Thiruvananthapuram: Centre for Development Studies.
Zachariah, K. C., and Rajan, S. I. 2010b. *Impact of the Global Recession on Migration and Remittances in Kerala: New Evidences from the Return Migration Study (RMS)*. Working Paper 432. Kerala Migration Report 2009. Thiruvananthapuram: Centre for Development Studies.
Zachariah, K. C., and Rajan, S. I. 2011. *From Kerala via Kerala Via the Gulf: Emigration Experiences of Return Emigrants*. Working Paper 443. Thiruvananthapuram: Centre for Development Studies.
Zachariah, K. C., and Rajan, S. I. 2012. *Inflexion in Kerala's Gulf Connection: Report on Kerala Migration Report 2011*. Working Paper 450. Thiruvananthapuram: Centre for Development Studies.
Zachariah, K. C., and Rajan, S. I. 2015. *Dynamics of Emigration and Remittances in Kerala: Results from the Kerala Migration Survey 2014*. Working Paper 463. Thiruvananthapuram: Centre for Development Studies.

8 COVID-19 pandemic, international remittances, and economic growth in Kerala

A macro analysis

K. Pushpangadan and G. Murugan

Introduction

The COVID-19 pandemic (covid-19) put severe strains on the world economy since starting its devastating journey from China to countries in Europe, Latin America, Asia, etc. At the time of writing, assessing its whole impact was extremely difficult since it was multidimensional – social, economic, environmental, and demographic etc. - in nature. Most studies on the economic impact in this area of specialization are at the national level but only a few at the sub-national level. If at all sub-national studies exist, they lack a macroeconomic framework in most of the cases. The present attempt is to develop a macroeconomic framework for measuring the impact of COVID-19 on the aggregate economic growth of Kerala, the sub-national economy in India, where international remittances play a crucial role in the growth of the service sector.

The second objective of the chapter is to put forth an alternative route and data source for the estimation of the State Domestic Product/Gross State Domestic product, in a scenario where the conventional set out methodologies of estimation becomes in operational due to constraints of a lockdown phenomena when all institutions and machinery are under lockdown in a stand still.

The first section of the chapter provides the macroeconomic framework and the database for the analysis; the second section reports the empirical results; the third estimates the impact due to COVID-19 in the state domestic product; the fourth deals with the reduction in international remittances due to COVID-19 return migration and the slowdown in economic activity in Gulf countries; the fifth estimates the aggregate effect of COVID-19 on the economic growth of the region using the growth equation for the state; and the final section contains the summary and conclusions.

Macro-framework for the analysis of economic growth

The analytical framework for measuring economic growth was developed only in the 1950s by Solow (1956, 1957), one on the theory of economic growth and the other on the role of technological progress for sustainable

DOI: 10.4324/9781003601289-10

growth. Both ideas have produced several Nobel prize-winning theses as surveyed by Jones and Vollrath (2013). But its application at the sub-national level is hardly undertaken, especially in India. In the present study, only the theory of economic growth contained in the Solow's1956 paper is considered for the evaluation of COVID-19 impact.

Basic Solow growth model

The model has two equations – first, it assumes the economy produces a composite commodity, y, following the tradition of Harrod-Domar and Mahalanobis with two primary inputs, labour and capital. Since our purpose is to understand economic growth, the appropriate variable is per capita output and per capita physical capital. It is linked to the production function of the following form (equation 8.1):

$$y = f(k) \ldots \tag{8.1}$$

Where y is output per capita and k, stock of capital per capita. Solow (1956) specifies the simplest functional form for his analysis as given in equation 8.2:

$$y = k^{\alpha} \ldots \tag{8.2}$$

where α denotes the share of output paid to capital in the production process. It may be noted that the production is subject to diminishing marginal returns to capital per worker. The unexplained variation in (8.2) becomes the basis for Solow's 1957 paper on technical change for sustainable growth. His second equation is the capital accumulation in the economy as given in equation 8.3.

$$k = sy - (n - \delta)\ k \ldots \tag{8.3}$$

Equation (8.3) expresses the capital accumulation per worker terms, where s is the saving rate in the economy, n, labour force growth and, δ, the depreciation rate. In a closed economy, savings is equal to investment and the equation gives the net investment or the change in the capital stock in the economy. The highlights of growth in this economy are shown in Figure 8.1.

Figure 8.1 has two curves; both are functions of capital-labour ratio (k). The first curve is the amount of investment which is the scaled-down version of economy' wide production function by the saving rate in the economy. The second curve is the line indicating the net investment per person required to keep the capital–labour ratio constant. The difference between the two curves gives the change in the capital per worker in the economy. If the difference is positive, then capital per worker is increasing, which usually be termed as "capital deepening" On the other hand, if the change is zero and

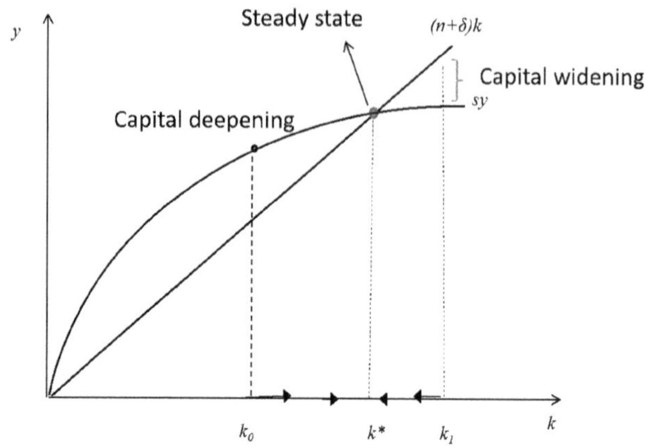

Figure 8.1 Basic Solow growth

Source: Adapted from Jones and Vollrath (2013), p. 29; Figure 2.2.

k is growing, then only "capital widening" is taking place due to population growth. Suppose an economy starts from k_0, then the investment per worker is higher than it is required for the capital–labour ratio . Capital deepening occurs (*k* increases overtime) in an economy so that capital–labour ratio becomes constant. Such a point, k*, is called "steady-state equilibrium" in the Solow diagram. Instead, say, the capital stock per worker is higher than that is available from the investment in the economy, as in k_1, then investment will be used for widening the capital base of the economy so that capital–labour ratio becomes constant.

Now let us examine the response of the Solow model for changes in parameters such as saving rate (*s*) and/or population growth (*n*) in the economy. This is the standard comparative statics analysis. This is examined in Figure 8.2 in the case of the change in saving rate.

Let us consider the response of the Solow growth model for a positive change in the savings rate of the consumers. The investment function will move upward, and the capital deepening takes place so that the new steady-state equilibrium is reached, as shown in the Figure 8.2. Similarly, it can be shown that an increase in population will reduce per capita output because of capital widening to reach a constant capital–labour ratio (Jones and Vollrath 2013).

Our objective is to estimate the Solow growth equation for a sub-national economy, Kerala, where migration has been playing an important role since the 1970s (Zachariah et al. 2003; Pushpangadan 2003, 2012; Acemoglu 2009, chapter 20; Pushpangadan and Murugan 2019; Kannan and Hari 2002 and 2020). This is possible only if the economy is open so that international remittances positively affect saving rates and economic growth. This would mean that international remittances become an exogenous variable in

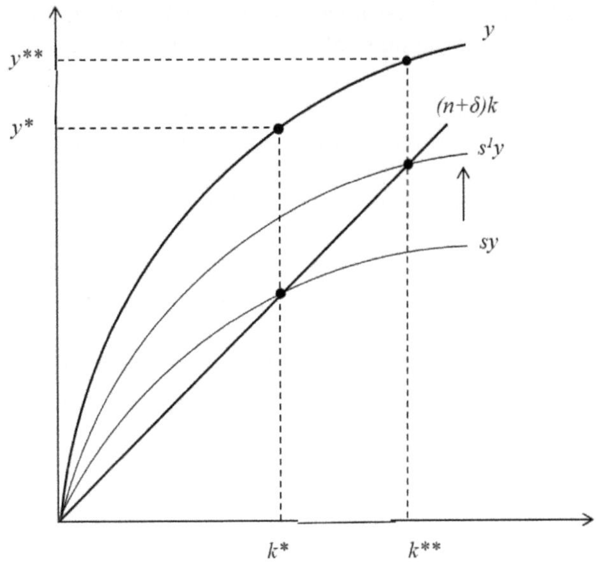

Figure 8.2 Comparative statistics of investment rate

Source: adapted from Jones and Vollrath (2013); Figure 2.4

the Solow model. The modified growth equation of Solow model is given in equation 8.4.

output = F (stock of physical capital, international remittances) ... (8.4)

Log specification of equation (8.4) is used for estimating the aggregate (overall) growth of the regional economy.

Data sources

(i) Per capita real output series: The net state domestic product (SDP) in constant series per capita published by the Department of Economics and Statistics, Government of Kerala.
(ii) Stock of physical capital - is not available on a continuous basis for the state. The time series for the period, 1970–80, is published by the Department of Economics and Statistics, but the department was unable to locate the series from their collection. The department has published the series for the periods, 1990–1997 and 2011–2015. Our data search shows that EPW Research Foundation has (1993) published a series for the period starting from 1982 to 1987. Our task is to generate time series data on the capital stock by generating the missing values. The following methodology is applied for estimating the missing values from the capital

stock of all India. It is assumed that the share of capital stock of the region is the same as the share of GDP of the region in all-India GDP. The growth rate of the capital stock estimated for the region is then applied for generating missing values for completing the series for the period, 1983–2015. The investment rate is obtained by normalizing the capital stock series with the GDP series in current prices. The deflation process is adjusted partly for the price effect and unadjusted for depreciation.

(iii) Per capita real remittances = total remittances deflated by national income deflator of Net SDP. The remittances figure is taken from Kannan and Hari (2020). Number of migrants from Kerala is also taken from Kannan and Hari (2020).

(iv) Data for the computation of COVID-19-impacted SDP, for the year 2020–21 is collected from many primary and secondary sources. Details are given along with the appropriate texts.

Empirical results

The following regression is estimated from the data generated in the section above The Solow open economy growth equation used for the estimation in log form is given below:

$$\ln PCNSDP = a + a_1 \ln INVR + a_2 \ln PCREM + u \quad (8.5)$$

where, lnPCNSDP is the Log of Per capita net SDP;
lnINVR is the investment rate defined as log Capital stock/GDP;
lnPCREM is the log per capita remittance and u the random error

Equation (8.5) is estimated for the period 1981–2015. and the results are reported in Table 8.1.

Table 8.1 Results of Economic growth for Kerala, 1981–2015

Dep. Variable: lnPCNSDP	*Coefficient*
lnINVR	0.16
	(0.131)
lnPCREM	0.285***
	(0.033)
Constant	6.226***
	(0.189)
Number of observations	36
F (2, 33)	278.23
Prob > F	0
Adj R-squared	0.94

Source: Authors' calculation.
Note: *** indicates significance at 1% level; standard errors are in parenthesis.

The equation as revealed in Table 8.1 has an explanatory power of 94%. The only problem is that the investment rate is not significant. Obviously, the investment rate generates growth with a lagged effect. Therefore, a lag structure has to be included in the specification for estimating the growth equation.

Three lag structures were considered for the investment rate in the growth equation: (1) Ad-hoc lags; (2) Koyck lag; and (3) Almon's lag (Gujarati 1988).

The two ad-hoc results were estimated, and the results are reported in Table 8.2. and Table 8.3.

The equation has been adjusted for autocorrelation using the CORC method results do not yield any meaningful result.

There is no statistical significance in the lagged investment variables with inappropriate signs (negative) instead of positive, especially in the investment. We also examined the validity of Koyck and Almon's lag for the investment rate but did not find any significance for such models.

Among the equations, the equation with one ad-hoc lag is the only promising one, though it does not yield a meaningful result. Hence the equation is re-estimated using Robust Method gives significant results. However the lag structure in the sources of investment rate on economic growth requires further research in a remittance economy. The results from the Robust Method are given in Table 8.4.

The equation with a single lag was the only result worth pursuing for the analysis. The use of this version also justified the instrumental variable method in the Koyck scheme (Liviatan 1963; Gujarati 1988;). The results are reported in Table 8.4.

Table 8.2 Growth equation with ad-hoc lags in investment rates

Dep. Variable: lnPCNSDP	*Coefficient*
lnINVR	0.428*
	(0.215)
lnINVR(_1)	-0.193
	(0.221)
lnPCREM	0.277***
	(0.038)
Constant	6.047***
	(0.207)
Number of observations	35
F (3, 31)	194.83
Prob > F	0
Adj R-squared	0.944
Durbin-Watson d-statistic (4, 35) =	0.47

Source: Same as in Table 8.1

Note: *** indicates significance at 1% level; * indicates significance at 10% level; standard errors are in parenthesis.

Table 8.3 Growth equation with two ad-hoc lags for investment rate

Dep. Variable: lnPCNSDP	*Coefficient*
ln INVR	0.423*
	(0.23)
ln PCREM	0.272***
	(0.045)
ln INVR (−1)	−0.034
	(0.273)
ln INVR (−2)	−0.115
	(0.228)
Constant	5.958***
	(0.23)
Number of obs	34
F (4, 29)	136.19
Prob > F	0
Adj R-squared	0.94

Source: Same as in Table 8.1
Note: *** indicates significance at 1% level; * indicates significance at 10% level; standard errors are in parenthesis.

Table 8.4 Robust regression of growth equation

Dep. Variable: lnPCNSDP	*Coefficient*
lnINVR	0.428***
	(0.152)
lnINVR(_1)	−0.193
	(0.184)
lnPCREM	0.277***
	(0.038)
Constant	6.047***
	(0.173)
Number of observations	35
F (3, 31)	275.74
Prob > F	0
R-squared	0.950
Root MSE	0.122

Source: Same as in Table 8.1
Note: *** indicates significance at 1% level; Robust standard errors are in parenthesis.

The Robust growth equation (Table 8.4) explains about 95% of the variation in real per capita income. Moreover, 43% of the growth is explained by the investment rate, 28% by real per capita remittances, and the remaining [{100−(43+28)} =29] 29% by all other factors. Let us evaluate the model for COVID-19 effect. First is the investment rate. How do we arrive at the investment rate after COVID-19? Let us explore.

The overall impact of COVID-19 on economic growth is estimated only if the pandemic's effect on investment rate and remittances is estimated. The next two sections undertake such estimation.

COVID-19 and investment reduction

Hitherto, we saw the pattern of growth of the sub-regional economy in the long run. Having done that, our next attempt is to measure the impact of COVID-19 and the ramifications it can make on the SDP, particularly on its reductions in Kerala during 2020–21. For conducting the exercise, ideally, one should follow the guidelines issued by the Ministry of Statistics and programme implementation for the measurement of national income. Considering the peculiar lockdown and restrictions, which were forced to be implemented not only in the state or country but across the globe in many countries and continents there were practical difficulties and unavailability of required data and information. Even in places where the data are available it do not permit us to follow as they are not based on the guidelines for measurement of SDP. However, though we have used alternative sources of data, by and large we made a point to follow the computational methodologies as laid down in the guidelines of Government of India.

In this scenario despite of the limitations we attempted to devise methodologies that more or less give an idea of how COVID-19 has impacted the SDP. Measurements like the use of collection of the total goods and services (GST) in the state as a proxy measure to assess the losses in SDP are found to be defective, since these contain productions and should account for the GST due to be collected from the previous year as well. Another possible measure is to make use of the per-day losses in SDP, using the previous year's total SDP and then estimating losses for the number of days for which lockdown in the economy was affected. Yet, both the measures cited are found to be defective. In the first case, it contains the SDP already accounted in the previous year. In the second case, the measure does not completely contain the effect of COVID-19 on the economy for the year, but only the estimates, based on the assumption that the economy ought to have continued to produce as in the previous year, but for the occurrence of COVID-19. Apart from this there can also slowdown in the production process since there can have partial clocures and lockdowns, which drives to a lower estimate than the reality.

Both measures do not account for the real situation or the near-real situation in the state. To find a near-real situation, we have devised a methodology, which could provide a nearby truth of the losses. One should be aware that the measurements in all the sectors of the economy and all the sub-sectors do not behave in the same way. Considering this, we attempted to measure the impact in the sub-sectors of the economy based on the estimated data available and collected from various sources. Data have been collected and published by the Department of Economics and Statistics, Government of Kerala, also have been used effectively to measure the reflections of COVID-19 in the state economy. By and large, we have followed the sub-classifications used in the computation of SDP by the state to maintain comparability.

Estimates on SDP are available only up to the year 2018–19. To make the computation easier and more accurate to the point, we have made a projection for the year 2019–20, based on the growth trend of the previous year, assuming the economy would not reverse in that year as it is known. These estimated figures of SDP during 2019–20 are used as the base for making the COVID-19 impact measurement during 2020–21.[1] Our main aim is to measure the losses due to COVID-19 in the SDP of the year 2020–21 and the losses in the remittance.

As stated, it is not possible to have the estimates from the same source of data for each of the sub-sectors and sectors. Even within the sector, it is very difficult, unless some rationale is followed and different sources are used. The SDP thus computed for the years 2019–20, projection based on earlier growth, assuming that the same rate of growth will be continued, is used. For the year 2020–21, it is estimated based on the quick data collected from secondary and primary sources by the author. The computation in the abstract is presented in Table 8.5.

Primary sector

To measure the effect of Covid-19 on the production of crops, we used data from the Agmark network (Agmarknet.gov.in) of the Government of India for the state of Kerala. Rawal and Verma (2020) also attempted to explore the arrivals of commodities in 1331 *mandi*s during the lockdown period for India as a whole. A study conducted by the Public Health Foundation of India (PHFI) in 12 states found that the farmers, in many cases, stored their commodities since the markets were not functioning in a routine manner. Kerala was not included in the survey by PHFI. Further, in Kerala, too, it was not possible for the farmers to cultivate during the post-monsoon season because of the shortage of labours and fertilizers. Data on marketable surplus for each of the crops for each date and market in the state are available on the web page of Agmarknet.[2] This was extracted for the periods from April to November 2020 and April to October 2019. The difference between market arrivals was taken as the loss due to COVID-19 for 2020–21.[3] The SDP estimated for crops was re-estimated for 2020–21 using the values so arrived at from Agmarknet. It may be noted that this could be the minimum though there can be a larger figure, than the estimates. The restrictions of lockdown in many areas and support systems could have reduced the figure. However this could be the minimum.

The deficiency in market arrivals of agricultural commodities in the state was attributed to either loss of production due to COVID-19 or might not have been sold out in the market since there were problems of transport that

Table 8.5 COVID-19 effect on estimated gross state value added by economic activity at current prices: 2020–21

Base Year 2011–12		*(INR in lakhs)*					
S. N.	*Item*	*GSDP 2019–20(EST)**	*Est. GSDP 2020/21*	*Growth in SDP from 18–19 to19–20*	*% change during 2019–20*	*Covid loss % in SDP*	*Remarks*
1	Agriculture, forestry, and fishing	7,481,704.31	4,666,523.30	8335	0.11	**–37.63**	
1.1	Crops	2,855,456.37	1,970,264.90	–158,192	–5	–0.31	Agrinet data market arrivals+ untimely rain
1.2	Livestock	2,398,991.11	1,655,303.90	114,344	5.28	–0.4	ISS data and MILMA
1.3	Forestry and logging	1,066,157.42	477,851.75	23,904	2.35	–55.18	Estimated from Forest dept.
1.4	Fishing and aquaculture	1,176,316.63	563,102.77	28,279	2.53	–52.13	Estimated from CMFRI (2019) data and primary information on fish landing from CMFRI
2	Mining and quarrying	260,996.40	180,087.51	–52,390	–14.63	–50	Estimation in discussion with Mining and geology
	Primary	7,735,277.08	4,846,610.80	–44,054	–0.56	**–37.34**	
3	Manufacturing	8,523,656.82	5,305,976.40	872,550	13.09	–44	Estimates based on DES data
4	Electricity, gas, water supply and other	1,011,368.98	910,232.08	109,082	14.02	–10	Estimates based on CEA data
5	Construction	10,103,431.12	5,051,715.60	823,808	9.84	–50	estimated based on discussions with builders
	Secondary	19,633,965.88	11,267,924	1,805,440	11.41	**–42.61**	

(*Continued*)

Table 8.5 (Continued)

Base Year 2011–12		*(INR in lakhs)*					
S. N.	*Item*	*GSDP 2019–20(EST)**	*Est. GSDP 2020/21*	*Growth in SDP from 18–19 to19–20*	*% change during 2019–20*	*Covid loss % in SDP*	*Remarks*
6	Trade, repair, hotels, and restaurants	15,121,891.78	11,416,879	1,492,707	12.49		
6.1	Trade and repair services	13,880,872.27	10,757,676	1,387,565	12.7	−23	Estimates based on DES data
6.2	Hotels and restaurants	1,241,553.45	659,202.80	105,142	10.3	−53.095	Estimates based on DES data
7	Transport, storage, and communication	4,727,516.53	2,770,663.20	149,169	3.37		
7.1	Railways	235,732.29	78,593.15	16,812	8.38	−66.66	Estimated from railway data
7.2	Road transport	3,058,889.56	1,794,421.10	84,312	2.92	−58.66	Estimates based on DES data
7.3	Water transport	49,609.35	9,477.45	7292	21.81	−79	Estimates based on DES data
7.4	Air transport	137,178.87	30,179.35	2436	1.84	−78	Est from AAI data
7.5	Services incidental to transport	200,096.19	100,048.09	22,202	14.56	−50	Estimates based on DES data
7.6	Storage	8960.53	5641.9963	1183	18.56	−38	Estimates based on DES data
7.7	Communication and services	1,041,200.54	752,302.10	14,933	1.48	−27.75	Estimates based on DES data
8	Financial services	2,991,065.63	2,535,551.30	215,597	8.48	−15.23	Estimates based on DES data
9	Real estate, and ownership of dwelling	12,900,074.82	4,758,300.10	1,320,191	13.09	−63.12	Estimates based on DES data

10	Public administration	3,021,211.52	3,293,120.60	258,122	10.42	9	Kerala Budget
11	Other services	11,443,643.65	6,549,292.60	1,468,851	17.82	–42.77	Estimates based on DES data
	Tertiary	50,139,803.08	31,323,807	4,904,637	**12.35**	**–37.53**	
12	**Total GSVA at basic prices**	77,398,431.93	47,438,341	6,666,023	**10.52**	**–38.71**	
13	Taxes on Products	10,436,253.93	6,404,176.10	1,357,825	18.17	–38.635	
14	Subsidies on products	714,210.06	1,114,801	16,260	2.39		
15	**Gross state domestic product**	87,086,875.42	52,727,716	8,007,588	11.41	**–39.45**	
16	Population ('00)*	348,388.62	357,267.58	1724	0.5		
17	**Per Capita GSDP (Rs)**	249,970.67	147,586.10	22,088	10.86	–40.96	

Subsidies as% GSVA in 2012–13 2.35

SDP for 2020–21 is 60.5461% of 2019–20

Decline in SDP is 39.45% from previous year

The computations are not strictly according to the Guidelines for computation of National Accounts, which is possible only if real data and measures are available. Indirect methods and alternative estimations are used for quick measurements.

* denotes estimated figures

Source: Computed by the authors based on the latest data available.

had some impact. However, one cannot fully attribute to the transport issue. Transport was not available only for the lockdown period. Even after the lockdown was lifted, there was a shortage of arrivals in the market; hence, it was purely an impact of COVID-19 on agricrops. One possible source of underestimates in crops was that people used the lockdown situation and after for self-cultivation and home-grown use of commodities. This was also attributable to the SDP, but it was short to that extent. Despite all these, it is evident that this was only a negligible quantity. Evidence from data shows that there was a minimum reduction of 31% in the share of crops in the 2020–21 SDP compared to that of the previous year. A similar exercise was conducted in the case of livestock, too, which showed a decline of 40% from that of the previous year. The Integrated Sample Survey (ISS) data available with the Aniumal husbandry Department was used for the estimation during the precovid period. Data collected from the Kerala State Milk Marketing Agency (MILMA) and other agencies were used for estimation of milk and milk products during covid period and was readily available. Since slaughter houses were not functioning there were relatively less production of meat and meat products, only local slaughtering were there and that too was highly limited since the consumers were not dare enough to purchase combined with the covid restrictions. data so obtained was used for estimation of livestock and livestock products.

Information on the revenue receipts received under the forest department, both from logging and for minor forest products, until the end of November 2020 was collected from the Principal Chief Conservator of Forests. The information difference from that of the previous year was computed, and this was attributed to the impact of COVID-19. It worked out to a possible reduction of 55.18% from that of the previous year. Details on fisheries were collected from the Central Marine Fisheries Research Institute (CMFRI), Kochi, on the fish landings in major centres in Kerala for the periods from April 2020 to November 2020. The percentage differences in the landings of fish were worked out for the same periods, and the difference in the same was attributed to the pandemic. Accounting for indegenous fresh water fisheries and hatcheries were also explored, from the Fisheries Department, who were of the opinion that there was not much owing to severe lockdown restrictions. Estimation of the mining and quarrying was conducted based on the discussions with the Mining and Geology Department. Because of stringent restrictions in environmental laws and the restrictions on the movement of vehicles and lockdown, it was estimated that a minimum of 50% reduction was possible in this field. Moreover, the construction activities and real estate were also in a deadlock consequent to COVID-19, where the products of quarrying and mining were largely used. This was reflected in the income generation in the mining and quarrying sector. This approach was followed in the case of the primary sector. In the case of the secondary sector, an altogether different approach was deemed necessary.

Secondary sector

Manufacturing, electricity, gas and water supply, and construction are the constituent components of the secondary sector. Data based on the study conducted by the Department of Economics and Statistics (DES) is available, and it gives a detailed view of the impact of COVID-based lockdown and post-lockdown periods in the secondary and tertiary sectors of the state. Data collected from the field provides us with information on how many percentage of days in each month the manufacturing sector could carry out their work. Loss in operational days in each month is taken as the yardstick for calculating the losses in the manufacturing sector. If one considers the loss in receipts by the units, it comes to (–)44% during the year, whereas if we consider the periods under lockdown and closure due to local regional lockdowns, it comes to about 38% loss for the year.

Regarding electricity, the Central Electricity Authority provides information on the state-wise use of power. The use for the period from April 2020 to November 2020 was compared with the use of the previous year for the same period and we could find that there is only a marginal difference of 7% during 2020–21 compared to that of the previous year. Gas and water are basic necessities; hence, only a marginal decline to the tune of 3% in gas and water supply does not have any significant change. It might be an underestimate; still, we accounted for a 10% reduction altogether in this sub-sector as the impact of COVID-19.

The construction sector faced the deepest slowdown during the period. Based on quick discussions with some of the skilled workers, such as masons, carpenters, builders and painters, we concluded the possibility of a 50% reduction in this sub-sector, though it is possible that the losses could be more. The paucity of materials like cement, steel, iron, and other building materials also contributed to the reduction.

Now we attempt to estimate the sector that provided the largest contribution to economic growth, viz., the services sector.

Tertiary sector[4]

All the service sectors, like trade, hotels and restaurants, transport, railways, airlines, storage, communications, financial services, and real estate, are the components of the tertiary sector. There is no unique methodology that can be applied for making the estimation in all these. Hence, we followed different sources of data and in some cases different methodologies, for arriving at the estimation of losses. To estimate the loss in trade and repair services, we used the data collected and made available by the Department of Economics and Statistics (DES 2020).

Trade and repair services are estimated by adopting the principle of percentage of the number of days in which it could not function for each month, which is available from the survey data. This percentage is taken to estimate the losses, as there is no other acceptable data available. The estimates show the possibility of a decline of 23% minimum from this sub-sector to the SDP for the year 2020–21. Effective trade during these periods could also be low when compared to normal days. Many consumers, particularly in towns and cities, preferred online trading and purchasing of goods through home delivery, since there was no person-to-person contact or crowd. Hotels and restaurants could not function, and if at all they started some activity, there were restrictions on takeaway orders or limited availability of seats for maintaining distance between seats. As for trade, the percentage of days it could not function was taken as the criteria for the calculation of the losses. This is available from the data published by the Department of Economics and Statistics (DES).

For transport and storage, we followed different approaches from different sources. The Indian Railway Board provides data on monthly revenue from both cargo and passenger fares. This is available for each railway zone. The percentage reduction in the Southern Railway Zone in respect of both goods and passengers were aggregated, and the difference between 2020–21 for the period from April to November 2020 and for the same period in 2019 was taken as the losses for the railways. This difference was then adjusted with that of the previous year. Losses on account of road transport and water transport were estimated from the data available from the DES. The percentage number of days in a month could not function for each month was calculated, and their corresponding losses were accounted for the year, assuming if there was no pandemic, at least the return from that of the previous year would have been attained. This was aggregated to form the annual loss and compared with that of the same period in the previous year. The loss from road transport was estimated to be 58.66% as compared to that of 2019–20, and that of water transport was 79% less. Data obtained from the Airports Authority of India (AAI) for each month on passenger traffic and goods traffic was used to find the proportion of losses in air transport in the country. The same proportion was used to estimate the loss for the state too. Services incidental to transport were calculated using the survey data from DES as in the case of other services. There was a loss of 50% on this account. Data obtained from the survey results of DES were used for measuring the contribution of storage, as in the earlier cases on the use of data from DES. It yielded a negative result of a decline of 38% in the value addition from that of the previous year. DES data also provided us with information under the communications sub-sector, and the same was used. It yielded a result of a 27.25% loss compared to that of the previous year. Data on various sub-categories of financial services in the state were also available in the DES publication. The results yield a result that the loss would be to the tune of 15.23% in the financial services. Compared to other sub sectors the reduction in losses in the financial sector could have been because of the increased technological innovation in transactions in the state. The real estate sub-sector faced very high difficulties in the period. DES data provided us with month-wise information on this, and we used these for estimation purposes. The results show that a reduction to the tune of 63.12% is likely to have occurred in this sub-sector. Public administration, as in the case of the earlier years, could foresee a growth of 9%, as the administration during the covid period itself required large amounts, apart from the inflation factor. Data from the DES survey were used to estimate the contribution of other services. It is seen that there was a likely decline of 42.77% in this, too.

As there was an overall decline in almost all sub-sectors of the economy, the consequences of the same would be reflected in the taxes and duties collected from the state. A quick assessment and discussion with the tax authorities reveals that a minimum of 21% decline could be expected from the revenue from taxes. Subsidies, on the other hand, doubled against that of the previous years. To cope with the situation and to avoid hunger and poverty, free ration and other facilities were extended to all the people, irrespective of whether they were or were not under lockdown and ignoring the capability to pay and class of people. Thus, subsidies were assumed to be 2.39%, which was equivalent to the highest accounted in the SDP for 2012–13.

Considering all these, it was seen that the SDP for 2020–21 was likely to be 39.45% less than that of the previous year in current prices. How far this would influence the growth of the economy is estimated further. The reflections of the reduction in remittance from abroad, to the state consequent on the COVID-19 pandemic, which is also one of the important sources of funds for daily spending for the households on consumtion are measured in the next section.

COVID-19 and reduction in international remittances

India, being the largest and topmost recipient of remittances in the world in the recent past, and Kerala, having the major share of migrants to the Middle East and other European and US economies, enjoys a sizeable share of remittances. The COVID-19 pandemic left its scar on all economies of the world, though in varying degrees. It also negatively impacted the income of the migrants in the foreign economy thereby on the share of that income remitted to the host country. COVID-19 affected the migrants in two ways: (i) They lost employment in the foreign economy where they undertake job. At the same time those who were on leave to visit their family in the host country on expiry of their stay-period visa, could not return in time because of the lockdown restrictions, where too the situation had worsened, forcing them to return to their native country, thereby loosing their job. (ii) The forced reductions in wages and salaries in the migrant country has driven the migrants to reduce remittances to their host country. Both the reduction in the salaries in the migrant country and the loss of employment has resulted in returning, large numbers of migrants to their native country as there was no option but to face a catastrophic situation. The reduction in wages because of lockdowns and reduced production, combined with the decline in demand for commodities across the globe because of the restrictions and reduced income in the hands of the people, specifically in oil-producing economies, constrained the economies and reduced the prevailing wages and in many cases could not make prompt payments, quite often forced the migrant workers to return to their home country, leaving everything. Later some of the labourers could not get back their pending wages. This, in turn, reduced substantially the remittance to the host country too.

This was estimated using the following, and its impact on the growth of Kerala was measured. The number of migrants who returned to Kerala was available from the data provided by the State Planning Board. It is as follows from different countries till the end of November 20 as observed in Table 8.6.

Of the total 713,758 returnees, some had to return out of sheer necessity, and a lion's share either lost their jobs or their visa period had expired. They are categorized as given in Table 8.7.

We considered only categories one and two in Table 8.7, for our analysis since there was every possibility that pregnant women and their spouses would likely return at a future date, whereas children and senior citizens were non-earning members and there was no possibility of a loss of remittance, as

Table 8.6 Return of migrants due to COVID-19

Migrant returnees till Nov. 2020		
No.	*Country*	*No. of migrants returned*
1	UAE	390,056
2	Saudi Arabia	98,401
3	Qatar	62,773
4	Oman	64,451
5	Kuwait	33,323
6	Bahrain	25,272
7	USA	6560
8	Other countries	32,922
	Total	713,758

Source: Kerala State Planning Board.

Table 8.7 Categories of migrants and reason for return

No.	*Reason*	*No. of returnees*
1	Loss of job	452,258
2	Visa expiry and others	187,716
3	Children below 10 years	43,024
4	Senior citizens	18,172
5	Pregnant women	10,842
6	Spouses of pregnant women	1746
	Total	713,758

Source: Same as Table 8.6.

in the case of the effective returnees. Data for remittance from abroad in total was available from the studies of Kannan and Hari (2020). Although they are not methodologically as stipulated in the UN System of National Accounts 2008 (UN 2009) or as in Murugan (2018) for the accounting of remittances, in the absence of any other data we used that as the total remittance to the state. This was converted to per capita terms of remittance by using the total number of estimated migrants. Using this per capita, we arrived at the loss for the year 2020–21 due to COVID-19. However, this formed only one part of the story, as this loss constituted the reduction in remittance by way of returnees alone. This is summarized in the following equation.

$LRRM_t = PCR_{t-i} * RM_t$

where $LRRM_t$ = Loss in remittance through Return Migrants in Year "t"

PCR_{t-1} = Per capita remittance of year t–1 and

RM_t = No. of Return Migrants in year t and

$PCR_{t-1} = TRYr_{t-1} / TM_{t-1}$

where TRYrt–1 is the total annual remittance to the country from various sources abroad in the year t–1 and TMt–1 is the total number of migrants serving abroad in year t–1.

The second aspect that needs consideration in the estimation of total loss of remittance is the loss that plausibly emanated from the decline or losses in the wages among migrants still serving in the foreign country. There was a sure possibility of reduction in the total remittance to the state from among those migrants residing abroad, consequent on reduction and loss of wages among them, though they were continuing in the migrant country in anticipation of the fact that the situation might improve in the near future, as the preventive vaccine implementation took off in a big scale. On the other hand, it was also possible that even if they returned, they would not be able to acquire a reasonable job in the host country. Loss from this was estimated using a different approach as stated subsequently.

Further, we had no idea of the extent of the reduction in the wages that were affected in the countries abroad, as it could vary from country to country and under different circumstances. To make a more or less accurate estimation and measurement of this loss, we have devised a methodology as shown subsequently. Since many migrants returned to their host countries, it was certain that there was a likely reduction in the total remittance to the host countries, which, in turn, was reflected in the per capita remittance as well. Besides, the migrant countries were facing a situation of reduction in their growth, rather a negative growth in many countries as opined by the World Bank, IMF, and other UN agencies. Consequently, the employment and wages to the employees were also likely to be affected at least until the situation improved.

In the absence of a clearer picture, we took a proxy. The report of the World Bank and UN Migration and Development Brief No. 33 (Oct-2020),

KONRAD, showed that there might be a negative growth to the tune of 14% in the Middle East. Since the Middle East still constituted a major share of the migrant working population, we reduced that much of 14% in the per capita remittance amount of 2019–20 and attempted to re-estimate the total likely remittance. As many migrants returned and thereby the total declined, we reduced that from the total migrant population. Then, the revised per capita remittance was multiplied with the remaining migrant strength to arrive at the total revised remittance. This was expressed as follows:

> The per capita remittance PCRyt-1 was adjusted to suit for year Yt, current year. The revised per capita remittance during 2020–21 was calculated using the following:
>
> RPCRyt = PCRYt–1 – (PCRYt–1*%LGDPM/100)

where PCRYt is the current per capita remittance from abroad in year t.

LGDPM is the percentage loss in GDP expected in the migrant country (as given in Migration Brief 33).

The total revised remittance was calculated using the RPCRYt. Thus TR, the total remittance in year t to the host country was

TRt = RPCRYt*(TMt–1 – RMt),

where TRt is the total remittance in the host country after adjusting for the COVID-19 impact in the migrant country.

Using the preceding equations, we estimated the total remittance, TR for Kerala in the revised scenario. The total loss by way of remittance to the host country is LRRMt+TRt, i.e. the sum of losses by way of reductions in remittance occurred through the return of migrant labour from abroad to Kerala and the loss in remittance from the migrant country by way of reduction in wages because of the reduction in their GDP owing to COVID-19. The estimates are shown in Table 8.8.

It was expected that substantial losses likely took place as described earlier.

Table 8.8 Estimates on percentage of losses from remittance

No.	*Item*	*Loss in %*
1	Loss due to return migrants	30.1
2	Loss due to reduction in wages abroad and remittance Based on loss of national Income	9
	Total loss	39.1

Source: Author's computation.

Overall effects of COVID-19 on economic growth

The overall effect was the combined weighted average of the effect on economic growth and on international remittances. It was estimated earlier (see "COVID-19 and investment reduction") that COVID-19 reduced the growth of the region by 39.45%. The investment rate corresponding to the reduction was estimated from the trend rate of the capital-output series for the year 2019–20. The trend rate of the ratio was estimated as 63.1%. The corresponding reduction in the investment rate was equal to 39.45% of 63.1 = 24.9%.

The reduction in per capita real international remittances was estimated to be 39.1% (see "COVID-19 and reduction in international remittances"). The overall impact was a weighted average of the growth and remittances effects, the weights taken from the Solow growth equation. The weight for the reduction in growth was 0.47 and for international remittances, it was 0.27, as given by the Robust Regression of the Solow Open Economy Growth Model. The weighted average was given as follows:

$$\text{Overall reduction in growth} = 0.47 * 24.9 + 0.27 * 39.1$$
$$= 22.26$$

This indicates a total reduction of 22.3% in the per capita income in the state.

Table 8.9 shows that the weight of international remittances was more than half of that of investment, and when it came to the weighted contribution, it became almost the same. This indicates that in the economy, the welfare implication of the return migrants was as important as that of the non-emigrants. This reduction in the growth is unlikely to be reflected in the conventional method of estimation of SDP, since there is very heavy shortage of appropriate data to capture the reductions in the generation of production in the economy.

Summary and conclusions

The chapter develops a macroeconomic framework for the measurement of the impact of COVID-19 pandemic on the overall economic growth of the

Table 8.9 Overall impact of COVID-19 on economic growth in Kerala for the 2020–21

Source	*Weight*	*Reduction*	*Weighted reduction*
Investment	0.47	24.9	11.7
International remittances	0.27	39.1	10.56
Overall reduction	–	–	22.3

Source: Sections "COVID-19 and reduction in international remittances" and "Overall effects of COVID-19 on economic growth" and Table 8.4.

sub-national economy of Kerala. The evaluation was based on a modified simple Solow Growth Model for an open economy, determined by the stock of physical capital, and international remittances. The chapter undertook an estimation of the comprehensive growth impact of the regional economy and found a reduction of 39.45% of SDP during the COVID-19 period. During the same period, the reduction in international remittances was about 39.1% due to the slowdown in the economic activity of the Gulf countries, where the migrant population was concentrated, and for the home country, there was job loss of the return migrants. The overall impact depended on the relative contribution of both the components on per capita real output for the COVID-19 period. The growth equation of the region shows that the contribution of physical capital was about 47% and that of international remittances was about 27%. Only the remaining 26% of the growth needed to be accounted for the growth of the regional economy. The investment reduction was estimated from the trend value of the capital-output series in 2019–20 at 22%. The weighted average of the investment reduction and reduction in international remittances shows the reduction of per capita income as 23% during COVID-19 period.

The weight of remittances was more than half that of investment, and when it came to the weighted contribution, it became almost the same. This indicates that in the economy, the welfare implication of the return migrants was as important as the non-emigrants.

Future area of research is the sensitivity analysis of these growth rates. In order to measure the impact of any such shocks in the economy such as, epidemics or war, top priority should be given to develop appropriate methodologies to deal with such exogenous shocks. Methodologies of estimation of GDP should be developed when conventional data sources fail to provide the information required, particularalry by the National Accounts researchers.

Notes

1 These projected estimates are available upon request from the authors.
2 Agmarknet is administered by the Ministry of Agriculture, Government of India.
3 For details on methodology and computation procedures, see Murugan (forthcoming).
4 Please note that it is very difficult and voluminous to describe each of the estimation procedures followed. Hence we have not described each methodology used. As far as possible we have attempted to follow the methodologies of estimation followed by the National Income authorities, but wherever it was not possible we have deviced our own methodologies and data sources.

References

Acemoglu, D. 2009. *Introduction to Modern Economic Growth*. Princeton: Princeton University Press.

Central Marine Fisheries Research Institute (ICAR). 2019. *Marine Fish Landings in India*. Booklet No. 15, Kochi.

Department of Economics and Statistics. *Gross Fixed Capital Formation at State Level*. Thiruvananthapuram: Government of Kerala. http://www.ecostat.kerala.gov.in/images/pdf/publications/State_Income/data/gross_fixed_capital_formation_1112_1516.pdf.

Department of Economics and Statistics. Trivandrum *State Income (Various Issues)*. Thiruvananthapuram: Government of Kerala. http://www.ecostat.kerala.gov.in/index.php/state-income (Accessed 20 January 2021).

Department of Economics and Statistics. 2020. "Impact of COVID-19 in Unincorporated Sector Enterprises in Kerala – A Quick Study Report." Trivandrum.

EPW Research Foundation. 1993. "Domestic Product of States of India." Mumbai.

Government of India. 2015. *Changes in the Methodology and Data Sources in the New Series of National Accounts: Base Year 2011–12*. New Delhi: Ministry of Statistics and Program Implementation.

Gujarati, D. N. 1988. *Basic Econometrics*. 2nd ed. New Delhi: McGraw-Hill Book Company.

Jones, Charles I., and Vollrath, D. 2013. *Introduction to Economic Growth*. 3rd Edition. New York: W. W. Norton & Co.

Kannan, K. P., and Hari, K. S. 2002. *Emigration, Remittances and Their Macro Economic Impact*. Working Chapter No. 328. Thiruvananthapuram: Centre for Development Studies.

Kannan, K. P., and Hari, K. S. 2020. "Revisiting Kerala's Gulf Connection: Half a Century of Emigration, Remittances and Their Macroeconomic Impact, 1972–2020." *The Indian Journal of Labour Economics*. https://doi.org/10.1007/s41027-020-00280-z

Liviatan, N. 1963. "Consistent estimation of distributed lags." *International Economic Review* 4(1): 44–52.

Murugan, G. 2018. "Accounting International Remittance in Gross State Disposable Income (GSDI) of a Sub-National Economy: Some Explorations." *The Journal of Income and Wealth* 40(2). https://doi.org/10.1111/j.1475-4991.1994.tb00061.x

Murugan, G., and Hari, K. S. 2018. *International Remittances External Shock and Economic Growth – Their Influence on a Regional Economy – Kerala*. Thiruvananthapuram: Centre for Development Studies.

Pushpangadan, K. 2003. *Remittances, Consumption and Economic Growth in Kerala: 1980–2000*. Working Chapter No. 343. Thiruvananthapuram: Centre for Development Studies.

Pushpangadan, K. 2012. "Analytics of Migration and Growth: Exploring Kerala's Economic Performance. In *Growth, Development and Diversity: India's Record Since Liberalisation*, edited by K. Pushpangadan and V. N. Balasubramanian, 1–22. New Delhi: Oxford University Press.

Pushpangadan, K., and Murugan, G. 2019. *International Remittances and Economic Growth: A Dynamic Analysis*. Thiruvananthapuram: Gulati Institute of Finance and Taxation.

Rawal, Vikas and Verma, Ankur. 2020. "Agricultural Supply Chains During the COVID-19 Lockdown: A Study of Market Arrivals of Seven Key Food Commodities." SSER Monograph 20/1, Society for Social and Economic Research, New Delhi. http://archive.indianstatistics.org/sserwp/sserwp2001.pdf.

Solow, R. M. 1956. "A Contribution to the Theory of Economic Growth." *The Quarterly Journal of Economics* 70(1): 65–94.

Solow, R. M. 1957. "Technical Change and Aggregate Production Function." *Review of Economics and Statistics* 39(3): 312–20.

United Nations (UN). 2009. *System of National Accounts – 2008*. New York: United Nations and World Bank.

Zachariah, K. C., Mathew, E. T., and Rajan, S. I. 2003. *Dynamics of Migration in Kerala: Dimensions, Differentials, and Consequences*. New Delhi: Orient Black Swan.

Further Reading

Government of India. 2015. *National Accounts Statistics: Manual on Estimation of State and District Income, 2008*. New Delhi: Ministry of Statistics and Program Implementation.

9 Remittances and golden Kerala

The economics of productive consumption or conspicuous consumption?

Sumeetha Mokkil Maruthur

Introduction

All production is for the purpose of ultimately satisfying a consumer.

—John Maynard Keynes, *The General Theory of Employment, Interest and Money*

The term "consumption" was originally derived from the word "consumer", which meant using up and physical exhaustion of matter. Between the seventeenth and twentieth centuries, consumption progressively ceased to mean waste or destruction and instead became something positive and creative. This was because of the economic argument that the purchase of goods and services not only satisfied individual wants but, in the process, also enriched a nation by enlarging the market for producers and investors (Trentmann 2016). Consumption in all societies is an aspect of the political economy of societies. This, in turn, implies that demand for commodities emerges as a function of a variety of social practices (Appadurai 1986). Consumption expenditure is one crucial component of aggregate demand. Keynesian consumption function has modelled consumption to be a simple function of income. Modern consumption theories like the life-cycle hypothesis and permanent income rest on the assumption that individuals always aim to maintain a smooth consumption pattern throughout their lifetimes. So not only disposable income but wealth and expected income also play a role in determining consumption patterns. The assumption of consumer preferences as being exogenous has also been criticized for preventing a full understanding of behaviour and decision-making in the long run. Observed preferences are subject to multiple factors, such as education, advertising, and social groups. From an economic point of view, consumption is often treated as an unproductive activity precisely because durable consumption – although a large part of investment on the part of a household – is not added as investment in national income accounts.

The Indian economy is the largest recipient of remittances in the world. According to a World Bank (2006) study, most remittance-receiving households in India reported receiving these remittances in cash. Among those households reporting receipt of remittances, 82% reported cash, about 15%

DOI: 10.4324/9781003601289-11

checks or drafts, and close to 2% postal money orders. By the mid-1970s, the remittance-fuelled economy had completely altered the consumption landscape of Kerala. As consumption patterns have triggered new analyzes, this chapter tries to explore the relationship between remittances in Kerala and the pattern of gold consumption. The economics of productive consumption is the theoretical base that will attempt to analyze the role of gold in migrant households in Kerala. As of 2020, Kerala emigrants, at 2.12 million, who have an identifiable household to report in Kerala, work out to a little more than 6% of the population but 17%–18% of its workforce. Six countries in the Arabian Peninsula, called Gulf countries (Bahrain, Kuwait, Oman, Qatar, Saudi Arabia, and the United Arab Emirates), accounted for 96.8% of the total emigrants in 1998; it came down to 89.4% in 2018 (Sunny et al. 2020, 21) The emigrants, including semi-skilled and unskilled labourers from Kerala in the Gulf, sending money to family left behind, have used this for building houses, buying consumer durables, and financing other emergencies at home.

Background

India's gems and jewellery sector is one of the largest in the world, contributing 29% to global jewellery consumption. The sector is home to more than 300,000 gems and jewellery players. Its market size is expected to grow by US$ 103.06 billion during 2019–2023 (World Gold Council 2021). India is one of the largest markets for gold, and a remittance-fuelled economy is driving this demand. Gold is considered a store of value, a symbol of wealth and status, and a fundamental part of many rituals. Among the country's rural population, jewellery serves as an investment option as people pawn it to meet unforeseen emergencies. Jeffries (1964) puts forth the argument that gold as a commodity has a double life both because of its use value as a commodity and its monetary value. Emerging markets like India and China account for over 70% of the global gold demand. These countries' purchasing power patterns and consumption behaviour are expected to influence the global gold market in the long run. India added 48.5 tonnes to its gold reserves in 2018–19, thereby increasing its reserves to 608.8 tonnes (India Gold Policy Centre 2019). India is the second-largest importer of gold in the world. The Ministry of Commerce and Industry data suggests that gold is the third biggest item on India's import list and that its share in total imports was 7.2%.

A commodity is, in the first place, an object outside us, a thing that by its properties satisfies human wants of some sort or another (Marx 1971). Gold as a commodity has a unique place in the economic and social milieu of Kerala. The increasing remittances and the existing socioeconomic practices have allowed for the widespread consumption of gold jewellery in Kerala. With the reduction in the migrant flow to the Middle East and the pandemic pressure on Kerala's economy, gold is seen as a major instrument to meet financial needs. This chapter tries to explore the argument that gold can no longer be seen as a luxury item alone. A huge amount of gold in the country is used as collateral for raising funds. Often small business firms survive with the help of these funds. It is also a buffer stock that households use during times of crises. The Inverted Pyramid, presented by John Exter,[1] shows gold as an asset at the bottom of the pyramid with the least risk. The nature of the commodity acting as a hedge against inflation has resulted in remittances being used to buy gold jewellery. Although new financial instruments such as Gold Sovereign Bonds and Gold Metal Loans have been launched in the Indian market, households still prefer gold jewellery purchases, with their social conditions structuring their purchasing preferences. The RBI study in 2017 on Indian Household Debt shows that about 18% of debt in Kerala is in the form of a gold loan, which is the highest for any Indian state (RBI 2017).

Reviewing the literature

Macroeconomic evidence suggests that gold by itself does not add much to the productive capacity. In the early 1990s, household savings including gold averaged around 12.2%, and in the 1980s 14.1%, which increased to 21% by the mid-1990s (Vaidyanathan 1999). Gold is a valuable asset as it mitigates risks and acts as a good store of value. Demand for gold depends on various factors, including price, remittance income, magnitude of black income generated, rate of return on alternate assets, and the general price level. Following the steady flow of remittances to Kerala, the main channels for investing became real estate and gold because of the low rate of returns from bank deposits and migrants' dependence on investment in gold jewellery. Most of the studies in the Kerala context have found that remittances led to higher income for migrant households and poverty reduction, but price increases in real estate, food, consumables, education, and healthcare, all of which, in turn, affected non-migrant households (Prakash 1978). In India, gold behaviour keeps the gold industry buoyant. The case of demonetization in November 2016 illustrates this point. Despite a slowdown in the initial days of demonetization, the gold industry showed signs of recovery within a month, thanks to the wedding season (Kanungo and Chakrabarti 2021)

The literature also deals with the determinants and the impact of Gulf migration on communities and districts in Kerala (Mathew and Nair 1978; Kurian 1979). These studies have extremely relevant findings and stress on migrant remittances being channelized to productive uses. This chapter, however, departs from the usual analysis to understand if remittances changed the consumption pattern of gold in Kerala and if gold could be considered a productive mechanism because of this change.

Gold jewellery purchase is often regarded as conspicuous consumption and as private purchases that do not add to productive capacity in the economy. In Kerala's case, gold jewellery is no longer a luxury item. It is used to finance education, innovation, and small enterprises. Almost all households, irrespective of social status, purchase gold. The growth of NBFCs that provide gold loans is a case in point. Adams (1998) found that in Pakistan the saving propensities out of remittances are higher than those from other sources. Migration and remittances in Kerala have been analyzed in detail in various studies (Kannan and Hari 2002; Zachariah et al. 2003; Pushpangadan 2003; Zachariah, K C and Irudaya, R2005; Sil 2013; Kannan and Hari 2020; Sunny et al. 2020). Remittances into Kerala's economy led to an increase in the demand for consumer durables, which, in turn, led to trade as the domestic sector was not enough to meet the demand (Pushpangadan 2003). Emigrants to the Gulf from Kerala are mostly those of lower socioeconomic status, but they regularly send remittances back home. Contrary to permanent migration, the ties between the Gulf emigrant and his family do not loosen over time (Pelletier 2011, 406).

Earlier studies on the pattern of use of remittances in Kerala (Commerce Research Bureau 1978) show that due to poverty, remittances were used to meet the immediate consumption needs of households. Later, with the start of a steady flow, remittances were allocated to house construction and improvement and diverted to asset purchases like land and gold jewellery. The study also found that the average value of assets of remittance households to be always greater than the average value of assets of other households in Kerala. Mathew and Nair (1978) in their case study of two remittance-receiving villages of Kerala tried to find out how migrant households distributed their newly gained income among the purchase of alternative items. This was seen mainly as expenditure on housing, education, and consumption goods. Radhakrishnan and Ibrahim (1981) showed that at low levels of remittances, the major investment in Kerala is land purchase. With a rise in remittances, there is a shift to the purchase of land, buildings, and jewellery. Zachariah et al. (2003) noted in their study that migrant households exhibited a greater propensity to acquire consumer durables like refrigerators, televisions, and VCRs. They also pointed out the possession of gold jewellery by migrant households, even though gold is regarded as a conspicuous consumption item. The savings rate in the Kerala economy seems to have increased tremendously since the early 1990s. In the Kerala context, much of the savings have gone into house construction, investment in gold, and acquiring financial assets (Kannan and Hari 2020). The revival of the growth in Kerala's economy since the late 1980s, after more than a decade of economic stagnation, brought into prominence the role of remittances. The major findings of a study (Sunny et al. 2020) shows that remittances improved households' per capita income and changed their spending patterns. Households receiving remittances on average spared a relatively larger share of monthly income on the consumption of non-food durable goods. Moreover, receipts of remittances also enabled the households to save; invest more in assets, land, and buildings; and to form human capital (through increased share of spending on education and health).

While the studies investigate the macroeconomic impact of remittances in Kerala economy, they do not analyze how remittances are used in the economy. The consumer culture argument has been discussed in mainstream literature. Although excessive consumption of gold has had its socioeconomic impact in Kerala – for example, the increase in dowry spending – it can now be seen in the context of use in productive channels. Gold as an asset is a useful investment option for the emigrants as it provides them some buffer or security during crises. With remittances to India reducing by nearly 22% due to the COVID-19 pandemic, most dependent families could no longer rely on remittance income alone. The COVID-19 situation has further shown how gold can act as collateral in case of financial distress and how also it could provide loans to start small ventures. International remittances have shown a steady, increasing trend in India, but the question is how these remittances can be channelized and used efficiently.

(i) The chapter thus tries to explore two questions: Have remittances changed the consumption pattern of gold in Kerala?
(ii) Can gold be considered a productive consumption mechanism in this context?

Methodology

The chapter uses KMS 2013 and 2018 data, the NSSO survey for consumer expenditure, the author's field data, and World Gold Council data.

Theoretical framework

According to neoclassical economics, the consumer is oriented on maximizing utility in the sense of a subjective experience, and consumption has effects only in the form of a subjectively perceived experience. The economics of productive consumption, however, considers consumption productive in the sense that it brings substantial income effects. The mechanism of subjectively perceived experience is solely decisive; consumers (the economic subject) maximize the current value of their future income over a long-term timeframe in accordance with their life strategy in the given social conditions. The economics of productive consumption, unlike the standard concept of neoclassical economics, presumes that consuming a series of consumption goods does not suffice solely for satisfying current needs or achieving current utility but has a productive character and is a source of future income (Valencik and Wawrosz 2016).

Economics of productive consumption emphasizes that a large part of human behaviour is related to the future (more or less remotely). People value individual needs as well as objects (resources), activities, and situations by which the given needs are satisfied – returns that will be derived in the future from current consumption (Valencik and Wawrosz, 2016). The theory is rooted in the belief that human behaviour is such that people use their current income to maximize future income. In other words, according to the economics of productive consumption, people act in the creation and operation of their assets (their asset portfolio), which is composed of tangible and financial assets, from human and non-human capital, to maximize the current value of future income. The economics of productive consumption acknowledges that individuals have the ability to relate their current behaviour to all manner of future returns.

Yet, to presume that they do not have them at all, or that people in their decision-making do not take future returns into consideration, or that they take them into consideration only when making decisions about whether to save and how to invest, is not realistic. The neoclassical approach to consumer theory sees individuals as isolated entities and alienates them from the social institutions that guide them. Veblen's conspicuous consumption theory considers the institutional perspective in consumption decisions. He divides consumption into technological and ceremonial (Cosgel 1997). He, therefore, divides consumption as natural and artificial, classifying ceremonial consumption as waste. Dugger (1985) uses Veblen's theory to develop an interdependent utility function, which states that as consumption increases consumers become worse off. According to the concept of "pecuniary emulation" introduced by Veblen in his theory of conspicuous consumption, individuals tend to imitate the consumption habits of other ones, situated at higher positions in the social hierarchy (Memushi 2013). Lietchy (2003) argues that consumption is not an epiphenomenon of middle-class lifestyle but is central to middle-class identities.

Gold jewellery consumption is often regarded as pecuniary, as it is often wasteful expenditure. But if we see it as productive consumption because it provides a future flow of income, the gold considered "wasteful" can be used to maximize future returns. Also, as a store of value, it can enhance the productive capacity of individuals.

Golden Kerala

Historically, gold jewellery consumption in Kerala was restricted to the landed aristocracy and royalty. Each locality had a goldsmith who fulfilled their demands, and thus the extent of the market was limited. The past restrictions on the usage of gold and jewellery contributed to their current lavish use, as those who were formerly denied these ornaments enthusiastically purchase and wear them. Jewellery designs said to be traditionally *Nayar* or *Brahman* are especially popular (Osella and Osella 1999, 1004). The inflow of Gulf remittances from the early 1970s and the elevation of the status of gold as a secure investment option was a boost to jewellery consumption in the state.

The cultural, religious, and social norms placed on gold made it a prized possession for all kinds of consumers. The consumer market has expanded to other states in India, where retail houses from Kerala have ventured out to open new outlets. Dowry in Kerala involves transfer of land, gold, cash, household appliances, and cars from the bride's family to the groom's. The last decade has seen an increase in gold being given as dowry.

By the mid-1990s, there was an effort to expand these operations outside the country. Kerala-based retailers have shifted to the policy of opening new, sophisticated retail outlets in the Middle East. Since the estimated number of emigrants in the Middle East was around 23.63 lakhs in 2014 (KMS 2013), this move is seen as a step to cater to the demands of the expatriate population in the Middle East. Consumers' purchase of gold jewellery has been entirely manipulated by the utilization of eloquent space, by attributing gold jewellery an ethereal charm, and by offering a wide array of designs (Sumeetha 2017). The erosion of trust in the neighbourhood goldsmith and the manipulation of consumer choices by large retailers have substantially increased the universal demand for gold jewellery. Kerala's lightweight jewellery is also in demand in global markets with consumers preferring lightweight ornaments due to the rising price of gold. Trissur district in Kerala is a centre for manufacturing lightweight jewellery.

The marketing of gold jewellery up to the mid-1960s was direct and involved a simple transaction between the artisan and the customer. The artisan would directly take orders from the customer and complete the work. It was a lengthy process and hence took time. The artisan directly marketing finished jewellery to customers is at present a rarity in Kerala. The erosion of trustworthiness of the local *thattan* (goldsmith) and the demand for a diverse set of designs at short notice prompted the industry to rechannelize its marketing (Sumeetha 2020). Some consumers depend on the direct service of the goldsmith even now, especially for traditional ornaments.

Access to the market, however, is beset with difficulties. Most independent and subcontracting units depend on wholesalers to market finished jewellery. A variety of ornaments made by these production units are supplied to the wholesaler. The wholesaler finds sets of retailers who demand various kinds of jewellery. Independent small retailers, who have their own production units, also engage in marketing. Their market share has been dwindling over the years and most of these retailers have now completely shifted their role from being independent producers to becoming wholesalers in the industry. The increasingly popular method of large retailers controlling the entire market chain and winning over consumers has become more prevalent since the mid-1990s.

The emigration of workers from Kerala to the Middle East since the late 1970s has fuelled a consumption boom in the state. The remittances sent by these workers are extensively used to purchase gold jewellery (Rajan 1988). Stark (1991) puts forward the "the implicit co-insurance" approach in which he shows us that remittances are part of the family's risk reduction strategy as they tend to diversify their sources of income. Stahl and Arnold (1986) notes the substantial contribution of remittances to economic development in Asian countries. Their view is that remittances provides a major source of foreign exchange, increase household income, and can be used for investment in education, healthcare, and other productive activities. Cash and gold consumption have a gendered association. In a patriarchal setup, as women are traditionally marginalized in terms of inheritance, they logically try to invest in something non-controversial and socially acceptable, such as purchasing gold jewellery (Mehrotra 2004, 34). Remittances have led to an increase in cash flows and gold purchases – gold is especially associated with women, while cash appears especially linked with men (Osella and Osella 1999). Jewellery is preferred as a form of saving, as it is less liquid than cash but serves the purpose of holding money. The choice of Middle East-based Kerala industrialists to invest in gold has prompted the expansion of gold retailing within the state.

Beyond its sheer size, India's jewellery market is diverse – heavy, chunky 22k chains are common in Kerala while lighter, bejewelled pieces are popular in Rajasthan. It depends on the culture and practices followed in different parts of India. While there is diversity in gold jewellery pieces, the purchasing pattern also varies across states in India. The southern region accounts for around 40% of all of India's demand. Southern India dominates India's gold jewellery consumption, accounting for nearly 40% of the total volume (World Gold Council 2019).Policy regulations like hall marking of jewellery has increased trust in gold purchases (World Gold Council, 2023). As per NSSO 68th Round, per capita gold consumption is the highest in southern India (NSSO 2018).

With the abolition of the Gold Control Act and the opening up of Indian gold bullion imports, the deregulation of the gold jewellery industry in the 1990s changed the role of NRIs in the jewellery industry. Prior to its abolition, NRIs were the main carriers of gold into the country, both officially and otherwise. Broad estimates put the supply of gold from NRIs during the 22 years of the Gold Control Act (GCA) regime at around 1000 tonnes (World Gold Council 2019). The NRI scheme, introduced in 1992, permitted returning NRIs to import up to 5 kg of gold bars and other approved gold items if they had been away for at least six months. After 1997, the allowance was increased to 10 kg. Between 1992 and 1997, NRIs brought in around 1300 tonnes. With the introduction of the Open General Licence (OGL) scheme in 1997, the dependence on NRIs for bringing gold reduced. The OGL allowed 20 banks and four public sector bodies to import gold. By 2001, 99% of gold imported into India was through the OGL scheme. Following these regulatory changes, NRIs changed themselves into gold consumers. India's global diaspora and the rise in incomes earned in countries like the United States, the United Kingdom, and the Middle East became important drivers of gold demand (World Gold Council 2019).

The removal of restrictions on the import of gold led to large-scale investment into the sector. In Kerala, most investors venturing into the gold industry were NRIs, who opened large retail outlets offering a wide array of designs and variety to customers. The Malabar Gold group, Alukkas, and Kalyan group, all of which had modest beginnings in the early 1990s, have grown into enormous business conglomerates. In the early 1990s, retail houses largely depended on independent workshops to meet their production needs. Work orders were urgent and demanding. By the mid-1990s, workshops that exclusively produced machine-made jewellery began operations in Kerala. These units facilitated bulk production that minimized wastage of gold and saved production time. More recently, the state has witnessed a spurt in machine-made units with sophisticated machinery for stone setting. The scale and spread of different kinds of production units have been rapid due to policy changes. In the first decade of liberalization, numerous independent workshops supplied a variety of designs to the retail outlets, giving goldsmiths an opportunity to revive their traditional work. But after ten years of liberalization, unabated supply of labour overshot the industry's actual requirement. From early 2000 onwards, most small workshops have become appendages to large retail houses. Thus, retail houses have successfully extended an indirect control mechanism to regulate production structures and arrangements. Workshops increasingly relied on the division of labour and streamlining workers into narrower specializations. The retail gold market became highly competitive, and this altered the nature of production in the industry.

The NRIs find their own hometowns as excellent places to buy gold. They look for intricate designs, vintage craftsmanship, and prefer Indian gold due to lower taxes and labour charges. Jewellers in states with large NRI populations – Punjab, Gujarat, Maharashtra, Telangana, Andhra Pradesh, Karnataka, Tamil Nadu, and Kerala – believe that NRIs make up between 10% and 20% of their sales (World Gold Council 2019). A sudden hike in NRIs purchasing gold jewellery occurs during festivals (Diwali, Ramzan, or Christmas), as many return home to celebrate with their families. Higher taxes levied on gold during 2013–14 hit this market, with many NRIs deciding to buy elsewhere. For example, a rise in 22-carat hallmarking in the United Kingdom was reflective of NRIs choosing to buy in the country rather than India.

Demand for gold jewellery in the southern states is linked to the relatively high levels of wealth in these states. Kerala and Tamil Nadu, for example, have lower than average poverty levels and have higher than average per capita income, and both benefit from strong NRI demand. Much of household spending goes beyond conversion into prestige for the immediate benefit of the current household; it can be seen as investment in the long-term improvement of the family (Osella and Osella 1999, 1014). Southern India, predominantly a 22-carat traditional, handmade market, remains the most diverse marketplace in the country. About half of the gold mined at present is converted into jewellery. Heavy floods and incessant rains in the important gold-buying centres of Kerala during July and August 2018 negatively impacted gold demand, and jewellers in the region reported negligible sales during Onam (the harvest festival of Kerala). But demand slowly picked up with marriages during the quarter, helping to tide over the crisis period. While the price dip in August was a helpful boost to the industry, it highlighted a structural challenge jewellers face. Retailers' main strategy for generating sales has been to compete on price. Huge retailers in Kerala pursue the aggressive strategy of signalling through advertisements. For example, they offer price discounts, advanced booking facilities, bulk order discounts, lightweight special collections, etc., to capture the imagination of the large emigrant population.

Worker remittances can be seen as a strategy to diversify sources of income and as type of insurance policy to provide a safety net during an economic downturn (Hunte 2004,86). Kerala and Tamil Nadu saw higher reportage of using remittances towards debt repayment, possibly due to the debts incurred in overcoming the high transaction costs of migrating to the Gulf and higher income levels in these states require less expenditure on household items (Tumbe 2011). India is the largest recipient of international remittances and hosts the second-largest domestic remittance market in the developing world. The share of expenditure on gold has risen sharply in both rural and urban parts of the country between 2004–05 and 2011–12, the survey shows. On the other hand, the spending trend on real estate in this duration has revealed that the proportionate share of expenditure on residential buildings was down by almost half. Kerala has the highest monthly per capita expenditure (MPCE) on gold ornaments among all Indian states, according to an NSSO survey (NSSO 2015). Kerala is the top consumer of gold in the country: rural Kerala's per capita expenditure on gold is INR 208.55, while for urban Kerala, it is INR 189.95 (NSSO 2015). The KMS surveys (2013, 2018) suggest the investment portfolio of households receiving remittances consists of shares, mutual funds, gold jewellery, capital investment, land, buildings, other construction, livestock, and others. Households with return emigrants and those with emigrants in the Gulf tend to hold gold jewellery worth 3.5 lakhs (average stock). Non-migrant households also spend money on gold jewellery as a preferred investment option for the household. For migrant households, the portfolio has been diversified into shares and land acquisition.

Gold demand trends show that gold exchange-traded funds (ETFs) are a preferred source of investment over the last year. But the more educated and highly skilled migrants invest in ETFs.

The pandemic and gold

With the easing of lockdown restrictions from September 2020, and a reported steady reduction in COVID-19 daily cases, some positive signals of domestic economic recovery came through in the last quarter of 2020

(World Gold Council 2021). When the domestic prices stabilized, the recovery was faster. With restrictions being eased and the announcement of new vaccines, consumer sentiment improved. The Reserve Bank of India's Consumer Confidence Index increased from 49.9 in September 2020 to 52.3 in November 2020. To enable an understanding of the economy recovering slowly, goods and sales tax revenues reached a record high of INR 1.15 trillion in December – the highest since the introduction of the tax was in 2017. Gold jewellery retailers in Tier 2 and Tier 3 cities,[2] where economic activity is more dependent on agricultural and allied activities, reported better volume sales in the last quarter of 2020. Although jewellery consumption declined during the pandemic, the steady increase in sales indicates that gold is no longer a luxury commodity, and people were trying to reopen or restart small businesses post-pandemic. They raised urgent funds by taking gold loans – the most convenient and quickest option that does not require a credit check. For small business owners, gold makes for the most preferred collateral because of minimized procedural delays. Consumption offers the chance to make hard-earned money work twice in the act of spending economic capital as it is simultaneously publicly displayed and converted into symbolic capital (Osella and Osella 1999, 1004).

The new online purchases of gold, especially an active digital gold market on e-commerce retail sites post-August 2019, are also indicative of a robust gold market. A challenge facing India's gold industry is that some of the transactions are through illegal channels. Some sections engaged in gold trade have benefited from anonymity and a lack of transparency on price, purity, taxes, and supply sources. While still highly fragmented, the industry is becoming more organized, and retailers with large regional and national chains are gaining market share. The government has also made hallmarking for gold mandatory, ensuring the safety of consumers.

Two crucial determinants of gold demand are prices and the consumer's income. Demand responds more to income than it does to price. This helps explain why gold demand increased from around 700 tonnes in 2000 to around 1000 tonnes in 2010, despite a dramatic increase in the gold price over the period. The impact of the 137% increase in the rupee gold price was outweighed by the 78% increase in per capita income (World Gold Council 2021). The responsiveness to income, therefore, is much larger to that than price. In the ICE 360° Survey (2014), 93% of respondents said jewellery shops were their preferred point to buy bars and coins. Gold's accessibility through the nationwide network of jewellers in urban and rural areas is one of its strengths. Also, the low rate of banking penetration in India makes gold a preferred investment option. Buying gold gives the purchaser a notion of attaining financial security and saving for a daughter's marriage, though its returns are unclear (ICE 360° Survey 2014, 549).

With all these factors and digital gold being given a push, the industry is set to be on a recovery path. Return migrants who have faced job losses depend largely on the gold jewellery they have accumulated over the years to tide over the crisis. Gold jewellery, although ingrained in the culture of Kerala, has far-reaching economic implications that need further exploration. Consumption no longer is about just purchasing goods, it also reflects power and meaning.

Notes

1 American economist, member of the Board of Governors of the United States Federal Reserve System, and founder of the Central Bank of Sri Lanka.
2 The Reserve Bank of India's population-based classification of Indian cities categorises Tier 2 cities as those with a population of 50,000 to 99,999 and Tier 3 as those with 20,000 to 49,999 people.

References

Adams, R. H., Jr. 1998. "Remittances, Investment, and Rural Asset Accumulation in Pakistan." *Economic Development and Cultural Change* 1998: 155–73.
Appadurai, A. (ed.). 1986 *The Social Life of Things: Commodities in Cultural Perspective*. New York: Cambridge University Press.
Commerce Research Bureau. 1978. "Inward Remittances in Kerala." *Commerce* December 9: 976–80.
Cosgel, M. 1997. "Consumption Institutions." *Review of Social Economy* 55(2): 153–71.
Dugger, W. 1985. "The Analytics of Consumption Externalities." *Review of Social Economy* 43(3): 212–33.
Hunte, C. K. 2004. "Workers, Remittances, Remittance Decay, and Financial Deepening in Developing Countries." *The American Economist* 48(2): 82–94.
ICE 360° Survey. 2014. *National Survey on Indian Consumers Middle India: Key to Inclusive Growth and a Prosperous Future India (Wave1.0)*. New Delhi: PRICE.
India Gold Policy Centre. 2019. "5th Annual Report." Ahmedabad, IIM Ahmedabad.
Jeffries Zay. 1964. "Gold." *Proceedings of the American Philosophical Society* 108(5): 437–42.
Kannan, K. P., and Hari, K. S. 2002. *Kerala's Gulf Connection: Emigration, Remittances and their Macroeconomic Impact, 1972–2000*. Working Chapter No: 328. Thiruvananthapuram: Centre for Development Studies.
Kannan, K. P., and Hari, K. S. 2020. "Revisiting Kerala's Gulf Connection: Half a Century of Emigration, Remittances and their Macroeconomic Impact, 1972–2020." *The Indian Society of Labour Economics* 63(4): 941–67.
Kanungo, S., and Chakrabarti, A. 2021. Gold Governance and Goldsmithery: Economic Sociology of an Informal Manufacturing Sector in India." *Contributions to Indian Sociology* 55(2): 172–99.
Kerala Migration Survey (KMS). 2013. Thiruvananthapuram: Centre for Development Studies.
Kerala Migration Survey (KMS). 2018. Thiruvananthapuram: Centre for Development Studies.
Kurian, R. 1979. "Patterns of Emigration from Kerala." *Social Scientist* 7(6): 32–53.
Liechty, M. 2003. *Suitably Modern: Making Middle-Class Culture in a New Consumer Society*. Princeton: Princeton University Press.
Marx, K. 1971. *Theories of Surplus Value* (Pt. 3). Moscow: Progress.

Mathew, E. T., and Nair, P. R. G. 1978. "Socio Economic Characteristics of Emigrant Households – A Case Study of Two Villages in Kerala." *Economic and Political Weekly* 13(28): 1141–53.
Mehrotra, Nilika. 2004. "Gold and Gender in India: Some Observations from Southern Orissa." *Indian Anthropologist* 34(1): 27–39.
Memushi, Amando. 2013. "Conspicuous Consumption of Luxury Goods: Long Run Theoretical and Empirical Evidences." *International Journal of Scientific and Engineering Research* 4(12): 250–55.
NSSO. 2015. *Household Consumption of Various Goods and Services in Kerala, NSS 66th Round 2009–10*. Thiruvananthapuram: Directorate of Economics and Statistics.
NSSO. 2018. *Household Consumption Expenditure, NSS 68th Round, July 2011–12*. India: MOSPI.
Osella, F., and Osella, C. 1999. "From Transience to Immanence: Commodities, Life Cycle and Social Mobility in Kerala, South India." *Modern Indian Studies* 33(4): 989–1020.
Pelletier, A. 2011. "Household Remittances, Inequality and Poverty: Evidence from the State of Kerala." In *Dynamics of Indian Migration: Historical and Current Perspectives*, edited by Irudaya Rajan and Marie Percot. New Delhi: Routledge.
Prakash, B. A. 1978 "Impact of Foreign Remittance: A Case Sstudy of Chavakkad Village." *Economic and Political Weekly* 13(27): 1107–11.
Pushpangadan, K. 2003. *Remittances, Consumption and Economic Growth in Kerala, 1980–2000*. Working Chapter No. 343. Thiruvananthapuram: Centre for Development Studies.
Radhakrishnan, C., and Ibrahim, P. 1981. "Emigration, Inward Remittances, Economic Development (with particular reference to Emigration from Kerala to the Gulf countries)." *Manpower Journal* 16(40): 15–52.
Rajan, D. 1988. *Report on the Survey of Utilisation of Gulf Remittances in Kerala*. Thiruvananthapuram: CDC.
Reserve Bank of India (RBI). 2017. *Indian House Finance: Report of the Household Finance Committee*. New Delhi: RBI.
Sil, M. 2013. "Remittances to India: Performance, Relative Stability and Current Research Concerns." In *India Migration Report 2013*, edited by Irudaya Rajan. New Delhi: Routledge.
Stahl, W. C., and Arnold, F. 1986. "Overseas Workers Remittances in Asian Development." *The International Migration Review* 20(4): 899–925.
Stark. 1991. *The Migration of Labour*. Cambridge: Basil Blackwell Inc.
Sumeetha, M 2017 "Exploring the Capital –Labour Dynamics: Migrants in the Gold Jewellery Making Industry in Kerala, India." In *India Migration Report 2017: Forced Migration*, edited by Irudaya Rajan. New Delhi: Routledge.
Sumeetha, M. 2020. "Labour Process in Migration." In *Handbook of Internal Migration in India*, edited by Irudaya Rajan and Sumeetha Mokkil. New Delhi: Sage.
Sunny, J., Parida, J. K., and Azurudeen, M. 2020. "Remittances, Investment and New Emigration Trends in Kerala." *Review of Development and Change* 25(1): 5–29.
Trentmann, F. 2016. *Empire of Things*. London: Penguin.
Tumbe, C. 2011. "Remittance in India: Facts and Issues." Research Chapter, IIM Bangalore, No. 331.
Vaidyanathan, A. 1999. "Consumption of Gold in India: Trends and Determinants." *Economic and Political Weekly* 34(8): 471–76.
Valencik, R., and Wawrosz, P. 2016. "Economics of Productive Consumption as an Offshoot of Main Currents of Economic Theory." *ACTAVSFS Journal* 13(2): 113–34.

World Bank Survey. 2006. *Global Economic Prospects: Economic Implications of Remittances*. Washington: World Bank.
World Gold Council. 2017. *India's Gold Market, Evolution and Innovation*. World Gold Council Report. Mumbai: World Gold Council.
World Gold Council. 2021. *Gold Demand Trends Full Year: 2020*. World Gold Council Report. Mumbai: World Gold Council.
World Gold Council. 2023. *India's Gold Market: Reform and Growth*. Mumbai: World Gold Council Report.
Zachariah, K. C., and Irudaya, R. 2005. *Unemployment in Kerala at the Turn of the Century: Insights from CDS Gulf Migration Studies*. Working Chapter No. 374. Thiruvananthapuram: Centre for Development Studies.
Zachariah, K. C., Mathew, E. T., and Irudaya R., eds. 2003. *Dynamics of Migration in Kerala: Dimensions, Differentials and Consequences*. New Delhi: Orient Blackswan.

10 Economic impact of lockdown on common people in Kerala

A survey report

Surajit Das and Soni T. L.

Introduction

The Government of India imposed a country-wide lockdown on 24 March 2020 in response to the Coronavirus (COVID-19) outbreak. We conducted a telephonic survey in Kerala in July 2020, three months after the first lockdown, to understand its economic impact on the common people. The survey was telephonic because any direct field visit for a primary survey was impossible under the circumstances and a huge health risk at the time. The sample size was 480 households comprising 2056 people from various locations in Kerala. In this anonymous survey, we posed questions about the pre- and post-lockdown income and expenditures of the households; indebtedness and coping strategy in the face of income loss; future expectations; and the benefits from the PM Garib Kalyan Yojana (PMGKY – subsequently made part of the Atmanirbhar Bharat Abhiyan package). In the absence of any other more reliable data based on a more scientifically designed larger sample survey, our study highlights the ground-level situation after the first three months of lockdown.

In the first three months of the first lockdown, the employment and livelihood of an overwhelming majority of workers took a huge hit, with massive uncertainty looming over their immediate foreseeable future (Jha and Kumar 2021). However, the summary results of the Periodic Labour Force Survey (PLFS) data of 2019–20 (including the first three months – April–June 2020 – of lockdown) do not reflect that while reporting a decline in the unemployment rate and an increase in the work participation rate. Kannan and Khan (2022) have argued that the category of self-employment is a default sector for a significant segment of people to earn a living. "The low per capita earnings in self-employment – lower than even the wages of the casual workers – is an indicator of this survival sector" (Kannan and Khan 2022). Therefore, the overall measurement of employment and unemployment rates that includes the category of self-employment initially may seem counterintuitive. Anand and Thampi (2021) used the same PLFS 2019–20 data to argue that the lockdown quarter saw a substantial increase in the category of employed labour force with zero income. This data also suggested a significant decline in the labour force participation rate (LFPR,

DOI: 10.4324/9781003601289-12

mainly for the female labour force) during the same quarter compared to the average of the three-quarters.

Several studies have also attributed this fall in LFPR to the "discouraged" worker effect, i.e., the lockdown and the ensuing socio-economic crisis likely discouraged workers in that those "who are willing to secure a job but have stopped job searches" (Roychowdhury et al. 2022). Further, the issue is particularly vexing for the female labour force. The pandemic exacerbated the impact on women LFPR vis-à-vis men as a higher burden of unpaid care and household work fell on women during lockdowns across the globe (International Labour Organization 2022). Placing the COVID-19 at the centre of the job crisis, the International Labour Organization (2021) suggested that the pandemic had "severely affected labour markets around the world, hurting young people more than other age groups".

A primary survey to study the impact of COVID-19 on livelihoods in India found that around two-thirds of the respondents reported employment loss during the lockdown and those employed witnessed a sharp decline in earnings (Kesar et al. 2021). A survey conducted by Azim Premji University (2021) in India also found that women and younger workers were hit particularly hard both in terms of loss of work and the ability to re-enter the labour market. It found that significant losses of income forced households to sell assets or borrow even for daily consumption or health expenditure (Azim Premji University 2021). As pointed out earlier, the lockdown also took a heavy toll on Kerala households (Das and Soni 2020). Our survey of 15 Indian states during 2020–21 estimated that 72% of families received free ration, 25% had some direct benefit transfers made to their Jan-Dhan accounts, and 23% received free cooking gas cylinders as promised under the Atmanirbhar Bharat Abhiyan package. These average numbers (of 15 states) varied widely from state to state (Das 2022b).

Respondents' characteristics

We talked to 135 female and 345 male respondents aged between 18 and 75 years. They were chosen from diverse occupational backgrounds and locations from the available phone numbers. Of these, 90 were school dropouts, 153 had completed their tenth standard, 97 their twelfth standard, 86 were graduates, 30 were professionally qualified, and 24 were post-graduates or had higher educational qualifications. The religious composition of the respondent families was as follows: 50 Muslim, 89 Christian, 334 Hindu, and 7 others. The caste composition of the households was: 5 scheduled tribe (ST), 56 scheduled caste (SC), 258 other backward caste (OBC), and the remaining 159 from the other, unreserved (UR), or general (GEN) caste backgrounds. Among the respondents were 9 NRI families from Dubai, Kuwait, Bahrain, UAE, Oman, Riyadh, Lebanon, and Muscat, and 8 migrant families from Karnataka, Tamil Nadu, Maharashtra, Chhattisgarh, etc., in our sample.

As mentioned earlier, the respondents were from diverse occupational backgrounds, including AC mechanics, academicians, accountants, agro-businessmen, *anganwadi* workers, auditors, autorickshaw drivers, bankers, beauticians, business persons, car mechanics, carpenters, caterers, clerks, cooks, coolies, construction workers, contractors, daily-wage earners, data entry operators, designers, domestic help, drivers, electricians, farmers, fabric workers, factory workers, fashion designers, fishermen, fitters, flooring workers, footwear sellers, fruit sellers, gas suppliers, glass workers, government employees, homemakers, hotel employees, housekeepers, house painting workers, journalists, laboratory workers, librarians, managers, machine operators, mechanics, medical representatives, merchants, MGNREGS workers, mobile repairing workers, nurses, peons, petrol pump employees, pharmacists, photographers, plumbers, priests, private sector employees, researchers, restaurant workers, rubber tappers, shopkeepers, sales girls and boys, software engineers, students, supervisors, tailors, teachers, technicians, temple employees, textile employees, traders, toddy tappers, temple employees, vegetable vendors, welders, and workshop employees.

Sample characteristics

Of the 14 districts in Kerala, the sample households belonged to various locations across seven districts (Thrissur, Kozhikode, Wayanad, Malappuram, Kottayam, Ernakulam, Alappuzha, and Thiruvananthapuram). The families were from Akkikavu, Alapad, Alapuzha, Alathur, Aloor, Aluva, Ambalavayal, Amballur, Ambalore, Anandapuram, Anchelpetty, Anchery, Anjoor, Annalloor, Anthikad, Arattupuzha, Arimpur, Anthimahakalan, Avanoor, Avinissery, Calicut, Chalakudy, Chavakkad, Chelakkara, Chembankunnu, Chembuthra, Chenchengaloor, Chengaloor, Kizkkedath, Chengannur, Cherakekood, Cheroor, Cherpu, Cheruchenam, Cheruthurethy, Chettuva, Chirakkakode, Chittanjoor, Chittissery, Edamuttam, Edavilangu, Elanad, Enamakkal, Eravimangalam, Ernakulam, Irinjalakuda, Kachery, Kadalassery, Kadavallur, Kalathode, Kallettumkara, Kallur, Kalpetta, Kanippayyur, Kaniyamangalam, Kanjiramuck, Kannapuram, Kannara, Kannimangalam, Kannur, Karikulam, Karumathra, Karuvanchal, Karuvannur, Karyamattom, Kattakampal, Kavu, Kechery, Manakody, Kilinikadavu, Kiliyinikadavu, Kizhakkumpaattukkara, Kodakara, Kodaly, Kodunga, Kodungallur, Kolangattukara, Kolathur, Kolazhy, Kollangattukara, Koorkenchery, Koottala, Koramkulam, Koratty, Kottala, Kottapuram, Kottayam, Kanjirappally, Kottekad, Kozhukkully, Kunnamkulam, Kurukkanjeri, Kurumpilavu, Kurumpilavu, Kuthampully, Kuttanellur, Kuttumuck, Kuttur, Laloor, Madakkathara, Mala, Mambra, Kottala, Kottapuram, Kottayam, Kanjirappally, Kottekad, Kozhukkully, Kunnamkulam, Kurukkanjeri, Kurumpilavu, Kurumpilavu, Kuthampully, Kuttanellur, Kuttumuck, Kuttur, Laloor, Madakkathara, Mala, Mambra, Meppadi, Moorkanikkara,

Mudikkodu, Mukkatukara, Mukkola, Mulavukadu, Mullakara, Mullassery, Mundathicode, Mundoor, Mupliyam, Murikkungal, Muriyad, Muthuvara, Nandipulam, Narokkavu, Nedupuzha, Nellangara, Nellayi, Nenmanikkara, Nettissery, Nilambur, Nooluvally, North Chellanam (Kochi), Ollur, Oorakam, Padukkad, Palakkad, Palappuram, Palazhy, Paliyekkara, Pallimoola, Pallippuram, Panamukku, Paravattani, Pattambi, Pattepadam, Pazhanji, Pazhayannur, Pazhayi, Pazhuvil, Peechi, Peramangalm, Perambra, Perinjery, Ponganamkad, Ponjanam Kattoor, Ponnukkara, Poovathumkadavu, Pottore Minipark, Poyya, Pozhuthana, Pulakode, Pullur, Puranatukara, Puthoor, Puttore, Ramavarmapuram, Thalicode, Thallur, Thalore, Thannikudam, Thannyam, Thayyur, Thazhe Sambarkode, Thekkumkkara, Thiroorangadi, Thiruvananthapuram, Thiruvangoor, Tholanur, Thozhiyoor, Thrikkur, Urokad, Vadakkenchery, Vallachira, Vallarkavu, Vaniampara, Varaakara, Varadiyam, Varandharappilly, Vazhani, Vazhukkumpara, Veeranchira, Velappaya, Vellakkarithadam, Vellanikkara, Vellithiruthi, Velupadam, Veluthur, Villadam, Viyur, Wadakkanchery, Wandoor, and Wayanad.

The average monthly income of these 480 households was around INR 20,500 before the lockdown. The monthly per capita income of one-fourth of the families was less than INR 1875, that of another one-fourth was INR 1875 to less than INR 3750, for yet another one-fourth, it was INR 3750–INR 6000, and from above INR 6000 to INR 80,000 per month for the remaining families. Therefore, this implies that the per capita income of three-fourth of the families was less than or equal to INR 6000 and one-fourth of the families was higher than that before the lockdown. The average pre-lockdown per capita monthly income of the unreserved, general caste category households was INR 5125. The same for the OBC and SC households was INR 4677 and INR 3282, respectively. The per capita family income of Christian, Hindu, and Muslim families before the lockdown was INR 6002, INR 4612, and INR 3612, respectively. However, it is important to mention here that our sample may not be representative of the entire population of Kerala as the sampling technique is not random sampling in a strict sense.

The questionnaire

The survey involved anonymous telephonic interviews. Considering attention span is relatively shorter in a telephonic survey and most respondents were under tremendous distress due to the lockdown, we kept the questionnaire short and precise. Included among the 36 questions we asked were the respondents' age, gender, educational qualification, the family's caste (SC, ST, OBC, or general caste category), their religion (Christian, Muslim, or Hindu), occupation, place of work, and place of origin. We also sought information from respondents on the number of family members and working members gender-wise, pre- and post-lockdown individual and family income, and pre- and post-lockdown family expenditures. We then calculated the per capita pre- and post-lockdown income and expenditures of each of the 480 households on the basis of this information and, subsequently, the change in income and expenditure due to the lockdown.

We asked questions on whether indebtedness had risen because of the lockdown as a coping strategy, whether the respondents decided to continue in the same profession, and about their expected income in the next six months from July 2020. We also asked them whether their families had received free rations, free cooking gas cylinders, and some money in their Jan-Dhan accounts as promised in the PMGKY. Our sample had a huge urban bias with very little reach in the rural areas because of the unavailability of phone numbers; however, we sought information on their possession of MGNREGS job cards. We asked migrant workers whether they wanted to go back to their native places. We also asked whether any member of the family was suffering from an ailment other than COVID-19 and whether they faced any treatment issues because of the lockdown from April through June 2020. We not only asked whether staying at home was otherwise comfortable aside from the income loss but also sought their opinion on the need for an urban employment guarantee scheme in the country and their suggestions to the government and comments on the overall situation. The Results section summarizes the respondents' answers.

The results

The average monthly income of these 480 families became almost halved (52%) because of the lockdown. Only 72 out of 480 families (15%) could retain their income during April–June. Income decreased for 85% of the families and became less than half for 60% (287) of them during the first three months of the lockdown versus their pre-lockdown income. As many as 60 families reported absolutely zero income during the lockdown. On average, the family expenditure during the lockdown reportedly increased (not decreased) by 4.8% compared to that in the pre-lockdown situation in Kerala because of the inflation in essential commodities during the lockdown. The expenditure for these 480 households in Kerala rose to 113% of the income because of the lockdown, which was just about half (56%) before the lockdown (Table 10.1). A little more than half (280) of the 480 respondents (i.e., 59%) reported an increase in the indebtedness of their families – the others (41%) coped by depleting their savings during the first three months of the lockdown.

The survey data (Table 10.1) shows that the average per capita monthly pre-lockdown income of all 480 families was INR 4914, which dropped to only INR 2530 during the lockdown months under study, registering a 48.5% fall. The average monthly per capita expenditures increased from INR 2737 to INR 2869 (by 4.8%). As a result, the average expenditure-income ratio increased from 0.56 to 1.13 during the first three months of lockdown. This ratio increased from 0.56 to as high as 1.44 for the Muslim families in the sample. For the scheduled caste families, this ratio went up from 0.52

Table 10.1 Per capita monthly income and expenditure before and during lockdown (INR)

Caste category (average)	*Before lockdown income*	*During lockdown income*	*Before lockdown expenditure*	*During lockdown expenditure*	*Expd.-Income ratio before lockdown*	*Expd.-Income ratio during lockdown*
Unreserved	5125	2637	2775	2859	0.54	1.08
OBC	4677	2390	2824	2996	0.60	1.25
SC	3282	1537	1722	1993	0.52	1.30
Hindu	4612	2392	2680	2863	0.58	1.20
Muslim	3612	1450	2025	2093	0.56	1.44
Christian	6002	3473	2908	2818	0.48	0.81
Total	4914	2530	2737	2869	0.56	1.13

Source: Authors' calculations based on the survey data.

to 1.30 because of the income fall and the increase in average monthly per capita expenditure under the lockdown. As mentioned previously, dividing the sample families into four groups based on the pre-lockdown per capita income of the sample households reveals a slightly lower fall in income for the top 25% of families than for the other three classes. However, more striking is the increase in expenditure for the poorest 25% of families – it was the highest (by 15.8%). Instead, the expenditure rose only by 1.5% for the top 25% of families and by slightly above 5% for the middle 50% of families.

The pre-lockdown average per capita monthly income for the SC families was only INR 3282, and that for the Muslim families was INR 3612; this came down by 53% and 60%, respectively, during the lockdown months (see Figure 10.1). The per capita average monthly income of Christian families was relatively higher (INR 6002) before the lockdown, which dwindled by 42%. The income of Hindu, OBC, and unreserved families dropped by around 49%. The average monthly per capita expenditure went up dramatically for the SC families (by 15.7%) in the sample. It remained similar for the Christian families, went up by almost 7% for the Hindu families, and by 3.5% for the Muslim families. The expenditure for the OBC families went up by more than 6% and by more than 3% for the unreserved families during the lockdown (see Figure 10.1). Overall, income fell by 48.5% and expenditure increased by 4.8%.

The Central Government (in the PMGKY) had promised in March that households would receive free rations, free cooking gas cylinders, and INR 500 per month in their Jan-Dhan accounts. Because of the efficient public distribution system (PDS) in Kerala, 97% of the sample families got free rations during the lockdown. However, only 17% of respondents reported having received the cash transfer, and less than 4% of families received free cooking gas cylinders during April–June. Many respondents reported that they were unaware of the PMJDY in Kerala.

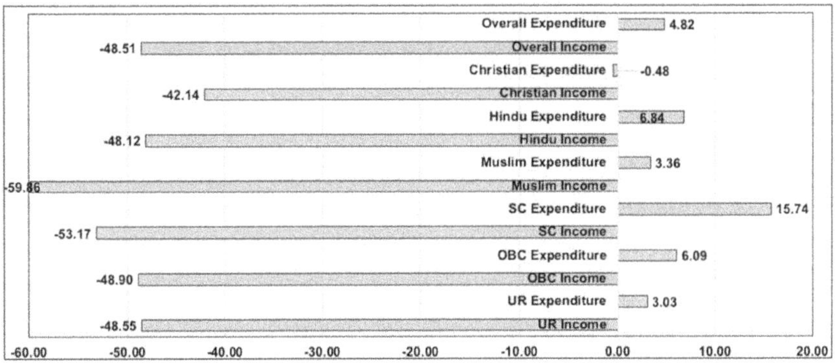

Figure 10.1 Average percentage change in income and expenditure due to lockdown

Source: Authors' calculations based on the survey data.

According to our survey data, 120 of the 480 families (25%) had some member who was a patient (other than with COVID-19) and more than 50% of them faced treatment-related difficulties because of the lockdown through April 2020. While more than one-third of the respondents said that staying at home during the lockdown was not at all comfortable for them because of various reasons, the remaining two-thirds did not face any issues apart from job and income loss. Most respondents in the sample were engaged in some activities in the unorganized, informal sectors of the economy. Almost 80% were expecting their average monthly income to reduce in the following six months compared to their pre-lockdown income. The responses revealed extreme job insecurities and income vulnerabilities. While almost 70% of respondents expressed an urgent need for an urban employment guarantee scheme, 30% were not sure. It is important to remember that most sample households of our survey were from the urban or suburban areas, with only 8% (39 out of 480 of them) possessing MGNREGS job cards till July 2020.

Policy suggestions

On being asked for suggestions, many respondents made extremely interesting and insightful comments from a policy perspective. Most suggestions centred around job creation, food security, inflation control, growth revival, public health, and education. The common people's main expectations could be summarized as follows.

1. Following huge lockdown-related job losses, respondents demanded jobs under the employers of last resort (ELR) scheme in both rural and urban areas to ensure minimum income security for all families, at least to eradicate the phenomenon of extreme poverty. In this context, the State of Kerala already has in place an Urban Employment Guarantee Scheme, along with the MGNREGS (for the rural areas), called Ayyankali Urban Employment Guarantee Programme. However, less than 10% of the respondents in our sample reported having job cards of the employment guarantee scheme, but 70% demanded it, especially in the urban areas. So, this indicates that the government needs to pay more attention to this area.

Respondents also demanded an unemployment allowance. One respondent interestingly commented, "Don't compel people to sit at home without providing financial support." Some respondents also separately mentioned the need for creating employment opportunities for the educated youth and for Gulf-returned *pravasi*s (overseas Indians). One of the prominent demands was also job creation in the private sector, besides that in the government sector, and ensuring remunerative salary/wages in the formal and informal private sectors with some job stability or existence of some labour laws. The major suggestion focused on early economic recovery and job creation in all sectors.

2. The next set of suggestions revolved around food security and supporting the vulnerable and needy. Many respondents talked about the demand for direct cash transfers of at least INR 10,000 per family for the poorer (non-direct tax payee) households after the first three months of the lockdown. Many expressed the need for a lengthier continuation of the free food distribution system. Some felt that distinction should not be made between the Above Poverty Line (APL) and Below Poverty Line (BPL) families vis-à-vis food distribution and other welfare measures during the crisis, considering everyone, the middle class included, was equally affected and that many APL families were poor.

While some demanded the distribution of more necessary commodities through the PDS in Kerala, some suggested providing free medicines and food to the poor, shelter to the homeless, and travel concessions for the workers.

Some demanded loan waivers and asked for the provision of interest-free loans or loans at subsidized interest rates as many families had become indebted because of the lockdown. Many respondents also raised the need for properly identifying the affected and providing some sort of financial support to the poorer people. Some sought relief on electricity bills and cooking gas prices during the lockdown. Some respondents highlighted the fact that while some people were categorized as APL because of certain parameters, their actual situation was similar to or worse than those in the BPL category, so relief measures should not only be BPL-targeted but must have wider coverage. Some others pointed out the special need for supporting daily-wage earners and migrant workers in Kerala. Some respondents highlighted the need to deliver cooked food to people who did not have the means to eat.

3. Some common comments were related to controlling inflation and reviving growth. While many suggested that the government try to control the inflation of food and other necessities that occurred following the huge income loss, some proposed reducing the GST rates on essential commodities and grocery and medicine prices, as well as lowering tax rates on petroleum products. Some also suggested that the government provide free, good-quality medical treatment in hospitals.

"Money should be pumped into the society only then will consumption increase" and "Support farmers in farming" were some of the other suggestions. One person also suggested privatizing some public sector units (PSUs) in the state because of their inefficiencies. The person felt that while in the short run, this could cause unemployment (which could be compensated by unemployment benefits schemes), in the long run, it could increase private investment and boost the economy. Some respondents also suggested tax deduction/exemption for small- and medium-scale businesses.

One of the policy suggestions in this context was to collect maximum tax and loan returns from corporates and to provide interest-free loans to small businesses for the revival of economic growth and employment. Some recommendations also included providing start-ups with financial help and loans with less interest and more subsidy; skill development programmes for the youth; training programmes to make people self-reliant, particularly in the rural areas; liquid fund release into the economy to increase the purchasing power of common people for their loan repayment; and enhancing consumption demand in the economy to ensure quicker recovery under a severe demand depression.

4. Public health under the COVID-19 lockdown was of great concern for many respondents. Some suggested free vaccination to control the spread of the Coronavirus; more free-of-cost medical facilities, care, and better hospitality services; stricter implementation of the quarantine rule for people returning from abroad; and stopping the spread of the virus instead of locking down the economy. Some suggested that there be no more lockdowns in the month of July 2020. However, some living in regions close to district borders suggested closing the state borders to reduce the virus spread. Some respondents emphasized that the government must manage unwanted social gatherings to control the spread of the virus and provide a safe working environment for people. Some also suggested addressing the mental health situation. Many advocated providing medical insurance to all families and ensuring insurance facilities in all hospitals, while some suggested a free supply of medicines to patients other than those afflicted with COVID. Allotting more budget to develop the health infrastructure was also considered important. Some felt that government regulation should be introduced to increase the salary of nurses working in the private sector.
5. A major set of suggestions dealt with education. Many respondents demanded laptops or smartphones for poor students to ensure all students and their families had access to online classes and study materials during the lockdown. Some suggested waiving school fees in private schools. Some suggested that freshers and underemployed persons be provided more facilities in the educational space, while some others felt special care to the affected people and proper action in professional college education were important and the need for conducting more research studies. Other miscellaneous suggestions included highlighting issues such as providing flexibility on loan repayment instalments, employment and residential facilities for transgenders, awareness programmes for *pravasi*s returning home, reduction in bus fares, reduction in plastic usage, closure of liquor shops and bars, drain cleaning, protection of poorer people from the next flood, increase in old age pension, more

kshemanidhi pensions for the needy, timely distribution of all social security funds, etc.

Government policymakers are expected to take note and try to address the issues soon. Many respondents praised the Kerala government's role during this difficult time; however, post the arrival of non-residential Keralites, the situation became more challenging.

Conclusion

The lockdown affected all sections of the population to various degrees; however, the poorer section suffered the most. The monthly average family income became less than half for 60% of the households and more than half the families became more indebted during the first three months of lockdown. On average, SC households suffered more than households from other castes. Muslim households suffered more than Hindu and Christian households. Families in Kerala faced extreme income vulnerabilities and huge job uncertainties. People felt the need for ELR programmes in urban and rural areas. The food distribution through the PDS also provided some relief to the common people.

Government planning for faster recovery and support, particularly for the poor and vulnerable sections of the population, is crucial. The universal employment guarantee programme can eradicate extreme poverty in the country using just 1% of the GDP amount of government expenditure (Das 2022a). Government health expenditure must be enhanced to ensure quality health services for all. Expansionary demand management policy seems to be the present need to get rid of the unemployment crisis accruing from the demand depression – fiscal conservatism would be imprudent in the current situation. The suggestions raised during this primary survey may help design the policy for minimizing the losses caused by the lockdown not only in Kerala but also in India. This study may also give a broad direction to the policymakers and the planners of the entire developing world vis-à-vis the post-lockdown policy formulation to tackle the humanitarian crisis caused by the COVID-19 pandemic-induced lockdown all over the globe.

References

Anand, I., and Thampi, A. 2021, August 18. "Do PLFS Numbers Underestimate the Pain of Lockdown?" *Hindustan Times*. https://www.hindustantimes.com/business/do-plfs-numbers-underestimate-the-pain-of-lockdown-101629229850220.html.

Azim Premji University. 2021. *State of Working India 2021: One Year of Covid*. Bengaluru: Centre for Sustainable Development, APU. https://cse.azimpremjiuniversity.edu.in/wp-content/uploads/2021/05/State_of_Working_India_2021-One_year_of_Covid-19.pdf.

Das, S. 2022a, March 18. "Opinion: Guarantee Universal Employment." *Telangana Today*. https://telanganatoday.com/opinion-guarantee-universal-employment.

Das, S. 2022b. “Some Aspects of Impact of Lockdown in India and the Way Forward.” In *COVID-19 Pandemic, Public Policy, and Institutions in India Issues of Labour, Income, and Human Development*, edited by Indranil De, Soumyadip Chattopadhyay, Hippu Salk Kristle Nathan, and Kingshuk Sarkar, and Routledge Research in Public Administration and Public Policy. UK: Routledge.

Das, S., and Soni, T. L. 2020, September 16. “Opinion: Lockdown Takes a Heavy Toll on Kerala Households.” *The Hindu Business Line*. https://www.thehindubusinessline.com/opinion/lockdown-takes-a-heavy-toll-on-kerala-households/article32623010.ece.

International Labour Organization. 2021. *An Update on the Youth Labour Market Impact of the COVID-19 Crisis*. Geneva: ILO. https://www.ilo.org/emppolicy/pubs/WCMS_795479/lang--en/index.htm#:~:text=The%20COVID%2D19%20crisis%20has,3.7%20per%20cent%20for%20adults.

International Labour Organization. 2022. *World Employment and Economic Outlook (2021)*. Geneva: ILO. https://www.ilo.org/global/research/global-reports/weso/trends2021/lang--en/index.htm.

Jha, P., and Kumar, M. 2020. “Labour in India and the COVID-19 Pandemic.” *The Indian Economic Journal* 68(3): 417–37.

Kannan, K. P., and Khan, Md. Imran. 2021 “Loss of Job, Work, and Income in the Time of COVID-19: An Analysis of PLFS Data.” *Economic and Political Weekly* 57(2): 37–41.

Kesar, S., Abraham, R., Lahoti, R., Nath, P., and Basole, A. 2021. “Pandemic, Informality, and Vulnerability: Impact of COVID-19 on Livelihoods in India.” *Canadian Journal of Development Studies/Revue Canadienne d’Études du Développement* 42(1–2): 145–64.

Roychowdhury, A., Bose, M., and Roy, S. D. 2022. “The Great Indian Lockdown 1.0: Exploring the Labour Market Dynamics.” *Canadian Journal of Development Studies / Revue Canadienne d’Études du Développement* 43(4). https://doi.org/10.1080/02255189.2022.2038093.

Part III

Structural Transformation and Distributional Issues

11 Structural change, social groups, and mobility

A state-level analysis of Kerala and Tamil Nadu

Anjali Rajan and Mritiunjoy Mohanty

Introduction

This chapter analyzes how the process of structural transformation in output and employment has played out in Kerala and Tamil Nadu (TN) and its implications for social mobility across social groups (as defined by the NSSO). Using NSSO unit-level data and PLFS unit-level data, we explore social group dynamics of structural change in output and employment in these two southern Indian states with an enviable record of delivering, substantially if not wholly, what Amartya Sen has called "Development as freedom".

They have consistently performed well in economic (per capita income) as well as human and social development indicators (see Table 11.1 below). As the table indicates, Kerala and TN, which rank ninth and seventh, respectively, in terms of per capita income, rank first and third in terms of overall sustainable development goals (SDG) performance.[1] Gujarat, which is ranked third in terms of per capita income, ranks seventh in terms of overall SDG performance.[2] Perhaps equally important is the quality and consistency of the SDG performance: both states have "frontrunner" status in 13 out of 15 SDG indicators, Gujarat in 10. Neither is present in the "aspirant" category, Gujarat is in one. In the indicator SDG1, both states have "achiever" status, Gujarat achieves this in none. In SDG2 (hunger and malnutrition), which has serious implications for the development of long-term human capabilities, both states have substantially solved the problem (frontrunner), while Gujarat has not (aspirant).

From the standpoint of this chapter – structural change and mobility – what is also important is that Kerala and TN have witnessed land and social reform movements led by the lower caste and peasant groups (see for example, Pandian 1987; Kurup 1994; Heller and Törnquist 2021; and Kalaiyarasan and Vijayabaskar 2021). These movements around land and caste from below have influenced and shaped the social, economic, and political mobility of all social groups, including their own. Kerala's social movement was led by SCs and small and marginal, mostly Muslim, peasant groups (see for example, Kurup 1994, Heller and Törnquist 2021). Tamil Nadu's social movement was led by OBCs (Pandian 1987; Kalaiyarasan and Vijayabaskar (2021). Despite movements from below and associated social

DOI: 10.4324/9781003601289-14

Table 11.1 Per capita income and sustainable development goals (SDG) index of select Indian States

State	*Per capita income Rank (2022–23)*	*Overall SDG rank*	*Number of indicators as Aspirant (0–49)*	*Number of indicators as Performer (50–64)*	*Number of indicators as Frontrunner (65–99)*	*Number of indicators as Achiever (100)*	*Lowest indicators*
Kerala	9	1	0	1	13	1	SDG 12
Tamil Nadu	7	2	0	1	13	1	SDG 5
Karnataka	4	6	0	4	10	1	SDG 5, SDG 2
Gujarat	3	7	1	3	10	0	SDG 5, SDG 2
Maharashtra	8	9	1	2	11	1	SDG 5, SDG 2

Source: Compiled by authors based on SDG India Index 2023–24 report published by NITI Aayog. Per capital income data is compiled by authors based on state level aggregates published by Ministry of Statistics and Programme Implementation (https://www.mospi.gov.in/data).

Note: 15 SDGs are evaluated at state level. SDG 13 and SDG 17 are evaluated at national level. SDG 2 pertains to hunger and malnutrition, SDG 5 pertains to gender equality, and SDG 12 pertains to sustainable consumption and production patterns. The per capita income (constant prices, 2011–12 base year) rankings are based on 28 states of India. Among the large states, Gujarat ranks 1. Data for 2023–24 is incomplete, therefore rankings based on 2022–23 data are reported.

development, relatively speaking, social and economic gains have eluded lower caste Dalits and Adivasis (Devika 2010; Harriss 2015).

This chapter seeks to understand mobility patterns seen in the context of structural change, particularly among SC and OBC population groups in Kerala and TN, through an analysis of employment composition, both in terms of sectors and quality, of these two social groups. Successful episodes of industrialization in particular and non-agrarian growth in general are driven by prior agrarian transformations fuelled by agricultural labour productivity growth, food security, and institutional change (see for example, Wade 2003; Storm and Naastepad 2005). In addition, successful institutional changes (such as land reform and anti-caste movements) from below can counter and overcome the inevitable blocking strategies of elites, both rural and urban (see Saith 1990; Heller and Törnquist 2021). As Kalaiyarasan and Vijayabaskar (2021) establish in the case of TN, an industrialization strategy premised on an anti-caste movement from below was similarly transformative. Therefore, both Kerala and TN have followed distinctive paths towards economic and social transformation driven by institutional change from below. This chapter seeks to understand the role of structural change in this transformation and the nature of mobility that may or may not have resulted.

This chapter is organized into six sections, excluding the introduction. The first section elucidates the structural change in output and employment in Kerala and TN. The second enumerates the population and workforce composition by social groups, followed by sectoral and employment status-based analysis in the third. The fourth section presents the educational attainments of SC and OBC population groups in Kerala and TN. In the preceding context, the fifth section analyzes the employment mobility of social groups using likelihood ratios. Finally, our conclusions are presented in the final section.

Structural change in output and employment and relative surplusness of labour

One of the most important and robust stylizations in growth literature is the association between growth in income and the nature of structural change. In his account of Simon Kuznets's scholarly career, Fogel (2000) notes that according to Kuznets, the essential characteristic of the "modern epoch of growth" was a "sustained increase in per capita income accompanied by an increase in total population and sweeping changes in the structure of the economy". So, a successful structural transformation must feature structural change in output and employment from low productivity (agrarian activities) to high productivity (non-agrarian activities) sectors along with a convergence of sectoral labour productivities. The sectoral composition of output and employment of Kerala and TN (for selected periods) is given in Table 11.2. The table also lists the relative surplusness of labour in the farm sector (L/O) vis-à-vis the non-farm sector. Following (Mohanty 2009), relative surplusness of labour is defined as the ratio of two other ratios: the share of

Table 11.2 Output and employment composition of Kerala and Tamil Nadu

Kerala								
Employment composition	*Agriculture and allied activities*	*Industry*	*Services*	*Output composition*	*Agricultureand alliedactivities*	*Industry*	*Services*	*L/O*
1999–00	38.5	25.8	35.7	1999–00	28.6	28.7	42.7	1.3
2004–05	36.1	26.7	37.2	2004–05	23.2	31.1	45.7	1.6
2009–10	29.5	29.5	41	2009–10	16.3	27.9	55.8	1.8
2011–12	25.5	31.8	42.7	2011–12	14.4	28.2	57.5	1.8
2017–18	19.9	31.3	48.8	2017–18	9.6	28.9	61.5	2.1
2021–22	23.5	30.8	45.7	2021–22	9.0	28.4	62.6	2.6
Tamil Nadu								
Employment composition	*Agricultureand alliedactivities*	*Industry*	*Services*	*Output composition*	*Agricultureand alliedactivities*	*Industry*	*Services*	*L/O*
1999-00	50.3	24.0	25.7	1999–00	21.2	41.3	37.5	2.4
2004–05	46.4	26.3	27.3	2004–05	15.6	42.6	41.8	3.0
2009–10	44.6	27.9	27.5	2009–10	12.8	38.8	48.4	3.5
2011–12	35.2	33.9	30.9	2011–12	12.7	36.9	50.5	2.8
2017–18	27.7	34.9	37.3	2017–18	11.0	37.6	51.5	2.5
2021–22	31.0	34.9	34.1	2021–22	11.7	37.3	50.9	2.6

Source: Calculations by authors based on NSSO and PLFS unit level data on employment and MoSPI GSDP data (2011–12 base year), calculated based on methodology presented in the Report of the Committee on Real Sector Statistics (National Statitical Commission, 2018) (Mundle Commission Report 2018). All figures are in percentage terms.

agriculture in employment (L) to the share of agriculture in output (O). *What the L/O ratio allows us to do is to compare the nature of structural change over time from the standpoint of transfer of labour out of agriculture.* The L/O ratio is a relative measure of the extent to which labour moves out of the farm to the non-farm sector as the share of both farm output and farm employment declines, as expected in successful episodes of structural transformation. Equally important, it allows us to compare relative labour transfer over time and between geographies.

On the assumption that agriculture is the lower labour productivity sector, if labour productivities in the agricultural and non-agricultural sectors converge[3] and the share of both agricultural employment and output is declining, we would expect the L/O ratio to move towards one, indicating that structural change has been able to move labour out of agriculture (and absorbed by non-agriculture) in a way that reduces surplus labour, in both absolute and relative terms, in the sector over time (see fn3 for labour productivity conditions). On the other hand, if sectoral labour productivities diverge, then the L/O ratio will move away from one, implying that even is labour is transferred out of agriculture (both agricultural employment and output ratios are declining), the pace of transfer is such that agriculture is left holding increasing amounts of relatively surplus labour, despite being the lower productivity sector.

Table 11.2, therefore, tells us that for Kerala the L/O ratio, secularly, if incrementally, increased from 1.3 in 1999–2000 to 2.1 in 2017–18, suggesting a slowing pace of labour transfer out of agriculture. Between 2017–18 and 2021–22, the share of agricultural employment increases from 19.9% to 23.5%, suggesting structural retrogression[4] with labour moving back into agriculture. *The associated L/O ratio increases to 2.6 but is qualitatively not comparable to L/O ratios of earlier periods because of the retrogression.*

For TN, the L/O ratios tell a very different story. Between 1999–2000 and 2009–10, there is a sharp increase in the L/O ratio from 2.4 to 3.5, suggesting a marked increase in the divergence between sectoral productivities[5] and therefore a relative inability to transfer labour out of agriculture, increasing sharply the relative surplusness of labour in the sector. Between 2009–10 and 2017–18 this process reverses itself, with the L/O ratio declining to 2.5, suggesting a convergence of sectoral productivities and accelerated labour transfer out of agriculture with the agricultural employment ratio falling significantly faster than in the earlier period. As in Kerala, in TN as well, the share of agricultural employment increases from 27.7% to 31% between 2017–18 and 2021–22, indicating a structural retrogression and an increase in the L/O ratio to 2.6. The period of structural retrogression aside, in TN, structural change from the standpoint of agrarian change divides into two distinct periods, with the period between 2009–10 to 2017–18, witnessing accelerated transfer of labour out of agriculture.

We learnt from NSSO (2012) that for the entire Indian economy, the level of agrarian workforce fell, for the first time, below 50% in 2011–12. As

Table 11.2 indicates, however, this Lewisian transformation happened much earlier in Kerala and TN. In Kerala, the proportion of the workforce engaged in agriculture and allied activities was below 40% in 1999–2000. For TN, the proportion of the workforce in the primary sector fell below 50% in 2004–05.

In Kerala, between 1999–2000 and 2017–18, the decline of output share of farm sector (19%) is only slightly higher than the decline in employment share (18.6%). If the period of structural retrogression is included, i.e. up to 2021–22, the decline in output share (19.6%) is strictly greater than the decline in employment share (15%). The decline in the share of farm output is mostly counterbalanced by an increase in the share of services sector output (18.8% up to 2017–18) while the share of industry in output has fluctuated within a tight band of 28%–29% between 1999–2000 and 2021–22, with a very mild uptrend between 2009–10 and 2017–18 within that band. In employment share terms, up to 2017–18, industry and services shares increased by 5.5% and 13.1%, respectively. Given that industry's output share was almost stagnant, the increase in the employment share of 5.5% suggests a lower-than-average sectoral labour productivity growth. Both industry and services employment shares declined during the period of structural retrogression, which saw agriculture's employment share rise after a consistent two-decade decline.

It is also worth noting that right through the period under analysis (1999–2000 to 2017–18 or 2021–22), *services have been the dominant output-producing sector*. In employment terms, the dominant sector changes. In 1999–2000, agriculture had the highest share followed by services. From 2004–05, however, services sector has the highest employment share, followed by industry. Therefore, it is the services sector that is the dominant sector both in output and employment terms in Kerala from 2004–05.

Finally, we have noted earlier that Kerala's L/O ratio has slowly and incrementally risen – from 1.3 (1999–2000) to 2.1 (2017–18), suggesting a slow increase in the relative surplusness of labour in agriculture. A little more flesh can now be put to the bones of this statement. Of the two non-agricultural sectors – industry and services – the former has, given its size, absorbed more labour than the latter and, therefore, in this instance, seen relatively slower labour productivity growth (as compared with the latter). As we have noted earlier industry's share in output remains range bound between 28% and 29% over 1999–2000 and 2017–18, whereas its share in employment rises from almost 26% to more than 31%. Services absorb relatively much less labour and exhibit significantly higher labour productivity growth.

Tamil Nadu's trajectory of structural change has been quite different from Kerala's. As we have already noted, TN's L/O ratio exhibits two distinct phases: the first where it increases significantly from 2.4 to 3.5 between 1999–2000 and 2009–10, suggesting a very slow pace of transfer of the labour out of agriculture; and second, where the L/O declines from 3.5 to 2.5 between 2009–10 to 2017–18, implying an accelerated pace of transfer of labour out of agriculture.[6] In 1999–2000, in output terms, industry was the dominant sector, accounting for more than 41%. This was followed by services with almost 38% and agriculture with 21%. In that year, in employment terms, agriculture was the dominant sector, accounting for more than 50%, with industry and services accounting for roughly similar shares, with the latter having a slight edge. The first phase, which saw a steep increase in the L/O ratio, is also very consequent in terms of structural change. In 2004–05, the share of industry peaked at almost 43%. The share of services increased as well to almost 42%. Agriculture's share declined by nearly 6%–15.6%. By 2009–10, agriculture's share declined by another 3%–12.8%. Interestingly, industry's share declined as well – from 43% to 39%, marking the beginning of a secular decline for the rest of the period under analysis. Services became the clear driver of output growth, increasing its share by 7% to more than 48%.

On the employment side, the transfer of labour out of agriculture was relatively slow, as implied by the increase in the L/O ratio. By 2004–5, agriculture's share in employment fell by 4% as opposed to a decline in output share by 6%. This decline in agriculture's share happened alongside an increase of roughly 2% each in the employment share of industry and services. Whereas industry's employment share increased by 2%, roughly matching its increase in output share – i.e. industry growth was labour absorbing – services increase was much less than its increase of output share of almost 4%, suggesting non-labour-absorbing growth. By 2009–10, these trends had become more entrenched – even as the pace of labour transfer out of agriculture slowed down and employment shares declined by less than 2% even as output share fell by 3% – with industry share of employment share *increasing* by 1.5% even as its share in output *declined* by 4%. The services share in employment *stagnated* even as its share in output *increased by a whopping 7%*.

Overall, in the first phase (the non-labour-absorbing phase), agriculture's output and employment shares declined by 8.4% and 5.7%, respectively; industry's output share *declined* by 2.5%, whereas its employment share *increased* by 3.9%; and finally, the service sector's output share increased by 11%, whereas employment share increased by 1.8%. Therefore, in this non-labour-absorbing phase of TN's growth, not only was the pace of transfer slow, *but it was the relatively slower-growing labour productivity sector (industry) that absorbed the bulk of the labour.*[7]

In the second phase (2009–10 to 2017–18), when TN's L/O ratio declined from 3.5 to 2.5, implying an accelerated pace of transfer of labour out of agriculture, agriculture's output share declines by only 2% *whereas employment share fell by a phenomenal 17%*. Over this period, industry's output share continued to fall, *declining* 2% by 2011–12. Industry's *employment share*, however, continued to rise, *increasing by* 6% by 2011–12. Between 2011–12 and 2017–18, the decline in industry's output share reversed partially, increasing by nearly 1%. Over the same period, the industry's employment share increased by 1% as well. *Overall, between 2004–05 and 2011–12, when industry's output share decreased by nearly 6%, its employment share increased by more than 7%.*

Taking the entire second phase (2009–10 to 2017–18) into account, industry's output share declined by more than 1%, whereas employment share increased by 7%. The pace of increase in the service sector output share slowed down, rising by a little more than 3% as opposed to 11% in the earlier phase. However, it is much more labour absorbing, with an almost 10% increase in its employment share. Therefore, in the second, more labour-absorbing phase of structural change in TN, the bulk of labour was absorbed by the higher labour productivity growth sector, services, even as the relatively lower productivity growth sector continued to absorb labour. This contradicted the first phase, where most of the labour absorption was done by the latter sector. Again, similar to Kerala, 2017–18 to 2021–22 is a period of structural retrogression, with the agricultural sector gaining in both output and employment shares at the expense of both industry and services sectors.

In 1999–2000, in TN, employment was dominated by agriculture, accounting for more than 50%. Output was dominated by industry (41%), followed closely by services (37.5%). By 2017–18, the economic structure was substantially different, services was the largest employer with a 37% share followed closely by industry with 35%. In output terms services was clearly dominant accounting for more than 51% of the total followed by industry with 38%. And even though agriculture was the smallest sector in both employment (28%) and output (11%) terms, the first phase of non-labour-absorbing growth of the fastest growing sector – services – meant that the relative surplusness of labour had barely budged, with the L/O ratio almost the same as in 1999–2000.

To conclude this discussion, in comparative terms, the following trends in structural change emerge when comparing Kerala and TN:

(1) Even though L/O ratios for both worsened, TN ended the period under review, not taking the period of structural retrogression into account, with a relatively higher degree of surplus labour in agriculture. This is largely due to the first phase of non-labour-absorbing growth of the services sector in TN. That is to say that Kerala was relatively more successful in transferring labour out of agriculture.
(2) In both states, however, services were the dominant sector in output and employment.
(3) In TN, the rise to dominance of the services sector in output terms happened alongside the declining share – deindustrialization – of the once dominant industry sector. *Right through this process of deindustrialization, industry's share in employment continued to rise*, i.e. the slower productivity growth sector (as compared with services and the consequent divergence in labour productivities) remained an important driver of labour absorption. This had implications for

inequality as well as the nature and quality of jobs generated in the industrial sector. In comparison, for Kerala, even though the output share of the relatively smaller industry sector stagnates, there was no deindustrialization.

Population and workforce composition by social groups

Having established the baseline in terms of structural change in output and employment and the related relative surplusness of labour, let us explore the population and workforce composition by social groups. The composition in terms of social groups for population and workforce in Kerala and TN is listed in Table 11.3.

OBCs are the most dominant social group in Kerala and TN, but they are of a different order. In Kerala, the population composition is more diverse despite the high proportion of the OBC population. The share of the OBC population *rose from 52% to 65%* between 1999–2000 and 2021–22. The share of the SC population also rose. *The share of all other social groups reduced.* Reflecting the increasing weight of OBCs in the population, their share in the workforce (WF) also increased – from 50% to 61%. *However, OBCs were under-represented in the* workforce, *given their share in the population steadily.*

Similarly, SC WF participation in Kerala has tracked its population share movements, *with the proviso that SCs were overrepresented in the WF.* The SC population and *WF share rose in 2021–22* (only social grouping other than OBC for whom it does) after declining during 2010–11 and 2017–18. The SC and OBC groups together accounted for 75% of the population and 73% of the workforce.

The shares of other religions (OR) and upper-caste Hindus (UCH) in the population and WF declined consistently. The fall in the share of OR is higher – 8.8% as compared to a 3.4% decline in the UCH share in the population. *OR accounts for less than 10% of the total population in 2021–22 as compared to 18.5% in 1999–2000.*

In TN, the OBC share in the population increased from 65% to 75%, and its share in the WF has also increased proportionately, from 66% to 75%. *The share of the SC population declined from 24% to 21%, and its WF from 26% to 22%, approximately.*

Perhaps the most remarkable decrease is that of the UCH population share – from 7% to 2.3% of the overall population and the WF, from 6% to ~2%.

In both Kerala and TN, the scheduled tribes (ST) account for a small proportion (1.25%) of the population. STs were overrepresented in the WF as compared to the population in 1999–2000 across both states. However, the share of ST workers declined in Kerala while it increased slightly in TN.

In TN, the OR population share (which is already very small) declined from 1.85% to 0.15% by 2021–22. The OR workforce share also declined from 1.3% to 0.06%. The share of UCH in population and workforce also

Table 11.3 Population and workforce composition by social groups

	Population composition					
Kerala	*1999–00*	*2004–05*	*2009–10*	*2011–12*	*2017–18*	*2021–22*
ST	1.7	1.71	1.73	1.07	1.0	1.25
SC	9.47	10.51	10.82	8.39	8.31	10.7
OBC	52.21	61.63	60.33	65.31	63.21	64.6
UCH	18.14	12.88	13.58	13.79	14.95	14.26
OR	18.48	13.28	13.54	11.45	12.53	9.71
TN	**1999–00**	**2004–05**	**2009–10**	**2011–12**	**2017–18**	**2021–22**
ST	1.34	0.55	0.97	1.09	1.56	1.25
SC	24.39	21.72	19.08	20.22	22.75	21.17
OBC	65.29	73.47	76.37	76.07	71.96	75.1
UCH	7.13	3.49	2.93	1.98	3.42	2.33
OR	1.85	0.77	0.65	0.64	0.31	0.15

	Workforce composition					
Kerala	*1999–00*	*2004–05*	*2009–10*	*2011–12*	*2017–18*	*2021–22*
ST	2.45	2.17	1.65	1.54	1.37	1.11
SC	10.93	12.4	12.86	10.46	10.31	12.31
OBC	50.09	56.94	56.74	61.5	59.51	60.97
UCH	18.75	13.95	14.07	14.1	16.52	15.55
OR	17.79	14.54	14.69	12.4	12.29	10.06
TN	**1999–00**	**2004–05**	**2009–10**	**2011–12**	**2017–18**	**2021–22**
ST	1.52	0.63	1.08	1.32	1.75	1.74
SC	25.66	22.46	20.66	20.86	24.29	21.82
OBC	65.79	73.61	75.45	75.66	70.7	74.45
UCH	5.7	2.66	2.29	1.71	2.99	1.93
OR	1.32	0.64	0.53	0.44	0.27	0.06

Source: Author calculations based on NSSO unit level data. All figures are in percentage terms.
Note: ST- Scheduled Tribe; SC – Scheduled Caste; OBC – Other Backward Castes; UCH – Upper Caste Hindus; OR – Other Religions. For the methodology used to disaggregate UCH and OR from NSSO data see Mohanty (2006). For methodology used for population and workforce estimates, see Chapter 3 in Rajan (2021)

declined in TN. *In Kerala, though declining, the UCH population share is substantially greater compared to TN.* The SC and OBC population in TN together account for almost *96% of the WF and population in 2021–22.* The increase is entirely the result of the rise in the share of OBC and not SC.

This chapter focuses on the OBC and SC social groups due to the small sample size of ST in Kerala and ST, UCH, and OR in TN. The OBC and SC social groups are of particular relevance to our analysis, as these groups initiated the social movements in Kerala and TN. We will also enumerate UCH and OR for Kerala to highlight the contrast in employment composition and outcomes as compared with SCs and OBCs.

Workforce composition by sector and activity status

This section analyzes the sectoral and activity status-based employment composition of SC and OBC social groups in Kerala and TN. We know that the economic and social mobility associated with labour market participation is contingent on the sector and quality of employment (see, for example, Himanshu et al., 2013; Reddy and Swaminathan, 2014). Table 11.4 outlines the sectoral employment composition between 1999–2000 and 2021–22. In both Kerala and TN, agriculture was the largest employer of SC workers to begin with. By 2021–22, the proportion of SC in agriculture fell sharply (more than 30%), and industry became the largest employer of the SC workforce. In 2021–22, the farm sector had the lowest share among SC workforce, followed by the OBC workforce. Whereas employment shares in agriculture across all social groups declined in Kerala – the UCH declined the least, followed by OR and OBCs. Therefore, in 1999–2000 more than 50% of the SC workforce worked in agriculture. By 2017–18, this had fallen to 21% and it continued to decline through the period of structural retrogression. All other social groups saw an increase in the agricultural workforce during this period (i.e. retrogression).

In 1999–2000, services were the largest employer of OBC workers, followed by agriculture. Post 2004–05, the decline in the farm sector share in employment made industry the second-highest employer of the OBC workforce in Kerala. The drop in farm employment between 1999–2000 and 2021–22 was smaller among the OBC than SC. For OBCs, the overall employment composition and movement out of agriculture are dominated by the services sector. The OBC workforce was dominated by services employment. Given, as was noted earlier, the increase in the contribution of the services sector to output and employment, the OBC workforce stood to gain from this trend.

In TN, the proportion of SC and OBC workforce engaged in the farm sector is higher than in Kerala. *Unlike Kerala, SC continues to have a higher proportion of its workforce engaged in agriculture despite experiencing a similar decline (30%) in the share of farm sector in employment.* This is due to the disparity in the initial levels of sectoral shares in employment.

Table 11.4 Employment composition of social groups by sector

	Agriculture and allied activities						
Kerala	*1999–00*	*2004–05*	*2009–10*	*2011–12*	*2017–18*	*2021–22*	*change*
SC	52.7	42	35.8	31.3	21.27	20.74	-31.96
OBC	33.2	30.5	22.8	21.6	17.62	21.35	-11.85
UCH	36.7	33.8	31.9	23.5	18.01	29.61	-7.09
OR	44.1	50.4	44.6	39.6	27.6	29.87	-14.23
Tamil Nadu	*1999–00*	*2004–05*	*2009–10*	*2011–12*	*2017–18*	*2021–22*	*change*
SC	69.1	61.8	59.1	45.8	35.78	38.44	-30.66
OBC	45.9	43.2	41.5	32.5	25.1	28.09	-17.81
				Industry			
Kerala	*1999–00*	*2004–05*	*2009–10*	*2011–12*	*2017–18*	*2021–22*	*change*
SC	25.5	33	38.4	42.2	46.02	44.22	18.72
OBC	29.5	30.6	33.1	34.2	32.62	33.53	4.03
UCH	19.6	19.7	19.9	24.9	23.9	16.32	-3.28
OR	19.8	15.4	17.3	20.1	23.68	17.56	-2.24
Tamil Nadu	*1999–00*	*2004–05*	*2009–10*	*2011–12*	*2017–18*	*2021–22*	*change*
SC	16.9	19.9	22.6	32.5	33.15	36.49	19.59
OBC	26.8	28.6	29.7	34.6	36.3	35.07	8.27
				Services			
Kerala	*1999–00*	*2004–05*	*2009–10*	*2011–12*	*2017–18*	*2021–22*	*change*
SC	21.8	25	25.8	26.5	32.51	35.04	13.24
OBC	37.3	38.9	44.1	44.2	49.76	45.12	7.82
UCH	43.7	46.5	48.1	51.6	58.1	54.07	10.37
OR	36.1	34.1	38.1	40.2	48.72	52.58	16.48
Tamil Nadu	*1999–00*	*2004–05*	*2009–10*	*2011–12*	*2017–18*	*2021–22*	*change*
SC	14	18.3	18.2	21.7	31.07	25.06	11.1
OBC	27.4	28.1	28.8	32.9	38.61	36.84	9.4

Source: Calculations based on NSSO and PLFS unit level data. For methodology used to disaggregate UCH and OR from NSSO data see Mohanty (2006). For methodology used for population and workforce estimates see Chapter 3 in Rajan (2021). All figures are in percentage terms. The change represents the difference between 1999–00 and 2021–22.

Therefore, among the SC, there is no change in the ranking (in terms of sectors they were most employed) over time, even with a large fall in the proportion of the agrarian workforce. Similar to that in Kerala, for SC, the movement out of the agrarian sector is industry dominated employment in TN .

In the case of the OBC workforce, agriculture was the largest employer until 2009–10. In 2011–12, the industrial sector took the spot. By 2017–18, the services sector became the largest employer of the OBC workforce, absorbing most of the workforce out of the farm sector. As mentioned earlier (see section Population and workforce composition by social groups), this was in the second phase, where L/O ratios narrowed and labour absorption in the services improved dramatically. However, the difference in the share of industry and services sector among OBC workforce was narrow. The difference emanated from the higher agrarian workforce and lower services sector workforce presence in TN (see section Population and workforce composition by social groups).

The slower pace of the structural change in employment, along with the increasing relative surplusness of labour in TN, the results in a larger proportion of the workforce (SC and OBC) remained stuck in agriculture. The movements within the SC workforce composition were similar between Kerala and TN, but the levels were clearly very different. Given the de-industrialization in TN (see Table 11.2) and its implications for labour productivity growth, the high share of SC in farm and industry as compared to the services sector is not desirable.

The pace of structural change in employment is slower for OBCs in TN than in Kerala. For example, in 2017–18, 50% of OBCs in Kerala were employed in the service sector as opposed to 39% in TN. The issues are the high initial share of agrarian employment and a possible move into the agrarian sector due to distress post the pandemic. During the period of structural retrogression, between 2017–18 and 2021–22, it is important to note the *uptick in the share of the farm sector* in employment among the OBC and SC in TN and OBC in Kerala, but not among the SC. Also, the decline in farm employment among the SC in Kerala almost halted (registered only a 1% decline in share). This could be distress-driven employment (Abraham 2013) due to the pandemic response.

The difference in the sectoral composition of workforce will have an impact on the activity status-based composition as well. At the national level, the services sector produces more regular/salaried employment than other sectors (see appendix Table A1). There is an increasing casualization of the industrial sector. The trajectory of structural change in employment of SC and OBC workforces will be differentially affected by these trends, given their sectoral distribution of employment.

The national-level trends indicate that the proportion of casual employment is the most prevalent activity status among the SC workforce. In 2021–22, the share of self-employment increased among SC workforce. Currently, self-employment has the largest share among the SC and OBC workforce in India.

This national-level trend is not reflected in Kerala or TN. Table 11.5 presents the activity status-wise employment composition by social groups. Within the SC workforce in Kerala and TN, casual employment has the highest share followed by regular employment and self-employment. And even though in both states the share of regular and self-employment has gone up and that of casual employment has gone down, in 2017–18 work for SCs was overwhelmingly casual – 54% in Kerala and 47% in TN. This percentage worsened during the period of structural retrogression up to 2021–22. In 2017–18, the proportion of regular/salaried SC workers was higher in TN than in Kerala, but in 2021–22, it was roughly the same, with the former seeing a significant decline. This is particularly important considering the lower levels of employment of SC in agriculture in Kerala. If we read this conclusion in conjunction with the sectoral trends, *we can infer that the casualization of non-farm sectors, especially industry, is more prevalent in Kerala compared to TN*. There is a significant switch from casual employment to regular employment among SC workforce in TN and Kerala between 1999–2000 and 2017–18. In 2021–22, a significant decline (~5%) occurred in regular/salaried employment among the SC in TN and a minor (1%) decline among SC workforce in Kerala. At the same time, the share of casual employment increased among SC WF during the period of structural retrogression between 2017–18 and 2021–22 in Kerala and TN. *The bottom line remains the same – the bulk of the SC workforce is still in casual employment in Kerala and TN.*

Self-employment is the dominant type of employment status among the OBC workforce at national level and in both states. This is true in both 2017–18 and 2021–22. The steady trend is the consistent decline in casual employment among OBC workforce in Kerala and TN. The share of regular employment increased in tandem with the decline in casual employment between 2009–10 and 2017–18. This trend was consistent with the increase in the share of the services sector in employment and the decline in the share of the farm sector. After 2017–18, casual employment increased among OBC in Kerala and TN, while the regular/salaried employment share declined. *These changes are more noticeable in TN than in Kerala, where the share of agrarian sector employment increased, and the share of services and industrial sector employment decreased (refer to Table 11.5) between 2017–18 and 2021–22. In Kerala, the decline in share of services sector employment is counterbalanced by the increase in industrial sector employment share. Hence, the activity status-wise employment share for OBCs mostly remains stable between 2017–18 and 2021–22.*

Finally, an important distinction between Kerala and TN emanates from the diversity in the composition of social groups in population and workforce. The proportion of regular/salaried employment among OBC workforce in TN has remained higher than that of the OBC workforce in Kerala.

Table 11.5 Employment composition of social groups by activity status

	Self-employment						
Kerala	*1999–00*	*2004–05*	*2009–10*	*2011–12*	**2017–18**	*2021–22*	*change*
SC	15.9	20.8	14.7	16.1	18.95	18.4	2.5
OBC	45.2	45.6	39.3	38.3	40.18	39.41	–5.79
UCH	44.5	49.4	39.9	42.5	35.94	45.35	0.85
OR	50.7	59.4	55.3	49.6	46.13	48.28	–2.42
All	42.56	44.45	38.36	37.67	37.8	38.26	–4.3
TN	*1999–00*	*2004–05*	*2009–10*	*2011–12*	*2017–18*	*2021–22*	*change*
SC	16.6	22.5	14.9	16.3	21.55	23.23	6.63
OBC	43.7	47.6	38	36	37.11	40.31	–3.39
All	36.04	41.72	32.98	31.7	32.76	36.77	0.73
	Regular employment						
Kerala	*1999–00*	*2004–05*	*2009–10*	*2011–12*	*2017–18*	*2021–22*	*change*
SC	16.3	15.8	19.6	16.5	26.6	25.59	9.29
OBC	14	17.6	21.5	20.7	30.37	29.17	15.17
UCH	26.1	30.9	33.4	34.6	45.42	37.66	11.56
OR	19.9	18.3	23.7	22.8	35.45	37.06	17.16
All	17.48	19.19	23.15	22.48	32.9	30.9	13.42
TN	*1999–00*	*2004–05*	*2009–10*	*2011–12*	*2017–18*	*2021–22*	*change*
SC	12.6	18.4	14.6	22.4	31.02	25.72	13.12
OBC	22.1	21.4	21.9	25.8	34.02	31.55	9.45
All	21.57	21.64	21.37	25.54	33.77	30.33	8.76
	Casual employment						
Kerala	*1999–00*	*2004–05*	*2009–10*	*2011–12*	*2017–18*	*2021–22*	*change*
SC	67.8	63.4	65.7	67.4	54.44	56.01	–11.79
OBC	40.9	36.9	39.3	41	29.44	31.42	–9.48
UCH	29.4	19.6	26.7	22.9	18.64	16.99	–12.41
OR	29.4	22.3	21.1	27.6	18.42	14.66	–14.74
All	39.96	36.36	38.49	39.85	29.3	30.84	–9.12
TN	*1999–00*	*2004–05*	*2009–10*	*2011–12*	*2017–18*	*2021–22*	*change*
SC	70.8	59.1	70.6	61.3	47.43	51.04	–19.76
OBC	34.2	31.1	40.1	38.3	28.87	28.14	–6.06
All	42.39	36.64	45.65	42.75	33.47	32.9	–9.49

Source: Calculations based on NSSO and PLFS unit level data. All figures are in percentage terms. The change represents the difference between 1999–00 and 2021–22.

TN has become a two-caste (OBC–SC) state, where the OBCs are dominant. Effectively, the OBCs do not have to contest and share space with either the UCH or the OR (see Table 11.3). On the other hand, in Kerala, even though the OBCs are numerically dominant, both the OR and the UCH are significant minorities (see Table 11.3), and OBCs have to compete with them and the SCs as well. *In a way, both for OBCs and SCs, mobility is relatively easier in TN because important social groups such as the UCH and the OR are relatively marginal as compared with Kerala.* In other words, intergroup competition for jobs tends to be more muted in TN than in Kerala. And, as the Kerala experience tells us, the UCH and the OR are effective competitors in the job market, particularly when it comes to preferred jobs. *The OR and the UCH have a consistently higher proportion of regular/salaried employment in Kerala than the OBC and SC workforce. Between 1999–2000 and 2017–18, the UCH and the OR consistently increased their share of regular employment. As a result, in 2017–18, regular employment as a proportion of total employment was highest for the UCH, followed by the OR. However, between 2017–18 and 2021–22, the regular employment proportion for the UCH declined and that for the OR increased, reversing the ranking.* Between 2017–18 and 2021–22, self-employment increases and regular/salaried employment decreases among the UCH.

Educational attainments of social groups in Kerala and TN

Along with social group membership, the educational attainments of the population are an important determinant of mobility. According to PLFS 2023, 50% of the workforce engaged in regular/salaried employment has higher secondary education and above. Table 11.6 depicts the proportion of 15+ population with educational attainment of higher secondary or above in Kerala and TN by social groups. *We can infer from Table 11.6 that inter-social group differences are higher than inter-state differences. Educational attainment levels of SC and OBC in Kerala and TN are at similar levels.*

The proportion of tertiary-educated UCH is higher in TN than in Kerala, with the proviso that the UCH population in TN, as we have already noted, is really small. The SC and OBC populations have made large strides in educational attainments in TN and Kerala. However, the ranking in terms of proportion of tertiary educated in the population – the UCH, followed by the OBC, and finally the SC – has remained the same owing to the initial differences in levels of education. Indeed, the gap between the SCs and UCHs have narrowed very slowly, helping maintain the initial advantage, with all its ramifications for social capital (see for example, Mohanty 2006) and networks (see Munshi 2017), areas that we have not explored at all in this chapter.

The convergence in the share of the tertiary educated among the SCs and OBCs in Kerala and TN is also reflected in the share of regular/salaried employment of the social groups in both states. The SC in Kerala and

Table 11.6 Proportion of 15+ population with higher secondary education or more

SC	*1999–00*	*2004–05*	*2009–10*	*2011–12*	*2017–18*	*2021–22*	*change*
Kerala	4.65	10.21	12.18	16.25	20.65	26.94	22.29
Tamil Nadu	5.36	8.5	11.3	16.55	22.6	26.07	20.71
OBC	*1999–00*	*2004–05*	*2009–10*	*2011–12*	*2017–18*	*2021–22*	*change*
Kerala	7.92	15.66	20.68	20.65	28.75	33.76	25.84
Tamil Nadu	10.56	15.06	20.31	24.25	28.82	33.89	23.33
UCH	*1999–00*	*2004–05*	*2009–10*	*2011–12*	*2017–18*	*2021–22*	*change*
Kerala	18.84	27.43	34.68	33.51	42.07	47.02	28.18
Tamil Nadu	37.05	53	51.86	51.9	49.11	53.28	16.23

Source: Author calculations based on unit level NSSO and PLFS data of respective rounds. Change represents the difference between 1999–00 and 2021–22.

TN and the OBC in Kerala and TN have a similar share of their workforce engaged in regular salaried employment. *A higher proportion of regular/salaried employment among the UCH (in Kerala) is expected, given the higher levels of educational attainment of the UCH population.*

Again, we need to contextualize the achievements of the OBC and SC workforce in TN compared to Kerala within the overall workforce composition. The significant presence of UCH with high educational qualifications (47% of the UCH have completed higher secondary education or have higher degrees as opposed to 34% and 27% for OBCs and SCs, respectively (see Table 11.6). This implies a relatively more difficult path for the SC and OBC in Kerala towards securing regular employment, involving greater labour market competition. As mentioned earlier, in TN, competition from the UCH and the OR is relatively more muted, given their marginal presence both in the population and the workforce, creating potential space for higher mobility among the educationally qualified SC and OBC workforce aspiring for regular jobs.

To conclude, the analysis of employment composition by social groups depicts the differential impact of structural transformation on different social groups, shaped in part by the educational qualifications attained. Analyzing the sectoral aspect of structural change in employment for SC and OBC in Kerala and TN, we find that the same social group has dissimilar experiences of structural change in the two states. This is particularly true of the SC social group.

As Table 11.4 indicates, in 2017–18, at 36%, agriculture is still the principal employer of the SC workforce in TN, and the sector is characterized by increasing relative surplusness of labour. This is followed by industry (33%) and services (31%). The period of structural retrogression (2017–18 to 2021–22) saw a worsening, with the share of services declining and that of agriculture and industry rising. In Kerala, in 2017–18, it is the industrial sector (46%) is the principal employer of the SC workforce, followed by services (32%) and agriculture (22%). Interestingly, during the period of structural retrogression, the share of services increased (35%) and industry fell (44%). On the other hand, as we have already noted, casualization of employment, particularly in the non-farm sector, was more prevalent in Kerala than in TN. In 2017–18, 54% of the SC workforce was in casual employment in Kerala as opposed to 47% in TN. This casualization worsened during the period of structural retrogression in both states, and the difference between the two narrowed.

In 2017–18, for the OBC, services sector (50%) was the chief employer in Kerala, followed by industry (33%) and agriculture (18%). An OBC in Kerala was mostly self-employed (40%), followed by regular employment (30%) and casual employment (29%) in roughly similar proportions. Just for the sake of comparison, an UCH in Kerala roughly had a similar sectoral distribution of employment as the OBC, with a greater skew towards services (58%), followed by industry (24%) and agriculture (18%). In quality of employment, however, the UCH were significantly better off with regular employment, accounting for 45% of jobs, followed by self-employment (36%) and casual employment (19%). It is worth noting that the period of structural retrogression affected the UCH more than the OBC in the quality of jobs – regular employment declined to 38% in 2021–22 and self-employment increased to 45%. Casual employment also declined to 17%. For OBC the decline in regular employment was marginal – a little more than 1%.

In 2017–18, for OBC in TN, the services sector was the leading employer (39%), closely followed by industry (37%). Agriculture accounted for 25% of OBC jobs. OBC were mostly self-employed (37%), followed by regular employment (34%) and casual employment (29%). *It is interesting to note that for OBC occupational distribution and quality of employment in Kerala and TN are not that dissimilar.* That said, an OBC in Kerala is more likely to be in services and less likely in agriculture than in TN. On the other hand, an OBC in TN is slightly more likely to hold a regular job. In TN, the period of structural retrogression affects OBCs negatively with an increase in the share of agriculture (28%) and a decline in the share of both industry and services, with no change in the ranking, however. In terms of quality of employment, it reinforced the dominance of self-employment (40%) with a decline in regular employment (31%).

Likelihood Ratio-based analysis of employment mobility

With this analysis of structural change in Kerala and TN as the context, in this section, we formalize the preceding discussion around mobility by calculating the statistical likelihood of mobility based on activity status-based employment composition.

Statistical likelihood is calculated by dividing the number of self-employed/regular employed/casual employed in a social group by the total number of self-employed/regular employed/casual employed in a certain geography. *The likelihoods are derived based on the actual sample size of self-employed, regular employed, or casual employed in a social group (ST, SC, OBC, UCH, OR). The likelihoods calculated will help us understand the likelihood of a worker of a specific employment status belonging to the ST, SC, OBC, UCH, or OR.* For example, what is the likelihood that a casually employed person will belong to the SC social grouping? Or what is the likelihood that a person with regular employment will belong to the SC social grouping?

Our starting assumption is that in the absence of any bias, the likelihood of a worker of an employment status being in a specific social group equals the proportion of that social group in the total workforce. This statement will hold true if we assume that there are no underlying economic and social biases that hinder the participation of any social group in the workforce. If the likelihood of one employment status is consistently higher than other/s within the social group across rounds, we can conclude that there is a bias. *For example, if the likelihood that a self-employed worker is ST is significantly higher than the likelihood that a regular employed worker is ST, it implies a bias.* Comparing the likelihood of biases across different social groups will enable us to understand how social group membership affects the composition of employment.

As stated previously, the likelihood ratios of employment statuses in any social group should be equal if no biases exist. It is equivalent to saying that the difference in likelihood ratios between any two statuses of employment is zero. Based on the assumption of equality of likelihood ratios, we formulate the null hypothesis as the following:

H_0: $p_1 - p_2 = 0$

H_1: $p_1 - p_2 \neq 0$; where p_1, p_2 are the population proportions of different employment statuses. Because the employment status is categorized into three, we arrive at the following set of hypotheses.

1. $H_0{:}\, p_{SE} - p_{RE} = 0$ $\quad$ $H_1{:}\, p_{SE} - p_{RE} \neq 0$
2. $H_0{:}\, p_{SE} - p_{CE} = 0$ $\quad$ $H_1{:}\, p_{SE} - p_{CE} \neq 0$
3. $H_0{:}\, p_{RE} - p_{CE} = 0$ $\quad$ $H_1{:}\, p_{RE} - p_{CE} \neq 0$

The subscripts refer to casual employment (CE), regular/salaried employment (RE), and self-employment (SE). To prove that over-representation or under-representation exists, we only need to demonstrate that any one of the three cases is valid within each social group. We employ z-test[8] for testing the equality of proportions given by:

$$z_t = \frac{\left(\widehat{p_1} - \widehat{p_2}\right) - \left(p_1 - p_2\right)}{s_{\widehat{p_1} - \widehat{p_2}}}$$

We present the results of our analysis in the form of a mobility matrix for SC and OBC social groups in Kerala and TN. *Again, we are not presenting the other social groups due to sample size restrictions.*

In Table 11.7, the z statistics are given, and the significance is based on the ±1.96 cut-off. In the table, we have the three different activity statuses of employment, and the comparisons mentioned in the three hypotheses described earlier are presented in the corresponding cells. For example, cell 1 of column 2 contains the result of the likelihood analysis based on Hypothesis 1. The result presented in the cell implies that the likelihood of a self-employed person being SC is significantly less than the likelihood of a regular employed person is SC in Kerala.

In this section, we will analyze the likelihoods of employment for SC in Kerala and TN. *The likelihood of a casual employed worker being SC is consistently higher than the probability of a regular employed worker being*

Table 11.7 Mobility matrix based on likelihood analysis for SC and OBC workforce in Kerala and Tamil Nadu

	Kerala – SC		*Tamil Nadu – SC*		*Kerala – OBC*		*Tamil Nadu – OBC*	
1999–00	*RE*	*CE*	*RE*	*CE*	*RE*	*CE*	*RE*	*CE*
SE	-2.1	-5.8	-1.5	-18.2	6.8	0.76	9.9	22.7
RE	–	-2.7	–	-14.3	–	-5.9	–	11.2
2004–05	*RE*	*CE*	*RE*	*CE*	*RE*	*CE*	*RE*	*CE*
SE	-1.2	-6.9	-4.4	-12.7	3.02	-0.46	11.4	17.7
RE	–	-4.5	–	-7.1	–	-3.2	–	5.8
2009–10	*RE*	*CE*	*RE*	*CE*	*RE*	*CE*	*RE*	*CE*
SE	-1.94	-6.2	-1.8	-8.9	4.3	-0.99	6.9	14.6
RE	–	-3.5	–	-6	–	-5.02	–	6.2
2011–12	*RE*	*CE*	*RE*	*CE*	*RE*	*CE*	*RE*	*CE*
SE	-1.1	-4.5	-3.03	-7.6	3.4	-1.5	8.1	14.02
RE	–	-2.89	–	-3.96	–	-4.7	–	5.1
2017–18	*RE*	*CE*	*RE*	*CE*	*RE*	*CE*	*RE*	*CE*
SE	-0.82	-3.9	-3.1	-8.6	3.8	2.0	7.6	13.9
RE	–	-2.9	–	-5.6	–	-1.7	–	6.9
2021–22	*RE*	*CE*	*RE*	*CE*	*RE*	*CE*	*RE*	*CE*
SE	-1.6	-5.7	-2.6	-9.95	2.7	1.04	5.99	15.7
RE	–	-3.8	–	-6.9	–	-1.6	–	9.7

Source: Calculations based on unit level NSSO data. The figures are the test statistics of the two tailed z-test conducted. Assuming a normal distribution, a z statistic of ±1.96 translates as significant at 5% level. SE – self-employment, RE – regular employment, CE – casual employment.

SC or a self-employed worker being SC. This observation is true in the case of both TN and Kerala consistently during our period of analysis. In 1999–2000, the likelihood of a self-employed worker being SC was lower than the likelihood of a regular employed worker being SC. However, from 2004–05 onwards, we are not able to see a statistically significant difference between the likelihood of a self-employed worker being SC and a regular employed worker being SC in Kerala. In TN, from 2011–12 onwards, the likelihood of a regular employed worker being SC is higher than the likelihood of a selfemployed worker being SC.

The central conclusion we can draw from the likelihood of SC in Kerala and TN is the preponderance of casual employment. *The likelihood of a casual employed worker being SC is higher than the other two activity statuses consistently across the rounds analyzed.* The important distinction, however, *is the trend in TN where the likelihood of regular employed being SC is higher than a self-employed worker being SC.* It also implies that the *mobility among SC workforce in TN in terms of activity status is better despite a relatively less favourable sectoral employment composition. Kerala has a lower proportion of an agrarian SC workforce.* But despite the high pace of structural change in employment, *casual employment dominates among SC workforce in Kerala.* What this means is that while successful agrarian transition has certainly enabled the SC population in Kerala to move out of agriculture, but the SC population has not been able to *convert these gains into higher regular/ salaried employment in the non-farm sectors* consistently. *In TN, on the other hand, the SC workforce has higher mobility, even though the higher education attainments are similar to that of Kerala* (refer Table 11.6). It is remarkable considering the slower pace of structural transformation and the higher presence of industry among the SC workforce in TN than in Kerala.

In the case of the OBC workforce, *the likelihood of a self-employed worker being OBC is higher than the likelihood of a regular employed worker being OBC.* We observe this trend consistently across Kerala and TN during our period of analysis. There exists no statistically significant difference in the likelihood of a casual employed worker being OBC and a self-employed worker being OBC between 1999–2000 and 2011–12. However, in 2017–18, we observe that the likelihood ratio is significant (and positive) and consistent with the uptick in self-employment among OBC (refer Table 11.6). However, in 2021–22, the likelihood ratio between casual employment and self-employment is not significant for OBC. In general, there is no significant difference between the likelihood of a casual employed worker being OBC and a self-employed worker being OBC in Kerala.

In contrast, the likelihood of a self-employed worker belonging to OBC is higher than the likelihood of a casual employed worker being OBC across all periods of analysis in TN. Self-employment is the predominant activity status among the OBC in TN (refer Table 11.5). The results of the likelihood analysis are consistent with the activity status-based analysis. Another key point of distinction between OBC workers in TN and Kerala can be understood based on the likelihood ratio between regular employment and casual employment. Consistently, in TN, the likelihood of a regular employed worker being OBC is higher than the likelihood of a casual employed worker being OBC. Two aspects are important here – first, the distinction between SC and OBC workforces in TN, and second, the difference in likelihoods among OBC workers across states. The higher levels of educational attainment among OBCs compared to SCs (refer Table 11.6) in TN, along with the higher share of services sector employment among OBC workers compared to the SC could be the reason for the divergence in likelihoods among the SC and the OBC in TN. Despite similar levels of educational attainment among OBCs of Kerala and TN and more favourable workforce composition, the likelihood of a casual employed worker being OBC is higher than the likelihood of a regular employed worker being OBC. The stability of the likelihoods across rounds in Kerala and TN underscores our observation about the impediments to mobility faced by the OBC workforce in Kerala than in TN. Clearly, despite a slower pace of structural change in output, the OBC workforce in TN has made significant achievements in mobility.

The difference in the mobility of SC and OBC in Kerala and in TN appears to be heavily influenced by the population composition and the nature of structural change. If the total number of jobs in each employment category are to be shared between the two groups (SC and OBC) in one case and the four groups (SC – scheduled caste, OBC – other backward class, UCH – upper-class Hindu, and OR – other religion) in another case, then, naturally, the likelihoods in the first group case will be higher. In regular employment, it will matter because all the groups in Kerala will vie for that pool. If we calculate, for Kerala, the likelihood that a regular employed person will be UCH, it is significantly higher than self-employment in all years except 2021–22, when as we have noted earlier, the share of regular employment falls (our analysis did not find a statistically significant difference for 2021–22). The likelihood that a regular employed person will be UCH is significantly higher than casual employment in all rounds considered. *Essentially, the presence of UCH in regular employment continues to be high and this presents challenges for the mobility of SC and OBC in Kerala.*

To conclude, the SC and OBC have better mobility in TN than in Kerala, especially when we are looking at the likelihood ratios with respect to regular/salaried employment. Despite the higher pace of structural transformation and more favourable employment composition among the SC and OBC workforce in Kerala, the gains have not materialized as mobility in terms of job quality. In Kerala, the OR and UCH constitute a small but significant proportion of workforce unlike in TN. The results for the SC and OBC indicate that the *OR and UCH workforce in Kerala has significant mobility in the labour market in terms of accessing regular employment.* What does this mean in the context of movements around land and caste pioneered by the SC in Kerala and the OBC in TN? The mobility experience of SC and OBC in these two South Indian states is better than the national average. However, whereas movements from below have challenged the hegemony of the UCH and rural elites in both states, the relative mobility of the SC and the OBC is better in TN.

Conclusion

At the aggregate level, both Kerala and TN have undergone a Lewisian transformation before India as a whole. In both states, the service sector dominates output and employment. However, reflecting the fact that industrialization was the centrepiece of TN's growth strategy (see Kalaiyarasan and Vijayabaskar 2021), industry accounts for a substantially greater share of output in TN than in Kerala. That said, Kerala has been much more successful in moving the workforce out of agriculture. TN, on the other hand, has been much less successful in moving the workforce out of agriculture and is stuck with, relatively speaking, much more surplus labour in the sector.[9] This is in part because service growth in TN was not labour-absorbing, particularly in the period 1999–2000 to 2009–10. In addition, in TN, the bulk of the non-agrarian labour absorption is done by industry, with its share in employment consistently rising, whereas its share of output declines almost secularly. This, then, has clear adverse implications for sectoral labour productivity growth.

In both states, tertiary education attainment has improved significantly across social groups and is not dissimilar between the two. However, the gaps between social groups in terms of tertiary education attainment have narrowed very slowly, with the UCH retaining primacy in this regard and this has implications for mobility. Given that the SC were far more likely to be employed in agriculture than any other social group, moving the workforce out of agriculture has benefited them the most. And given Kerala's success, compared with that in TN, in moving the workforce out of agriculture, the SC in Kerala has benefited from structural change than in TN. An SC in Kerala is more likely to be in industry than in TN. That said, whereas the dominant employment contract in both Kerala and TN is casual employment, an SC in Kerala is less likely to access regular employment than in TN. Similarly, whereas for the OBC in Kerala and TN have similar sectoral employment profiles, an OBC in the latter is more likely to access regular employment than in the former. In Kerala, despite their diminishing weight in the workforce, the UCH and OR in Kerala have improved their primacy in labour market outcomes, continuing to disproportionately access the best jobs – regular employment in the service sector. As a result, paradoxically, despite Kerala's better performance in terms of structural change (particularly in moving the workforce out of agriculture), TN affords better mobility to the SC and OBC in terms of quality of employment, largely because inter-social group competition for the best jobs is more muted.

Shifting our lens to what has been termed the "dynamic bonus" of structural change (see for example, Storm 2015) where structural change *contributes to raising the average labour productivity growth over time*. Kaldor (1966, 1967) identified three empirical regularities which have been collectively termed Kaldor's Growth Laws in the heterodox structural change literature, which contribute towards this dynamic bonus. Central to these laws is the role of manufacturing in not only sustaining economy-wide productivity growth, but also enlarging the market through a process of cumulative causation as well as generating employment in other sectors through a process of backward and forward linkages (see Storm 2015, 67–74, for a discussion around the importance of Kaldorian Growth Laws for dynamic structural change). Seen in that light, TN's secular decline in manufacturing output share even as the employment share rises and the consequent low rate of growth of sectoral labour productivity becomes a particular point of concern, constraining mobility gains as well. Seen from a Kaldorian perspective, the relative smallness of Kerala's manufacturing sector becomes an issue, constraining it from dealing with mobility issues outlined earlier. That said, the performance of Kerala and TN has to be assessed keeping in mind that for the national economy, this has been a period of "jobless growth" (see Kannan and Srinivasan 2009). Equally, the structural retrogression witnessed in the recent past (see Mehrotra 2024) is likely to constrain both Kerala and TN as they seek to look ahead.

However, propelled by movements from below around issues related to caste and land, Kerala and TN's remarkable achievements in human and social development and capacities for institutional renewal suggest that both are well-positioned to address these new challenges.

We have not included in this chapter two major aspects that have a bearing on the issues discussed – migration (Zachariah et al. 2001; Srivastava 2011; Zachariah and Rajan 2015; Rajan et al. 2017) and wages (Jose 1978, 2017). Both Kerala and TN are part of very active migration corridors – both internal and external. Therefore, migration is an important contributor to household incomes in these states. Also, migration affects wages in states along with a whole host of factors such as the implementation of employment guarantee programmes, collective bargaining, minimum wage implementation, etc. We hope to incorporate them in future research.

Notes

1 Uttarakhand and Kerala rank joint first (see NITI Aayog 2024: p69). If we consider only large states, TN ranks second.
2 If only large states are taken into account, Gujarat ranks first in terms of per capita income.
3 Implying, *rate of growth* of labour productivity in agriculture is greater than in non-agriculture.
4 It is important to note that this is an economy-wide phenomena. As Mehrotra (2024) notes "Worse still, a return to agriculture is reversing the structural change in employment in the economy." Calling it "structural retrogression" is our characterization.
5 Implying that the rate of growth of non-agricultural labour productivity is much higher than that of agricultural labour productivity, therefore impeding the transfer of labour out of agriculture.
6 The first phase, therefore, implies a divergence between agricultural and non-agricultural labour productivities, with the latter growing much faster than the former. The second phase implies a convergence.
7 As we have noted in fn3, in the first phase, there was divergence between agricultural and non-agricultural productivity growth. We now note that within the non-agricultural sector, there was a divergence in labour productivity growth between industrial (slower) and service (faster) sectors as well.
8 In the formula, note that p1–p2=0 as per our hypothesis.

Also, the standard error is $s_{\widehat{p_1}-\widehat{p_2}} = \sqrt{\frac{p_1 * (1-p_1)}{n_1} + \frac{p_2 * (1-p_2)}{n_2}}$

9 The Kerala growth model has been less successful at job creation and has relatively high unemployment (see Heller and Tornquist (2021).

References

Abraham, V. 2013. "Missing Labour or Consistent 'De-Feminisation'"? *Economic and Political Weekly* 99–108.
Devika, J. 2010. "Egalitarian Developmentalism, Communist Mobilization, and the Question of Caste in Kerala State, India." *The Journal of Asian Studies* 69(3): 799–820. https://doi.org/10.1017/S0021911810001506.
Fogel, R. W. 2000. *Simon S. Kuznets: April 30, 1901-July 9, 1985*. Cambridge, Massachusetts: National Bureau of Economic Research Cambridge. https://www.nber.org/papers/w7787
Harriss, J. 2015. "Privilege in Dispute: Economic and Political Change and Caste Relations in Tamil Nadu Early in the 21st Century (SWP 44)." *Null*. https://doi.org/null.
Heller, P. and Törnquist, O. 2021. "Making Sense of Kerala.' *The Hindu*, December 13, 2013.
Himanshu, Lanjouw, P., Murgai, R., and Stern, N. 2013. "Nonfarm Diversification, Poverty, Economic Mobility, and Income Inequality: A Case Study in Village India." *Agricultural Economics* 44(4–5): 461–73. https://doi.org/10.1111/agec.12029.
Jose, A. V. 1978. "Real Wages, Employment, and Income of Agricultural Labourers." *Economic and Political Weekly* A16–A20.
Jose, A. V. 2017. "Agricultural Wages in Indian States." *The Indian Journal of Labour Economics* 60(3): 333–45. https://doi.org/10.1007/s41027-018-0111-x.
Kalaiyarasan, A. and Vijayabaskar, M. 2021. *The Dravidian Model: Interpreting the Political Economy of Tamil Nadu*. Cambridge: Cambridge University Press.
Kaldor, N. 1966. *Causes of the Slow Rate of Economic Growth of the United Kingdom*. Cambridge University Press.
Kaldor, Nicholas. 1967. *Strategic Factors in Economic Development*. Cornell University Press.
Kannan, K.P. and Raveendran, G. 2009. "Growth Sans Employment: A Quarter Century of Jobless Growth in India's Organized Manufacturing." *Economic and Political Weekly* 44(10): 80–91.
Kurup, K. K. N. 1994. "The Intellectual Movements and Anti-Caste Struggles in Kerala." *Proceedings of the Indian History Congress* 55: 673–77.
Mehrotra, S. 2024. "Some Proof Required: Modi Government's Abysmal Record of No Jobs." *The Wire*. May 8, 2024. https://thewire.in/labour/some-proof-required-modi-government-abysmal-record-no-jobs.
Mohanty, M. 2009. *Structural Change and Employment: An Empirical Exploration*. Working Paper WPS No. 639; Indian Institute of Management Calcutta Working Paper Series. Kolkata: Indian Institute of Management. https://www.iimcal.ac.in/sites/default/files/pdfs/wps-639_1_0.pdf.
Mohanty, M. 2006. "Social Inequality, Labour Market Dynamics and Reservation." *Economic and Political Weekly* 41(35): 2–8.
Munshi, K. 2017. "Caste and Economic Mobility in India." *VoxDev*. https://voxdev.org/topic/labour-markets-migration/caste-and-economic-mobility-india.
National Statistical Commission. 2018. "Report of the Commitee on Real Sector Statistics". New Delhi: Ministry of Statistics and Programme Implementation.
NITI Aayog. 2024. *SDG India Index 2023–24*. NITI Aayog, Government of India. New Delhi: Niti Aayog. https://www.niti.gov.in/sites/default/files/2024-07/SDG_India_Index_2023-24.pdf.
Pandian, J. 1987. *Caste, Nationalism and Ethnicity: An Interpretation of Tamil Cultural History and Social Order*. Mumbai: Popular Prakashan.

Rajan, A. 2021. "Essays in Structural Change in Labour Force-A View from the Standpoint of Caste, Gender and Informality." Unpublished PhD dissertation, Indian Institute of Management Calcutta.

Rajan, S. Irudaya, D'Sami, Bernard., Raj, S. S. A. 2017. Tamil Nadu Migration Survey 2015. *Economic and Political Weekly* 52(21): 85–94.

Reddy, A. B., and Swaminathan, M. 2014. "Intergenerational Occupational Mobility in Rural India: Evidence from Ten Villages." *Review of Agrarian Studies* 4(1): 95–134. https://ageconsearch.umn.edu/record/308509/files/Occupational%20Mobility%20in%20Rural%20India.pdf.

Saith, A. 1990. "Development Strategies and the Rural Poor." *Journal of Peasant Studies* 17(2): 171–244.

Srivastava, R. 2011. "Internal Migration in India." *Human Development in India.* https://ruralindiaonline.org/media/documents/16wkshpReportInternalMigrationHumanDevelopmentIndia2EN20111231.pdf#page=7.

Storm, S. 2015. "Structural Change." *Development and Change* 46(4): 666–99. https://doi.org/10.1111/dech.12169.

Storm, S., and Naastepad, C. W. M. 2005. "Strategic Factors in Economic Development: East Asian Industrialization 1950–2003," *Development and Change* 36(6): 1059–94.

Wade, R. 2003. "Introduction: Creating Capitalisms." In *Governing the Market: Economic Theory and the Role of Government in East Asian Industrialization*, R. edited by R. Wade, xiii–iiv. Princeton, NJ: Princeton University Press.

Zachariah, K. C., and Rajan, S. Irudaya. 2015. *Dynamics of Emigration and Remittances in Kerala: Results from the Kerala Migration Survey 2014.* http://14.139.171.199:8080/xmlui/bitstream/handle/123456789/81/WP463.pdf?sequence=1&isAllowed=y.

Zachariah, K. C., Mathew, E. T., and Rajan, S. I. 2001. Impact of Migration on Kerala's Economy and Society. *International Migration* 39(1): 63–87. https://doi.org/10.1111/1468-2435.00135

Appendix Table A1 Employment composition of social groups by sector and activity status – all India level

	1999–2000			*2004–05*			*2017–18*			*2021–22*		
Sector	*Farm*	*Industry*	*Service*	*Farm*	*Industry*	*Service*	*Farm*	*Industry*	**Service**	*Farm*	*Industry*	*Service*
SC												
SE	22.38	5.19	7.58	21.43	6.43	8.89	23.83	5.61	9.51	25.71	6.37	9.99
RE	1.22	2.62	6.58	0.34	4.51	10.46	0.42	5.57	13.83	0.44	5.4	13.93
CE	43.4	8.21	2.81	27.19	18.52	2.25	19.86	19.36	2.01	16.19	19.85	2.12
Total	67	16.03	16.98	48.96	29.45	21.59	44.11	30.54	25.35	42.34	31.62	26.04
OBC												
SE	38.8	7.33	10.91	34.39	8.03	12.89	33.76	7.48	14.41	38.18	7.67	14.05
RE	0.74	3.7	7.09	0.4	4.86	10.54	0.56	6.19	14.67	0.5	6.21	13.35
CE	23.37	5.59	2.48	15.79	10.92	2.17	9.35	11.65	1.93	7.76	10.81	1.48
Total	62.91	16.62	20.48	50.58	23.81	25.6	43.67	25.32	31.01	46.44	24.69	28.88
All												
SE	35.63	6.18	10.8	31.85	7.39	12.98	32.32	6.5	13.39	35.54	6.89	13.4
RE	0.9	3.93	9.23	0.41	5.44	12	0.54	6.34	15.96	0.42	6.27	14.81
CE	25.26	5.6	2.48	16.64	11.43	1.86	11.27	11.96	1.71	9.51	11.72	1.44
Total	61.79	15.7	22.51	48.9	24.26	26.84	44.13	24.8	31.06	45.47	24.88	29.65

Source: Data collected by authors based on NSSO and PLFS unit level data for the years under consideration.

12 Organized peasant migration and intergenerational mobility

A case of Madambam settlement in Kannur District, Kerala

Govindaprasad P. K. and Syam Prasad

Introduction

The migration of peasants from Travancore to Malabar[1] is an important chapter in the developmental history of the hilly areas of North Kerala due to its significant consequences on the socio-economic spheres. In their studies on different aspects of this migration, several scholars and experts, such as Tharakan (1976), Joseph (1988), Viswanathan (2015), and Varghese (2009), have discussed the causes and consequences of the unorganized peasant migration in Kerala. Although organized peasant migration, too, occurred in the region around the same time (Sebastian 2002), there is a dearth of detailed study. Our study is an attempt to trace the history of organized peasant migration in Malabar and tries to analyze its consequences.

The organized peasant migration of the Knanayas, a Christian community, into Malabar is of great significance. In AD 345, the Knanaya community first immigrated from Mesopotamia to Kodungallur under the leadership of Knanaya Thomman, and later their family members migrated from Travancore to Malabar. The Syro-Malabar Catholic Archeparchy of Kottayam (commonly known as Kottayam Diocese) organized this migration of farmers from Kottayam to Rajapuram, Madambam, and Ranipuram. The Knanaya community undertook three such organized migrations – the first from Travancore to Rajapuram in Kasaragod district (2–4 February 1943), the second from Travancore to Madambam in Kannur district (6–8 May 1943), and the third from Travancore to Ranipuram (26–27 January 1970) (Sebastian 2002 and Kappukalayil 2017).

The important causes of peasant migration were high population density in Travancore, near exhaustion of cultivable land, the economic depression of the 1930s, famine, poverty, availability of vast areas of cultivable and forest land in Malabar at cheap prices, and changes in the peasants' economic conditions. The major consequences of this migration include an increase in the Christian population, an increase in the capital formation in agriculture, a change in the cropping pattern, an improvement in the social infrastructure of the migrant centres, and a decline in the forest area (Netumgattu 2014).

Besides these, it is critical to understand the intergenerational mobility of peasant migrant households for assessing the long-term impact of peasant

DOI: 10.4324/9781003601289-15

migration on the development of the settlement area. To analyze the early consequences of peasant migration and the intergenerational mobility of peasant migrant households in the settlement area, we chose Madambam village in the Kannur district. In this chapter, we delve into the history of peasant migration of the Knanaya community into Madambam and its contribution to the early development of this area. We also analyze the intergenerational mobility among the members of peasant migrant households in the Madambam region over three generations to understand (i) the impact of organized peasant migration on the development of the region, (ii) the intergenerational educational mobility among the male members of the peasant migrant households, (iii) the Intergenerational occupational mobility among the male members of the peasant migrant households, and (iv) the impact of the COVID-19 pandemic on peasant migrant households in the peasant migrant settlement.

The descriptive study is based on the primary data we collected from 50 peasant migrant households in the Madambam region. We used a mobility transition matrix to evaluate intergenerational mobility, including educational and occupational mobility. We also conducted five interviews to probe the impact of the COVID-19 pandemic on peasant migrant households. Subsequent sections provide a brief history of the migration and a comprehensive account of the data analysis and interpretation.

Organized peasant migration in Madambam

Peasant migration in Madambam

Madambam is a small village in the Sreekandapuram panchayat of Kannur district, Kerala. The name Madambam is derived from the Malayalam word *madamb*, which means the confluence of a small stream and a river. While initially named Alex Nagar Colony in memory of Mar Alexander Choolaparambil, it is also popular as the Madambam colony (Netumgattu 2014).

Migration to Alex Nagar

Bishop Mar Alexander Choolaparambil and Chevaliar V. J. Joseph Kandoth of the Kottayam Diocese led the immigration into North Malabar after purchasing 2000 acres of land in Payyavoor and Madambam from Seemanathakam Karakkattitam Unnamman Nair in March 1943. From 10 May 1943 onwards, the surveyor divided this land. The diocese then distributed this land among 100 selected households on 10 May 1943.

The low-income families, mainly from Meenachil *taluk*, then migrated to Madambam or Alex Nagar, which already had settlers belonging to the *thekkum bhagam* (southern) Catholic sect of the Kottayam Diocese. Their prime occupation was agriculture, and they only had primary education. When they first settled in the region, they cultivated rice and tapioca. Their initial years were full of struggle, with minimal access to transportation, health services, and education.

To help the people overcome these difficulties, the church began undertaking various developmental activities in the settlement. In 1945, it established the Mary Land Higher Elementary School in Madambam, followed by the Sacred Heart Elementary School in Payyavoor in 1946. It also set up an elementary school in Kotoor Vayal. With the help of the people in both dioceses (Madambam and Payyavoor) and under the leadership of Father Mannathumakkil, the church also expanded the Payyavoor–Potikkalam road in 1953.

Father Muthukattil was appointed as the vicar of Madambam in 1961. Father Muthukattil's plans for the development of Madambam included giving importance to growth in agriculture, financial self-sufficiency, and health and education of the people. He also had plans to construct a dam near Madambam. The vicar had also initiated a small yet successful savings scheme, a rubber plantation scheme, the construction of Mercy Hospital, a lift irrigation project in Madambam, and the development of several schools for the betterment of the people in Madambam (Netumgattu 2014).

Development in both dioceses (Madambam and Payyavoor) occurred under the aegis of the church, particularly the policies of the vicars appointed in the Payyavoor and Madambam dioceses. These vicars had focused on investing in social overhead capital and commercial agriculture, which had a significant impact on the educational and occupational changes in the settlement area.

Intergenerational mobility

Intergenerational educational mobility reflects the association between parents' and adult children's educational attainment. While a strong association means low mobility, a weak association refers to high mobility. Educational attainment has high perceived value because it is a predictor of several social impacts, including income, health, longevity, marriage, parenting, fertility, political participation, and attitude. Education not only plays a critical role in intergenerational economic and occupational mobility; it also determines economic persistence and intergenerational mobility (Torche 2019). The important factors that influence intergenerational educational mobility are economic development, gender (Aydemir and Yazici 2017), parents' financial and educational status (Dustman 2008; Tansel 2015; Azomabou and Yitbarek 2016; Torul and Oztunali 2017; Latif 2019; Lam and Liu 2019; Emran et al. 2019) public expenditure in education (Iyigun1999), credit constraint (Lee and Lee 2019), state incentive for pursuing education (Andrade and Thomsen, 2018), local public education policy (Card, Domnisoru, and Taylor 2018), and supply of schooling (Assaad and Saleh, 2018).

Table 12.1 shows the intergenerational educational mobility between the first- and second-generation male members of Madambam's peasant migrant households.

Table 12.1 Intergenerational educational mobility between first and second generation (male)

	Second generation											
First generation	*Level of education*	*Pre-primary*	*Primary*	*Upper primary*	*Secondary*	*Higher secondary*	*Vocational education*	*Under graduation*	*Post-graduation*	*Diploma*	*Professional*	*Total*
	Pre-primary	0	4	2	3	0	0	0	0	0	0	9
	Raw (%)	0	44.44	22.22	33.34	0	0	0	0	0	0	5.14
	Primary	0	21	46	41	15	0	11	2	3	12	151
	Raw (%)	0	13.91	30.46	27.16	9.93	0	7.28	1.32	1.99	7.95	86.29
	Upper primary	0	0	0	3	5	0	2	0	0	1	11
	Raw (%)	0	0	0	27.28	45.45	0	18.18	0	0	9.09	6.29
	Secondary	0	0	1	0	0	0	0	0	0	0	1
	Raw (%)	0	0	100	0	0	0	0	0	0	0	0.57
	Higher secondary	0	0	0	0	0	0	1	0	0	2	3
	Raw (%)	0	0	0	0	0	0	33.33	0	0	66.67	1.71
	Vocational education	0	0	0	0	0	0	0	0	0	0	0
	Raw (%)	0	0	0	0	0	0	0	0	0	0	0
	Undergraduation	0	0	0	0	0	0	0	0	0	0	0
	Raw (%)	0	0	0	0	0	0	0	0	0	0	0
	Post-graduation	0	0	0	0	0	0	0	0	0	0	0
	Raw (%)	0	0	0	0	0	0	0	0	0	0	0
	Diploma	0	0	0	0	0	0	0	0	0	0	0
	Raw (%)	0	0	0	0	0	0	0	0	0	0	0
	Professional	0	0	0	0	0	0	0	0	0	0	0
	Raw (%)	0	0	0	0	0	0	0	0	0	0	0
	Total	0	25	49	47	20	0	14	2	3	15	175
	Raw (%)	0	14.29	28	26.86	11.43	0	8	1.14	1.71	8.57	100

Source: Primary data collected from field survey by authors in 2020.

While many cases of upward educational mobility between the two generations of male members are evident, some instances of immobility and downward mobility also exist. Of all the pairs studied, 87.4% reflect upward educational mobility, 12% immobility, and 0.57% downward mobility.

The key reason for the upward educational mobility is the church-facilitated access to education. Most second-generation people were born and raised in Madambam, and their parents prioritized educating their children. However, due to poverty, lack of infrastructure, and other institutional bottlenecks, most could not enrol for higher studies.

Table 12.2 shows the intergenerational educational mobility between the second and third-generation male members of Madambam's peasant migrant households. The third-generation men were more educated than their second-generation counterparts and had completed professional and diploma courses compared to other levels of education. Our intergenerational educational mobility analysis reveals both intergenerational educational immobility and upward intergenerational educational mobility. Of all the pairs studied, the upward mobility rate (98.07%) is higher than the immobility rate (1.92%). The intergenerational upward educational mobility between the second and third generation is higher than between the first- and second-generation male members of the peasant migrant households. This shows that the influence of parents' level of education on their children is less among the third generation than among the second generation.

Intergenerational occupational mobility

Occupation mobility is the relationship between occupation origins (or parents' occupation) and destinations (individual occupation outcomes) (Chapman T, 2020). A movement from a low-wage to a high-wage occupation shows upward occupational mobility. And a movement from a high-wage to a low-wage occupation shows downward occupational mobility (Gabriel 2003). Many factors influence occupational mobility, including the level of education. Studies by Sicherman (1990), Ruiz (2016), Borjas (1993), and Mayer et al. (1979) show the positive and significant influence of education on occupational mobility. Rajarshi (2010) observed that along with education, parents' occupation also significantly influences a child's occupational status. Landholding, caste, and educational and economic factors also affect an individual's intergenerational occupational mobility (Tiwari 2016).

Table 12.3 shows the intergenerational occupational mobility between the first- and second-generation male members of peasant migrant households in Madambam.

Most (98.28%) first-generation peasant migrants (male) are farmers. Most of their sons (69.71%) also chose farming as their main occupation. The occupational choices of the second-generation male members include jobs in the following areas: construction, electricity board, transportation, accommodation and food service, information and communication, doctors,

Table 12.2 Intergenerational educational mobility between second and third generation (male)

		Third generation										
Second generation	*Level of education*	*Pre-primary*	*Primary*	*Upper primary*	*Secondary*	*Higher secondary*	*Vocational education*	*Undergraduation*	*Post-graduation*	*Diploma*	*Professional*	*Total*
	Pre-primary	0	0	0	0	0	0	0	0	0	0	0
	Raw (%)	0	0	0	0	0	0	0	0	0	0	0
	Primary	0	0	0	0	1	5	4	0	3	0	13
	Raw (%)	0	0	0	0	7.69	38.46	30.77	0	23.08	0	25
	Upper primary	0	0	0	2	5	2	2	0	10	1	22
	Raw (%)	0	0	0	9.09	22.73	9.09	9.09	0	45.45	4.55	42.31
	Secondary	0	0	0	1	2	0	1	2	3	3	12
	Raw (%)	0	0	0	8.33	16.67	0	8.33	16.67	25	25	23.08
	Higher secondary	0	0	0	0	0	1	1	0	1	1	4
	Raw (%)	0	0	0	0	0	25	25	0	25	25	7.69
	Vocational education	0	0	0	0	0	0	0	0	0	0	0
	Raw (%)	0	0	0	0	0	0	0	0	0	0	0
	Undergraduation	0	0	0	0	0	0	0	0	0	0	0
	Raw (%)	0	0	0	0	0	0	0	0	0	0	0
	Post-graduation	0	0	0	0	0	0	0	0	0	0	0
	Raw (%)	0	0	0	0	0	0	0	0	0	0	0
	Diploma	0	0	0	0	0	0	0	0	0	0	0
	Raw (%)	0	0	0	0	0	0	0	0	0	0	0
	Professional	0	0	0	0	0	0	0	0	1	0	1
	Raw (%)	0	0	0	0	0	0	0	0	100	0	1.92
	Total	0	0	0	3	8	8	8	2	18	5	52
	Raw (%)	0	0	0	5.77	15.38	15.38	15.38	3.85	34.62	9.62	100

Source: Primary data collected from field survey by authors in 2020.

Table 12.3 Intergenerational occupational mobility between first and second generation (male)

	Occupation	*Second generation*				
		Unskilled	*Farmer*	*Skilled*	*White collar*	*Total*
First generation	Unskilled	0	0	0	0	0
	Raw (%)	0	0	0	0	0
	Farmer	0	122	28	22	172
	Raw (%)	0	70.93	16.28	12.79	98.2
	Skilled	0	0	1	2	3
	Raw (%)	0	0	33.33	66.66	1.71
	White Collar	0	0	0	0	0
	Raw (%)	0	0	0	0	0
	Total	0	122	29	24	175
	Raw (%)	0	69.71	16.57	13.71	100

Source: Primary data collected from field survey by the authors in 2020.

nurses, private- and public-sector administration, defence, religious institutions, finance, insurance, and self-employment.

Most sons of farmers chose farming as their occupation. Most sons of men with skilled jobs moved to white-collar jobs.

The preceding analysis reveals that of the total number of pairs, the intergenerational occupational immobility (70.28%) between the first and second generation is greater than the mobility (29.7%), with immobility higher in farming than in skilled jobs.

Table 12.4 shows the intergenerational occupational mobility between the second and third-generation male members of peasant migrant households in Madambam.

Of the 52 third-generation male members studied, 90.38% men work in the agricultural sector, with 72.3% of their sons engaged in non-agricultural activities, most moving to white-collar jobs.

Most sons of men with skilled jobs remained in skilled jobs just as most sons of men with white-collar jobs remained in the same jobs. Only 25% of sons of men with skilled jobs moved to white-collar jobs, with the rest remaining in skilled jobs. However, none of the sons of men in white-collar jobs moved jobs.

The occupational choices of the third-generation male members included self-employment, vehicle repair, transportation, accommodation and food services-related jobs, telephone-related jobs, activity in the financial and insurance sector, administrative activity, public administration and defence, and other services. Most third-generation members are emigrants who moved abroad in search of better employment.

The analysis shows that intergenerational occupational mobility (67.30%) is greater than immobility (32.69%). Intergenerational occupational

Table 12.4 Intergenerational occupational mobility between second and third generation (male)

	Occupation	*Third generation*				
		Unskilled	*Farmer*	*Skilled*	*White collar*	*Total*
Second generation	Unskilled	0	0	0	0	0
	Raw (%)	0	0	0	0	0
	Farmer	0	13	13	21	47
	Raw (%)	0	27.66	27.66	44.68	90.38
	Skilled	0	0	3	1	4
	Raw (%)	0	0	75	25	7.69
	White Collar	0	0	0	1	1
	Raw (%)	0	0	0	100	3.45
	Total	0	13	16	23	52
	Raw (%)	0	25	30.77	44.23	100

Source: Primary data collected from field survey by the authors in 2020.

immobility is prevalent in farming, skilled jobs, and white-collar jobs, with high immobility in white-collar jobs followed by skilled jobs.

Impact of COVID-19 on migrant peasant households

The COVID-19 pandemic intensely impacted international migration, reshaping patterns, and trends in unprecedented ways. Stringent government-implemented regulations worldwide to curb virus spread, such as border closures, travel bans, and restrictions on mobility, led to a drastic decline in global human movement. These measures also created significant challenges for migrants, including economic hardships, social isolation, and limited access to essential services (Guadagno 2020).

The pandemic's impact on migration has been particularly severe in certain regions. Before the pandemic, India was the leading country of origin for international migrants, with many individuals moving abroad for different reasons. Mexico, China, Russia, and Syria also had large populations of migrants residing outside their borders, collectively accounting for slightly more than one-third of all international migrants in 2019 (Chamie 2020). Thus, it is likely the COVID-19 pandemic severely affected different segments of these countries. For instance, Nithya N. R. (2021) found considerable strain on the local economy following the COVID-19-propelled significant return migration to Kerala, adversely affecting household investments in land, housing, education, and healthcare. Additionally, student mobility trends shifted, with a significant reduction in students' interest in studying abroad (Mok et al. 2021). A study by Kikkawa Takenaka et al. (2020) observed that the pandemic had resulted in a significant reduction in remittances in Asia, especially in South Asia. Migrants from Asia and the Pacific region also faced job insecurity, especially those in the retail, hospitality, manufacturing, and food services sectors. In this section, we attempt to analyze the impact of COVID-19 pandemic on peasant migrant households and the post-pandemic scenario of international migration among the migrant peasant households in Madambam.

To understand the impact of COVID-19 in the Madambam region, we conducted interviews with five respondents from peasant migrant households. All respondents agreed that during the pandemic, members of their family permanently settled in the United States, United Kingdom, Canada, and Israel did not return to Kerala. There was also a slight decline in remittance income for these peasant migrant families. After the pandemic, the flow of international migrants increased in this region, with most younger generation members emigrating for better employment opportunities and higher education. The following is the response of a peasant migrant household member regarding the impact of the COVID-19 pandemic in the Madambam region.

> *My family migrated to Madambam in 1947. The first generation engaged in agriculture. I am currently running a business, and my son, who is settled in the US, is also involved in business. In Kerala, many people prefer to leave due to unemployment, low economic growth, and corruption. Even during the COVID-19 pandemic, most emigrants did not return to Madambam, choosing instead to remain in their destination countries, where many have settled permanently. Although there was a slight decline in remittance income during the pandemic, families mitigated this issue through farming. Despite agriculture not being a highly profitable venture, many increased their agricultural activities during the pandemic. Post-pandemic, the younger generation of peasant families is migrating to other countries for higher education and job opportunities.*

Discussion

Our analysis clarifies that peasant migration in Madambam was organized. Many development initiatives – focused mainly on investment in social overhead capital and commercial cultivation – were launched under the aegis of the church. This formed the basis for the development of the Madambam/Alex Nagar colony. Most peasant migrants were less educated and engaged in cultivation. The investments in social overhead capital and in primary and upper primary schools increased the access to education, helping improve the educational attainment of second-generation members.

However, the increased educational attainment was not sufficient to procure other skilled jobs. Moreover, as employment opportunities were minimal during the time, most second-generation members sought employment in the primary sector, cultivating more commercial crops. The increased income from commercial crops improved their financial status, facilitating more investment in the education of their children. The increase in public spending and gradation of the school, rise in higher educational opportunities, and the improvement in parents' financial status resulted in an upward intergenerational educational mobility between the second and third generations. This supports the arguments of other studies.

Important factors that influenced intergenerational educational mobility were economic development (Aydemor and Yazici 2017) financial status, and educational attainment of parents (Dustman 2008; Torul and Oztunali 2017; Latif 2019), public expenditure in education (Iyigun 1999), credit constraints (Lee and Lee 2019), and supply of schooling (Assaad and Saleh 2018). The high educational attainment helped the third generation find employment in nursing, hotel management, teaching, engineering, and medicine. Our analysis found that educational attainment had a significant positive impact on occupational mobility, which supports Torche's arguments that education plays a significant role in intergenerational economic and occupational mobility (Torche 2019).

Our study shows that only the second-generation members of peasant migrant households work in the primary sector, whereas most third-generation members are engaged in the tertiary sector. This indicates the rural settlement's transformation from an agrarian to a non-agrarian village. This supports the arguments of Pani and Jafar (2010), who suggested that mass education led to growth in Kerala, leading to non-agrarian villages. Here, the education-led growth converted the settlement area (Madambam colony) into a non-agrarian village, with the major share of income of the peasant migrant households over the past few decades coming from the non-farm sector.

Meanwhile, most emigrants did not return to Madambam because of the COVID-19 pandemic, and remittance income among the migrant families also saw a slight fall.

Conclusion

Church-led organized peasant migration resulted in the development of social overhead capital and the agricultural sector in the Madambam colony. With the state government supporting these efforts and expanding the educational sector, improved education and financial positions enabled the younger generation to pursue job-oriented courses, such as engineering, medicine, nursing, and hotel management. While this led to upward educational and occupational mobility, especially between the second and third generations, occupational mobility moved downwards, indicating unemployment issues in the labour market. Consequently, many young people migrated abroad for better remuneration, reducing dependence on the primary sector and increasing foreign earnings. Currently, only second-generation members and less-educated third-generation members work in the primary sector. Although still agrarian, most households now rely on non-farm income, with remittances being a major source. This education-led development transformed Madambam from an agrarian to a non-agrarian village, with many NRIs primarily settled in the United Kingdom, United States, and Canada. During the COVID-19 pandemic, minimal return migration resulted in a slight decline in remittance income. Our study suggests strengthening the agricultural sector and creating more employment opportunities alongside educational development to reduce the brain drain.

Acknowledgement

We thank the Indian Council of Social Science Research for providing financial assistance. We also thank Dr S. Ramaswamy and Dr T. J. Joseph for their valuable comments. We acknowledge the support and cooperation of the sample respondents.

Govindaprasad P. K. is a recipient of the Indian Council of Social Science Research Doctoral Fellowship. His article is largely an outcome of his doctoral work sponsored by ICSSR. However, the responsibility for the facts stated, opinions expressed, and the conclusions drawn is entirely that of the author.

Note

1 All regions mentioned in this chapter are in Kerala unless otherwise specified.

References

Andrade, S. B., and Thomsen, J.-P. 2018. "Intergenerational Educational Mobility in Denmark and the United States." *Sociological Science* 5: 93–113.

Assaad, R., and Saleh, M. 2018. "Does Improved Local Supply of Schooling Enhance Intergenerational Mobility in Education? Evidence from Jordan." *The World Bank Economic Review* 633–55.

Aydemir, A. B., and Yazici, H. 2017. *Intergenerational Education Mobility and the Level of Development:Evidence from Turkey*. Germany: IZA-Institute of Labour Economics.

Azomabou, T. T., and Yitbarek, E. A. 2016. *Intergenerational Educational Mobility in Africa: Has Progress Been Inclusive?* Washington: World Bank Group.

Borjas, G. J. 1992. "Ethnic Capital and Intergeneratioanl Mobility." *The Quaterly Journal of Economics* 107: 123–50.

Card, D., Domnisoru, C., and Taylor, L. 2018, October 06. *Public Education and Intergenerational Mobility*. Retrieved 7 19, 2020, from Research-Based Policy Analysis and Commentary from Leading Economists. https//:voxeu.org/article/public-education-and-intergenerational-mobility

Chamie, J. 2020. "International Migration Amid a World in Crisis." *Journal on Migration and Human Security* 8(3): 230–45. https://doi.org/10.1177/2331502420948796.

Chapman, T. 2020, March 1. *ORF Issue Brief*. Retrieved July 17, 2020, from ORF https://www.orfonline.org/research/social-mobility-in-india-63480

Dustmann, C. 2008. "Return Migration, Investment in Children, and Intergenerational Mobility: Comparing Sons of Foreign-and Native-Born Fathers." *Journal of Human Resources* 43: 299–324.

Emran, M., Ferreira, F., Jiang, Y., and Sun, Y. 2019. *Intergenerational Educational Mobility in Rural Economy:Evidence fromChina and India*. Germany: University Library of Munich.

Gabriel, P. E. 2013. "An Examination of Occupational Mobility Among Fulltime Workers." *Monthly Labor Review* 32–6.

Guadagno, L., 2020. *Migrants and the COVID-19 Pandemic: An Initial Analysis*. Geneva: Migration Research Series N° 60. International Organization for Migration (IOM).

Iyigun, M. F. 1999. "Public Education and Intergeneratioanl Economic Mobility." *Internatioanl Economic Review* 697–710.

Joseph, K. 1988. *Migration and the Changing Pattern of Land Use in Malabar*. Delhi: Mittal Publications.

Kappukalayil, G. 2017. "Malabarilekkulla Knanaya Kudiyettam." In *Kottayam Athiroopataha Malabar Regional Platinum Jubilee Knanaya Malabar Kudiyettam Symbosium*, 1–22. Kottayam: Kottayam Athiroopatha.

Kikkawa Takenaka, A., Villafuerte, J., Gaspar, R., and Narayanan, B. 2020. COVID-19 "Impact on International Migration, Remittances, and Recipient Households in Developing Asia." ADB Briefs No. 148. https://www.adb.org/publications/covid-19-impact-migration-remittances-asia

Lam, K. C., and Liu, P. -W. 2019. "Intergenerational Educational Mobility in Hong Kong: Are Immmigrants More Mobile Than Natives?" *Pacific Economic Review* 400.

Latif, E. 2019. "Trends in Intergenerational Educational Mobility in Canada." *The Australian Economic Review* 61–75.

Lee, H., and Lee, J. -W. 2019. *Patterns and Determinants of Intergenerational Educational Mobility: Evidence Across Countries*. Korea: Asian Growth Research Institute.

Mayer, J. W., Tuma, N. B., and Zagorski, K. 1979. "Education and Occupational Mobility: A Comparison of Polish and American Men." *American Journal of Sociology* 84: 978–86.

Mok, K. H., Xiong, W., Ke, G., and Cheung, J. O. W. 2021. "Impact of COVID-19 Pandemic on International Higher Education and Student Mobility: Student Perspectives from Mainland China and Hong Kong." *International Journal of Educational Research* 105. https://doi.org/10.1016/j.ijer.2020.101718

Netumgattu, A. 2014. *Muthalavayanum Amsavadium Abhishiktharum*. Chicago: Abraham Netumgattu.

Nithya N. R. 2021. "The Impact of Covid 19 on Kerala Diaspora." *International Journal of Multidisciplinary Educational Research1* 9(2): 75–81. http://ijmer.in/pdf/e-Certificate%20of%20Publication-IJMER.pdf.

Pani, N., and Jafar, K. 2010. "Mass Education-Led Growth and Non-Agrarian Villages: Long-Term Results of the Kerala Model." *Oxford Development Studies* 25–42.

Rajarshi, M. 2010. *Intergenerational Mobility in Educational and Occupational Attainment: A Comparative Study of Social Classes in India*. Germany: University Library of Munich.

Ruiz, A. C. 2016. "The Impact of Education on Intergenerational Occupational Mobility in Spain." *Journal of Vocational Behaviour* 92: 94–104.

Sebastian, P. T. 2002. *Christian Migration to Malabar*. Kozhikode: University of Calicut.

Sicherman, N. 1990. Education and Occupational Mobility. *Economics of Education Review* 163–179.
Tansel, A. 2015. *Intergenerational Educational Mobility in Turkey*. Germany: IZA.
Tharakan, M. P. 1976. *Migration of Farmers from Travancore to Malabar from 1930 to 1960: An Analysis of Its Economic Causes*. Thiruvananthapuram: Centre for Development Studies.
Tiwari, C. 2016. "Factors Behind Intergenerational Occupational Mobility:Evidences from Uttar Pradesh (India)." *Journal of Business Management and Social Science Research* 5: 21–27.
Torche, F. 2019. *Educational Mobility in Developing Countries*. Finland: UNU-Wider.
Torul, O., and Oztunali, O. 2017, June 22. *Intergenerational Educational Mobility in Europe*. Turkey: Bogazici University. http://www.econ.boun.edu.tr/torul/ieme.pdf.
Varghese, V. 2009. *Land, Labour, and Migrations: Understanding Kerala's Economic Modernity*. Thiruvananthapuram: Centre for Development Studies.
Viswanathan, P. 2015. *Farmer Migration and Agrarian Transformation in Kerala: Impacts on the Local Economy, Society and the Agrarian Landscape in the Erstwhile Malabar Region*. Thiruvananthapuaram: Centre for Development Studies.

13 What perpetuates multidimensional inequalities in plantations?

A study of tea plantations in Kerala in a comparative setting

P. K. Viswanathan and A. Sajitha

Introduction

The concept of inequality is not alien to the population in developing countries like India, where the top 1% of the population controls more than 60% of the total national wealth. This gap between the rich and the poor has also been widening over the years, despite having regulatory as well as distributive public policies in place. Various theories are put forth by philosophers, social and political scientists, and development theorists to conceptualize inequality and the contributory factors. Initially, economic development models were used to explain the degree of differences in inequality among nations, with postulations that income inequalities decrease as countries achieve economic growth. The much-celebrated Inverted U-hypothesis of Simon Kuznets (1971) is a case in point, which postulated that inequality in income distribution would increase in the initial stages of growth with a rise in per capita income, followed by a decline in inequality with income levels reaching the highest degrees in the intermediate level. However, several of the later and recent studies (Rubinson 1976; Hewitt 1977; Stiglitz 2013; Piketty 2014; Atkinson 2015) pointed out the inadequacy of such theories and focused on economic and social factors that contribute to perpetuating inequalities in societies. In this regard, Sen's Capability Approach[1] (Sen 1993, 30–53) may be considered the most convincing explanation of multidimensional social and economic inequalities due to "lack of capabilities and functionings".

The persistent social and economic inequalities of the sorts that prevail in the tea plantations in India may be traced back to the path-dependent outcome of the historical processes of appropriation and control of resources by the colonial powers, as argued by some scholars (Gupta 1986; Angeles 2007; Acemoglu and Robinson 2017). Tea plantations are labour intensive in terms of harvesting (plucking of tea leaves) and processing of tea, and the labour force (an overwhelming majority being women) is mostly kept as "indentured labour" staying put in the plantations with the most adverse working and living conditions. The "family-based recruitment and employment system" being widely followed by the plantations helped them economize production costs and maximize profits.

DOI: 10.4324/9781003601289-16

The situation in tea plantations underwent certain changes following Independence in 1947, leading to a change in ownership of tea plantations from the colonial companies/operators to indigenous private/corporate entities. The launching of economic planning at the national level also coincided with the enunciation of the Plantation Labour Act (PLA) (1951), followed by the setting up of the Tea Board (1953) to promote the growth and expansion of the tea industry in India. As per the PL Act 1951, the plantation companies have been mandated to implement various labour welfare measures, including employment protection and security for the plantation workers. Most provisions under the PLA 1951 offered to provide protection to the plantation and factory workers and included basic minimum wages, housing, sanitation, primary healthcare, and education.

However, even after more than seven decades of Independence and a planned economic development process, the workers in India's tea plantations across states, including Kerala, are still in distress, mainly due to the worsening economic prospects of the tea plantation industry in the context of globalization and liberalization of trade reforms, which adversely affect the working and living conditions of the workers. The historically persistent low wage and earning conditions along with sub-optimal working and living conditions in the tea plantations have led to multidimensional inequalities, which are further exacerbated by the poor socio-economic status of workers. Most suffer from multiple deficiencies/deprivations, such as landlessness, illiteracy, and tribal status, the most critical factors for building "capabilities and functionings" as envisaged under the capabilities approach.

Objectives, data, and methods

Against this conceptual background, this chapter explores the multidimensional aspects of the lingering inequalities in the case of tea plantations in Kerala in a comparative setting of Tamil Nadu, which continues to bear the brunt of the colonial legacy involving "regimented labour force" and "command and control-based governance regime". In the backdrop of the adoption of Fairtrade certification by the tea plantations, the chapter also examines whether the Fairtrade certification[2] has made any significant change in the socio-economic conditions of the workers and the working conditions prevailing in the plantations. The chapter is based on a historical analysis of the development and status of tea plantation workers with case studies of working and living conditions from Kerala and Tamil Nadu in a comparative setting. Apart from income inequality, the perpetuation of inequality in various forms prevalent in tea plantations is also considered.

The chapter uses mainly primary data to explore the objective in detail. The survey covered 143 sample respondents from five tea plantation estates from two districts (Idukki and Nilgiri), one each from Kerala and Tamil Nadu. To examine if Fairtrade certification has made any impact in addressing the inequalities in tea plantations, both Fairtrade and non-Fairtrade

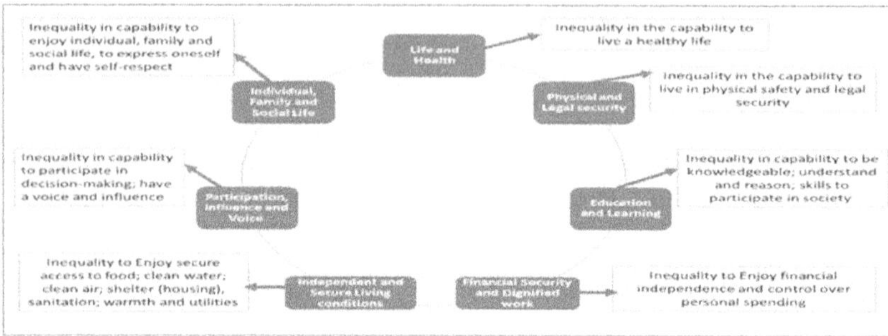

Figure 13.1 Framework for assessing multidimensional inequality in tea plantations

estates were covered for the survey. The estates chosen for inquiry from the Nilgiri district comprised two Fairtrade–certified estates – Chamraj (26 samples) and Burnside (30 samples) and one non-Fairtrade certified estate – Havukal, whereas from Idukki, the study covered one Fairtrade (Chenduvurrai) and one non-Fairtrade (Penshrust) estate. To choose the sample respondents, a purposive random sampling method was followed. Apart from the sample survey, the survey included focus group discussions (FGD) with male workers, female workers, worker representatives, Fairtrade Joint Body Committee members, and a semi-structured interview with estate management.

To explore the research questions, multidimensional inequalities were analyzed to identify the possible reasons. Potential solutions were derived by the governments and the plantation sector in terms of policies and interventions, which could be formulated to sustain the economic dynamism cast by the tea plantations over the past century since the colonial era. To do this, a multidimensional inequality framework designed by (McKnight, Loureiro, and Vizard, n.d.) based on Sen's (1993) Capability Approach, was used, mainly to understand the inequality prevalent in the tea plantation industry across the two regions, in terms of wages, living and working conditions of the workers and workers' representation in plantation management activities. Chart 13.1 presents the conceptual framework of the Multidimensional Inequality Approach as used in the study.

Results and discussion

It was made mandatory for all the plantations to comply with the provisions of the PLA in matters of working and living conditions within the plantations, along with appropriate provisioning for housing, healthcare, maternity benefits to women workers, childcare, education of children, and food grains, to mention the most critical ones. The key workers' rights to form/join associations that represent workers' interests/grievances were also important considerations under the PLA. However, while the provisions of the PLA were to be effectively implemented by all the plantations, the changing economic and financial fortunes of the plantation sectors had significantly impacted the compliance efforts of the plantations over time. As a result, there has not been any perceptible change in the economic and social conditions of the workers in a vast majority of the plantations, especially tea plantations in the country (Joseph and Viswanathan 2016).

Socio-economic profile of the sample respondents

Age: It is generally argued by many scholars that the life and working conditions in the plantation sector are not attractive for the younger generation (John and Mansingh 2016; Joseph and Viswanathan 2016). In line with the findings of these studies, it has been observed that the majority of the workers in the tea plantation in both the states were above 40 years old. In Tamil Nadu, it has been observed that the majority of the sample workers (57.9%) are above 50 years old, while in Kerala, the majority of the workers (43.3%) were in the 40-year-old age group. Further, it was noted that almost 39% of the tea plantation workers in Kerala were in the 30–40 year-old age group as against 5.3% in Tamil Nadu (Table 13.1).

Family Size: With respect to family size, almost 60% of the tea plantation workers in Kerala reported an average family size of four members, as against 39.5% in Tamil Nadu. The relatively larger family size in Kerala could be attributed to the fact that the retired plantation workers continue to stay in the labour lines, as many of them are landless and were staying in the plantations over generations. This aspect of landlessness forces the retired plantation workers to continue to stay with their children who are currently working in the plantations.

Migration: The migration status of the workers in the estate appears to be interesting as the majority of the existing old workers have been migrants from the neighbouring regions of the same state or bordering states. From the survey,[3] it was observed that the proportion of migrant workers was reported at very high levels in the estates in both states (67.8%), with Tamil Nadu having the largest share (80.3%) compared to Kerala (53.7%). The majority of the male old workers in Tamil Nadu have reported that they had migrated or followed their parents/brothers to join work in the plantations from the neighbouring district of Palakkad in Kerala or districts of Tamil Nadu (Madurai, Theni, Karur, Trichy, Erode, and Thirunelveli, to mention a few). A few workers also identified themselves as emigrants from Sri Lanka. A large number of the old female workers also reported that they had migrated either with their parents or after marriage. Many workers also reported that they were born and raised inside the plantation. In contrast, the sample estates in the Nilgiris reported the inflow of migrants from the distant states of Odisha, Jharkhand, and Chattisgarh, and this situation has emerged in recent years in view of the increasing shortage of local workers. In principle, therefore, although they associate with their place of origin, the

Table 13.1 Socio-economic and demographic profile of sample workers

Variable	*Tamil Nadu (n = 76)*		*Kerala (n = 67)*		*Total (n = 143)*	
	Workers (#)	*Share (%)*	*Workers (#)*	*Share (%)*	*Workers (#)*	*Share (%)*
1. Age group (years)						
30–40	4	5.3	25	38.8	30	21
40–50	28	36.8	29	43.3	57	39.9
50–60	44	57.9	12	17.9	56	39.2
2. Family size						
One member	1	1.3	-	-	1	0.7
Two members	15	19.7	1	1.5	16	11.2
Three members	29	38.2	8	11.9	37	25.9
Four members	30	39.5	40	59.7	70	49
5 and above	1	1.3	18	26.9	19	13.3
3. Migration status						
Migrant	61	80.3	36	53.7	97	67.8
Non-migrant	15	19.7	31	46.3	46	32.2
4. Social group status (Caste/Community)						
SC	58	76.3	53	79.1	111	77.6
OBC	16	21.1	1	1.5	17	11.9
Christian	1	1.3	11	16.4	12	8.4
OEC	1	1.3	2	3	3	2.1
5. Occupation						
Tea leaf Plucking	58	76.3	50	74.6	108	75.5
Supervision of Plucking	2	2.6	2	3	4	2.8
Weeding	1	1.3	3	4.5	4	2.8
Fertilizer Application	1	1.3	2	3	3	2.1
Spraying	3	3.9	4	6	7	4.9
Tea Factory Work	8	10.5	3	4.5	11	7.7
Other works	3	3.9	3	4.5	6	4.2
6. Education						
Completed Primary	46	60.5	61	91	107	74.8
Completed Secondary	2	2.6	1	1.5	3	2.1
No formal schooling	28	36.8	5	7.5	33	23.1

Source: Survey in Tea Plantations, 2016.

reality is that they are part of a settled workforce. Most of the workers in the tea estates in Kerala consider Tamil as their native language, which is not the native language of Kerala, thus differentiating them from the surrounding villages.

The predominance of less privileged sections of labourers in the tea estates has been reported in the earlier works by several scholars (John and Mansingh 2016; Joseph and Viswanathan 2016). In tune with the findings of these studies, the present survey also noted that an overwhelming majority of the workers in the surveyed estates belonging to the scheduled caste category (77.6 %) of which 76.3% belong to Tamil Nadu and 79.1% from Kerala.

Occupation Status: The occupation status of the workers reveals that more than 75% of the workers in both the states were engaged in plucking activities, followed by other plantation-related activities, including upkeep and management.

Education: Access to education is likely to have an important role in inducing workers participate in trade unions, bargaining with the management and the state for better conditions of work and labour rights. Nevertheless, the plantation workers appear to have not been able to make significant progress in educational attainments, with a notable proportion of plantation workers reporting low levels of literacy. While the All-India literacy rate in 2011 (Census Data 2011) was 74%, Kerala topped among the Indian states with a literacy rate of 93%, followed by Tamil Nadu with a relatively high score of 80%. But it is observed that the plantation workers in both states had extremely low levels of literacy. About 23% of the total workers across states reported that they never attended school. The state-wise data shows that Tamil Nadu has the highest share of workers (36.8%) who never attended school as compared to Kerala (7.5%). In Kerala, 91% have completed primary schooling. This indicates that the social status (in terms of educational attainment) of the workers and their educational attainment is positively associated, as 91% of plantation workers in Kerala have completed primary schooling against only 61% in Tamil Nadu (How).

Life and health of plantation workers

The conditions of plantation workers have undergone significant transformation over time in terms of changes in working conditions and livelihoods, which also included measures providing secure life and health to the workers. The construction of new roads within the estate and the implementation of weighing stations at different points have helped the workers to reduce several health-related problems such as back pain and shoulder pain. As one of the workers from an estate in Tamil Nadu said: "To reduce the women's burden of carrying heavy leaf sacks on their shoulders and to walk a long distance, the estate has constructed roads to reach jeeps on the top of the hill and constructed weighing machines almost everywhere in the estate." Another worker from Tamil Nadu has also shared a similar opinion: "Infrastructure in the estate has improved. Initially, women workers had to walk at least three kilometers to reach the weighing station, carrying heavy leaf bags on their shoulders. This created a lot of health issues for them. Later, the estate constructed roads and put weighing machines everywhere. This reduced the burden." The workers from Kerala also mentioned that infrastructure development in the estate helped the field workers reduce the burden of carrying heavy loads on their shoulders. Further, the sample workers noted that the estates introduced technological advancements for plucking activities, such as shear plucking and machine plucking, to improve productivity.

The workers reported that although machine plucking results in increased productivity, it requires technical skills as well as stamina to carry the machine. Male workers are usually engaged in machine plucking activities and, as a result, suffer from pain in the knees, shoulders, and back. A worker during the discussion reported that: "Due to machine plucking, we are having several health issues. We need a lot of energy to carry the machine and operate it. Walking with the machine through the tea plantation is a tedious task – we get shoulder pain more often. Hence, there is a need for medical benefit to us."

Primary health centre (PHC) lacks enough facilities in non-Fairtrade estates

To provide free treatment for the workers, the estates are mandated to establish primary health care facilities within the estate. Among the workers surveyed, it has been reported that all the workers in Tamil Nadu and 70% of the workers from Kerala have approached PHCs at least once for treatment (Table 13.2).

However, interactions with the workers further revealed that the facilities in the primary health care centres in most estates are not adequate to provide better healthcare for the workers. There is a notable difference in the availability of facilities in primary healthcare centres across the states and between Fairtrade and non-Fairtrade-certified estates. By using the Fairtrade premium, the estate could improve the facilities in the PHCs by increasing the number of doctors' visits to the hospital, providing additional bed facilities, etc. A worker in one of the non-Fairtrade estates reported, "In our PHC, there is no doctor for consultation. If we go for any medical urgency, the nurse provides only a paracetamol tablet. So, we don't have trust in the kind of treatment available here." Whenever the workers demanded that doctors be appointed in the PHC, the estate management raised the issue of lack of adequate funds to do so. A similar experience was observed in one of the non-Fairtrade estates in Kerala as well. A woman worker during the discussion

Table 13.2 Details regarding visit and medical cost covered

Particulars	*Tamil Nadu (76 workers)*	*Kerala (67 workers)*
Approached primary health centre in estate	76 (100)	47 (70.1)
Approached private hospital	3 (4.0)	8 (11.9)
Approached government hospital	20 (26.7)	30 (44.8)
Illness during last 5 years	33 (44.0)	30 (44.8)
Cost covered by estate for treatment outside (partially)	27 (36.0)	25 (37.3)
Cost covered by self or family for outside treatment	18 (24.0)	13 (19.4)

Source: Survey in Tea Plantations, 2016.

pointed out, "We actually asked the management about not appointing doctors in the estate dispensary and for that they cited the reason of shortage of facilities to keep a doctor here."

One of the Fairtrade-certified estates in Tamil Nadu reported that they utilized Fairtrade premium to improve the facilities in the estate hospital. An interview with management revealed that

> compared to the initial years, there has been an improvement in the facilities in the estate hospital. New facilities such as dentistry, diabetology, ophthalmology etc have been included and salaries for these doctors are paid from Fraitrade premium. The estate workers can avail hospital service for free whereas the outsiders have to pay a minimum fee of INR 10 to consult the doctor and three meals for INR 100 and INR 25 for bed for admitting the patient in the hospital.

Interview with another Fairtrade estate management rationalized, "The estate has many divisions, and only one has Fairtrade certification. Hence it is not possible for us to improve PHC facilities in one division." The manager stated, "Suppose there is contingency with a family, then we are stuck, we will not be able to cover the entire expenses. So, we decided to be uniform, and the maximum amount that we can allot for one case is INR 20,000, so whatever the expense, this estate likes to support to them. Some treatment might be expensive, up to more than 1 lakh. On a case-to-case basis, it will be unfair on us because there might be other people who are also in need. Then we decided a policy of maximum can be given – this much amount – and that has been approved by the General Body."

Partial reimbursement of medical bills, that too, restricted to government hospitals

As compared to PHCs in the estate and the government hospitals, the proportion of workers who approached private hospitals is very minimal. This may be because workers do not have the option to claim reimbursement for private hospital medical bills. Even during the time of emergency, the workers are supposed to seek treatment either at the estate PHCs or a nearby government hospital. A worker stated,

> If we need to get reimbursement for our medical bill, we have to go only to government hospital. Suppose we go to any nearby private hospital due to an emergency; we will not get any money from the estate. Hence, there is a need to remove the restriction of going only to government hospital for claiming medical bills if they really consider our health.

The workers need to approach estate PHCs in the initial stages. If the staff concerned in the PHCs refers the workers for further treatment, they could undergo treatment in hospitals outside the estate. In such cases, the workers are supposed to go to only government hospitals, as they do not have enough money to meet private hospital expenses. For advanced treatment, they usually "go to Kottayam Medical College, which is far away from our estate", a worker from one of the estates in Kerala stated. However, the estate partially reimburses the medical bills. This leads to a financial burden on the workers. With the limited income received from the estate, most workers cannot afford to undergo further treatment outside. Hence, a worker stated the

> need for the full reimbursement of both medical and travel expenses if we go to other hospitals for further treatment, because we also have a major role in earning profits for the estate. So, it is the responsibility of the estate to take care of our health.

Another worker revealed, "Initially we used to get full travel fare. But now, the estate reimburses only half of the expense."

The workers in the non-Fairtrade estate in Kerala reported that

> the estate should do something to improve the medical facilities in the estate. The primary dispensary at the estate provides only minor treatment to the workers. For severe cases, the estate refers the workers to the government hospital. Sometimes we may need to spend nearly INR 5,000 for our treatment. Suppose we produce the full medical bills; the estate will reimburse only INR 2,500. This creates a problem for us.

Another worker reported that "there is no reimbursement for X-ray, if we go to other hospitals." Further, the daily bata provided by the estate to meet their daily expenses at the hospital is very minimal. A worker stated that

> if we go to nearby taluk hospital or medical college, the estate provides transportation charge and daily bata of INR 50 which is inadequate to meet our daily expenses. They do not provide any allowance for the bystander. When I was hospitalized last month, my wife was there to care for me. I got sickness benefits, but my wife lost her full salary. So, there should be some benefits for the bystander as well.

It shows that the bystanders lose their salary if they take leave to go to the hospital with their family.

During emergencies, the workers take a loan from their provident fund and chit funds or borrow from money lenders at high interest rates. This, in turn, adversely affects their financial savings for the future. To reduce the financial burden to a certain extent, some estates in Tamil Nadu (one

Fairtrade and one non-Fairtrade) provide interest-free loans to the workers, and the estate deducts a small amount from their wage every month.

No health/medical insurance for the workers

The survey reveals that none of the estates offer health insurance facilities to the workers. The survey revealed that only 11.8% of workers from Tamil Nadu and 14.9% of workers in Kerala had a health insurance card, and only 17% of workers from Tamil Nadu and 35.8% of workers from Kerala had an LIC policy. Most workers did not have any type of insurance policy, perhaps due to lack of money to pay for the insurance premium.

During a discussion, a member of the Fairtrade-certified estate management stated that, "since all the medical facilitates are provided at free of cost in the estate, there is no need of providing any medical insurance separately." However, this has not been the case with other estates irrespective of Fairtrade certification. Most estates find it difficult to provide free of cost treatment within the estate or reimburse the full amount of the medical bills. Hence, there is a need for arrangements for the workers to have a health insurance card that can cover the medical costs.

Independent and secure living conditions

In the PLA, every tea plantation is mandated to provide free accommodation to the workers within the estate. The survey showed that all the workers interviewed in Tamil Nadu utilize the accommodation provided by the estate, whereas in Kerala, 86.6% of the workers preferred to stay within the estate and rest stayed in their own houses outside the estates.

Labour lines lack enough facilities

Further discussions with the workers revealed that the accommodation provided by the estates was insufficient to accommodate a family with a household size of more than four members. A worker from one of the Fairtrade estates in Tamil Nadu reported,

> My family has six members, and only two of work. My two children are not working. My parents are also staying with me; they are very old and cannot work. We cannot allow them to work. Also, the house provided by the estate is not sufficient for all of us to have a better stay.

Similar observations have been made in the tea estates in Kerala as well. The workers have raised the issue of lack of enough space to accommodate their family members. A worker stated, "I have a temporary arrangement to make space to accommodate all my six family members. I extended my house with a tarpaulin sheet with the permission of estate management. My aged parents sleep there."

Since these places are prone to the movement of wild animals and cold during the night, there is a need to provide safe, secure, and spacious housing for the workers, considering their prime role in bringing revenue to the estate. Another worker has argued, "There is a need for renovation in the housing provided by the estate... actually, the estate repairs the labour lines only during the rainy season, when it is difficult to finish the work properly. We also face difficulties." The workers unanimously reported the need for better housing for them as most (both migrant and non-migrant) lack accommodation facilities outside the estate, especially the migrants. Only a few workers own land in their hometowns where they plan to build houses after retirement. However, a worker stated, "My parents had thought of moving back to our native place after their retirement, but now they plan to stay back here with me due to health issues." Hence, there is a need for better housing facilities, considering the health conditions of the workers' parents.

To improve the facilities in labour lines, the management in one of the non-Fairtrade estates in Kerala has taken necessary measures to enlarge the existing houses in the labour lines by merging two vacant houses together. One of the managers said,

> Out of all workers, only 46 are staying inside the estate. The rest have their own accommodation outside the estate. Hence, many of the labour lines are kept vacant. To utilize the resource properly, we have started expanding the existing house by merging two houses together. The new lines under construction have 2 bedrooms, one hall, and one kitchen each. It is an ongoing project, and we are hoping to complete them as soon as possible.

Tea estate labour lines prone to landslides

The tea plantations are situated in hilly areas, and the labour lines are constructed within the estates. These areas are prone to landslides during the rainy season, which raises serious concerns over the safety and security of staying in those labour lines. This issue became important in the backdrop of the Pettimudi incident at one of the tea plantations in Munnar, which took the lives of nearly 58 people who stayed at the labour lines.

Participation, influence, and voice

To understand workers' efforts to make improvements in working as well as living conditions in the estates concerned, the workers were asked to reflect upon their individual and collective initiatives that would result in addressing their concerns. Although individual efforts in achieving notable changes in working conditions were hardly reported, workers stated that their individual efforts were mainly to seek help towards addressing their financial or living-related requirements (especially personal needs), which did not require collective action. A male worker from one of the Fairtrade estates stated, "If I have any personal requirement, I don't ask 10 persons to accompany me to meet the management. I will go directly and meet the manager."

However, collective initiatives by the workers have played an important role in improving/altering the working and living conditions across estates. To do so, workers have utilized platforms such as workers' committees and trade unions to convey their requirements to the management. The collective efforts helped not only to improve the working conditions but also to resolve any individual concerns of the workers. A male worker from one of the Fairtrade estates stated, "If we have any common issues, we organize meeting with everyone and find a solution."

Workers were observed to actively participate in the meeting organized within the estate to discuss their grievances and seek solutions (see Table 13.3). Women's participation was higher in Tamil Nadu (97.9%) than in Kerala (74.75%). The FGD with women workers pointed to the fact that when free from work, they preferred to do household chores. However, mirroring the larger representation among the respondents in the worker survey, women tea pluckers represented the majority of those engaged in the meeting. Yet, workers with higher education levels, settled, and from higher caste backgrounds were better represented among those involved in collective action, especially on certified estates.

Many relevant topics not addressed in individual or collective meeting

The workers have noted that the individual meetings usually focused on topics related to financial needs, health concerns, and housing needs, and that the collective meetings focused mostly on bonuses, hikes, weather protectives and gears, housing-related matters, educational scholarships for children, and other labour-related issues in the field, if any.

However, there are many areas where workers do not have the power to raise their voices to demand. One such example is the recent strike by women workers in one of the tea plantations in Munnar for a hike in daily wages and a bonus along with the proper implementation of all welfare measures (Raj

Table 13.3 Details regarding participation in the meetings organized

Particulars	*Tamil Nadu (76 workers)*	*Kerala (67 workers)*
Participation in meeting	66 (86.8)	63 (94.0)
Women participation	46 (97.9)	44 (74.57)

Source: Survey in Tea Plantations, 2016.

2019). The study observed a reduction in the funds allocated for most labour welfare schemes as stipulated by PLA. Even after the strike by women workers in the Munnar tea plantation, the wage was not increased much. This itself shows that the workers have a limited voice in demanding their needs.

The workers, however, were aware that beyond the topics covered earlier, critical areas, such as wages, needed addressing, as they felt the existing wage levels were insufficient to meet their daily needs. However, the workers felt that wage-related decisions were stipulated by the management.

Physical and legal security

Physical and legal security are imperative for ensuring the physical, economic, and psychological well-being of the workers. The discussion with the workers suggested that estates were implementing adequate measures to ensure the workers' rights as stipulated in the PLA.

Table 13.4 shows that all the workers' rights, except wages, were guaranteed by the estate management. Similar observations were made during the discussion with workers as well. During FGD, they reported that the estate took adequate measures to guarantee the workers' rights as mandated in PLA. However, considering the increase in consumption expenditure and the price of daily required goods and services, there was a need to increase wages to meet the expenditure. The workers in both states felt that their current wages did not help them lead a decent standard of living. For instance, Table 13.4 reveals that when only around 39% of workers in Tamil Nadu reported that the wages enabled the family to afford a decent standard of living, whereas in Kerala, the proportion was hardly 12%.

Table 13.4 Workers' responses concerning guaranteeing of their rights by the tea estate

Particulars of worker's rights (Guaranteed or Not)	*Tamil Nadu*	*Kerala*
Workers get freedom to form workers' associations and bargain with management (Yes)	76 (100)	67 (100)
Workers do not face discrimination of any kind, for instance, on the basis of sex, caste, nationality, etc. (Yes)	76 (100)	67 (100)
No forced labour (Yes)	76 (100)	67 (100)
No child labour (Yes)	76 (100)	67 (100)
Wages enabling family to afford a decent standard of living (Yes)	30 (39.4)	8 (11.9)
Working environment is free from risks to health and safety (Yes)	76 (100)	67 (100)
Workers get treated with dignity and respect (Yes)	76 (100)	67 (100)

Source: Survey in Tea Plantations, 2016.
Note: Figures in parentheses indicate the percentage responses of the workers against each item.

The workers during the discussion stated that "Decent wage should be there... Even though wage has been increased over the years, cost of living has also increased along with it." Further, the workers mentioned an increase in the expenses for education. Hence, to meet the expenses, one of the workers stated that "We are taking loans."

Financial security and dignified work

Providing financial support to workers to enjoy financial independence, promoting decent working conditions, and removing all the barriers that restrict equity in the workplace ensure economic empowerment for the workers. The survey data suggests that Fairtrade play an imperative role in providing financial support to the workers versus non-Fairtrade estates.

Improvement in facilities due to Fairtrade

The workers reported that the Fairtrade premium helped attain financial security in many ways. Among the five estates surveyed, three estates had Fairtrade certification. Compared to non-Fairtrade estates, the Fairtrade premium the estates receive helps the management provide their workers with several facilities related to health, educational scholarships for children, retirement benefits, and annual bonuses. (Table 13.5).

The interactions with the workers pointed to the fact that facilities offered under Fairtrade ensure financial security for the workers. For instance, Chamraj Estate uses the Fairtrade premium to provide an annual bonus to the workers based on the number of days they have worked in the estate. Suppose a worker is engaged in 240 days' work at the estate, they are eligible for INR 10,000 as bonus. The estate deposits the money directly to the worker's bank account, and the worker can withdraw the amount during the time of retirement.

During the discussion, a worker stated, "Whatever money we get, we are using it to meet our daily expenses. We do not have any money. But we have a feeling that there is some deposit in our bank, which makes us happy now." Another worker reported,

> I was raised here. My parents faced a lot of difficulties raising us. Using their limited income, they provided education and satisfied our needs. After ninth std, there was no way to continue our education. During those days, there was no Fairtrade. After that, I joined the estate, and now it has been 26 years. I became permanent in 1994. During that time, the estate got Fairtrade. After that, we get good facilities to provide education to our children. My son has completed his degree, and daughter is in first-year degree.

The Fairtrade premium received and the facilities offered are positively related. Compared to the other two estates, Burnside Estate offers fewer facilities

Table 13.5 Details regarding the facilities provided using FT premium

Particulars	*Chamraj*	*Burnside*	*Chenduvurrai division in KDHP Estate*
Certification	Certified in 1994 but started providing facilities after 2000	Certified in 1994 but started providing facilities after 2000	Certified in 2009 but started providing facilities after 2013
Coverage of FT	Entire estate is covered	Entire estate is covered	Only one division among the total nine other divisions in the estate, and the benefit is restricted only to this division
Activities undertaken	• Improvement in school facilities • Scholarship for higher education • Improvement in hospital facilities • Annual bonus • Pension scheme • Retirement housing scheme • Funeral fund	• Educational Scholarship • Distribution of weather protectives • Annual bonus	• Annual bonus • Educational scholarship • Financial support for medical • Sport activities • Facilities for hospital, crèche and school • Computer training • Training on income generating activities

Source: Sample Survey and Focus Group Discussion, 2016.

because of the lesser premium it receives from Fairtrade. Further, Table 13.5 shows that among the estates under Kannan Devan Hills Plantation, only the Chenduvurrai division has adopted a Fairtrade certification. Although management wants to extend the activities to other divisions, the Fairtrade premium amount is insufficient to meet the expenditure on the activities. Hence, the estate management has restricted their Fairtrade activities in this division. Further, the estate management could not undertake more activities in this division as workers could create problems in other estates.

Education and learning

As already mentioned, most workers have less education and belong to the above 40-year-old age group. Further, most workers concentrate on one work for a long time, which does not require continuous learning. Hence, the scope for education and learning in tea estates is limited. On further probing about "whether the workers had ever thought of continuing their education beyond the primary schooling," we learnt that all the workers had thought of continuing education beyond their existing level. However, most workers responded that they did not get any opportunity to continue their education due to difficulties in their family. Other reasons, such as lack of interest, laziness, and difficulty in learning, were also indicated as reasons for not continuing education. Most belonged to the less privileged sections of the society. As for migrant labourers, the older age cohorts (more than 40 years) had lower educational attainments, and most were engaged in tea leaf plucking. In comparison, a marginally higher proportion of younger generation workers were found in Fairtrade estates. A larger proportion of workers in Fairtrade estates belonged to less privileged communities, and their educational attainment was considerably lower.

When asked about information on PLA in the FDG, it was observed that most did not have an idea about the Act. Many women workers said that there was lack of adequate knowledge regarding the terminology used in PLA. However, they had knowledge regarding the workers' rights included in the Act. Similarly, the workers were also not aware of the term "Fairtrade premium" and called it "foreign money or half dollar". This shows that they were well-informed about the changes happening in the estate, even though they could not remember the exact terminologies.

Individual, family, and social life in tea plantations

New migrant workers cooperate less with existing workers

Since most workers in the tea plantation are migrants from neighbouring states and districts, they form different sub-groups based on their origin and ethnic identity. However, their customs and norms vary even within the same religious group. Even though they migrated from different places and have been living in the estate for a long time, they still follow their ethnic identities.

This identity distinguishes them from the natives. These workers celebrate their festivals at the estate, and they invite other people to join in the celebrations. In this way, the workers maintain unity and harmony within the estate. However, the existing workers feel that the newly migrated workers find some difficulty in cooperating with them. The new migrants are mainly from Jharkhand, Uttar Pradesh, etc., and they mainly speak Hindi, which is not familiar to the existing workers. However, the discussion revealed that the existing workers still took the initiative to teach them about the work and invite them to their houses to create a friendly environment, although the new migrant workers often rejected the invitation. A worker engaged in factory activity stated that "if we teach them, they say that who are you to teach us. Ego issue is there. Cooperation is very less among them and... once I asked a worker to do my work for some time, as I had to go urgently to the washroom, he replied to me in such a rude way, asking how I could ask him to do my work also."

Poor social status

The social status of the tea plantation workers is mainly isolation from mainstream communities, as they live and work inside the estate itself. Since these estates are situated in hilly regions, these workers have less connection with the outside world. However, the workers go outside the tea garden for manly activities such as purchasing groceries and attending functions. The respondents have mixed experiences regarding interactions with the outside community. According to a worker,

> Wherever we go, they treat us as estate labour because of our job status issue. People think that these people get only INR 300 per day, so even if we invite them, they are not going to provide any help to us. Hence, if we go for any function like marriage, many of them don't treat us properly.

Another worker reported, "Social status issue is a major problem for us." One of the estate managements in Kerala also pointed, "The mainstream community treats estate workers as low-profile category people." Compared to Kerala, the situation in Tamil Nadu is different. The discussions with the workers did not raise the concern of ill treatment by the outside community.

Conclusions and policy imperatives

The chapter examines the historical factors that perpetuate multidimensional inequalities in tea plantations in India in a comparative perspective of Kerala and Tamil Nadu. The analysis also looks at whether the changing trade policy environment in the advent of globalization has made any significant improvement in the working and living conditions of the workers. For analysis, we took up the case of Fairtrade certification adopted by tea plantations, covering a few sample estates that adopted Fairtrade certification. The analysis was done from a comparative perspective of Fairtrade-certified versus non-Fairtrade-certified estates in the two states.

Our analysis shows that historically, tea plantation workers face multiple deprivations, especially with respect to accessing educational facilities. Lack of education beyond the primary level, general backwardness of the plantation-growing regions, virtual absence of the urban informal sector, and the lack of demand for industrial goods on the part of plantation workers are some other inherent structural problems that lead to multidimensional inequalities and marginalization of plantation workers. The factors mainly include institutional ones that are historically responsible for the overall lack of inclusive development in the plantation regions in Kerala, Tamil Nadu, Assam, and West Bengal. The August 2020 landslide at Pettimudi, Idukki district that killed 58 plantation workers at the Kannan Devan Hills Plantations Company (P) Ltd. is a narrative of the tragic outcomes of historic deprivation of the tea plantation workers in Kerala, whose lives and livelihoods are severely affected by natural hazards of the sorts.

The multidimensional inequality in tea plantations also depicts an inseparable gender dimension attached to it, as women workers constitute the majority of plantation workers most vulnerable to various inequalities in terms of education, working and living conditions, good health, poverty, malnutrition, water, and sanitation. While the implementation of the provisions of the PL Act 1950 is mandatory for all plantations, there are huge deviations in this regard. It is observed that the unfair wages, disinterest from management, and improper implementation of labour laws by the state governments have pushed the workers into impoverishment (Viswanathan and Kavya 2019), perpetuating and rather exacerbating the inequalities in the plantations.

While trade reforms and market integration policies have also penetrated the plantation sectors, including tea, we found that such reforms and policies do not significantly help alleviate the multidimensional deprivations of the tea plantation workers. It also emerges from a large number of recent empirical studies that the economic as well as trade reform measures in the various forms of new certifications and standards, involving tea plantations, such as Fairtrade, Rainforest Alliance, UTZ, Trustea, and HACCP, seem to have made little impact on the economic and social well-being of the workers due to various reasons, including lack of stable returns from tea exports, the meagre volume of trade occurring through the certified channels, and lack of clarity in terms of development and welfare projects (Viswanathan 2021).

From a policy angle, we propose that the sustainability of the tea plantation industry in Kerala and other states depends on how the sector can reinvent in terms of addressing the challenges posed by the multidimensional inequalities historically faced by the plantation workers. The continued dynamism of the tea plantation sector also depends on a thorough overhauling of the production relations as well as the invention of new models of plantation management with proper collaborations or partnerships between the plantation companies, the emerging segment of small producers, the state as well as the workers and their associations. Such a process of restructuring the plantation industry and the key stakeholders becomes imperative if the historic inequalities perpetuated by the colonial style of plantation management being followed by the plantation entities are to be curtailed.

Notes

1 As observed by Burchardt and Hick (2017), the Capability Approach has emphasized the distinction between means and ends and has broadened the focus of poverty research from monetary resources to multiple dimensions of deprivation.
2 Fair trade certification is a type of product certification given by Fairtrade International that aims to ensure a product or its brand meets certain standards related to environment, labour and development. The certification helps producers in developing countries to attain equitable and sustainable trade relations with the rest of the world.
3 The sample does not cover the recent migrant workers in the estate due to the specific definition of the research population. The survey basically covered those workers who joined the estate before receiving Fairtrade certification.

References

Acemoglu, Daron, and Robinson, James A. 2017. "The Economic Impact of Colonialism". In *The Long Economic and Political Shadow of History*, Vol. 1. A Global View, edited by Stelios Michalopoulos and Elias Papaioannou, 81–89. London: Vox EU.org and CEPR Press.
Angeles, L. 2007. "Income Inequality and Colonialism." *European Economic Review* 51(5): 1155–76.
Atkinson, A. B. 2015. *Inequality: What Can Be Done*? London: Harvard University Press.
Burchardt, T., and Hick, R. 2017. *Inequality and the Capability Approach*, CASE/201. Centre for Analysis of Social Exclusion, London School of Economics, 20p. http://sticerd.lse.ac.uk/dps/case/cp/casechapter201.pdf.
Census. 20ss11. Government of India. http://censusindia.gov.in.
Gupta, R. D. 1986. "From Peasants and Tribesmen to Plantation Workers: Colonial Capitalism, Reproduction of Labour Power and Proletarianisation in North East India, 1850s to 1947." *Economic and Political Weekly* 21(4): PE2–PE10.
Hewitt, C. 1977. "The Effect of Political Democracy and Social Democracy on Equality in Industrial Societies: A Cross-National Comparison." *American Sociological Review* 450–464.
John, J., and Mansingh, P. 2016. "Plantation Labour Act 1951 and Social Cost – the Case of the Tea Industry." In *Globalisation, Development and Plantation Labour in India*, edited by Joseph K. J. and P. K. Viswanathan, 131–166. London and New York: Routledge.
Joseph K. J., and Viswanathan, P. K., editors. 2016. *Globalisation, Development and Plantation Labour in India*. London and New York: Routledge.
Kuznets, Simon, 1971. "Modern Economic Growth: Findings and Reflections." Nobel Prize in Economics Documents 1971–2, Nobel Prize Committee.

McKnight, A., Loureiro, P. M., and Vizard, P. (n.d.). *Multidimensional Inequality Framework*. http://sticerd.lse.ac.uk/inequality/the-framework/media/mif-framework.pdf.
Piketty, T. 2014. *Capital in the Twenty-First Century*. Cambridge, MA: Harvard University Press.
Raj, J. 2019. "Beyond the Unions: *Pembillai Orumai* Women's Strike in South Indian Tea Belt." *Journal of Agrarian Change* 19(4): 671–89.
Rubinson, R. 1976. "The World-Economy and the Distribution of Income Within States: A Cross-National Study." *American Sociological Review* 638–59.
Sen, A. K. 1993. "Capability and Well-being." In *The Quality of Life*, edited by Martha C. Nussbaum and Amartya K. Sen, 30–53. Oxford: Clarendon Press.
Stiglitz, J. 2013. *The Price of Inequality*. London: Penguin.
Viswanathan, P. K. 2021. Do Trade Certifications Alleviate Economic and Social Deprivations of Plantation Workers? A Study of the Tea Plantation Sector in India." *Work Organisation, Labour & Globalisation* 15(2): 46–72. https://doi.org/10.13169/workorgalaboglob.15.2.0046.
Viswanathan, P. K., and Kavya, K. 2019. "Contesting Social Deprivations in a Dynamic Trade Reforms Context: The Curious Case of Tea Plantation Workers in India." In *Second Policy Conference of the Network of Rural and Agrarian Studies (NRAS)*, 144–153. New Delhi: Indian Institute of Technology (IIT).

Index

Page numbers in **bold** indicate tables, while page numbers in *italics* indicate figures.

For Product Safety Concerns and Information please contact our EU
representative GPSR@taylorandfrancis.com
Taylor & Francis Verlag GmbH, Kaufingerstraße 24, 80331 München, Germany

www.ingramcontent.com/pod-product-compliance
Ingram Content Group UK Ltd.
Pitfield, Milton Keynes, MK11 3LW, UK
UKHW020151200926
475702UK00016B/2650
9781032989037